Transforming Authority

Beihefte zur Zeitschrift
für die alttestamentliche
Wissenschaft

Edited by
John Barton, Reinhard G. Kratz, Nathan MacDonald,
Sara Milstein, and Markus Witte

Volume 518

Transforming Authority

Concepts of Leadership in Prophetic
and Chronistic Literature

Edited by
Katharina Pyschny and Sarah Schulz

DE GRUYTER

ISBN 978-3-11-125600-9
e-ISBN (PDF) 978-3-11-065035-8
e-ISBN (EPUB) 978-3-11-064715-0
ISSN 0934-2575

Library of Congress Control Number: 2021934874

Bibliografische Information der Deutschen Nationalbibliothek
The Deutsche Nationalbibliothek lists this publication in the Deutsche Nationalbibliografie; detailed bibliographic data are available on the Internet at http://dnb.dnb.de.

© 2023 Walter de Gruyter GmbH, Berlin/Boston
This volume is text- and page-identical with the hardback published in 2021.
Typesetting: Meta Systems Publishing & Printservices GmbH, Wustermark
Printing and binding: CPI books GmbH, Leck

www.degruyter.com

Preface and Acknowledgements

There can be no doubt that the theme of leadership played an important role in ancient Israel and the discourses represented in the Hebrew Bible. Even though aspects of leadership are omnipresent within biblical scholarship, an all-encompassing systematic monograph or volume dealing with the diversity and complexity of leadership concepts in the Hebrew Bible or selected canonical parts is still lacking. With the volume entitled *Debating Authority* (BZAW 507) we took a first step into the direction of a comprehensive investigation of the topic by providing a resource for scholars studying questions of leadership within the Pentateuch and the Former Prophets. The present volume entitled *Transforming Authority* is to be understood as a follow-up expanding the perspective onto selected texts from prophetic and Chronistic literature.

The volume originated in four sessions of our EABS Research Unit "Concepts of Leadership in the Hebrew Bible" conducted at the EABS Annual Conferences 2017 and 2018 in Berlin (Germany) and Helsinki (Finland). The papers and responses, the intense and thought-provoking discussions as well as the questions evolving from the sessions encouraged us to plan a second comprehensive volume and to invite several additional contributions.

Editing this volume was a long, albeit fascinating journey. It would not have been possible without the collaboration of several persons and the support of various institutions. Firstly, our thanks go to the European Association of Biblical Studies (EABS) for accepting our proposal for a research unit and providing us for three years with an international platform for our research. Secondly, we would like to thank the participants of the sessions in Berlin and Helsinki and all contributors to the present volume who engaged with great interest in the questions and discussions related to the volume. Furthermore, we owe sincere thanks to Dr. Stephen Germany from the University of Basel for his outstanding work as copy editor. Veronika Bibelriether from the University of Erlangen supported us most effectively in preparing the manuscript. The Chair for Old Testament Studies (Old Testament Literature and its History) at the Friedrich-Alexander-University of Erlangen-Nuremberg, the *Frau Dorothea and Dr. Dr. Richard Zantner-Busch-Stiftung*, and the *North Rhine-Westphalian Academy of Sciences, Humanities and the Arts* generously provided financial support to this publication. Finally, we are deeply grateful to the editors of *Beihefte zur Zeitschrift für die Alttestamentliche Wissenschaft* for accepting this volume into their series as well as to Eva Frantz, Sabina Dabrowski, Sophie Wagenhofer, and Alice Meroz from de Gruyter for their indispensable help and support in preparing the manuscript.

To all these persons and institutions, we would like to express our most sincere thanks for making the completion of this journey possible. We hope that the volume will provide a forum for the current debate on leadership in the Hebrew Bible and become an initial point for further research.

Berlin/Erlangen, March 2021   Katharina Pyschny & Sarah Schulz

Contents

Preface and Acknowledgements —— v

I: Introduction

Katharina Pyschny and Sarah Schulz
Introduction —— 3

II: Concepts of Leadership in Selected Prophetic Literature

Christl M. Maier
Why Judean Monarchy Failed: A Discourse on Leadership
in Jer 21:1–23:8 —— 19

L. Juliana M. Claassens
Prophetic Leadership as Resistance: The Case of Baruch
and Ebed-melech (Jeremiah 36–38) —— 33

Johanna Erzberger
Kingship and Priesthood – Reloaded (Jer 33:14–26) —— 47

Jan Rückl
The Leadership of the Judean Community according to the Book
of Haggai —— 59

Martin Schott
Messianism in Transition: Zech 9:9–10 between First
and Second Zechariah —— 85

Hervé Gonzalez
Zechariah 9–14 and the Transformations of Judean Royal Ideology
during the Early Hellenistic Period —— 97

III: Concepts of Leadership in Chronistic Literature

Anna Maria Bortz
Conflicting Roles of Leadership in the Temple Building Account of Ezra 1–6 —— 155

Bob Becking
Was Ezra a Persian or a Yehudite Leader? —— 171

Ehud Ben Zvi
Leadership in the World of Memories Evoked by Chronicles in the Context of the Late Persian/Early Hellenistic Period —— 185

Louis C. Jonker
Reflections on Leadership in Achaemenid Yehud: Case Studies from the Chronicler's Imperial, Provincial, Tribal, and Cultic Rhetoric —— 201

Yigal Levin
Judges, Elders, and Officers in Chronicles —— 223

Isabel Cranz
Diseased Leadership —— 243

IV: Comprehensive Aspects of Leadership in Prophetic and Chronistic Literature

Sarah Schulz
Zerubbabel, Joshua and the Restoration of the Temple – A Comparative Approach to the Concepts of Leadership in Haggai/Zech 1–8 and Ezra 1–6 —— 263

Katharina Pyschny
Concepts of Prophetic Leadership in Chronicles and Their Relation to Prophetic Literature —— 293

List of Contributors —— 315

Index of Biblical References —— 317

I: Introduction

Katharina Pyschny and Sarah Schulz
Introduction

Throughout its literary scope, the Hebrew Bible offers a wide variety of different and sometimes even contradictory concepts of leadership. Various aspects of leadership are present not only on a superficial level but are deeply embedded in the structure of the biblical texts and their redactional history. Leadership can certainly be considered a cross-cutting issue within the Hebrew Bible, still in need of further research.[1]

Our first volume on leadership[2] shed light on the variety and diversity of concepts of leadership within the Pentateuch and the Former Prophets highlighting as well the literary dynamics and discursivity coinciding with these concepts and ideas. In comparison to other biblical texts, this phenomenon, i.e. the way in which the Pentateuch and the Former Prophets first constitute various concepts of leadership and then negotiate and debate them in regard to their authority, is a special feature of these literary corpora, as was hinted at by the title "Debating Authority." Even though these corpora also reflect the notion of reshaping and reinterpreting leadership concepts (e.g., the transformation of leadership and authority in the case of Moses' successor Joshua), it is not the most decisive tendency there.

The present volume, "Transforming Authority," focuses instead on biblical literature in which the notion of transforming leadership concepts is (more) characteristic: namely, prophetic and chronistic literature. The aspect of transformation can be understood on two levels: The volume deals with texts that not only reshape, reinterpret and transform "traditional" concepts of leadership on a literary level, but which also stem predominately from the postexilic period, a transformed time characterized by many social changes.

Aspects of Definition and Methodology

This volume is based on a rather broad or open understanding of leadership, which allows for analyzing the biblical concepts in their variety, complexity,

---

1 The following remarks refrain from referring to the numerous studies on leadership in prophetic and chronistic literature and serve specifically as an introduction to the present volume.
2 Pyschny, Katharina, and Sarah Schulz, eds. 2018. *Debating Authority: Concepts of Leadership in the Pentateuch and the Former Prophets*. BZAW 507. Berlin and Boston: de Gruyter.

and fluidity. Leadership is understood as the *power or ability to direct the actions of individuals or groups*. This direction is conducted via *(social) interaction(s)* and is always *goal-oriented*. Leadership constitutes *asymmetrical social relations* of super- and subordination, which are not simple, unidirectional relationships such as between leaders and their subordinates, but include several reciprocal dynamics. It is important to note that these asymmetrical social relations are not necessarily totalitarian in nature. Leadership claims can be restricted to specific areas, depending on the leader's competence and authority. Leadership is not necessarily institutionalized, but it always has a *public character or impact*. The stabilization or routinization of specific leadership claims, though, is often linked to processes of institutionalization. Every kind of leadership has at least one *basis of legitimation*, which can differ in concept and style. This is already evident from the typology of leadership established by Max Weber: legitimation via law, legitimation via tradition, and legitimation via charisma. In order to speak of legitimate leadership, the *authority of the leader must be acknowledged* at some point by his or her subordinates, at least to a certain degree.

In regard to the identification of concepts of leadership in the Hebrew Bible, the present volume takes into account not only lexical and semantic issues but also – given the almost complete lack of abstract terms for "leadership," "authority," "office," etc. in Biblical Hebrew – narrative constellations and structural analogies.[3]

Thus, as far as methodology is concerned, the contributions follow a wide range of approaches and seek to combine synchronic, diachronic, and sociological perspectives in a methodologically critical and conscious way. The volume intentionally does not concentrate on one specific concept of leadership, but seeks to group various concepts together and to contextualize them in terms of their synchronic scope or compositional structure, theological content, literary-historical background, and historical contexts. At the same time, the various concepts of leadership will be compared in order to shed new light on the leadership discourses in and behind the biblical texts. Given that biblical texts

---

3 As was pointed out by Francis Borchardt. 2017. "Leader, Leadership." *EBR* 15:1121–1124, 1121: "The philological discussion is only part of the presentation of leaders and leadership in the HB/OT. In addition, one can learn about the various functions and social roles played by leaders within the narratives by observing who is characterized as a leader and how they interact with those they lead. Because the variety of ways in which one could construct leaders or leadership in the HB/OT is virtually limitless, any such attempt at understanding leaders, either regarding specific terms or with respect to figures we might recognize as leaders from our contemporary perspective, is bound to be superficial."

seek to be read as "construed history," various concepts of leadership will be analyzed with regard to their theological perspectives on the one hand and their historical and socio-political contexts on the other. Taking into account the highly complex and reciprocal relationship between history and text, the biblical leadership claims are understood primarily as fictive or ideological in character. They can be assumed to have points of contact with the actual history of ancient Israel but are not taken as its one-to-one-reflection. However, even the most fictive authority or leadership claim has some kind of historical context and an actual (perhaps even de facto failed) agenda, which can only be explored by looking both at and behind the texts.

Leadership in Selected Prophetic Literature

The present volume deals with only a small selection of biblical texts and their respective concepts of leadership. Within the rather large corpus of prophetic texts, the essays here focus on the book of Jeremiah on the one hand and the books of Haggai and Zechariah on the other. Based on these selected case studies, the volume seeks to provide insights into various issues of leadership in prophetic literature. They are by no means comprehensive but rather aim to open up new perspectives and encourage further research.

The Book of Jeremiah

The book of Jeremiah is particularly interesting and challenging for this endeavor. This is due to the fact that aspects of leadership, legitimacy, authority, etc. are dealt with more or less explicitly throughout the whole book. They play a significant role on various levels of analysis:

On the *literary-synchronic level*, the book of Jeremiah constructs various types of human leadership, including prophetic, priestly, Levitical, and royal leadership. Of course, not every form of leadership is given the same amount of attention. The conceptualization of these types of leadership differs in terms of definition,[4] types of competencies they include, theological background or reasoning, relationship to divine leadership or institutions (e.g., the temple),

---

4 This holds true in general but also if one focuses on one specific model, such as royal leadership.

evaluation,[5] "modes,"[6] and strategies of legitimation or authorization. Especially considering that the use of Pentateuchal (and other biblical) traditions is a stylistic feature of the book, Jeremiah is an ideal candidate for transformations of leadership, as was already pointed out by Dalit Rom-Shiloni: "[T]he prophet's intertextual familiarity with earlier (or contemporaneous) traditions designates a transformation within prophetic intellectual leadership [...]".[7] In light of the various differences between the Hebrew and the Greek text, it is obvious that the issue of leadership could be also approached from the *perspective of textual history*. Regardless of how exactly the textual evidence is explained, there can be no doubt that significant textual phenomena or developments concern claims of leadership, legitimacy, and authority (see *J. Erzberger*). In addition, the book's textual (and literary) history is not totally independent from the evolving culture of writing in Israel. The textual (and literary) processes linked to the formation of the book as well as the ways it reflects on literacy and the nature of scripture were without doubt also influenced by aspects of leadership (see *L. J. M. Claassens*). Since the book of Jeremiah underwent a long and complex literary history that includes preexilic, exilic, early and probably also later postexilic strata and redactions, it is evident that aspects of leadership can be considered relevant also from a *diachronic perspective* (see *C. M. Maier*). Finally, it has to be stressed that questions of leadership and authority could be addressed from a *sociotheoretical and historical point of view*. The book of Jeremiah is set against the backdrop of the imperial invasion by the Babylonians that threatened not only Jerusalem and its inhabitants, but also Judah's political independence and the Judahite monarchy as a whole. It reflects a period of great affliction and social change just before and during the military attacks in Jerusalem (597, 587, and 581 BCE) on the one hand and restoration on the other, as is evident from the polarity between judgment and salvation. Theology and history are highly interconnected within the book. The historical events in the background of the book as well as its (theological-ideological) strategies to cope with them are very much linked to concepts of leadership and their transformation.

Since a significant amount of research has been done on Jeremiah as a prophetic leader, especially with a focus on him as a new Moses, the articles in the present volume follow a different approach by focusing on several key ques-

---

[5] It is noteworthy that the book of Jeremiah in particular often construes leadership *ex negativo* by criticizing specific types of leadership or specific leaders.
[6] Here, the term "mode" refers to the way in which leadership is distributed (e.g., dual leadership, with democratizing, channeling, or centralizing tendencies).
[7] Dalit M. Rom-Shiloni. 2018. "Prophets in Jeremiah in Struggle over Leadership, or Rather over Prophetic Authority?" *Biblica* 99:351–372, 370.

tions: the *evaluation of kingship*, the *notion of epistemic heroes within prophetic leadership*, and the *relationship between the people of Israel and its leadership* as well as the *competition between Davidic descendants and Levitical priests*.

Christl M. Maier focuses on the evaluation of kingship in Jeremiah by using Jer 21:1–23:8, the cycle of oracles against the kings, as an example of a discourse on (failed) leadership. This passage uses two concepts as criteria for judging the last kings of Judah. Within all diachronic strata of the text, the pursuit of justice and righteousness and the ability to uphold an equitable social order functions as a decisive criterion for effective (royal) leadership. This idea is complemented by the notion of the king as a shepherd who is responsible for nourishing and protecting his entire flock. Based on these two criteria, the oracle evaluates all of the later Judahite kings in a negative way. None of them was able to fulfill his royal duties towards his subjects. Interestingly, this explanation or coping strategy for the end of the Judahite monarchy holds on to the hope for a better son of David with two modifications. While the concept of justice is exclusively linked to YHWH and the arrival of the expected Davidic son is postponed to the indefinite future (Jer 23:5), the request to perform justice and righteousness is addressed to the whole community (Jer 22:1–5). This transformation not only democratizes a royal duty or responsibility but also strengthens the bond between the community and YHWH as the "source" of justice.

Drawing on José Medina's idea of "epistemic heroes," *L. Juliana M. Claassens* focuses on two characters, Baruch (Jer 36) and Ebed-melech (Jer 38), who join Jeremiah in resisting the abuse of power they are experiencing at the king's court and, ultimately, ensure the survival of the prophet and the prophetic word despite all immediate danger. By speaking truth to power, and continuing what Jeremiah started, Baruch, the scribe, as well as the scroll he has written and rewritten embody the survival of the prophetic ministry. Also Ebed-melech, a significant "other" in regard to ethnicity (foreigner), sexuality (eunuch), and status (servant), is crucial for the survival of Jeremiah and the prophetic ministry as a whole: Out of compassion he stands up to the king and names the injustice that is transpiring. It is precisely a marginalized person who plays a significant role in helping to resist imperial domination. Thus, in their respective ways, Baruch and Ebed-melech emerge as epistemic heroes in their own right, opening up some intriguing perspectives on prophetic leadership. The book of Jeremiah portrays not only prophets or intellectuals as epistemic heroes, but also ordinary people who, together with Jeremiah, resist injustice and the abuse of power. This observation significantly widens our understanding of prophetic leadership and its role of resistance, which is broader and deeper than usually assumed.

Johanna Erzberger, finally, addresses the royal oracle of Jer^{MT} 33:14–26. This passage builds heavily on intertextual links with the books of Samuel, Kings, and Jeremiah, indicating that the author was reflecting on other texts to develop a new understanding of the Davidic covenant applied to Jerusalem, the Levites, and the people. While the oracle is often understood to promote a dual model of leadership, Erzberger shows that it not only modifies earlier concepts of leadership but also reinterprets the relationship between the people and its leadership by identifying the urban elites of Jerusalem with "Israel." According to Jer^{MT} 33:14–26, Israel is defined and represented by its leadership. It is not a certain ideology or the Torah (as in Jer^{LXX}) what ensures Israel's identity and existence, but Israel's leadership. The relationship between David's descendants and the Levitical priests, however, remains ambiguous within the oracle. The contradictory textual dynamics of a consecutive de- and reevaluation of the Davidic figure, linked to the Levites (who ultimately disappear), is explained by their historical background: While the devaluation of a Davidic figure, whose description is based on earlier traditions which could not be ignored, goes back to its irrelevance in postexilic times, the Levitical priests are considered to represent one of the groups in power during this period. Thus, the passage holds on to a textual tradition in the case of the Davidic figure, but reflects an existing reality as far as the Levitical priests are concerned.

The Books of Haggai and Zechariah

The books of Haggai and Zechariah present an especially broad range of concepts of leadership. To begin with, in Haggai and Zech 1–8, issues of leadership are debated in a dense and detailed manner. Based on the events immediately following the return from exile, Haggai and Zech 1–8 negotiate the question of appropriate human leadership using the responsibility for and the power over the reconstruction of the temple as a cipher for the legitimate claim to leadership. Many different voices participated in this discourse, thus pointing to complex debates about legitimate claims to authority and leadership in the Persian and/or Hellenistic periods. In its present shape, the book depicts a diarchic form of leadership of the high priest Joshua and Zerubbabel, the governor of Davidic descent (cf. the narrative passages in Haggai framing the prophetic oracles), combined with royal or messianic expectations (Zerubbabel as the future royal leader in Hag 2:20–23; a mysterious future Davidic "shoot" in Zech 3:8; 6:12) and the idea of a politically powerful, if not to say royal, high priesthood (cf. the crowned high priest in Zech 6:9–15*). Thus, the book presents itself as the product of multiple transformations of concepts of leadership which can probably best be explained in terms of a multi-staged diachronic development of the text. The specific agendas regarding concepts of leadership behind the texts in Haggai and their socio-historical and political background are also a topic of scholarly debate, as is reflected by the contribution of *Jan Rückl*, who addresses two of the most prominent concepts of leadership in the book of Haggai, namely, a royal/messianic and a diarchic form of leadership. Regarding the oracle to Zerubbabel in Hag 2:20–23, Rückl opts against the frequent interpretation of the text in terms of a messianic promise that uses Zerubbabel as a cipher for future expectations. Instead, "Hag 2:21b–23 should be considered one of those clearly unfulfilled oracles in the Hebrew Bible that, precisely for that reason, have a good chance of being authentic prophecies." Clearly distinguishable from this, the narrative passages framing the prophetic oracles advance a diarchic form of leadership. According to Rückl, the attribution of the responsibility for the rebuilding of the temple (which is traditionally a royal prerogative) to the high priest (see esp. Zech 6:9–15) has a legitimating function with regard to the office: Ideas of a dyarchy, "as vague and utopian they may have been, could contribute to an increase in at least some kind of soft power for the high priest."

The articles by *Martin Schott* and *Hervé Gonzalez* focus on the latter parts of the book of Zechariah and deal with the complex and diverse interplay of concepts of leadership in Zech 9–14. The concepts of leadership presented in these chapters differ significantly from what we find in Haggai and Zech 1–8, which may point to a different political background, probably reflecting the downfall of the Persian Empire from the outset. Both authors agree that Zech 9–14 did not develop independently of Zech 1–8. Thus, especially as regards the concept of royal leadership, it is insightful to evaluate how traditional royal ideology in general and the reflections on it in Haggai and Zech 1–8 in particular are continued or transformed in Zech 9–14.

Focusing on Zech 9:9–10, *Martin Schott* argues that the messianic expectation of this text connects to the view of leadership in Haggai and Zech 1–8: The passiveness of the king is grounded in Hag 2:20–23, and the concentration on a royal figure fits together with the presumably late verses Zech 3:6 and Zech 6:12, which downgrade the high priest (who is presented as active and powerful in other parts of the text) "to a mere placeholder for the future Davidic *zemah*." At the same time, however, the ideals of Haggai and Zech 1–8 are considerably transformed into a unique messianic concept: In an incomparable way, Zech 9:9–10, which might be among the oldest parts of Deutero-Zechariah, stresses the passiveness of the king and his dependence on God, presenting a humble messiah riding on a donkey who is not involved in military actions at all. According to Schott, this clearly documents a shift from human power to divine power, which becomes more radicalized over the course of the redaction history of Zech 9–14: In Zech 14, there is no room left for a human leader at all. The redefinition of royal leadership in eschatological terms (in addition to the "shoot" passages in Zech 3:6 and 6:12, Schott also takes Hag 2:20–23 to be a messianic text) has been replaced by a purely theocratic eschatology (Zech 14:9).

Hervé Gonzalez evaluates the same material but sets a different focus by asking "how the monarchy and the royal house are envisaged in the utopian future that these prophetic materials depict," thus comparing Zech 9:9–10 with Zech 12:1–13:1. He argues that both texts revise traditional royal ideology. While Zech 9:9–10 promote the ideal of "Israel enjoying political independence on a large Levantine territory" with the humble king serving as an example of piety and reliance on YHWH, Zech 12:1–13:1 "attributes a *collective* form of leadership to the 'house of David,' restricted essentially to the city of Jerusalem and to military and ritual domains," i.e., without any further references to political (or royal) leadership. Gonzalez interprets this transformation of leadership functions regarding Davidic leadership against the background of socio-political changes in the early Hellenistic period, namely, in terms of a revision and a marginalization of the utopian idea of political independence under a royal figure. Thus, similar to Schott, he concludes that "[t]hese nuances can only be observed by accepting that chs. 9–14 form a complex literary ensemble rather than trying to harmonize the different notions they contain."

Leadership in Chronistic Literature

Leaving aside the complex and debated issue of a "Chronistic History," it cannot be doubted that the books of Ezra and Nehemiah on the one hand and the books of Chronicles on the other are, in their present shape, closely interrelated. Regarding these books' concepts of leadership, this applies at least insofar as the concepts of leadership both in Ezra/Nehemiah and Chronicles strongly reflect the complex processes of identity negotiation and (trans-)formation in Yehud during the Persian and Hellenistic periods.

The Books of Ezra and Nehemiah

The books of Ezra and Nehemiah reflect the multilayered processes of identity formation among the Judean community in Jerusalem in the Persian and early Hellenistic periods. Thus, it comes as no surprise that issues of leadership play a central role throughout these books. However, it should be noted that although Ezra and Nehemiah are contemporaneous with large parts of the historiographic and prophetic portions of the Hebrew Bible, they present their own concepts and ideals of leadership. Even Ezra 1–6, which obviously draw on the events reported in Hag and Zech 1–8, present a differentiated and detailed set of collective and individual leaders involved in the temple restoration and thus probably attest to distinct leadership agendas. Ezra 7–10 and Nehemiah, however, clearly aim to model the books' eponymous figures as leaders in a rather unique way, focusing on innovative concepts of leadership such as Nehemiah's office of governor or Ezra as a priestly scribe. As a piece of theology in the guise of historiography, the intense and direct reflection of the complex interplay between Persian and Judean authority is one of the books' defining features, as becomes clear from the two articles on Ezra and Nehemiah in this volume.

Anna-Maria Bortz investigates the complex interplay of concepts of leadership in the temple building account in Ezra 1–6 and comes to the conclusion that Ezra 1–6, imagining the new beginning after the exile from a Hellenistic perspective, integrates multiple restoration traditions and combines them into original concepts of leadership. Bortz underscores that Ezra 1–3 and Ezra 5–6 each have their own ideological and theological interests in presenting these historic events. By favoring the "Council of the Elders" as leaders of the community, the Aramaic Chronicle in Ezra 5–6 originally "bears witness to a concept of leadership during the restoration that differs significantly from what we know from other biblical texts." According to Bortz, the prophets and the individual leaders Zerubbabel and Joshua known from Haggai and Zech 1–8 were added later to the Aramaic Chronicle (5:1–2; 6:14) in order to emphasize the role of the prophets in the restoration of the temple.

As Bortz points out, Ezra 1–3 also adopts the prophetic tradition from Haggai and Zech 1–8 but not their concept of leadership, focusing instead on the leadership of the people, priests, and Levites as a whole. "Ezra 1–3 thus presents a compromise of different traditions. It combines the tradition of the Aramaic Chronicle in Ezra 5–6, which it seems to rewrite, as well as the prophetic traditions of Deutero-Isaiah and Haggai-Zechariah. In this way, the Hebrew prologue [...] gathers all the leaders of the early restoration that seem to have been associated with the rebuilding of the temple." By collecting all of the important figures associated with the temple's rebuilding, it creates "a glorious early phase of restoration that followed a second exodus and therefore epitomizes the beginning of the new *Heilszeit*" in which the focus is set on "the returnees as a whole – the community of the 'true Israel' and the primary protagonists of the early restoration."

Bob Becking's evaluation of the different leadership functions ascribed to Ezra takes as its starting point the "tension between Torah-based leadership and Persian commands." Interpreting Ezra and Nehemiah as "literary texts communicating a set of values through the guise of historical events," he considers whether Ezra is depicted as a Persian or rather as a Judean leader. By evaluating the diversity of the literary Ezra figures in terms of the Weberian categories of leadership, focusing on the Ezra in Neh 8 ("Ezra A") and the Ezra in Ezra 7–10 ("Ezra B"), he concludes that both Ezra A and Ezra B represent a multi-dimensional form of leadership combining charismatic, traditional, and juridical aspects, with the difference that Ezra A is dependent on the leadership of Nehemiah, while Ezra B is independent. As Ezra A and B are supported by king *and* God, "[b]oth the Israelite moral code and the Persian initiative drove their actions."

Becking interprets these literary findings in the context of the need for a twofold loyalty after the exile which arose out of Judah's loss of independence and incorporation into a vast empire and required a balancing act between the Persian government and the Yahwistic religion. "Apparently, Ezra A as well as Ezra B found ways to manoeuvre between the two, which also explains why neither can be classified fully as charismatic leaders. Both were restricted in their roles either of seconding Nehemiah or as an intermediary middleman." Thus, he concludes that "Ezra – and especially Ezra B – is best be seen as a middleman who was able to remain loyal to two sides: the Persian government and the Yahwistic religion (as he saw it). He was simultaneously a Persian and a Yehudite leader."

The Book of Chronicles

Since Chronicles presents a sophisticated "rewriting" of the monarchic period, issues of leadership are omnipresent within this book. Although several prior studies have dealt more or less explicitly with concepts of leadership in Chronicles, further research seems essential with regard to the following perspectives:

An extremely fruitful perspective is to look at the texts through the lens of *social theory*, that is social memory and social history in particular (see *E. Ben Zvi*). This perspective can facilitate an understanding of the processes of identity negotiation and reformulation in which Chronicles engages and the role of concepts of leadership within these processes. This is particularly interesting, since Chronicles provides a bridge between the monarchic past and the present Persian imperial rule. As a consequence, a *socio-historical perspective* is also worth exploring (see *L. Jonker*). Even though the concepts of leadership and claims to leadership found in Chronicles evidently do not reflect historical circumstances, they have a specific socio-historical context and setting that influenced the textual dynamics and *vice versa*. Moreover, they pose many challenges in *diachronic* respect. It is evident that the texts engage with traditions from both the Torah and the Former Prophets (esp. Samuel–Kings). However, Chronicles does not use biblical texts as a *Vorlage* by simply reproducing them, but shows a rather productive and innovative usage of traditions (see *Y. Levin* and *I. Cranz*). This observation is not only important for the redaction history of the Hebrew Bible but also raises the question of how and why Chronicles reshapes, re-conceptualizes, and transforms aspects of leadership.

The contributions of the present volume touch upon all of these perspectives and questions by focusing on four aspects: leadership in the world of memories and knowledge, the multilayered und multifaceted understanding of leadership on the imperial, provincial, tribal, and cultic level, the profile of judges, elders, and officers, and the motif of royal illness.

Using social theory and social memory as a lens, *Ehud Ben Zvi* provides insights into how multiple approaches, concepts, ideas and memories related to leadership that existed within the general world of knowledge and social mindscape of the postexilic literati interact and inform each other in Chronicles. This is exemplified by two case studies on the one hand (the heroic priest Azariah and the priest Jehoiada) and detailed observations regarding memories of kings evoked by Chronicles on the other. While guardianship is construed as the most essential form of leadership, it is not exclusively linked to the king. Centralized kingship is balanced by other models of (local) leaders with power, and even though Chronicles considers kings as historical agents, it stresses that they cooperate with others, such as officers or the people. In addition, Chronicles conveyed to the literati a sense that the king is neither a sufficient nor a necessary safeguard against chaos and that Israel is certainly able to remain faithful to YHWH without a king ruling over it. Thus, the need for a local and human king in terms of political thought seems to be downplayed. Chronicles helped the literati reading it to explore what leadership is about, while construing and remembering their (didactic, socializing) past, and as it did so it taught them why it was so important to remember that past also in the way their Chronicler did.

Louis C. Jonker investigates the varied leadership models that are reflected in Chronicles as a whole. Since the book of Chronicles communicates on at least four levels of socio-historical reality, instead of expecting one coherent understanding or portrayal of leadership, he opts for embedding and contextualizing the discourses on leadership on four different levels: imperial, provincial, tribal, and cultic. Based on case studies representing each of these levels (1 Chr 22:6–10; 2 Chr 13:1–14:1a; 2 Chr 13:23b–16:14 and 2 Chr 21:2–22:1; 1 Chr 10:1–14; 2 Chr 29–32), two insights become evident: First, even though the aforementioned socio-historical levels may overlap, coincide, and exert mutual influence on one another, each of them constitutes a unique rhetorical situation, which determines the ways notions of leadership are addressed and how they function in literature. Second, the narratives do not intend to provide an "applicable" model of leadership, but rather contribute to processes of identity negotiation and power-related processes of transformation in the late Persian period. Thus, Chronicles has a specific way of remembering models of leadership in the past in order to take part in ideological discourses in the present.

Yigal Levin examines the Chronicler's picture of the šōp^{e}ṭîm ("judges"), šōṭ^{e}rîm ("officers"), and z^{e}qenîm ("elders") using two guiding perspectives: first, a comparison between their appearances in Chronicles and the way they are presented in the Chronicler's "sources" (the Pentateuch and the Former Prophets), and second, a study of these office-holders as they are conceptualized in relation to the monarchy, priesthood, temple, and tribal institutions. Since there seems to be no relationship at all between the Chronicler's use of šōp^{e}ṭîm, šōṭ^{e}rîm, and z^{e}qenîm and that of other literature of the postexilic period, Levin argues that the Chronicler's picture of the "civil" leadership of preexilic Israel is not based on what he knew in his own day. Instead, the Chronicler's use of these terms seems to rely heavily on his sources. While in some cases the Chronicler simply retains the terms as he found them in his earlier source, in other cases (especially in his use of šōp^{e}ṭîm and šōṭ^{e}rîm) the Chronicler seems to have taken his understanding of their functions from other biblical traditions and incorporated them into his own narratives. His account of the monarchic period is based on the so-called Deuteronomistic History, and in many of the places in which Chronicles adds material to the account that he derives from it, the texts are informed by references to "the Torah of Moses" as a source of authority and a way to give his texts a more authoritative status.

Based on the analysis of how royal illnesses are represented in the so-called Deuteronomistic History and in Chronicles, *Isabel Cranz* shows how biblical historiography used the bodily integrity of the king as a starting point for formulating ideas about the expectations concerning Judah's and Israel's leadership. While in deuteronomistic texts instances of royal illness are used for casting aspersions on the institution of kingship and to anticipate the future annihilation of dynasties and nations, Chronicles takes up this motif and adapts it to the chronistic understanding of kingship and outlook on history. Even though the destruction of Judah and the end of the Davidic dynasty is never lost from view, the nature of kingship and the correct moral conduct of kings appear to be in the foreground. Taken together, it becomes evident that scribes living in post-monarchic Judah employed the motif of royal illness to draw attention to a broad array of different issues, such as problems relating to kingship, the conduct of individual kings, and the evaluation of dynasties. Despite the wide variety of issues that can be addressed through royal illness, when the motif occurs it typically points toward the eventual destruction of the nation and the end of Israel's and Judah's political independence. Thus, analyzing royal illness in the Bible provides insight into the articulation of national identity and the memory of kingship in Judah and Israel.

Comprehensive Aspects

In the last section of this volume, the editors present two studies which bring prophetic and chronistic literature together and offer some comprehensive and comparative remarks on the leadership concepts found therein. The contribution by *Sarah Schulz* focuses on the major point of contact between Haggai and Zech 1–8 on the one hand and Ezra 1–6 on the other: the parallel accounts of the rebuilding of the temple. The article takes a comparative perspective, with an emphasis on the leadership roles and functions ascribed to the individual leaders in both accounts, Zerubbabel and Joshua. On the basis of an evaluation of the concepts of leadership reflected in Haggai and Zech 1–8 and Ezra 1–6, Schulz concludes that they developed largely independently of each other. Haggai and Zech 1–8 present a complex set of concepts of leadership evolving around Zerubbabel and Joshua including messianic expectations, the ideal of a royal high priesthood, and perhaps even the attempt to promote the Persian governor of the province of Yehud as an indigenous Judean political leader. However, in Ezra 1–6 the notions of leadership at first developed independently of the two individuals. While the older parts in Ezra 5–6 and Ezra 1–3 favor the elders as the local leaders and the returnees as a collective entity respectively, Zerubbabel and Joshua are introduced into Ezra 1–6 only at an advanced stage of composition. The redaction draws on the older prophetic tradition in order to establish a totally distinct concept of leadership. Unlike in Haggai and Zech 1–8, in Ezra 1–6 the focus is not (and not even implicitly) on characterizing Zerubbabel and Joshua as leaders. Instead, in agreement with Bortz, Schulz concludes that their role as leading figures in the temple restoration is employed as a means of advancing a prophetic agenda.

Thus, the two accounts, as different as they are, at least have in common that they utilize the temple restoration as a crucial event to debate issues of leadership and authority during the postexilic period. By tying contemporary ideals to this historic event, for centuries the question "Who was responsible for the temple's restoration?" becomes a cipher for the question "Who is the legitimate leader of the community?"

In the final contribution of this volume, *Katharina Pyschny* reevaluates the concepts of prophetic leadership in Chronicles and its relationship to prophetic literature. Based on her analysis, the notion of the demise or decline of prophecy in the postexilic period proves, once again, to be a rather problematic oversimplification. In fact, Chronicles knows a remarkable variety of prophets and prophetic or inspired figures. These figures are first and foremost perceived in their role as mediators of God's words. The authority of prophetic leaders seems to be a given, either via the notion of prophecy as a divinely authorized institution (in the case of prophets known from Samuel–Kings) or via *ad hoc* inspirations by the divine spirit (in the case of inspired figures). This remarkable presence of prophetic figures not only serves to legitimize the Chronicler's presentation and interpretation of history but also reflects a transformed understanding of prophetic leadership characterized by a twofold democratization (with regard to the prophets on the one hand and the audience on the other). Furthermore, Chronicles attests to several transformations and distinctive emphases regarding prophetic functions. This is especially true of the prophet's role as preserver and interpreter of history, which is very pronounced in Chronicles. In addition, the prophetic function of warning is transformed into acts of counseling, preaching, and teaching. Especially in these contexts, prophetic speeches show an extensive appeal to and citation of the Torah in particular but also to prophetic literature. By portraying prophets as figures who cite and midrashically transform Scripture, prophetic leadership is characterized by proclaiming God's will (in accordance with the Torah) and interpreting it (in light of its "actualization" by the Prophets). In addition, prophetic utterances are not only an instrument for teaching the Torah but are qualitatively on a par with the Torah insofar as they likewise reveal the authoritative and normative words of God. Significantly, this authenticity and legitimacy of prophetic utterances is constituted by the Chronicler's engagement with Pentateuchal and prophetic traditions. For Chronicles, prophetic agency is, thus, closely linked to the interpretation of Scripture ("scribal prophetic leadership," *schriftgelehrte prophetische Führung*). Especially in the case of the inspired figures, it is exactly this phenomenon that not only characterizes prophetic agency but constitutes the prophet's legitimacy at the same time.

As editors, we hope that through its diversity and discursivity, our volume will spark new critical impulses and thus provide a helpful contribution to recent scholarship on leadership in prophetic and chronistic literature.

II: Concepts of Leadership in Selected Prophetic Literature

Christl M. Maier
Why Judean Monarchy Failed: A Discourse on Leadership in Jer 21:1–23:8

The book of Jeremiah focuses on the destruction of Jerusalem and its temple in 587 BCE by the Babylonians, which brought the Judean monarchy to an end. The book offers a host of reasons for how this catastrophe could happen and who is responsible for it. The most dominant argument within the book is that Judah neglected YHWH and instead followed other gods (Jer 1:16; 5:7; 7:9; 11:10; 16:11; 19:4; 22:9; 25:6; 35:15) – the so-called deuteronomistic view of exilic redactors (Thiel 1981, 107–112; but cf. Maier 2002, 19–37). While this reasoning targets Judah and Jerusalem as a whole, another strand specifically accuses Judah's last kings. Their corruption and self-confidence is portrayed in the cycle of oracles against the kings in Jer 21:1–23:8. In my view, these chapters present a discourse on failed leadership in preexilic Judah but also offer suggestions for how to avoid another disaster in the future.

After (1) introducing the structure of Jer 21–24, I will (2) briefly analyze the oracles against the kings Jehoahaz, Jehoiachin, and Jehoiakim. In the oracle against Jehoiakim (22:13–19), leadership is related to (3) the royal duty of upholding justice and righteousness, whereas Jer 23:1–4 presents (4) the concept of the king as shepherd. Since the Judean monarchy came to an end and could not be restored, in Jer 22:1–5 the first concept (upholding justice) is presented as (5) an obligation of the entire community.

1 The Structure of the Cycle of Words against the Kings

Jeremiah 21:1–24:10 assembles quite different passages ranging from short oracles of doom to Jeremiah's communication with a king and even a prose speech of the prophet that offers the alternative between doom and redemption. Jeremiah 21:1–10 and 24:1–10 frame the collection, and both passages mention the last

---

Note: The author is Extraordinary Professor in the disciplinary group Old and New Testament at the University of Stellenbosch, South Africa. The research for this article was supported by the German Research Foundation.

Judean king, Zedekiah. Within the cycle of oracles there are also some passages that address other figures, namely personified Jerusalem (21:13–14; 22:8–9, 20–23) and a group of prophets (23:9–20). The following structure distinguishes different speakers and addressees as well as text forms and contents.[1]

> 21:1–10 Jeremiah's words to a delegation sent by King Zedekiah
>   21:11–12 Introduction to oracles about the royal house
>   21:13–14 Oracle of doom addressed to a female figure (= Jerusalem)
>   *22:1–5 Prose sermon to the king, his court and the people in the king's palace*
>   22:6–7 Oracle about the royal house
>   22:8–9 Reflection about the fall of the city
>   22:10–12 Oracle about Shallum (= Jehoahaz)
>   22:13–19 Woe cry and oracle of doom addressed to Jehoiakim
>   22:20–23 A call to lament addressed to the city
>   22:24–30 Oracle of doom addressed to Coniah (= Jehoiachin)
>   23:1–4 Woe cry about the current shepherds and *announcement of new shepherds*
>   *23:5–6 The rise of a righteous sprout for David*
>   *23:7–8 The gathering of all dispersed people as a new exodus*
>   23:9–20 Oracles against the prophets
> 24:1–10 Jeremiah's vision of the two fig baskets (Zedekiah's generation = rotten figs)

With regard to concepts of leadership, my analysis of Jer 21:1–23:8 suggests a diachronic development of the text similar to John Job's thorough study on Jeremiah's kings (cf. Job 2006, 165–169). Some brief oracles directly address a certain monarch and his specific shortcomings (22:10–12, 13–19, 24–30). They refer to King Josiah as a positive counter-example (22:11, 15) and express the hope that King Zedekiah may be a better leader (23:5–6). As a criterion for good leadership, they point to the king's pursuit of justice and righteousness. This criterion later gets elaborated in more general statements about the royal house (21:11–12; 22:6–7; 23:7–8). Parallel to this development, the concept of the king as shepherd to his people serves as another criterion and a reason to condemn Judah's last kings (23:1–4). In a postexilic prose speech situated in the royal palace (22:1–5), upholding justice and righteousness becomes a duty not only of the king, but of the entire community. Finally, the collection was framed by two passages that focus on Zedekiah's failure and the impossibility of warding off the catastrophe (21:1–10; 24:1–10). I will substantiate this thesis by interpreting the passages in the order in which I just mentioned them.

---

[1] Passages that predict or include redemption are set in italics.

2 Oracles against Jehoahaz, Jehoiachin, and Jehoiakim

Several scholars argue that the three poetic oracles about a certain monarch in Jer 22:10–12, 13–19, 24–30 contain some authentic words of Jeremiah and are thus the earliest parts of chapters 21–24 (Hermisson 1998, 46; Thiel 1973, 241–244; Wanke 1995, 196–197, 201; Job 2006, 43–44, 53). Whereas the initial wording most probably did not name the king, in the written account the king was identified by name. All three oracles announce the demise of royal rule and predict an unusual death of the monarch.

2.1 Jehoahaz's Deportation and Death in a Foreign Land

Jeremiah 22:10–12 connects a rather vague prophetic call to lament with a divine announcement against a son of King Josiah. Due to its current context and its position in the cycle of oracles against the kings, the object of the unnamed audience's lament can be recognized as the heir to the throne, who is compared to his dead predecessor: "Do not weep for him who is dead, nor bemoan him; weep rather for him who goes away, for he shall return no more to see his native land" (Jer 22:10).[2]

With regard to the history of Judah, this situation may refer either to the transition from Josiah to his son Jehoahaz (2 Kgs 23:30–34) or from Jehoiakim to Jehoiachin (2 Kgs 23:36–24:16), since both sons were deported after only a short regency. Jeremiah's original audience certainly knew who is who in this saying (cf. Wanke 1995, 196). For later readers, the following prose verses identify the king to be mourned with Shallum, the fourth son of Josiah (1 Chr 3:15) whose throne name Jehoahaz is mentioned in 2 Kgs 23:30: "For thus says YHWH concerning Shallum, son of King Josiah of Judah, who succeeded his father Josiah as king and who went away from this place: 'He shall return here no more.' For in the place where they have carried him captive he shall die, and he shall never see this land again" (Jer 22:11–12).

Initially, the deportation of Shallum (= Jehoahaz) was presented as a reason for mourning (v. 10). Later, the call to mourn was transformed into an oracle about the king's fate in accordance with 2 Kgs 23:30–34: After Josiah's unexpected death at Megiddo, Jehoahaz was proclaimed king by the people of the land. Yet, Pharaoh Neco II exiled the young monarch to Egypt and installed another

---

[2] All translations from the Hebrew are my own.

son of Josiah, Jehoiakim, as vassal king. Shallum (= Jehoahaz) never returned to Judah and died in captivity. Thus, the editors of the initial, rather vague prophecy saw it fulfilled in the fate of Jehoahaz and thus identified the unnamed heir with this king who reigned for only three months in 609 BCE.

2.2 Jehoiachin's Deportation and the End of the Royal Line

Jeremiah 22:24–30 presents a divine oath that YHWH will cut off his signet ring, Coniah (= Jehoiachin; cf. Job 2006, 79–85),³ and hand him over to the Babylonians. The passages proclaim that the king and his mother will be cast away into a foreign land, from which they will not return. The announcement in v. 30a that Coniah will remain childless, however, was not fulfilled; 1 Chr 3:17–18 lists the names of seven sons, and 2 Kgs 25:27–30 reports Jehoiachin's release from prison and privileged treatment in Babylonia, which is supported by a Babylonian rations list mentioning the sons of the king (Weippert 2010, nos. 266–267). Therefore, a later editor attenuated the prediction by declaring that no man of his house will sit on David's throne again (22:30b). This predication came true, since all efforts to reestablish the Davidic dynasty in postexilic Judah failed.

2.3 Jehoiakim's Disreputable Death

While Jer 22:10–12, 24–30 do not include any critique of the king, Jer 22:13–19 accuses a Judean monarch of lavishness and lack of justice:

> ¹³ Woe to him who builds his house by unrighteousness (בלא־צדק), and his upper rooms by injustice (בלא משפט); who makes his neighbor work for nothing, and does not give him his wages; ¹⁴ who says, "I will build myself a spacious house with large upper rooms and cut out windows for it, paneled with cedar and painted with vermilion." ¹⁵ Are you a king because you compete in cedar? Did not your father eat and drink and do justice and righteousness (משפט וצדקה)? *Then it was well with him.*⁴ ¹⁶ He judged the cause of the afflicted and needy; *then it was well.* Is not this to know me? says YHWH. ¹⁷ But aren't your eyes and your heart only set on your dishonest gain *and on the blood of the innocent – shedding it, and on oppression and extortion – practicing it.* ¹⁸ Therefore thus says YHWH *concerning King Jehoiakim, son of Josiah of Judah*: They shall not lament for him, saying, "Alas, my brother!" or "Alas, sister!" They shall not lament for him, saying, "Alas, lord!" or "Alas, his majesty!" ¹⁹ With the burial of a donkey he shall be buried – dragged off and thrown out beyond the gates of Jerusalem.

---

3 For the different forms of the king's name in MT and LXX, see Job 2006, 79–85.
4 The sections in italics are, in my view, later additions.

The passage connects a woe-cry (vv. 13–14) with a direct accusation (vv. 16–17) and an oracle of doom (vv. 18–19). The king is criticized for building a luxurious palace with compulsory labor of his people and for augmenting his own wealth by unjust means. The king's father serves as a positive foil in that he is said to execute justice and righteousness, which includes the defense of the afflicted and the poor in court.

While the oracle's initial audience may have recognized the addressee, for later readers the name of Jehoiakim was added in v. 18. This identification led to the inclusion of more actions known of this king from other texts in v. 17b: His shedding of innocent blood probably refers to his order that the prophet Uriah be killed (Jer 26:23); the oppression of his people may be linked to his imposition of heavy taxes in order to pay tribute to Pharaoh Neco (2 Kgs 23:35). Jehoiakim's building of a palace, however, is not corroborated by other sources. With a climactic ending, v. 19 predicts a horrible fate for Jehoiakim, the "burial of a donkey," which implies that the dead body may be thrown to the dung heap outside of the city wall. The narrative about Jehoiakim's burning of the scroll with Jeremiah's words records a similar prophecy, namely that "his dead body shall be thrown out to the heat by day and the frost by night" (Jer 36:30). Not to be buried would be a disreputable death for any person, and especially for a king (cf. Jer 8:2; 9:21; 16:4; 25:33). The lack of proper lament for a dead king already deprives him of his royal status. As Saul Olyan (2014, 271–279) has argued, the "burial of a donkey" would suggest a ritual act of reclassification which dehumanizes the king and makes him an object of shame.

Contrary to this shameful end, 2 Kgs 24:6 reads "Jehoiakim slept with his ancestors" and thus uses the conventional phrase for a regular death but without the usual burial notice "and was buried in the city of David" (cf. 1 Kgs 11:43; 14:31; 15:24; 2 Kgs 16:20).[5] According to 2 Kgs 24:12, Jehoiakim's son Jehoiachin faced the Babylonian answer to his father's breach of covenant, surrendered to Nebuchadnezzar and was deported to Babylon with his family and officials (cf. Jer 24:1).

Due to the discrepancy in these notices about Jehoiakim's death, the problem arises that the announcement of the "donkey burial" in Jer 22:19 may entail

---

5 In contrast, 2 Chr 36:6 declares that Jehoiakim was deported to Babylon in fetters and thus correlates his fate with that of Zedekiah. Second Chronicles 36:8 LXX adds the note "and Jehoiakim slept with his ancestors and was buried in Ganoza with his ancestors." Ganoza transcribes the Hebrew גן־עזא "the garden of Uzza" where the tombs of Manasseh and Amon are located (2 Kgs 21:18, 26). While the first notice can be attributed to the Chronicler, who sought to link the fates of the last Judean kings, the addition in LXX may be a scribe's effort to balance Jehoiakim's death in 2 Kgs 24:6 with Jeremiah's prophecy by referring to the garden in which the 'apostate' kings Manasseh and Amon were also buried; cf. Lipschits 2002, 4.3–4.4.

false prophecy (Carroll 2006, 432),[6] which would support the conclusion that it may be an authentic word of Jeremiah (cf. Wanke 1995, 199). As Robert Carroll (2006, 433–434) rightly observes, the book of Jeremiah characterizes King Jehoiakim as a villain who defies all divine advice, and it does not record any encounter between Jehoiakim and a prophet. In analyzing all of the available sources, Oded Lipschits (2002, 3, 2, 11) argues that Jehoiakim probably died a natural death, but when the author of the Deuteronomistic History recorded this, he deliberately left out the burial notice because he, like Jeremiah, considered the king to be a sinner. Another way to explain this strange prophecy is that – without claiming that it is historically reliable – it was formulated as a sort of act-consequence relationship in that the king's neglected dead body corresponds to his neglect of his people during his lifetime. Thus, his shameful end would signify divine retribution for his violent and dishonorable deeds during his reign.

3 The Royal Duty of Upholding Justice and Righteousness

The concept of leadership mentioned in Jer 22:15–17 is the pursuit of מִשְׁפָּט וּצְדָקָה, most often translated as "justice and righteousness" (NRSV) or "justice and equity" (NJPS). The Hebrew term מִשְׁפָּט designates the preexisting order of things, an area of "what is right" in the world (Liedke 1996, 1005). In a narrower sense it may also designate the entire written law and, especially in the plural, a court decision. The term צְדָקָה refers to both a behavior that builds up the community (in German "gemeinschaftsgemäßes Verhalten") and the situation of *shalom* in that community (Koch 1996, 513, 515). Taken together, "[b]oth idioms express the totality of what is just and ethical" (Ho 1991, 147).

In the Hebrew Bible, doing מִשְׁפָּט וּצְדָקָה is an ideal of proverbial wisdom that is used as a yardstick by the social critiques of Amos (5:7, 24), Isaiah (1:21; 5:7; 28:17), and Jeremiah (5:28) (Wolff 1985, 287–288). According to Ezekiel (18:5, 19; 33:14, 16), pursuing justice and righteousness is seen as the responsibility of everyone. In Jer 9:23, YHWH is called the founder of justice and righteousness

---

[6] Other examples of failed prophecy are Huldah's prediction that Josiah would be gathered to his ancestors in peace (2 Kgs 22:20), although the king died by the hand of Pharaoh Neco (2 Kgs 23:29). Similarly, Jeremiah's announcement that Zedekiah will die in peace and not by the sword (34:4–5) does not match his violent treatment by the Babylonians narrated in Jer 39:4–7; cf. Carroll 2006, 432–433.

(cf. also Isa 33:5). This divine origin has a parallel in the Assyrian goddess *kittu(m)* "order, justice" and the god *mīšaru(m)* "justice, right," both of which symbolize righteousness in daily life and fair court procedures. Both deities accompany the sun god Shamash and guide the king in his reign (Koch 1996, 509–510). In Egypt, justice is related to Ma'at, a just world order established by the gods, which nevertheless has to be preserved daily by the Pharaoh. Within this ancient Near Eastern tradition, the Israelite king as YHWH's representative on earth is responsible for implementing justice and righteousness in Israel and sustaining the social order in his realm (see Pss 45:7–8; 72:1–4; 2 Sam 8:15 // 1 Chr 18:14; 1 Kgs 10:9 // 2 Chr 9:8). While this concept seems rather abstract, a specific application is that the king helps marginalized people to be treated fairly in court proceedings (Jer 22:16; Ps 72:2).

In Jer 22:15, Josiah is said to have fulfilled his royal duty, and such an assessment parallels Josiah's positive portrait in the Deuteronomistic History (2 Kgs 22–23). According to Jer 22:13–17, Jehoiakim failed because he disregarded the right of his subjects by using corvée labor and seeking his own advantage. In Jer 36, he is portrayed as the antipode of Josiah, because he has the scroll of Jeremiah's prophetic words burned and thus disregards the divine word, whereas Josiah honored it (2 Kgs 22:11).

The pursuit of justice and righteousness is also mentioned in an announcement of a future king in Jer 23:5–6, which has been widely interpreted as an exilic (Wanke 1995, 205–206) or early postexilic (Carroll 2006, 447) oracle of salvation that seeks to invigorate the hope of reestablishing the Davidic dynasty:

> ⁵ See, days are coming, oracle of YHWH, when I will raise for David a righteous sprout (צמח). He shall reign as king and deal wisely; he shall execute justice and righteousness in the land. ⁶ In his days, Judah will be saved and Israel will dwell securely. And this is his name by which he will be called: "YHWH is our righteousness" (יהוה צדקנו; LXX: Ιωσεδεκ).

The use of the word "sprout" for a royal descendant has parallels in Neo-Assyrian and Phoenician inscriptions (Maier 2016b, 883). The name of the Davidic heir to the throne, יהוה צדקנו "YHWH is our righteousness," forms a wordplay on King Zedekiah, whose name צדקיהו literally means "my righteousness is Yah." The connection is even more explicit in the LXX version, which renders the sprout's name as Ιω-σεδεκ, thus as an equivalent to the name *Zedek-iah*, since the theophoric element may be placed at the beginning or at the end of a name (Lust 2004, 43–44).[7]

---

[7] Further parallels are *Jecon-iah/Con-iah* in Jer 22:24, 24:1 and *Jeho-iachin* in 2 Kgs 24:6, 8.

In a meticulous study, Raik Heckl (2006, 190–193) has argued plausibly that Jer 23:5–6* originally praised Zedekiah as a righteous king due to his pro-Babylonian policy (cf. 2 Kgs 24:17).[8] Heckl's main arguments are based on the subtle differences between the MT and LXX as well as on a careful analysis of the wording and its context. Heckl's interpretation is strengthened by the observation that Zedekiah is not mentioned in the brief oracles, but only in the late framing of the collection. It is thus plausible that the first collection of oracles against Jehoahaz, Jehoiakim, and Jehoiachin initially had its climax in a positive outlook to the reign of Zedekiah, the last king of Judah.

As Hermann-Josef Stipp (1996, 630–632) has demonstrated, the narrative in Jer 37:3–43:7 characterizes Zedekiah as a God-fearing king who acknowledges Jeremiah's position, asks him twice to consult YHWH on his behalf, and even rescues him from the hands of his own officials (37:20–21; 38:9–10, 24–27). Although Jeremiah announces Zedekiah's defeat (37:9–10, 17; 38:17–23), he does not indict the king of any personal guilt, but blames his officials (38:22). While these narratives may have been composed close to the end of the Judean monarchy (Stipp 1996, 628), later passages such as the introduction in 37:1–2, the speech about the manumission of slaves in Jer 34:8–22, as well as the frame in Jer 21:1–7 and 24:1–10 reverse the portrait of Zedekiah.[9] They harshly dismiss Zedekiah's policy, yet again, they do not mention any personal failure, but portray the king as the representative of a doomed generation.

A further interpretation of the idea that the king should uphold justice is offered in Jer 21:11–12, which in its current context forms a general introduction to the oracles addressed to specific monarchs:

> [11] To the house of the king of Judah: Hear the word of YHWH, [12] House of David! Thus says YHWH: Execute justice in the morning (דינו לבקר משפט) and deliver from the hand of the oppressor anyone who has been robbed, or else my wrath will go forth like fire and burn, with no one to quench it, [because of your evil doings].[10]

---

[8] For a similar interpretation, although based on different arguments, cf. Sweeney 2007, 308–321. He sees in Jer 23:5–6 a thematic parallel to Isa 11:1–16, which he dates to the time of Josiah. Contrary to Heckl, however, Sweeney does not offer a detailed analysis of Jer 23:1–8.

[9] The assessment that Jer 37:1–2 and 21:1–7 are to be dated later than the narrative in Jer 37–43 is based on their function as introductions. Moreover, 21:1–7 elaborates on a note in 37:3, as I have shown in Maier 2013, 138–140. A Persian-period dating for Jer 34:8–22 is the result of my analysis in Maier 2002, 248–281. The vision of the two fig baskets in Jer 24:1–10 is a late postexilic text that declares the entire Babylonian Golah as descendants of the first deportation under Jehoiachin and writes off from history all those who survived in Judah or in Egypt; see Stipp 2015; Maier 2016a, 120–122. While Job (2006, 99–119) suggests somewhat different datings for these texts, he agrees that Zedekiah's portrait has been modified by later redactors.

[10] The bracketed words are absent in the LXX.

This passage states more precisely that upholding justice for the Davidic dynasty means to execute just verdicts in practice and to stop any unjust or oppressive treatment of marginalized persons. This introduction was probably added to the preexilic collection of oracles in order to stress the idea that God confronts the kings with his expectations for their rule and keeps watch over how they carry out their duty.

4 The Concept of the King as Shepherd

A different concept of leadership is presented in Jer 23:1–4, which connects a woe cry and an oracle of doom with an oracle of salvation for a remnant that has survived:

> [1] Woe to the shepherds who destroy and scatter the sheep of my pasture – [oracle of YHWH]! [2] Therefore thus says YHWH, [the God of Israel,] concerning [the shepherds] who shepherd my people: It is you who have scattered my flock! You drove them away and you have not attended to them. See, I am attending to you for your evil doings – [oracle of YHWH]. [3] *Yet, I myself will gather the remnant of my flock out of all the land[s] where I have dispersed them, and I will bring them back to their fold, and they shall be fruitful and multiply.* [4] I will raise up shepherds over them who will shepherd them, and they shall not fear any longer, or be dismayed, [nor shall any be missing] – oracle of YHWH.

The shepherd is a conventional ancient Near Eastern metaphor for the king known from ancient Sumer up to the first millennium (cf. Brettler 1989, 36–37). The role of a shepherd is to guard his flock, to nourish and to protect his animals (cf. Ezek 34:4–6). In the book of Jeremiah, the metaphor is used for kings, both Judean (2:8; 3:15; 10:21; 22:22; 50:6) and foreign (6:3; 12:10; 49:19), and in 31:10 YHWH is compared to a shepherd. The metaphor focuses on the relationship between the king and his entire people without distinguishing between wealthy and poor, oppressive and victimized subjects. The verdict in Jer 23:1–2 that the shepherds destroy and scatter their flock refers to the Judean kings' political failure to protect their people from Babylonian aggression. While their policy of changing alliances is not criticized explicitly, the metaphor holds the Judean kings, not the Babylonians, responsible for war and exile. In v. 4, the divine voice announces the commissioning of new shepherds who will guide the flock in peace and security – a situation that stands in stark contrast to the present conditions. This scenario of an exchange of shepherds is interrupted by v. 3, in which YHWH declares himself responsible for the dispersion of the flock and announces that he will gather its remnant and return it to its own fold – thus announcing the return of the exiled people to Judah.

The assessment of the Judean kings' failure and the motif of the remnant reveal that Jer 23:1–4 presupposes the fall of Jerusalem (cf. Wanke 1995, 203). Due to its differing picture, v. 3 may be a later comment that takes up motifs from Ezek 34:12–14 (Carroll 2006, 444). In its current context, the passage serves as a new introduction to the prediction of the Davidic sprout and transfers its fulfillment into the future, most probably because also Zedekiah proved to be a bad shepherd who could not protect his people.

In exploring these successive additions to the early oracles, one can see that the exilic redactors of the Jeremiah tradition agreed with the negative perspective of the preexilic cycle of words against Judah's kings but also sustained the hope for a new monarch. Their postexilic successors interpreted the return of the exiled as YHWH's willingness to guide his people. These reinterpretations, however, are not the last ones that can be discerned in Jer 21–24.

5 Upholding Justice and Righteousness as an Obligation of the Entire Community

Jeremiah 22:1–5 records a prose speech of Jeremiah to be delivered in the king's palace, which offers an alternative of doom or salvation depending on the behavior of the king and his court as well as the people:

> [1] Thus says YHWH: Go down to the house of the king of Judah, and speak there this word, [2] and say: Hear the word of YHWH, King of Judah who sits on the throne of David – you, and your servants, and your people who enter these gates. [3] Thus says YHWH: Do[11] justice and righteousness, and deliver from the hand of the oppressor anyone who has been robbed. And do not oppress or ill-treat the alien, the orphan, and the widow, nor shed innocent blood in this place. [4] For if you will indeed obey this word, then through the gates of this house shall enter kings who sit on the throne of David, riding in chariots and on horses – they, and their servants, and their people. [5] But if you will not heed these words, I swear by myself – oracle of YHWH – that this house shall become a desolation.

This speech follows the style of the temple sermon in Jer 7 and the Sabbath speech in Jer 17:19–27. The divine instructions in v. 3 reiterate phrases from the literary context. The call to act with justice and righteousness concords with the characterization of King Josiah in Jer 22:15–16. What the execution of justice and righteousness entails is then specified. The command to "deliver from the hand of the oppressor anyone who has been robbed" is a verbatim parallel to

---

[11] The verb forms in vv. 3–5 are plural.

Jer 21:12. The explicit prohibition to exploit or violate the alien, the orphan, and the widow has a parallel in Jer 7:6 and refers to the listing of marginalized community members in Deuteronomy (10:18; 24:19, 20, 21; 27:19). The prohibition to shed innocent blood recalls the concrete indictment of King Jehoiakim in Jer 22:17.[12]

In light of the plural imperatives in vv. 3–4, Jeremiah's exhortative speech expects the king, his court, and his people to do justice and righteousness, which would include fighting political and economic oppression. The speech offers an alternative scenario: If the addressees uphold these basic values of community loyalty, the Davidic dynasty will be preserved.[13] If they do not heed the divine commands, the king's house – that is, the dynasty and the palace – will be destroyed.

Although the speech is located in the king's palace, it is not clear which Judean king the prophet addresses. Rhetorically, all Judean kings, their officials, and the Judean people are addressed at the same time. Since the speech gathers explicit directives from the literary context and alludes to specific regulations in Deuteronomy, the passage cannot be part of the preexilic tradition in the book. Rather, the speech formulates a social ethos for the postexilic community and its alternative scenario serves a twofold purpose. The negative prediction explains why Davidic rule came to an end, whereas the positive one strengthens the hope for its restoration and promotes a community ethos that accords with the law in Deuteronomy. Moreover, the speech presents Jeremiah as a teacher of the Torah, who cites specific regulations that address the social order of the community. According to Deut 17:18–20, every Israelite king should have a copy of the Torah at hand and take it as a guideline for his policy. In Jer 22:1–5, however, Jeremiah addresses his teaching of the Torah to the entire community. Thus, the pursuit of justice and righteousness is no longer a prerogative of the king or any leading figure. If the whole community executes justice and righteousness, royal leaders are even superfluous – and this is the actual situation in postexilic Yehud.

6 Conclusion

The book of Jeremiah evaluates the last Judean kings in a differentiated way. Josiah is characterized as an ideal king who upheld righteousness and justice.

---
12 For a detailed analysis see Maier 2002, 225–249.
13 The view that the continuation of the Davidic dynasty depends on the right behavior of the king, his court, and his people is also raised in the Deuteronomistic History in exhortations to Solomon by David (1 Kgs 2:2–4) and by God (1 Kgs 9:4–9).

Jehoahaz and Jehoiachin are deplorable figures due to their short reign; they were deported by foreign rulers and did not see their land of birth again. Jehoiakim is characterized as a villain who was the negative antipode to his pious father Josiah. Zedekiah was first supposed to be a just and God-fearing leader, but turned out to be an insecure monarch who could not even control his own officials and in the end failed to protect his people from Babylonian aggression.

In Jer 21:1–23:8, there are two concepts used as criteria for judging the kings of Judah. The first is the pursuit of justice and righteousness, the upholding of an equitable social order, which in all stages of the text's development serves as a defining criterion for good leadership. The second is the idea that a king should act like a shepherd who nourishes and protects his entire flock. While the second concept focuses on the relationship between the monarch and his subjects, the first one differentiates between subjects and, in particular, addresses the power of the monarch to uphold justice in court and to end social and economic oppression of the marginalized.

In the overall perspective of the book, all of the last Judean kings fell short of these royal duties, and even Zedekiah, who first was expected to be a better leader, proved to be a failed monarch, which led to his negative portrayal in 21:1–7 and his designation as the first among the bad figs in the postexilic passage Jer 24:1–10.

Although the book of Jeremiah tries to cope with the loss of Jerusalem and the end of the Davidic monarchy, it is striking that the hope for a better son of David persisted, albeit with a twofold modification. First, the call to perform justice and righteousness is specified along the lines of the deuteronomic laws protecting the marginalized and is addressed to the entire community (Jer 22:1–5). Secondly, the concept of justice is related to YHWH alone, and the arrival of the expected Davidic "sprout of righteousness" is postponed to an indefinite future (Jer 23:5; cf. 33:15–16).

Bibliography

Brettler, Marc Zvi. 1989. *God is King: Understanding an Israelite Metaphor*. JSOTSup 76. Sheffield: Sheffield Academic Press.
Carroll, Robert P. 2006. *Jeremiah*. Vol. 1. Sheffield: Sheffield Phoenix Press.
Hermisson, Hans-Jürgen. 1998. "Die 'Königsspruch'-Sammlung im Jeremiabuch: Von der Anfangs- zur Endgestalt." In *Studien zu Prophetie und Weisheit: Gesammelte Aufsätze*, edited by Jörg Barthel, Hannelore Jaus, and Klaus Koenen, 37–58. FAT 23. Tübingen: Mohr Siebeck.
Heckl, Raik. 2006. "'Jhwh ist unsere Gerechtigkeit' (Jer 23,5 f.): Überlieferungsgeschichtliche Erwägungen zu Jer 21–24." In *Die unwiderstehliche Wahrheit: Studien zur*

alttestamentlichen Prophetie, edited by Rüdiger Lux and Ernst-Joachim Waschke, 181–198. ABIG 23. Leipzig: Evangelische Verlagsanstalt.

Ho, Ahuva. 1991. *Ṣedeq and Ṣedaqah in the Hebrew Bible*. New York et al.: Peter Lang.

Job, John B. 2006. *Jeremiah's Kings: A Study of the Monarchy in Jeremiah*. Aldershot: Ashgate.

Koch, Klaus. 1996. "צדק gemeinschaftstreu/heilvoll sein." *THAT* 2:508–530.

Liedke, Gerhard. 1996. "שפט richten." *THAT* 2:999–1009.

Lipschits, Oded. 2002. "'Jehoiakim Slept with His Fathers ...' (II Kings 24:6) – Did He?" *JHS* 4: Article 1.

Lust, Johan. 2004. "Messianism and the Greek Version of Jeremiah: Jer 23,5–6 and 33,14–16." In *Messianism and the Septuagint: Collected Essays by Johan Lust*, edited by Katrin Hauspie, 31–48. BEThL 178. Leuven: Leuven University Press and Peeters.

Maier, Christl M. 2002. *Jeremia als Lehrer der Tora: Soziale Gebote des Deuteronomiums in Fortschreibungen des Jeremiabuches*. FRLANT 196. Göttingen: Vandenhoeck & Ruprecht.

Maier, Christl M. 2013. "God's Cruelty and Jeremiah's Treason: Jer 21:1–10 in Postcolonial Perspective." In *Prophecy and Power: Jeremiah in Feminist and Postcolonial Perspective*, edited by Christl M. Maier and Carolyn J. Sharp, 133–149. LHBOTS 577. New York: Bloomsbury T&T Clark.

Maier, Christl M. 2016a. "The Nature of Deutero-Jeremianic Texts." In *Jeremiah's Scriptures: Production, Reception, Interaction, and Transformation*, edited by Hindy Najman and Konrad Schmid, 102–123. JSJ.S 173. Leiden: Brill.

Maier, Christl M. 2016b. "From Zedekiah to the Messiah: A Glimpse at the Early Reception of the Sprout." In *Sibyls, Scriptures, and Scrolls: John Collins at Seventy*. Vol. 2, edited by Joel Baden et al., 880–896. JSJ.S 175/2. Leiden: Brill.

Olyan, Saul M. 2014. "Jehoiakim's Dehumanizing Interment as a Ritual Act of Reclassification." *JBL* 133:271–279.

Stipp, Hermann-Josef. 1996. "Zedekiah in the Book of Jeremiah: On the Formation of a Biblical Character." *CBQ* 58:627–648.

Stipp, Hermann-Josef. 2015. "Jeremia 24: Geschichtsbild und historischer Ort." In *Studien zum Jeremiabuch: Text und Redaktion*, 349–378. FAT 96. Tübingen: Mohr Siebeck.

Sweeney, Marvin A. 2007. "Jeremiah's Reflections on the Isaian Royal Promise: Jeremiah 23:1–8 in Context." In *Uprooting and Planting: Essays on Jeremiah for Leslie Allen*, edited by John Goldingay, 308–321. LHBOTS 459. New York and London: Bloomsbury T&T Clark.

Thiel, Winfried. 1973. *Die deuteronomistische Redaktion von Jeremia 1–25*. WMANT 41. Neukirchen-Vluyn: Neukirchener Verlag.

Thiel, Winfried. 1981. *Die deuteronomistische Redaktion von Jer 26–45: Mit einer Gesamtbeurteilung der deuteronomistischen Redaktion des Buches Jeremia*. WMANT 52. Neukirchen-Vluyn: Neukirchener Verlag.

Wanke, Gunther. 1995. *Jeremia. Teilband 1: Jeremia 1,1–25,14*. ZBK.AT 20/1. Zurich: TVZ.

Weippert, Manfred. 2010. *Historisches Textbuch zum Alten Testament*. GAT 10. Göttingen: Vandenhoeck & Ruprecht.

Wolff, Hans-Walter. 1985. *Joel und Amos*. 3rd edition. BK.AT XIV/2. Neukirchen-Vluyn: Neukirchener Verlag.

L. Juliana M. Claassens
Prophetic Leadership as Resistance: The Case of Baruch and Ebed-melech (Jeremiah 36–38)

1 Introduction

In his book *The Epistemology of Resistance,* José Medina (2013) employs the intriguing notion of "epistemic heroes," which she defines as "extraordinary subjects who under conditions of epistemic oppression are able to develop epistemic virtues with a tremendous transformative potential." He writes as follow: "I argue that epistemic heroes should be understood as emblems: figures who become emblematic because they come to epitomize the daily struggles of resistance of ordinary people" (Medina 2013, 25).

Stories of such individuals rising up, and amidst the exceedingly challenging situations in which they find themselves, doing what they can to resist violence and injustice, play an important role in helping to forge what Medina (2013, 26) describes as "resistant ways of imagining" that may contribute to an alternative social imagination. In terms of the question of what constitutes a prophetic leader, particularly in a context of violence and injustice, one could say that emblematic figures such as envisioned here inspire others who find themselves in a context of oppression not to give up, and to continue their efforts in resisting what is deemed injurious and unjust.

The notion of prophetic leadership as resistance is an intriguing theme to consider with regard to the book of Jeremiah. Set against the backdrop of imperial invasion by the mighty Babylonian war machine that threatened to destroy the city of Jerusalem and its surroundings, the book of Jeremiah reflects a period of great violence just before and during three military attacks in 597, 587, and 581 BCE. These greatly traumatic events saw a large-scale destruction of property and human life, in addition to the mass deportation of a significant segment of its citizens (Stulman 2014, 180–181; O'Connor 2011, 7–17).

But beyond the turmoil caused by external geo-political forces, the prophet Jeremiah's immediate world is also fraught with violence as he becomes the victim of abuse by the leaders of the Judean people. Perhaps mimicking the violent actions of the imperial invaders, or perhaps an inevitable response because of these trying times, the fact is that Jeremiah is subjected throughout the book to a series of violent actions that can be said to be all the more painful given the fact that this maltreatment comes from his own people (Mills 2007, 9, 20–23).

https://doi.org/10.1515/9783110650358-003

Nevertheless, within this context where violence, fear and distrust abounds on so many different levels, one finds some remarkable stories of resistance when a number of individuals refuse to yield to the forces that seek to destroy them. In this regard, Kathleen O'Connor has compellingly described the prophet Jeremiah as the emblematic survivor. She argues that Jeremiah, throughout the book that bears his name, and in particular in what has been called the stories of his incarceration, comes to represent the people of Judah.[1] As she writes:

> A symbol of their fate, his suffering signifies their suffering; his survival points to their survival. [...] Like them, he is taken captive, battered, and starved. He faces death repeatedly and is exiled to a place he did not wish to go. Yet he survives that suffering again and again. Because he survives, they may as well (O'Connor 2002, 373; cf. also Stulman 2004, 56).

By refusing to succumb to the violence that threatens to engulf him, Jeremiah thus emerges as a symbol of hope (O'Connor 2011, 73–79).[2] In the trying times that form the backdrop to this prophetic book, Jeremiah's story of resistance offers a powerful alternative to those who hear and read it. In terms of Medina's description, the prophet could indeed be viewed as an "epistemic hero" that may inspire other ordinary people also to act in extraordinary ways in order to resist injustice.

Jeremiah is not alone though. In the latter part of the book, one finds in Jeremiah 36 and 38 two powerful stories of resistance that introduce two characters who demonstrate great courage as they, in an act of solidarity, join Jeremiah in resisting the violence and abuse of power they are experiencing in the king's court. These two very different characters – Baruch, the Judean scribe, and Ebed-melech, an Ethiopian eunuch who is, as his name suggests, an official of the king – act in such a way as to ensure that Jeremiah and ultimately the prophetic word will survive. Both Baruch and Ebed-melech are subsequently blessed by Jeremiah and promised that, because of their faithfulness to God, they will receive their lives as "booty of war" (Jer 21:9; 38:3; 39:18;

---

[1] Cf. Stulman (2004, 46, 55) who calls Jeremiah a "wounded survivor who triumphs over adversity" and whose "life and destiny" is presented in such a way "that parallels and intersects with that of the nation." Cf. also Mills' focus on prophetic embodiment as a means of telling the story of the traumatized community (Mills 2007, 116).
[2] O'Connor (2011, 79) writes: "Perhaps these stories helped survivors find their 'bearings in the world' or unlocked the future for them, gave them the energy to endure, and showed them a way forward in their life together with God, mysteriously obscured from view in these captivity stories."

45:5).[3] Indeed, one could say that in their respective ways, Baruch and Ebed-melech emerge as epistemic heroes in their own right, which may offer some intriguing perspectives on the meaning of "prophetic leadership."

In what follows, I will further explore the way in which resistance is narrated in the stories of Baruch (Jer 36) and Ebed-melech (Jer 38), considering what these stories may have to say about the nature of epistemological resistance. And in a final section, I will reflect on the way in which this view of resistance may affect our understanding of prophetic leadership in a context of violence such as reflected in the prophetic books and beyond.

2 Baruch, the Scribe (Jer 36)

One could say that Baruch, the scribe, is a bit of an accidental epistemic hero. As a scribe, Baruch's primary role is to faithfully write down all the words that God had spoken to Jeremiah (Jer 36:4). As Baruch describes his responsibility: "He dictated all these words to me, and I wrote them with ink on the scroll" (Jer 36:18). Baruch's resistance in Jer 36 thus takes the form of what he does best: reading and writing the prophetic word. What follows is hence an elaborate account of the public reading of the prophetic word that is underscored by the repeated reference to Baruch reading the scroll (Jer 36:10, 13, 14, 15).

The dramatic events of Jer 36 start with Jeremiah sending Baruch to the temple to read the divine words, which Jeremiah had asked Baruch to write down, so that people might hear them and "turn from their evil ways" (Jer 36:5–7). Baruch is sent because Jeremiah has been banned from the temple on account of the confounding nature of his message (Brueggemann 1998, 345).

Baruch's message is no less disturbing. The prophetic word is shown to have quite an effect on the officials of the king (Jer 36:11–15). Some "turned to one another in alarm" and warned Baruch that they had to report all that they had heard to the king (Jer 36:16). These officials acknowledge the dangerous nature of the prophetic word and implore Baruch and Jeremiah to go into hiding. One of these officials, Jehudi, who had heard Baruch reading the prophetic word, takes the scroll left behind by Baruch, and continues the public performance of the prophetic word by reading it to the king and his officials (Jer 36:20–21). At first it seems as if the prophetic word receives no reaction from the king and his

---

3 The expression "booty of war" means that at the war's end, all you will have left is your life. However, as O'Connor (2011, 74) rightly writes: "Yet having one's life is no small thing; it is the first requirement for a future, any future at all."

servants (Jer 36:24). Though in the next section, as Jehudi is reading the scroll left behind by Baruch, the king, who is sitting in front of the fire, cuts off one piece after another from the scroll, which he throws into the fire until the entire scroll has been burnt to ashes (Jer 36:22–23).[4]

The verb "to tear" is used in quite an ironic fashion by the biblical writer. Instead of "tearing" his clothes when hearing the prophetic word like his father Josiah in 2 Kgs 22:11, the king now "tears" the scroll to pieces (Jer 36:24; cf. Stulman 2005, 300; Brueggemann 1998, 350). The king's violent actions make it quite clear that he has heard all too well what has been said. Moreover, this stunning gesture by the king underscores just how fragile the prophetic word is as well as the tenuous nature of the prophetic ministry, since the words of the prophet may disappear into oblivion. The burning of the scroll with the prophetic words on it suggests that even if the prophetic word is written down, and thus technically might survive beyond the original performance of the prophet for future generations, it still may perish together with the people.[5]

However, in this context of violence in which the prophetic ministry is in great jeopardy, one finds an intriguing portrayal of resistance. First, the brave act of Baruch, the scribe, entering the temple in the place of Jeremiah, and continuing to read the prophetic word can be said to be a sure act of resistance. The scribe has now emerged as the proclaimer of the prophetic word (Seitz 2009, 17). In a context that is deemed to be too dangerous for Jeremiah to appear, Baruch, the scribe, exhibits great courage as he stands up and reads what he had written, thus doing what prophets do: speaking truth to power.[6]

Baruch's act of reading what had been written, moreover, points to the public nature of the prophetic witness – the prophetic word is meant to be heard (O'Connor 2002, 374; Brueggemann 1998, 347).[7] However, it is quite evident from this chapter that being a prophet is dangerous, and that Baruch – like Jeremiah before him – will likely be persecuted and conceivably imprisoned. Nevertheless, the message of this chapter is that despite danger and setbacks, Baruch will survive as well (O'Connor 2002, 375; Brueggemann 1998, 347). Even

---

4 Stulman (2005, 296) highlights the so-called "scroll motif," which points to one of the central themes of "the proclamation of the word of God, its rejection, and fulfilment in the history of Judah."
5 Stulman (2004, 55) writes that the king and his officials seek to destroy the scroll and furthermore arrest Jeremiah and Baruch "in a cunning attempt to silence both message and messenger."
6 Cf. Brueggemann's argument that "this narrative has contributed greatly to our understanding of 'prophetic ministry' as essentially confrontational" in nature (Brueggemann 1998, 345).
7 Brueggemann (1998, 347) argues that "the 'word of God' is intended precisely to be heard in public places, to impinge upon public policy, and to provoke public transformation."

when Baruch has to flee because the situation has become too dangerous, the scroll remains and continues to be read – in no small measure due to the helping hand of allies who not only warned Baruch that he is not safe, but also read the prophetic word in his stead.[8]

Second, the fact that Baruch continues what Jeremiah has started is also a sure sign of resistance. As Christopher Seitz (2009, 16–18) rightly points out, the proverbial prophetic mantel has fallen upon him. Baruch is commissioned at the same time that Jeremiah, in these final chapters, fades more and more into the background, finally disappearing into Egypt, not to be heard from again.[9] Moreover, it is significant that in Jer 45:5 Baruch receives the same promise of protection that Jeremiah had received in Jer 1:8, 19, thus confirming that the prophetic ministry will continue beyond the person of Jeremiah.[10] Read in this way, Baruch's presence in Jer 36 suggests that the struggle is much bigger than any one individual.

Finally, the scroll in itself can be said to be a powerful symbol of survival. The prophetic word is not limited to the prophetic body, but captured in a scroll, which suggests that it can go places, and will continue to be read, long after the individuals associated with these words have passed on.[11] Moreover, even though the scroll is fragile (as is made clear by Jehoiakim's violent actions), it can be recomposed in a remarkable act of resilience; written once again, with

---

[8] O'Connor (2002, 374) points to the role of allies in the story of Jeremiah and Baruch. She writes that Jeremiah and Baruch survive by means of some unexpected help. It is the allies who realize the danger that the prophetic witness poses to Jeremiah and Baruch, and it is they who tell Baruch to hide from the king's wrath as well (Jer 36:19).

[9] As Jeremiah fades from view, Seitz (2009, 16–18) considers how both Ebed-melech and Baruch are portrayed as role models of faith who are modelled upon Caleb and Joshua, who, because they remained obedient to God, were allowed to enter the Promised Land. This literary strategy, according to Seitz, demonstrates the "continuity between the Word of God delivered at Sinai and the Word destined to a new life with a new generation of faith." Cf. also the rabbinic view that "'[s]ince the day when the Temple was destroyed, prophecy has been taken from the prophets and given to the wise' (*B. Bathra 12a*)" (Seitz 2009, 18).

[10] According to Seitz (2009, 12), this transfer of the prophetic ministry can be said to relate to the theme of the death of the old and the birth of the new generation, suggested by Seitz to be one of the central themes of the book of Deuteronomy.

[11] Mark Brummitt and Yvonne Sherwood (2011, 55) poignantly describe the importance of writing given the fact that the scroll "surpass[es] the limits of the human body with its limited vocal chords in life and its endless silence after death." Jeremiah 36 reflects, moreover, the profound anxiety of what would happen when Jeremiah and Baruch are no longer there to reconstruct the scroll – an anxiety that is actually reinforced given the reality that the book of Jeremiah ends without the prophet. Towards the end of the book, Jeremiah is taken against his will to Egypt (Jer 43:6), to the very place concerning which he had vehemently dissuaded refugees from going to after the Mizpah massacre (Jer 42:7–22). Cf. Maier 2013, 84–85.

all these words and more (Jer 36:32).[12] This act of writing as resistance conveys a compelling message of the prophetic word that will continue against the odds, returning to the theme of power amidst vulnerability that runs through many of the prophetic books (cf., e.g., the Suffering Servant tradition as well as the female metaphors for God in Deutero-Isaiah).[13] Mark Brummitt and Yvonne Sherwood (2011, 59) put it well: "Defiantly the text proclaims the iteration and reiteration of God and his word over and against every opposition or threat of decomposition, just as Israel, stubbornly and impossibly, manages to overcome every opposition and every moment when its future is hanging by a thread" (cf. also Seitz 2009, 14).

For people who were feeling profoundly vulnerable, this example of the survival of the prophetic ministry as embodied in the survival of Baruch, the scribe, and the scroll that he has written and rewritten is exceedingly important in terms of their own struggle to endure.[14]

3 Ebed-melech, Servant of the King (Jer 38)

A second story of an unexpected epistemic hero is found in the figure of Ebed-melech, the Ethiopian eunuch whose story, as told in Jer 38, intersects with what has been called the Jeremiah in Prison stories (Jer 11:18–19, 21–23; 20:1–6; 26:1–24; 32:1–25; 37:11–21; 38:1–6). The Jeremiah in Prison stories have been associated with the theme of "survival against all odds," which is also at the heart of the story of Baruch discussed above (O'Connor 2011, 73–79).

Ebed-melech can be said to be the quintessential "other" in a number of ways: He is a foreigner; he is a eunuch[15] who transgresses what is considered

---

[12] Stulman (2005, 301) writes that "in a grand reversal, the powerless piece of papyrus defeats the king and his entourage," thus communicating that "the word of God" has "triumph[ed] over raw human power." Brueggemann (1998, 353) puts it well: "God is a scroll-maker and will continue to make scrolls."
[13] For a discussion of the role of female metaphors in Deutero-Isaiah that offer an alternative understanding of power, see Claassens 1997, 179–197; Brock 1997, 137–159.
[14] O'Connor (2011, 116) puts it well: "That potent [prophetic] word extends beyond the life of the prophet and has a kind of infinitude of its own. It lives into the future, and so it must, because the disaster's effects live into the future. That word is alive and growing, and recorded in a scroll." Cf. also Brueggemann 1998, 346.
[15] The reference to Ebed-melech being a eunuch is by no means clear in terms of its interpretative significance. Shelley Birdsong (2017, 112) outlines a variety of different interpretative options associated with Ebed-melech specifically being characterized as a eunuch. Interestingly enough, in the Old Greek there is no reference to Abdemelech's status as a servant nor his sexual status as a eunuch. This stands in contrast to the MT, which in terms of his name (Ebed-

to be heteronormative in terms of his sexuality; and he is a servant of the king – his social position being even embedded in his name (cf. the Hebrew meaning of his name, "servant of the king").¹⁶ But more important than all of these identifying factors of ethnicity, class, and sexuality that make Ebed-melech such an intriguing character is the way in which his actions are shown to be central to the survival of Jeremiah, as well the prophetic ministry as a whole. Moreover, on an epistemic level, Ebed-melech's acts of resistance play an important role in changing the way one looks at what Medina (2013, 3) describes as "oppressive normative structures and the complacent cognitive-affective functioning that sustains those structures." Ebed-melech's story of resistance in a significant way can be said to "undermine and change" these structures by cultivating a "resistant imagination" (Medina 2013, 7).

Jeremiah 37–38 recounts Jeremiah's ongoing incarceration against the backdrop of the looming threat of the Babylonian Empire. In Jer 38, the situation grows most dire when King Zedekiah's officials accuse Jeremiah of being a traitor because of his public opinions that implore people to accept the inevitable and surrender to the Babylonian forces (Brueggemann 1998, 362). These officials, whose names are mentioned in Jer 38:1 (Shephatiah son of Mattan, Gedaliah son of Pashhur, Jucal son of Shelemiah, and Pashhur son of Malchiah) collectively put tremendous pressure on the king to hand over the prophet, which results in Jeremiah being thrown into an empty cistern. Quite dramatically, Jer 38:6 describes how Jeremiah sank down into the mud, which according to O'Connor (2011, 77) should be viewed in symbolic terms as "the prophet sink[ing] into the mud of hopelessness, a place of abandonment and death."¹⁷

---

melech) refers to his status as the king's subordinate, but also in terms of the explicit reference to him being a male eunuch (אִישׁ סָרִיס). Birdsong writes that she is aware that the term סָרִיס could be translated as "official," which is the interpretation preferred by Walter Brueggemann and Robert Carroll, among others. However, she maintains that there is strong evidence that Ebed-melech ought to be viewed as a eunuch, given the fact that he is also referred to as a "male official" which seems superfluous given the context. Birdsong argues that these two terms work together to capture his gender and sexual identity. Cf. also the argument by Tom Parker (2007, 258–259), who maintains that Ebed-melech's identity as a eunuch is crucial for the irony of the story, which contrasts the inaction of the Judean king and the courageous action of an emasculated Ethiopian servant.

16 O'Connor (2002, 375) points to the irony associated with Ebed-melech's name. In terms of the Hebrew meaning of his name, one would expect him to be a loyal servant of the king; however, in the story it seems that this servant of the king is serving the divine ruler.

17 O'Connor (2011, 77) demonstrates how Jeremiah's experience of being in the cistern parallels the hopeless, desperate situation in which the people of Judah find themselves after the Babylonian invasion. Cf. also Carvalho's argument that "the story makes clear the horror of starvation. Jeremiah, with his feet stuck in a muddy cistern, represents the inhabitants of the city. Both will starve by staying where they stand" (Carvalho 2016, 124).

When things appear to be at their worst, help appears in the form of the Ethiopian eunuch, Ebed-melech. It is significant that Ebed-melech, who both in terms of his ethnic and sexual identity is an outsider to the community, is not only the one who is able to see the injustice done to Jeremiah, but also by reporting this abuse to the king, the one who does something to stop the violence. According to Birdsong (2017, 114) the problem in Ebed-melech's mind is that the king is not aware of the dire situation in which Jeremiah finds himself. She writes: "He assumes that his master will be shocked to hear about Jeremiah's treatment and will undoubtedly right the officials' wrong."[18] And indeed, the king listens to Ebed-melech and, going against his own officials, commands Ebed-melech to go and rescue Jeremiah before he dies (Jer 38:8–10). The story ends with Ebed-melech and his men saving Jeremiah from the cistern in a dramatic rescue.

On the one hand, the story told in Jer 38 is a classic story of salvation amidst disaster, which aligns with the central theme of the prophet Jeremiah and his prophetic ministry surviving despite the best attempts of his opponents to harm him (O'Connor 2011, 77–78).[19] This incredible story of survival against the odds speaks a word of hope to the people of Judah by opening up the possibility that salvation might well be possible when things are most dire (O'Connor 2011, 74). The choice of Ebed-melech as deliverer, particularly in terms of his ethnicity, sexuality, and his position in the king's court, underscores the point that salvation may come in the most unexpected places and from the most unexpected persons (Parker 2007, 258–259; cf. also O'Connor 2011, 77–78).

However, there are also some other striking perspectives concerning especially the nature of resistance that is recounted in the story of Ebed-melech that are most important in terms of our understanding of prophetic leadership in a context of trauma. First, one should recognize the great courage exemplified by Ebed-melech as he stands up to the king, naming the injustice that is transpiring. Tom Parker (2007, 257) underscores the significance of Ebed-melech going to speak to the king at the Benjamin Gate in a public setting (Jer 38:7), perhaps thus giving the king little choice but to acknowledge him. Even more so, though, the setting at the city gate is significant, since this is typically the place where legal matters are settled (Stulman 2005, 310). Ebed-melech thus can be said to bring a lawsuit before the king, daring to denounce the wickedness of the officials' actions: "These men have acted wickedly in all they did to the

---

[18] Birdsong (2017, 114) further remarks that this is a way for the king to redeem himself for his "inability to stop the brutish officials earlier."
[19] O'Connor (2011, 73) describes Jeremiah as "an action figure who escapes one catastrophe only to fall into another and survive every time."

prophet Jeremiah by throwing him into the cistern to die there of hunger, for there is no bread left in the city" (Jer 38:9). With a rampant famine in the city due to war, the officials did great evil by leaving Jeremiah to perish in the treacherous conditions of a cold, mud-filled cistern.[20]

The LXX goes even further than the MT, with Ebed-melech directly telling the king that he has done evil (Parker 2007, 257). Shelley Birdsong (2017, 114) notes that in the Old Greek version of the LXX, Abdemelech (as she calls him in order to distinguish him from Ebed-melech) does not "politely greet the king" but rather "bluntly exclaims: '*You* have been evil in what *you* have done – *to kill* this man because of famine.'"

This daring indictment of the officials – and in the Old Greek, the king himself – surely puts Ebed-melech in danger, risking retaliation and even death (Stulman 2005, 310). Yet, in this impressive show of resistance, Ebed-melech can be said to, in Parker's words, serve "an exemplar" in the book of Jeremiah, compelling the king to choose life. Parker puts it well: "Ebed-melech recognizes injustice and brings justice by doing right [...] He challenges the powers of the land – first the king in his appeal, then the officials by going into their territory to reverse their actions and their purposes" (Parker 2007, 258; cf. also Stulman 2005, 306).

Second, it is important to note that Ebed-melech's courageous actions that resist violence and injustice are rooted in compassion. In Jer 38:12 one finds the intriguing narrative detail of Ebed-melech's thoughtful gesture of taking along some old rags that could be put underneath the ropes so as to ensure that Jeremiah does not get hurt while being pulled up. This sincere act of gentleness and kindness, which speaks to Ebed-melech's attentiveness to Jeremiah's plight, is set against the backdrop of the brutality and force associated with the Babylonian invasion as well as the hostility of the officials who have been persecuting Jeremiah throughout the book.[21]

Perhaps it is *because* Ebed-melech likely has experienced his share of exclusion and hardship as a foreigner, a eunuch, and a slave in the king's court that he is able to act with compassion toward Jeremiah. Martha Nussbaum (2001, 315–316) has compellingly written that compassion inherently implies that one is able to forge a common connection, realizing that the other is hungry like

---

20 Birdsong (2017, 111–112) argues that "being thrown into the pit was likely a vehicle for a slow and painful death, which is supported by the lack of water in the pit and Ebed-melech's assertion that the prophet would die there if not rescued."

21 Carvalho (2016, 124) writes that the "level of humane treatment" on the part of Ebed-melech exemplified by the extent of his compassion "contrasts with the heartlessness of the Judean elite."

me, cold like me, afraid like me.[22] Nussbaum (2001, 438) speaks about the importance of being able to "create a unity in the disparate, seeing common human interests and sufferings across the sharpest of divisions." She argues that to be able "to imagine the experiences of others and to participate in their sufferings" is an essential prerequisite for compassion to transpire (cf. also Nussbaum 2013, 258). This incredible display of compassion on the part of Ebed-melech thus offers some poignant insights into the nature of resistance, showing how the very determination to do what is right cannot be disassociated from the ability to empathize with those who are wronged.

Third, Ebed-melech's position as a foreigner, as an emasculated man, and as a servant, is important in this story of resistance. Medina (2013, 22) writes that precisely "because their experiences have been silenced or rendered opaque, abnormal, unintelligible," individuals who can be considered to be outsiders, and who perhaps have had to face their share of oppression, are better able "to exert resistance and to pluralize the imagination." Outsiders see things that those in a position of power and privilege simply do not see. In this narrative one could say that it is precisely *because* of his marginalized position that Ebed-melech plays a vital role in helping to forge "resistant ways of imagining." One should not miss the fact that the king heeds the voice of his servant, going against the advice of his officials and seeing what Ebed-melech sees. It is Ebed-melech's courageous example of resisting what he deems wrong, accompanied by some incisive words, that finally opens the king's eyes to see what is good and right, moving him to redress a wrong. Medina reflects as follow on the role of practices of resistance in changing hearts and minds:

> Through practises of resistance we can learn to go beyond the structures of inherited cognitive and affective habits, and we can learn to envision new cognitive-affective attitudes and orientations towards others. Both our ability and our inability to relate to others [...] is mediated by the social imagination, the kind of imagination that opens our eyes and hearts to certain things and not others, enabling and constraining our social gaze (Medina 2013, 22).

However, at the same time, Medina (2013, 22) writes that given the fact that these individuals are also "often the most vulnerable, and we cannot overburden their already precarious agency with the task of pluralizing the social imagination for all of us." In addition, with reference to the story of the Rechabites in Jer 35, Steed Davidson (2013, 192) warns against the danger of exoticizing the

---

[22] Nussbaum (2001, 315–316) notes that "this is a judgment of *similar possibilities*; compassion concerns those misfortunes 'which [according to Aristotle] the person himself might expect to suffer, either himself or one of his loved ones' (1385b14)."

foreigners' faithfulness. He writes that through exoticization, the other "becomes not simply that which is different but that which is rendered different for the purpose of controlling and domesticating it." Indeed, in literature one quite often finds how "non-Western cultures and people" are subjected to "devices such as essentializing, stereotyping, infantilization, eroticization, debasement, [and] idealization" which work together to, as Davidson (2013, 191) warns us, control and domesticate what is deemed foreign or other to the norm.

In spite of these valid concerns about how the foreigner's faithfulness is depicted in this narrative, I nevertheless would deem it important that Ebed-melech's role in this story be recounted and recognized, as it offers some important perspectives on the role of prophetic leadership. I propose that the story of Ebed-melech should be read together with the story of Baruch in the preceding chapter, as these two examples of "epistemic heroes" collectively point to the importance of resistance as solidarity. Jeremiah would not have survived without Baruch or Ebed-melech. In terms of their unique social locations, and in their respective capacity as scribe and royal official, these two individuals emerge as prophetic leaders in their own right and communicate an important perspective about the power of solidarity when it comes to resistance. Indeed, as Medina (2013, 21) describes the intricate connection between "practices and habits of resistance" and solidarity:

> It is in and through resistance that relations of solidarity against domination and across different forms of oppression become possible and effective. It is in and through resistance that we discover new possibilities of social relationality by paying attention to new forms of social identification (Medina 2013, 21).

In the often difficult struggle to survive imperial domination, perhaps the most powerful message to the people as symbolized in the story of Jeremiah, Baruch, and Ebed-melech is the fact that one is not alone. In this regard, it is important not only to see Jeremiah as the emblematic survivor, but also how Baruch and Ebed-melech survive as well. Read together, the stories of resistance associated with these three figures suggest that the resistance amidst imperial domination – which is exacerbated by the abuse of power within the royal court – is much broader and deeper than it initially appears.

4 Conclusion

Louis Stulman (2013, 70) aptly calls the book of Jeremiah "literature of the losers." Indeed, particularly the narrative sections of this intriguing book can be said to constitute "coping strategies of the defeated and the subjugated who are able to fight injustice only by means of their words" (Fischer 2013, 250).[23]

The two stories of Baruch and Ebed-melech that intersect with the stories outlining the prophet Jeremiah's struggle to survive multiple levels of violence and abuse are designed to show readers that ordinary people may rise to the occasion and act for what is good and right and just. Moreover, the fact that both Baruch and Ebed-melech not only join Jeremiah in resisting oppression but also survive in the process serves as a powerful symbol of hope, ensuring people that, as O'Connor (2011, 376) has rightly argued, they can survive as well, often by unexpected means. Finally, expanding our view to include Baruch and Ebed-melech as epistemic heroes who, together with Jeremiah resist injustice and abuse, changes how one conceives of the phenomenon of prophetic leadership. It is not just the prophets or intellectuals who emerge as epistemic heroes, but also ordinary people – in the case of Ebed-melech, an outsider to the community in more than one way.

This point is corroborated by Medina's example of Rosa Parks to illustrate her notion of epistemic resistance. Rosa Parks was an ordinary person who amidst her ordinary daily commute acted in an unexpected way – her refusal to give up her seat becoming emblematic, and as we well know, an act of resistance that had an extraordinary effect in the Civil Rights movement and beyond. Rosa Park's courage captured people's imagination and encouraged them that perhaps they too could make a difference by resisting injustice and acts of violence and abuse wherever they find themselves. Medina (2013, 25) describes the effects of these examples of resistance in terms of the notion of "echoing," which he describes as "[...] the transformative impact of performance that we consider heroic is crucially dependent on social networks and daily practices of resistance in which the performance in question is taken up or re-enacted."

Stories of epistemic heroes who survive against the odds, who refuse to let injustice prevail, and who show great courage in living lives of integrity help us all to endure. Kathleen O'Connor (2011, 79) writes that the stories about Jeremiah – and I would add also about Baruch and Ebed-melech – may have helped survivors not to give up, to show them that an alternative reality from what they were experiencing might be possible after all. And ultimately, this ability to help others believe that their current reality is not the only reality is one of the core aspects of prophetic leadership in a context of injustice and violence.

---

23 Fischer (2013, 250) cites the metaphor of a woman in labor in Jer 31:7–9 as "an example of resistance that shows how the colonized within the dominant power survived by imagining an alternative reality." Cf. Claassens 2013, 129.

Bibliography

Birdsong, Shelley. 2017. *The Last King(s) of Judah: Zedekiah and Sedekias in the Hebrew and Old Greek Versions of Jeremiah 37(44):1–40(47):6*. FAT II/89. Tübingen: Mohr Siebeck.
Brock, Rita Nakashima. 1997. "A New Thing in the Land: The Female Surrounds the Warrior." In *Power, Powerlessness, and the Divine: New Inquiries in Bible and Theology*, edited by Cynthia L. Rigby, 137–159. Atlanta: Scholars Press.
Brueggemann, Walter. 1998. *A Commentary on Jeremiah: Exile and Homecoming*. Grand Rapids: Eerdmans.
Brummitt, Mark, and Yvonne Sherwood. 2011. "The Fear of Loss Inherent in Writing: Jeremiah 36 as the Tedious Self-Narration of a Highly Self-Conscious Scroll." In *Jeremiah (Dis)Placed: New Directions in Writing/Reading Jeremiah*, edited by Louis Stulman and A. R. Pete Diamond, 47–67. London: Bloomsbury T&T Clark.
Carvalho, Corrine. 2016. *Reading Jeremiah: A Literary and Theological Commentary*. Macon: Smyth & Helwys.
Claassens, L. Juliana. 2012. *Mourner, Mother, Midwife: Reimagining God's Liberating Presence*. Louisville: Westminster John Knox Press.
Claassens, L. Juliana. 2013. "'Like a Woman in Labor': Gender, Postcolonial, Queer, and Trauma Perspectives on the Book of Jeremiah." In *Prophecy and Power: Jeremiah in Feminist and Postcolonial Perspective*, edited by Christl M. Maier and Carolyn J. Sharp, 117–132. London: Bloomsbury T&T Clark.
Davidson, Steed Vernyl. 2013. "'Exoticizing the Otter': The Curious Case of the Rechabites in Jeremiah 35." In *Prophecy and Power: Jeremiah in Feminist and Postcolonial Perspective*, edited by Christl M. Maier and Carolyn J. Sharp, 189–207. London: Bloomsbury T&T Clark.
Fischer, Irmtraud. 2013. "On Writing a Feminist-Postcolonial Commentary." In *Prophecy and Power: Jeremiah in Feminist and Postcolonial Perspective*, edited by Christl M. Maier and Carolyn J. Sharp, 234–251. London: Bloomsbury T&T Clark.
Hanson, Paul D. 1997. "Divine Power in Powerlessness." In *Power, Powerlessness, and the Divine: New Inquiries in Bible and Theology*, edited by Cynthia L. Rigby, 179–197. Atlanta: Scholars Press.
Maier, Christl M. 2013. "After the 'One-Man Show': Multi-Authored and Multi-Voiced Commentary Writing." In *Prophecy and Power: Jeremiah in Feminist and Postcolonial Perspective*, edited by Christl M. Maier and Carolyn J. Sharp, 72–85. London: Bloomsbury T&T Clark.
Medina, José. 2013. *The Epistemology of Resistance: Gender and Racial Oppression, Epistemic Injustice, and Resistant Imaginations*. New York: Oxford University Press.
Mills, Mary E. 2007. *Alterity, Pain and Suffering in Isaiah, Jeremiah, and Ezekiel*. London: Bloomsbury T&T Clark.
Nussbaum, Martha. 2001. *Upheavals of Thought: The Intelligence of Emotions*. Cambridge: Cambridge University Press.
Nussbaum, Martha. 2013. *Political Emotions: Why Love Matters for Justice*. Cambridge: Harvard University Press.
O'Connor, Kathleen M. 2002. "Surviving Disaster in the Book of Jeremiah." *WW* 22:369–377.
O'Connor, Kathleen M. 2011. *Jeremiah: Pain and Promise*. Minneapolis: Fortress Press.
Parker, Tom. 2007. "Ebed-melech as Exemplar." In *Uprooting and Planting: Essays on Jeremiah for Leslie Allen*, edited by John Goldingay, 253–259. LHBOTS 459. New York: Bloomsbury T&T Clark.

Seitz, Christopher R. 2009. "The Prophet Moses and the Canonical Shape of Jeremiah" *ZAW* 101:3–27.
Stulman, Louis. 2004. "Jeremiah the Prophet: Astride Two Worlds." In *Reading the Book of Jeremiah: A Search for Coherence*, edited by Martin Kessler, 41–56. Winona Lake: Eisenbrauns.
Stulman, Louis. 2005. *Jeremiah*. Nashville: Abingdon Press.
Stulman, Louis. 2013. "Commentary as Memoir? Reflections on Writing/Reading War and Hegemony in Jeremiah and in Contemporary U. S. Foreign Policy." In *Prophecy and Power: Jeremiah in Feminist and Postcolonial Perspective*, edited by Christl M. Maier and Carolyn J. Sharp, 57–71. London: Bloomsbury T&T Clark.
Stulman, Louis. 2014. "Reading the Bible through the Lens of Trauma and Art." In *Trauma and Traumatization in Individual and Collective Dimensions: Insights from Biblical Studies and Beyond*, edited by Eve-Marie Becker, Jan Dochhorn, and Else Holt, 177–192. Göttingen: Vandenhoeck & Ruprecht.

Johanna Erzberger
Kingship and Priesthood – Reloaded (Jer 33:14–26)

1 Introduction

The Masoretic text of Jer 33:14–26 is the longest zero-variant in Jer^{MT}. It constitutes an announcement of salvation toward the houses of Israel and Judah and contains the announcement of a divine covenant with David and the Levitical priests. The passage has been read as promoting a dual leadership model and has been compared to similar models in other postexilic texts.[1] This article will argue that Jer 33:14–26, which builds heavily on intra- and intertextual links – particularly in Jer^{MT} – not only modifies earlier concepts of leadership but reinterprets the relationship between the people and its leadership by identifying the urban elites of Jerusalem with "Israel." In this context, both the Davidic heir and the Levitical priests play a specific role.

This article will analyze Jer^{MT} 33:14–26. Special attention will be paid to the intra- and intertextual links that it establishes and, in particular, to the way in which Jer^{MT} 33:20–26 makes use of Jer^{MT} 31:31–37. The article will then address the dynamics of the passage with regard to the presentation of both the Davidic heir and the Levitical priests, before inquiring into the passage's understanding of leadership in light of its most probable historical background.

2 The Righteous Branch

Verse 14 announces the fulfillment of a promise made to the houses of Israel and Judah in a not further specified future (הנה ימים באים "behold, days are coming"). The introduction in v. 14 is followed by the announcement of a branch of righteousness "in those days and at that time" (בימים ההם ובעת ההיא) in vv. 15–16. The announcement closely follows Jer 23:5–6, which closes a sequence of prophecies against the kings of Judah in 22:1–23:8.[2] However, there are several differences: Whereas in Jer 23:5–6 the announcement refers to a "righteous

---

[1] Cf. Hag 1:1; Zech 4:1–14; Sir 45:23–26. Gôldman 1992, 230; Lust 1994, 41–42; 2004, 61; Schenker 1994, 287.
[2] In the LXX these verses close the sequence of prophecies against the prophets. In the MT two verses (23:7–8) that juxtapose the Exodus from Egypt and the return from exile follow.

branch," who will rule as a king and execute justice and righteousness in the land, the actions of the righteous branch according to Jer 33:15–16 are confined to the execution of justice and righteousness. The branch is not said to rule as a king (Lust 1994, 38). The consequences, a life in safety, no longer applies to Judah and Israel, as is the case in Jer 23:6, but to Judah and Jerusalem. In both versions of Jer 23:6, God announces the name of the branch, either by giving the name of an individual, Josedec (Ιωσεδεκ) (Jer^{LXX}) or in terms of an abstract concept, "YHWH is our righteousness" (יהוה צדקנו) (Jer^{MT}).[3] Jeremiah 33:16, which more closely follows Jer^{MT} 23:5–6, attributes the name "YHWH is our righteousness" (יהוה צדקנו) to Jerusalem (Lust 1994, 38; Groß 1999, 84).

Verses 17–18 continue with a rationale (marked by כי) that further elaborates the announcement of the branch. The promise that David will never lack a successor on his throne in v. 17 quotes a frequent formula (לא־יכרת לדוד איש מעל כסא ישראל), which in 1 Kgs 2:4; 8:25; 9:5 and 2 Chr 6:16 alludes to the divine promise to David in 2 Sam 7:9. The latter verse is also in the background of Jer 23:5–6. The promise in v. 17 is supplemented by a parallel one in v. 18, according to which the Levites will never lack a man in God's presence (מלפני) offering sacrifices.

3 The Covenant with David and the Levites

The promise to David and the Levites is developed further in vv. 20–26. Introduced by a transmission formula (v. 19) and a messenger formula (v. 20a), vv. 20–26 proclaim a covenant each between God and David and God and the Levites that cannot be broken. The motif of the breaking of the covenant appears prominently in Jer^{MT} 31:32. Jer^{MT} 31:31–37 constitutes an important intertext for the entire passage Jer^{MT} 33:20–26 (Bogaert 1991, 241–247).

Excursus: The New Covenant
In Jer^{MT} 31:31–37 // Jer^{LXX} 28:31–37, the versions show a significantly high number of differences. Among these, only those that make a difference for the use and reinterpretation of the passage in Jer^{MT} 33:20–26 will be discussed in detail:

---

3 The masora has a *paseq* between יהוה and צדקנו, suggesting another possible reading according to which YHWH might function as the subject of the previous phrase, following the phrasing of the LXX. However, the difference between Jer 23:6 and Jer 33:16, according to which the name is given once to the branch (23:6) and once to the city (33:16) would remain even in that case.

Jer^MT 31:31 // Jer^LXX 38:31 announces a new covenant for an indefinite future (הנה ימים באים / ἰδοὺ ἡμέραι ἔρχονται, "behold, days are coming"), which differs from the covenant (לא כברית / οὐ κατὰ τὴν διαθήκην) made with the fathers on the day when God led the people out of Egypt. The former has been rejected by the people. Jer^MT uses הפר ("break") in order to address the rejection and thus creates a link to Jer^MT 33:20–21.[4] Jer^LXX uses οὐκ ἐμμένω ("not to keep").[5] The opposition between the covenant made with the fathers and the new covenant made in those days is underscored in the opening words of v. 33: כי זאת הברית אשר אכרת את־בית ישראל אחרי הימים ההם; ὅτι αὕτη ἡ διαθήκη ἣν διαθήσομαι τῷ οἴκῳ Ισραηλ μετὰ τὰς ἡμέρας ἐκείνας ("For this is the covenant that I will make with the house of Israel after those days"). What follows is a bipartite characterization of the new covenant that takes the form of a parallelism: The future covenant is characterized by God putting his laws (Jer^LXX: νόμοι, pl.) or law (Jer^MT: תורה, sg.) in the people's mind (Jer^LXX: διάνοια) or within them (Jer^MT literally: within their midst, קרב) and writing them/it on their hearts. With לב indicating the seat of understanding and καρδία indicating the seat of emotions (Wolff 2010, 75–97; Janowski 2019, 148–156), the inexact rendering of קרב by διάνοια might have compensated for the change in semantics accompanying the change of language and secured a parallelism referring to both understanding and emotion.[6] The writing of the law(s) on the people's

---

[4] הפר also creates a link to Jer 11:10.
[5] God's reaction also differs substantially between the versions: While in Jer^LXX God neglects (ἀμελέω) the fathers, who did not abide by the covenant, Jer^MT stresses God's unfailing attitude towards his people as their "owner," "lord" or even "husband" (ואנכי בעלתי בם). According to Schenker (2006, 24; 2010, 115) God's unconcern (Jer^LXX), as opposed to his continued act as Israel's בעל (Jer^MT), thus upholding the covenant, points to the irrevocable renunciation of the covenant in Jer^LXX, as opposed to its temporary suspension and renewal in Jer^MT. However, in both versions, the situation is reversed only by the making of a new covenant. Any distinction between a covenant that has been either cancelled or (temporarily) suspended should therefore be regarded with caution. At the same time, Jer^MT, which uses the motif of the breaking of the covenant elsewhere and contrasts it with God's unfailing loyalty, stresses both the rejection of the covenant by the people (using the terminology of "breaking") and God's unfailing loyalty and sets up a contrast between the behavior of the people and God's conduct.
[6] According to Schenker (2006, 34), the singular of תורה, the suffix conjugation נתתי, and קרב (which, in his view, signifies the midst of the people rather than of an individual) make v. 33a refer to the promulgation of the tablets on the Sinai. For Schenker, Jer^MT emphasizes the identity of the תורה promulgated at Sinai and the תורה that will be written on the people's hearts. The plural νόμοι in Jer^LXX and the participle followed by a future tense, a form which usually reflects the use of a figura ethymologica in Hebrew, refers to an unspecified and unfinished plurality of divine instructions that will be placed in the people's heart in the future and differ from the Sinaitic Torah (Schenker 2006, 34, 39; 2010, 121). However, the suffix conjugation in Jer^MT, if read as referring to the past, interrupts the opposition of past (v. 32) and future

hearts implies a contrast with the Sinai covenant, in whose context the law has been written on stone tablets.

The announcement of the new covenant is followed by a quotation of the covenant formula (Deut 26:17–19) in v. 33b. The following announcement, according to which any teaching of any knowledge of God will be superfluous, is justified (both introduced by ὅτι/כי) by a statement about the people's future general knowledge of God and an announcement of God's forgiveness of his people's sins in v. 34, which in Jer[LXX] concludes the announcement of the new covenant. In Jer[LXX] that announcement of God's steadfast commitment to Israel is confirmed by a final statement, according to which God's unconditioned favor for his people surpasses even the stability of heaven and earth (v. 35), a verse which, in a strongly divergent form, closes the following subunit in Jer[MT] (as Jer[MT] 31:37).

Jer[LXX] 38:36 // Jer[MT] 31:35 mark a new beginning with a prophetic messenger formula and introduce God, the speaker of the following statement, as the giver of sun, moon, and stars and the master of the ocean. According to Jer[LXX] 38:37 // Jer[MT] 31:36, only if "these ordinances" or "laws" (οἱ νόμοι οὗτοι / חוקים האלה), whose exact reference point deserves a separate discussion, cease from before him, will Israel cease to be God's people before God.

In the light of the preceding introduction of God as the giver of the sun, the order (חקת, having no equivalent in Jer[LXX])[7] of moon and stars, and the master of the ocean, חוקים in Jer[MT] 31:36 refers to the order of nature.[8] According to

---

(vv. 33–34), which is underscored by כי זאת הברית אשר אכרת את־בית ישראל אחרי הימים ההם introducing vv. 33–34. Within Jer[LXX] the plural of legal terms is repeatedly used with reference to the Sinai covenant, in particular in the second part of the book (cf. Jer[LXX] 51:10, 23). Though the more general meaning of קרב ("midst") applies to the majority of occurrences, several imply a meaning as it is usually assumed for Jer 31:33. In Ps 64:7; Prov 14:33 קרב is parallel to לב. Elsewhere, קרב refers to the individual in expressions such as "the middle of one's heart," "the heart within someone"; cf. 1 Sam 25:37; Pss 36:2; 39:4; 51:12; 55:5; 109:22; Jer 23:9; Lam 1:20; Ezek 11:19; 36:26. The precise meaning must be taken from the context.

7 חקת is absent in Jer[LXX]. Its addition by Jer[MT] seems unlikely in light of its inexact correspondence with חקים. Here, חקת is part of the expression חקת ירח וכוכבים, thus indicating the calendrical order. The fact that this expression is not taken up in the surrounding context, but is instead reinterpreted by חוקים in a more general sense in the following verse, suggests that it is part of earlier material. The word חקת might have fallen out in Jer[LXX] when חקים was translated by νόμοι and חקת lost its reference point in the following verse.

8 The subject of creation is even stronger following the verse order in Jer[LXX]. In both Jer[LXX] 38:36 // Jer[MT] 31:35 τὸν ἥλιον εἰς φῶς τῆς ἡμέρας σελήνην καὶ ἀστέρας εἰς φῶς τῆς νυκτός / שמש לאור יומם חקת ירח וכוכבים לאור לילה forms a unity of meaning. The incoherence of its combination with the sea is best explained in the context of Jer[LXX], where the sea completes a list of subjects of creation, including and reinterpreting heaven and earth in the preceding verse (Jer[LXX] 38:35) in this sense. The list roughly follows the example of Gen 1: the sky (second

Jer^MT 31:36 the enduring existence of Israel depends on the endurance of the order of nature, which is guaranteed by God the creator.

In Jer^LXX 38:36, οἱ νόμοι οὗτοι takes up νόμους μου in Jer^LXX 38:33 and refers to the laws of the Sinai covenant. If God, the creator, guarantees the enduring existence of Israel as God's people depending on the validity of the laws given at Sinai and later written on the people's hearts, the laws of the covenant trump the laws of nature. The fact that νόμοι in Jer^LXX 31:37 refers to Jer^LXX 31:33 rather than to the order of nature as the general topic of Jer^LXX 31:36–37 suggests that νόμοι has been chosen as a rendering for חוקים in order to create that link, which would thus be secondary.[9]

The conditional clause Jer^MT 31:37, which corresponds to Jer^LXX 38:35, parallels the conditional clause in Jer^MT 31:36:[10] The permanent existence of Israel is linked to the inscrutability of the order of creation in the same way as it is linked to its permanent existence. The terms מדד and חקר (both Niphal) in Jer^MT 31:37 differ from their equivalents ὑψόω and ταπεινόω in Jer^XXX 31:35. Neither of them has a reference point in the immediate context.[11] As both have a reference point in Jer^MT 33:22, Jer^MT 31:37, it is worth discussing whether both might have been chosen in order to fit Jer^MT 33:22 (Bogaert 1991, 246).
(End of excursus)

According to Jer^MT 33:20–21, God's covenant with David and the Levites cannot be broken, but if the addressees can break God's covenant with day and night. The covenants with David and the Levites mirror and build upon the promises made to David and the Levitical priests in vv. 17–18. The content of the covenant with David is further developed by taking up and varying the promise given to David according to v. 17. Instead of announcing a man (איש) who sits on the throne of the house of Israel as in v. 17, or the throne of Israel, as the formula from 1 Kgs quoted by v. 17 indicates, v. 21 announces a son (בן) who reigns as a king (מלך מלך) on his (David's) throne. In light of the parallel between v. 21

---

day) and the earth (third day) are supplemented by the creation of sun, moon, stars (fourth day), and sea (second day). This suggests the originality of the verse order in Jer^LXX.
9 Both Jer^LXX and Jer^MT are best explained as constituting revisions of a common *Vorlage*, which has a history itself and in which the unconditionality of the new covenant is illustrated by the stability of the order of nature. The common *Vorlage* would have followed the verse order of Jer^LXX and the wording of Jer^LXX in Jer^LXX 31:35 // Jer^MT 31:37 (with regard to the lack of מדד and חקר) but the wording of Jer^MT in Jer^LXX 31:36 // Jer^MT 31:35 (with regard to חקת) and Jer^LXX 31:37 // Jer^MT 31:36 (with regard to חקים rather than a term referring back to Jer 31:32).
10 Jer^MT 31:35–36, 37 constitute a bipartite subunit, both parts of which are introduced by a prophetic messenger formula.
11 The equivalent verse Jer^LXX 31:35 forms a more exact parallel to Jer^MT 31:37.

and vv. 17–18, the covenant with the Levites recalls the promise made to the Levitical priests in v. 18 without elaborating upon it. While the impossibility of breaking the covenant with David and the Levites as well as with day and night takes up – and opposes – the breaking of the covenant by the people according to Jer^{MT} 31:32, the ברית with day and night, recalls the order of night and day in Jer^{MT} 31:35, which elaborates upon the new covenant.

Verse 22 compares the impossibility of counting the stars of heaven and the sand of the sea with the impossibility of counting the descendants of David and the Levites. The host of heaven and the sand of the sea recall the stars and the sea in Jer^{MT} 31:35. Counting (ספר) the host of heaven and measuring (מדד) the grains of sand in the sea recall the measuring (מדד) of heaven and exploration of the foundations of the earth, which are found only in Jer^{MT} 31:37 and not in its equivalent Jer^{LXX} 31:35. The counting (ספר) of the host of heaven and the announcement of a multitude of descendants (זרה) both of David and of the Levites in 33:22 evoke the promise of countless descendants to Abraham according to Gen 15:5, introducing the Abrahamic covenant.[12] Another possible intertext is Gen 22:17, which compares the number of Abraham's descendants with the stars of heaven (צבא השמים) and the sand on the seashore (חול הים).[13] In Jer 33:22, an announcement of countless descendants to Abraham (that is, the people) is replaced by an announcement concerning David and the Levites. It is secured by the inexorability of creation that in Jer^{MT} 31:35 secures Israel's enduring existence.

In v. 23 another word transmission formula introduces a statement about "this people" (העם הזה) in v. 24. Verse 24 quotes "this people's" judgment about "the two families" (שתי המשפחות) as having been chosen by God, but as now being rejected. The reference to the two families (שתי המשפחות) occurs nowhere else in the passage. In light of v. 24b, the two families must be identified with God's people (עמי), whom "this people"[14] despise and might be understood as referring to Judah and Israel. God's people (עמי) not being a nation (גוי) in the eyes (גוי לפניהם) of "this people" (העם הזה) takes up – and opposes – the idea of Israel not ceasing to be a nation (גוי) in the eyes of God (גוי לפני) in Jer^{MT} 31:36. The use of the term מאס makes the rejection of "the two families" in Jer^{MT} 33:24 the object of the promise in Jer^{MT} 31:37, according to which God would not reject (מאס) all the offspring of Israel, and underscores the identification of the two families with the people of Israel and Judah. However, if these people's quote in v. 24 is presented as an objection to v. 20–22 by

---

12 The covenant with Abraham is referred to in Jer^{MT} 34:18.
13 Here no covenant is referred to.
14 "This people" (העם הזה) form an opposition to God's people (עמי).

the prophetic voice, the two families must be identified with the descendants of David and the Levites. Verses 23–24 function as a disruptive element.

If v. 24's objection is answered by vv. 25–26, the two families are identified with the descendants of Jacob and David. Only if God's covenant with night and day ceases to exist[15] and if God has not set the order of heaven and earth, will God reject (מאס) the descendants of Jacob and David, none of whom would rule any more over the descendants of Abraham, Isaac, and Jacob. The covenant with day and night, whose fictitious non-establishment makes up the first condition in v. 25, evokes the covenant with day and night in v. 20. As in v. 20, the ברית with day and night, recalls the order of night and day in Jer^{MT} 31:35. The non-establishment of the order (חקות) of heaven and earth, which makes up the second condition, points to the חקת in Jer^{MT} 31:35 and חקים in Jer^{MT} 31:36, referring to the order of nature and to the inscrutability of heaven and earth in Jer^{MT} 31:37. The conclusion of v. 26, according to which God would reject the offspring of Jacob and David, alludes to Jer 33:21. In both cases David is designated as God's servant (עבדי). However, v. 26 replaces the motif of the breaking of the covenant with the motif of rejection (מאס) taken from v. 24, dealing with the rejection of the two families. The motif of rejection also creates a link to Jer^{MT} 31:37 about God not rejecting his people. The juxtaposition of the descendants of Jacob and the descendants of David connects the people and its leadership. The rejection of the descendants of Jacob and David is further developed by God not placing rulers (משלים) from among David's descendants over the descendants of Abraham, Isaac, and Jacob.

Verse 26 closes with a final remark introduced by כי that announces a change of the people's fortune and God's mercy.

4 Jer^{MT} 33:14–26 as Part of Jer^{MT}

Jer^{MT} 33:14–26 is missing in Jer^{LXX}. Variants in the preceding passage Jer^{MT} 33:1–13, which anticipate Jer^{MT} 33:14–26, as well as the way in which Jer^{MT} 33:1–13 builds on MT variants elsewhere in the book of Jeremiah, argue against the possibility that the passage was deleted in Jer^{LXX} and in favor of its addition in Jer^{MT} and its late date of origin.

The passage's absence in Jer^{LXX} does not disturb the context's coherence, and it is to a large extent made up of quotations. Jer^{MT} 33:14–26 is thus usually

---

[15] Holladay (1989, 227–228) reads בריתי as a misreading for בראתי, but the parallel in Jer^{MT} 33:20 also has בריתי.

evaluated as a supplement (cf. Bogaert 1991, 238; Lust 1994, 37; 2004, 54; Tiňo 2010, 128). However, there are further arguments supporting this conclusion:[16]

A number of variants of Jer[MT] in the preceding passage Jer[MT] 33:1–13 are interlinked with Jer[MT] 33:14–26: Jer[MT] 33:5 has העיר הזאת, where Jer[LXX] has a third-person masculine plural personal pronoun, which might have been introduced in order to anticipate the identification of the branch of righteousness with Jerusalem in Jer[MT] 33:16 (Lust 1994, 37).[17] In JerMT 33:9 the city is said to be "a name of joy" (לשׁם שׂשׂון), whereas Jer[LXX] has "joy" (εἰς εὐφροσύνην). The word שׁם, which has no equivalent in Jer[LXX], might have been added in order to prepare for Jer[MT] 33:16 (Lust 2004, 54).[18]

The differences between the verbs ὑψόω and ταπεινόω and מדד and חקר (both Niphal) in the corresponding verses Jer[LXX] 38:35 and Jer[MT] 31:37 cannot be explained by their immediate context. The verb מדד, with חקר constituting a close synonym, has a reference point in Jer[MT] 33:22, where counting the host of heaven and measuring (מדד) the sand of the sea recall the measuring (מדד) of heaven and the exploration of the foundations of the earth in Jer[MT] 31:37. In light of this link, Jer[MT] 31:37 might be explained as revising the Hebrew *Vorlage* in light of Jer[LXX] 38:35.

5 David and the Levites versus the People

One line of reasoning, that characterizes the passage under discussion, is the replacement of Israel's role in several of the quoted sources by the descendant of David and the Levites in particular in Jer[MT] 33:20–26:

According to Jer 31:31–34 the breaking of the Sinai covenant is answered by the promise of an everlasting covenant and its individual internalization. According to Jer 31:35–37, even more clearly so in the MT version of the text, the enduring existence of Israel is guaranteed by the stability of the order of nature. In referring to Jer[MT] 31:31–34 and Jer[MT] 31:35–37, Jer[MT] 33:20–21 reinterprets God's everlasting covenant with Israel as an everlasting covenant with David

---

16 While even as a supplement Jer[MT] 33:14–26 could have been later on omitted by the Jer[LXX] or its Hebrew *Vorlage* – unconsciously or consciously so.
17 As an alternative, העיר הזאת might have been chosen under the influence of Jer 32:31. Cf. Janzen 1973, 49. However the unclear reference of the third-person plural personal pronoun in v. 5 as well as the mention of העיר הזאת in v. 4 might be sufficient in order to explain the introduction of העיר הזאת in v. 5.
18 Few exegetes consider שׁם to be original (Barthélemy 1986, 703). As an alternative לשׁם שׂשׂון might be a conflated לשׂשׂון (Duhm 1901, 273).

and the Levites with regard to their descendants, which is guaranteed by the order of nature. In this sense, the descendants of David and the Levites, the leaders, take on the function of the people.

Verse 22 quotes God's promise of countless descendants to Abraham when speaking about God's promise of countless descendants for David and the Levites. The transfer of the motif of the promise of countless descendants from Abraham to David and the Levites follows the same pattern of argumentation as the transfer of the covenant motif from the people to its leaders in vv. 20–21. The role of the descendants of Abraham – the people – is transferred to the descendants of David and the Levites and thus to Israel's leaders. The transfer occurs at the cost of conflating two dissimilar motifs: The promise of a long-standing royal succession does not require countless descendants, but only one descendant at a time.

Any identification of the two families (שתי המשפחות) in Jer^{MT} 33:24a remains ambiguous. In light of v. 24b, the two families introduced in v. 24a must be identified with God's people. In light of the broader textual dynamics, they would have to be identified with the descendants of David and the Levites. Verse 24 is being quoted as objecting to God's covenant with David and the Levitical priests. Once again, a statement referring to the people is transferred to the leading circles. This time the transfer does not take place between the text and its intertexts, but between a quote ascribed to an opponent by the prophetic voice and the voice of the prophetic narrator.

In vv. 25–26 the people reenter the scene in the form of the offspring of Jacob, who are placed alongside the descendants of David, and in the form of the offspring of Abraham, Isaac, and Jacob. The non-rejection of the people is expressed by the non-rejection of David and his descendants. However, this time, due to the parallelism of the offspring of Jacob and David, the distinction between the representative and the represented is more fluid and less clear cut.

6 Textual Dynamics: The De- and Revaluation of Kingship

A possible first impression of a strict parallelism between the passage's main protagonists, the Davidic heir and the Levitical priests, is undermined by the Davidic figure being described with reference to older traditions, whereas the Levitical priests are presented following the example of the Davidic figure. It is further questioned by shifting perspectives on both the Davidic descendant and the Levites over the course of the dynamics of the passage.

Jer^MT 33:15–16, which contains an allusion to God's promise to David in 2 Sam 7:9, devaluates the Davidic figure by denying the righteous branch the royal activity of ruling as a king (מלך מלך) that was attributed to him in Jer^MT 23:5 (Lust 1994, 38). When Jerusalem, which replaces Israel as the counterpart of Judah (Lust 1994, 38), is attributed the name of the branch, Jerusalem takes on the role of the righteous king.

Jer^MT 33:17–18 quotes 1 Kgs 2:4; 8:25; 9:5; 2 Chr 6:16, which also alludes to 2 Sam 7:9. Rather than fundamentally reworking their source,[19] vv. 17–18 put the Davidic heir into perspective by introducing the Levitical priests (הכהנים הלוים, v. 18) as parallel figures. The righteous branch from Jer 33:15–16 is reprised by the Davidic heir in v. 17. The Levitical priests in v. 18 have no reference point in vv. 15–16 other than representing an elite group in Jerusalem. In contrast to the Davidic king, they would have referred to a historical reality during the post-exilic period.

Following the new beginning set by the prophetic word transmission formula (v. 19) and the prophetic messenger formula (v. 20), vv. 20–22 further elaborate upon the pairing of the Davidic heir and the Levitical priests. With regard to the Davidic heir and in opposition to Jer 33:17 and its sources, where the reference to a Davidic descendant is clearly out of context, Jer 33:21 emphasizes the Davidic lineage. Jeremiah 33:17 and 1 Kgs 2:4 and its parallels announce an איש who will sit on the throne of Israel (על כסא ישראל, 1 Kgs 2:4) or on the throne of the house of Israel (על־כסא בית־ישראל, Jer 33:17). Jeremiah 33:21 refers to a son (בן) on "his" (David's) throne, making the reference to the lineage explicit. In contrast to vv. 15–16, v. 21 reintroduces the term מלך in its variation of the divine promise to David. At the same time, v. 21 only alludes to the promise to the Levites. Thus, v. 20–22 emphasize the Davidic figure and highlight his royal nature.[20]

In the two final verses 25–26, which are introduced by another prophetic word transmission formula, the Levites disappear. At the same time, the use of משלים rather than מלכים once again deprives the Davidic figure of his explicitly royal character.

---

[19] כסא בית־ישראל (Jer 33:17) and כסא ישראל (1 Kgs 2:4) hardly reflect any differences in meaning.

[20] The change of terminology in v. 21, which has "the Levites, the priests" or "the Levitical priests" (הלוים הכהנים) is striking. Verse 22 once again has simply "the Levites" (הלוים). With regard to the terminology cf. Pietsch 2003, 84–86. Apart from this article, Pietsch dates the passage into the early Second Temple period. In any case, Jer 33:14–26 identifies the Levites as priests (or the priests as Levites) and attributes the offering of sacrifices to them. Jeremiah 33 has a broadly aligned priesthood in mind.

The initial devaluation of the royal figure vis-à-vis those earlier traditions, which its presentation is drawing from is accompanied by the parallel reference to the Levites. Later, the Davidic figure (re-)gains importance following the dynamics of the narrative and the Levitical priests are ultimately ignored.

7 Conclusions

Elaborating upon the promise to David in 2 Sam 7 and on an announcement of salvation to Jerusalem (Jer 33:15–16), Jer 33:17–18 identify Israel's leadership with two figures, the royal figure of the descendant of David and the group of the Levitical priests. Jer^{MT} 33:19–26 transfers the promise of an everlasting (new) covenant with the people, as well as the promise of countless descendants made to Abraham in the context of God's covenant with him, to Israel's leadership. As the subject of both covenants, Israel's leadership takes over the role of the people. According to Jer^{MT} 33:14–26, Israel is defined and represented by its leadership. What ensures Israel's identity and existence is not a certain ideology, not the Torah (as in Jer^{LXX}), it is Israel's leadership.

The relationship between David's descendants and the Levitical priests remains ambiguous. The contradictory textual dynamics of a consecutive de- and reevaluation of the Davidic figure, who is "teamed" with the Levites (who ultimately disappear), might be illuminated by their likely historical background: Verses 15–16, with their focus on Jerusalem, resonate in a time in which Israel/Yehud is reduced to Jerusalem and its surroundings. During the postexilic period, the devaluation of a Davidic figure, whose description draws heavily from earlier traditions, would have been met and could be explained by its historical irrelevance. The quoted tradition could not be ignored. The Levitical priests, who are placed alongside the Davidic figure, might have represented one of the groups that actually held power during this period. The covenant interprets an existing reality with regard to the Levitical priests. It is striking that no high priest is mentioned. When the focus on the Davidic figure once again gains momentum in the last passage that might represent a later stage of textual development, the covenant (re-)gains a promissory character. If the passage is as late as suggested, the hopes and fantasies of the author of the final verses would have been met by the rise of the Maccabees, if they are not already in view.[21]

---

[21] For reasons that would take too long to discuss here, Duhm (1901, 274) and Schenker (1994, *passim*) both date Jer 33 to the early Hasmonean period.

Bibliography

Barthélemy, Dominique. 1986. *Critique Textuelle de L'Ancien Testament. Vol. 2: Isaïe, Jérémie, Lamentations.* OBO 50/2. Fribourg: Academic Press.

Bogaert, Pierre-Maurice. 1991. "Urtext, texte court et relecture: Jérémie XXXIII 14–26 TM et ses préparations." In *Congress Volume Leuven 1989*, edited by John A. Emerton, 236–247. Leiden: Brill.

Duhm, Bernhard. 1901. *Das Buch Jeremia.* Kurzer Hand-Commentar zum Alten Testament. Leipzig and Tübingen: Mohr Siebeck.

Gôldman, Yôhānan. 1992. *Prophétie et royauté au retour de l'exil: Les origines littéraires de la forme massorétique du livre de Jérémie.* OBO 118. Fribourg: Academic Press.

Groß, Walter. 1999. "Israels Hoffnung auf die Erneuerung des Staates." In *Studien zur Priesterschrift und zu alttestamentlichen Gottesbildern*. SBAB 30, 65–96. Stuttgart: Katholisches Bibelwerk.

Holladay, William L. 1989. *Jeremiah: A Commentary on the Book of the Prophet Jeremiah.* Vol. 2. Hermeneia. Minneapolis: Fortress Press.

Janowski, Bernd. 2019. *Anthropologie des Alten Testaments: Grundfragen – Kontexte – Themenfelder.* Tübingen: Mohr Siebeck.

Janzen, J. Gerald. 1973. *Studies in the Text of Jeremiah.* HSM 6. Cambridge: Harvard University Press.

Lust, Johan. 1994. "The Diverse Text Forms of Jeremiah and History Writing with Jer 33 as a Test Case." *JNSL* 20:31–48.

Lust, Johan. 2004. "Messianism and the Greek Version of Jeremiah: Jer 23,5–6 and 33,14–16." In *Messianism and the Septuagint: Collected Essays by Johan Lust*, edited by Katrin Hauspie, 41–67. BEThL 178. Leuven: Leuven University Press and Peeters.

Pietsch, Michael. 2003. *"Dieser ist der Spross Davids": Studien zur Rezeptionsgeschichte der Nathanverheißung im alttestamentlichen, zwischentestamentlichen und neutestamentlichen Schrifttum.* WMANT 100. Neukirchen-Vluyn: Neukirchener Verlag.

Schenker, Adrian. 1994. "La rédaction longue du livre de Jérémie doit-elle être datée au temps des premiers Hamonéens?" *ETL* 70:281–293.

Schenker, Adrian. 2006. *Das Neue am neuen Bund und das Alte am alten: Jer 31 in der hebräischen und griechischen Bibel, von der Textgeschichte zu Theologie, Synagoge und Kirche.* FRLANT 212. Göttingen: Vandenhoeck & Ruprecht.

Schenker, Adrian. 2010. "Welche Argumente wiegen schwerer auf der Waagschale?: Zwei Weisen, die Textunterschiede in Jer 31,32–33 zu erklären." *JNSL* 36:113–124.

Tiňo, Jozef. 2010. *King and Temple in Chronicles: A Contextual Approach to their Relations.* FRLANT 234. Göttingen: Vandenhoeck & Ruprecht.

Wolff, Hans Walter. 2010. *Anthropologie des Alten Testaments*, edited by Bernd Janowski. Gütersloh: Gütersloher Verlagshaus.

Jan Rückl
The Leadership of the Judean Community according to the Book of Haggai

1 Introduction

In Haggai, the theme of the Judean leadership explicitly appears only in the book's last oracle, which announces Zerubbabel's elevation (Hag 2:20–23). On the other hand, one might ask as well which idea of the community's leadership is reflected in 1:1, 12, 14 and 2:2, 4, where it is not only the governor Zerubbabel but also the high priest Joshua whom the prophet approaches as the people's representatives. Before addressing these two aspects of leadership in Haggai, I will briefly present my general idea of the book's formation, since all the above mentioned passages probably do not stem from one hand.

Most often, literary-critical treatments of Haggai are based on the distinction between the oracles themselves and a redactional framework, which speaks of the prophet in the third person. Many scholars assume that the first layer, i.e., a collection of Haggai's oracles, already existed in a written form, which was later processed by the author of the editorial framework (regardless of the transformations that the text underwent before or after the composition of the latter).[1] As we will see below, the redactional reworking is particularly well detectable at the boundary between the framework and the first oracle. In other parts of the book, the redactional seams are less apparent, yet they may be reconstructed on the basis of the distinction carried out in the first oracle. And although the author of the framework also partly reworked the text of the oracles he inherited, redactional separation of the oracles and the later framework seems feasible.

However, scholars sometimes reckon with a more complicated literary development of the book, detecting various layers and additions (*Fortschreibun-*

---

[1] See, among others, Ackroyd 1951/52; Beuken 1967, 27–83, 184–229; Steck 1971; Mason 1977; Wolff 1986, 3–6, and *passim*; Reventlow 1993, 5–6; Wöhrle 2006, 288–322; Hallaschka 2011, 42–43; Leuenberger 2015, 47–55, and *passim*.

Note: This study is a result of research supported by the Charles University through the program PRIMUS/20/HUM/010 "Textuality in the Second Temple Judaism: Composition, Function, and Transmission of Texts." I am grateful to Hervé Gonzalez for discussing with me an earlier version of this text, as well as to Stephen Germany and Petra Hudcová for correcting its English. All remaining mistakes are mine.

https://doi.org/10.1515/9783110650358-005

gen) in both the oracles and the editorial framework. A redactional model that goes very far in this direction has been suggested by R. G. Kratz[2] and subsequently elaborated in detail by M. Hallaschka.[3] According to these scholars, the book's core consisted of two prophetic sayings contained now in 1:1abα*, 4, 8; 1:15b–2:1, 3, 9a. Later on, Haggai went through several phases of development, acquiring real redactional layers ("Fluch-und-Segen-Bearbeitung" – 1:5–7; 2:15–16, 18a, 19; narrative framework – 1:1–3, 12a, 14–15a; 1:15b–2:2) as well as separate additions (e.g., the symbolic act in 2:10–14 and the promise to Zerubbabel in 2:20–23).[4]

I will return to some of Hallaschka's redactional-critical decisions when discussing the book's last oracle. Here, I will only note that redactional-critical models positing extremely short basic forms of Haggai and Zechariah (i.e., consisting of just a few verses) are, in my opinion, problematic in general. In the Persian period, the most common literary genre associated with prophets was probably a prophetic book, i.e., a collection of various texts, mainly oracles.[5] It is therefore unlikely that the original forms of prophetic books that emerged at this time were extremely different from the literary form that was in those days regarded as a typical prophetic book, and that they acquired only later (yet within a few decades, thus in a similar historical context) the usual form of a prophetic book.

The models suggested recently by J. Wöhrle and M. Leuenberger[6] seem much more plausible. These scholars posit a relatively large core of the book containing the prophet's oracles[7] and a fundamental reworking by the author of the redactional framework.[8] Their reconstructions are fairly close to some older models which distinguished between a collection of "Auftrittsskizzen" and

---

[2] Kratz 2004, 88–92.
[3] Hallaschka 2011, 15–138; see also the summary in Hallaschka 2012, 177–182.
[4] So Hallaschka; for a summary of his model, see Hallaschka 2011, 120–138.
[5] On the genre and concept of a "prophetic book," see Ben Zvi 2003; 2009. Ben Zvi is right that the concept of prophetic book as embodied by the fifteen canonical prophetic "books" could only have developed during the Persian period, since it often entails the ideology of exile and return. On the other hand, a larger genre of "prophetic book" as a collection of oracles ascribed to a particular prophet must have had existed already at the beginning of the Persian period; otherwise, it would be difficult to explain the preservation of collections of oracles stemming from preexilic and exilic prophets. Most likely these texts were not preserved in archives but survived as "literary" works.
[6] Wöhrle 2006, 288–322; Leuenberger 2015, 44–63.
[7] Wöhrle: 1:2, 4–11, 12b–13; 2:3, 4*, 5aβb, 9, 15–16, 18abβ, 19, 23; Leuenberger: 1:2, 4–11, 12b–13; 2:3–4aα, 4ay–b, 5b, 9a, 15–16, 18a, 19.
[8] Wöhrle: 1:1, 3, 12a, 14–15; 2:1–2, 4*, 10, 20–21a; Leuenberger: 1:1, 3, 12a, 14–15; 2:1–2, 4aβ, 10, 18b, 20–21a, 23aβ–bβ.

their redactional reworking, particularly to the one suggested by H. W. Wolff (1986, 3–6, and *passim*), who ascribed to the "Auftrittsskizzen" the text in 1:2, 4–11, 12b–13; 2:15–19*; 2:3–9*, 11–14; 2:21b–23,[9] and to the redactional framework the verses 1:1, 3; 1:12a, 14–15; 2:1–2, 10, 20–21a. Besides these two basic layers, all three of the aforementioned scholars believe that shorter texts were added to the book in various phases of its development.

My own idea of Haggai's literary development is relatively close to the models suggested by Wolff, Wöhrle, and Leuenberger, but differs from all three in some respects. Without entering into details, my model can be summarized as follows:[10] The material from the primitive collection may be found in 1:2, 4–11; 2:3, 4*, 5aβb, 6–9, 11–16, 18–19, 21b–23; the redactional reworking by the author of the narrative framework appears in 1:1, 3, 12–15; 2:1–2, 10, 20–21a (and the reference to Joshua in v. 4). Later on, the text was further expanded by several glosses.[11]

Besides editing the existing text, the author of the redactional framework may also have rearranged the order of the oracles that he found in his source. The most probable case of such a rearrangement concerns the text now contained in 2:3–9. As we will see below, the supposed original location of this passage would have some significance for Zerubbabel's portrayal in the primitive collection of Haggai's oracles, and it thus deserves a brief discussion here.

The steppingstone for considering another original location of Hag 2:2–9* is the textual crux in 2:6aβ. While MT has here עוֹד אַחַת מְעַט הִיא, LXX reads ἔτι ἅπαξ, in agreement with the Syriac text ܬܘܒ ܚܕܐ ܗܝ.[12] MT's problematic character cannot be overcome on synchronic level without unfounded speculation on the meaning of אַחַת.[13] At the same time, LXX's reading (together with that of Syr if the latter is not a result of LXX's secondary influence) should be taken as evidence of the short text עוֹד אַחַת.[14] The expression עוֹד אַחַת is possible: for אַחַת meaning "once," see especially 2 Kgs 6:10, and cf. also Exod 30:10;

---

9 As it may be seen, Wolff believes that the oracle in Hag 2:15–19* had a different place in the primitive collection than in the final form of the book.
10 For the moment, my detailed analysis is only accessible to Czech readers in my commentary on Haggai (Rückl 2018, 24–39, and *passim*). An enlarged version of it will be published in French.
11 Haggai 2:5aαMT; the expression מְעַט הִיא in 2:6MT; LXX contains secondary glosses in Hag 2:9, 14; the entire verse 2:17, appearing in all important witnesses, is most likely a gloss as well. For an overall treatment of glosses in Haggai, see already Ackroyd 1956.
12 For the history of research, see Kessler 2002, 160, 173–175; Koopmans 2017, 171–174.
13 Cf., e.g., Barthélemy 1992, 928, who argues that here the word means "period."
14 *Pace* Barthélemy 1992, 928–929, who believes that the short text is a result of simplifying translation.

Lev 16:34. It should also be noted that despite MT's problematic character, the Greek translator could easily have translated it in a meaningful way, conserving some equivalent of מעט had he read it in his *Vorlage* (cf. Vg and the translation of עוד מעט as ἔτι μικρὸν in Hos 1:4). J. Kessler (2002, 160) argues that the short reading attested in LXX and Syr is a result of omission due to the perceived postponement of the eschatological events described in vv. 6–9. However, MT's problematic character and the possibility to explain it diachronically make another development more likely.

Two textual variants should be considered as attested: עוד אחת מעט היא (proto-MT) and עוד אחת (LXX, Syr). MT's reading bears some similarity to the phrase עוד מעט that appears in Exod 17:4; Ps 37:10; Isa 10:25; 29:17; Jer 51:33; Hos 1:4. Therefore, Wellhausen suggested considering MT as a combination of two variants: עוד אחת and עוד מעט. Yet the postulated combination of variants (one of which is not separately attested in the witnesses of Hag 2:6) is unable to explain the problematic היא in proto-MT. The scribe responsible for combining the variants would have freely added the pronoun, creating *precisely by that addition* the problematic text of proto-MT even though he could have combined the presupposed variants into עוד מעט אחד, which would be simpler and would affect less the original wording of the two older readings. It seems better to consider מעט היא a gloss, i.e., a nominal clause qualifying the word אחת, added under the influence of the common phrase עוד מעט, with which the uncommon expression עוד אחת is more or less identified by means of the addition of the gloss. As a matter of fact, the expression מעט היא, absent in LXX, is a typical form of explicative gloss.[15] The nominal clause מעט היא is grammatically possible: מעט is an adverb and the feminine pronoun היא agrees with אחת (cf. esp. כי מעט המה in Josh 7:3). To conclude, the reading עוד אחת, meaning "once more," is preferable.[16]

Now, if Hag 2:6 announces that YHWH is going to shake the heaven and the earth "once more," it implies that this action will only come after another such shaking, whether this one happened in the past or will occur in the future as well. Can this first shaking of the heaven and the earth be identified?[17] The statement אני מרעיש את השמים ואת הארץ also appears in v. 21. The merism "the heaven and the earth" delineates the universe (cf., e.g., Gen 1:1), and in v. 21, the image of YHWH's shaking of the heavens and the earth aptly symbolizes the breakdown of the current political world order, an event described in a

---

[15] For the use of the personal pronouns הוא and היא in explicative glosses, see Fishbane 1988, 44–48.
[16] I am grateful to Johanna Erzberger for a stimulating discussion about this textual problem.
[17] For some suggestions, see Keil 1878, 191, and Rudolph 1976, 42–43.

more explicit way in v. 22. However, in v. 6, the cosmic cataclysm is a portent of the shaking of all nations that subsequently will bring their treasures to Jerusalem. Therefore, the vertical merism "the heaven and the earth" is supplemented with the horizontal merism "the sea and the dry land" in v. 7.[18] It thus seems that in v. 6, the phrase primarily coined for v. 21 is accommodated by the addition of a plus for its use in the context of vv. 6–8. This being so, the precedent for "once more" in v. 6 seems to be YHWH's shaking of the heaven and the earth in v. 21. This in turn may indicate that at a certain stage of the book's transmission, vv. 6–8, or – perhaps more likely – the whole oracle in vv. 3–9* followed after vv. 21–23*. In the absence of other indications of the point in time when the order of oracles was changed, it may be tentatively assumed that the relocation of vv. 3–9* (or 6–8) was carried out by the author of the redactional framework.

Can the individual phases of Haggai's literary development be dated? At first glance, Haggai's historical context is easily identifiable, since all the oracles in the book are precisely dated to four different days within the span of a few months of the second year of the Persian king Darius, who usually is identified with Darius I (521–485).[19] However, at least formally, the dates introducing the individual oracles are part of the redactional framework, and it is hardly possible to prove their historical reliability. D. Edelman (2005, 80–150), for instance, considers the dates in Haggai secondary and unreliable, and she situates the reconstruction of the temple together with the emergence of the oldest texts in Haggai during the reign of Artaxerxes I (465–424). Some scholars believe that there is a very large time gap between the composition of the original sayings and the narrative framework.[20]

Nevertheless, it appears quite likely that Haggai was indeed active under the reign of Darius I. Traditionally some credibility is given to the genealogy of the Davidides of the exilic and postexilic periods found in 1 Chr 3:17–24, according to which Zerubbabel was the son of Pedaiah (so v. 19MT), who was in turn the son of the next-to-last Judean king Jehoiachin. In Haggai, Zerubbabel is designated as the son of Shealtiel (in agreement with 1 Chr 3:19LXX), yet according to 1 Chr 3:17MT, Shealtiel was Jehoiachin's son as well, so that in both cases Zerubbabel would be Jehoiachin's grandson. (It should be noted, however, that

---

18 I adopt the terminology of "vertical" and "horizontal" merisms from Leuenberger 2015, 170–171.
19 It should be mentioned that L. DeQueker (1993) argued that the Second Temple was completed under Darius II (423–404). As I tried to show elsewhere (Rückl 2018, 43–49), his arguments are unconvincing.
20 E.g., Ackroyd 1951, 174, and *passim*.

we would not know that Shealtiel was Jehoiachin's son without 1 Chr 3.) Similarly, according to 1 Chr 5:27–41 and Neh 12:10–11, the high priest Joshua was son of Jehozadak, who was deported by the Babylonians. While all of the references to Joshua in Haggai (Hag 1:1, 12, 14; 2:2, 4) may be ascribed to the author of the redactional framework, Zerubbabel probably appeared already in the primitive collection of the prophet's oracles (2:4, 23; see below for more on all these passages). There are no extrabiblical indices confirming Zerubbabel's activity under Darius I, but this period corresponds to his place in the genealogy in 1 Chr 3:17–24. Moreover, there is extrabiblical evidence that combines well with the biblical depiction of the temple's reconstruction under Darius I. According to Ezra 5 (// 1 Esd 6:1–21), after Zerubbabel and Joshua had restarted the work on the temple, Tattenai, the governor of Transeuphratene, investigated whether the construction works were legal. His letter to Darius, quoted in Ezra 5:7–17, contains more elements testifying in favor of its authenticity than other alleged documents reproduced in Ezra, although even Tattenai's letter might, of course, have undergone some redactional reworking (Grabbe 1998, 128). Now, Tattenai, the governor of the Transeuphratene (which at this time was part of the mega-satrapy Babylonia and Transeuphratene) is attested in a cuneiform text dated to 502 BCE (Olmstead 1944). Therefore, the rebuilding of the Jerusalem temple most likely was undertaken under Darius I, and the primitive form of oracles gathered in Haggai stems from this period as well.

The redactional framework consists of rather scanty material, which adds to the difficulty of assigning a date to it. As we have seen, its author may have rearranged the pre-existent collection of Haggai's oracles, and is thus to some degree responsible for the book's composition, having it culminate with the promise to Zerubbabel in Hag 2:23. It may perhaps be inferred that this final oracle made some sense for him, and hence that he still worked during Zerubbabel's lifetime.[21] The basic form of the book as we know it today would thus have been created relatively early after Haggai's activity.

This is a fairly traditional dating of Haggai, but it can lead to less traditional conclusions regarding the book's place in the history of biblical literature. Like other "postexilic" books, Haggai was traditionally considered to be a "late" text. Until the middle of the twentieth century, this contributed to a rather negative appraisal of the prophet and his book by some scholars – Haggai was labeled as a mere epigone of the preexilic prophets, lacking their originality and moral loftiness.[22] Later on, with the rise in popularity of hermeneutics and intertextu-

---

[21] Cf. also Kessler 2002, 51–52 (with further references); Wöhrle 2006, 320; Leuenberger 2015, 232 (according to whom the redactor himself wrote the core of the promise).
[22] E.g., Weiser 1963, 236; for a more detailed presentation, see Kessler 2002, 2–3.

ality in philology, the processes of reception themselves became a favorite research topic, and several important studies published in the past decades paid great attention to the ways Haggai works with older literary traditions.[23] However, with the shifts in dating many biblical texts and entire literary traditions, the question arises which of these texts or literary traditions could have been known to the prophet or the redactor(s) of the book. As I demonstrate in more detail elsewhere, Haggai should in fact be considered a relatively old book that offers us a small yet interesting window onto several traditional aspects of Judean religion, mostly uninfluenced by some of the important theological developments of the "exilic" and Persian periods (Rückl, forthcoming). Also relatively traditional was the view of Zerubbabel's leadership in the book's oldest core, to which I will now turn.

2 Zerubbabel's Leadership according to Hag 2:21b–23

Zerubbabel appears in Haggai several times, but his leadership becomes an explicit theme only in the book's last oracle. After the prophetic word formula including the date of the prophecy's proclamation in v. 20, the oracle itself begins in v. 21a with YHWH's command to the prophet to address Zerubbabel. The latter is referred to with his title of "governor of Judah," yet, unlike in 1:1, 14; 2:2, without the patronym. The absence of the patronym may be linked to the fact that in v. 23 Zerubbabel on the contrary appears with the patronym and without his function in the Persian administration.

A very similar command to prophesy appears also at the beginning of the book's second oracle in 2:2, where the prophet is asked to approach Zerubbabel, the high priest Joshua, and the "rest of the people" (cf. also 2:11). Based on the agreement of the addressees mentioned in 2:2 with the list of the actors of the temple rebuilding in 1:12, 14, Hag 2:2 is often ascribed to the author of the redactional framework together with 1:15b–2:1.[24] Provided that 2:2 belongs to the framework, v. 21a should be ascribed to it as well.[25]

Verses 21b–23 are composed of two elements: vv. 21b–22 describe the breakdown of the current geopolitical world order, v. 23 announces Zerubbabel's ele-

---

23 Above all Kessler 2002; Koopmans 2017; cf. already Beuken 1967.
24 Reventlow 1993, 19; Wöhrle 2006, 291; Hallaschka 2011, 62, 75 (with further references); Leuenberger 2015, 152–153, 158; see also the last section of the present study.
25 So also Wöhrle 2006, 292; similarly Leuenberger 2015, 235.

vation that will follow upon it. Some scholars believe that these two elements belong to different redactional layers, or that these verses as a whole were not present in the core of Haggai's oracles. A few arguments in favor of the oracle's unity and its ascription to the book's basic text will be adduced at the end of this section.

The proclamation of Zerubbabel's elevation in v. 23 runs as follows:

ביום ההוא נאם יהוה צבאות אקחך זרבבל בן שאלתיאל עבדי נאם יהוה ושמתיך כחותם כי בך בחרתי נאם יהוה צבאות

> On that day, saying of YHWH of hosts, I will take you, O Zerubbabel, the son of Shealtiel, my servant, saying of YHWH, and make you like a seal, for I have chosen you, saying of YHWH of hosts. (Hag 2:23)

The position of the verse at the book's end may be deemed emphatic; its importance also emerges from the accumulation of the formulae of YHWH's saying (נאם יהוה), which appear here three times and comprise eight of the verse's twenty words. There is, however, a debate over how the text's author envisioned the concrete political consequences that YHWH's announced acts concerning Zerubbabel would have for him and the Judean community. According to most scholars, the oracle proclaims no less than the restoration of the Judean monarchy. However, in recent research another trend has also appeared that tries to reduce the concrete political dimension of the promise. In this connection, it is often pointed out that the oracle does not use terms such as "to reign," "king," "throne," etc., and Zerubbabel's royal status is thus not explicitly stated. As will become apparent, I tend to agree more or less with the traditional position – Zerubbabel's elevation is described in terms that connote his future royal status, even if the term "king" is not used explicitly. Some allusiveness is characteristic already for the preceding vv. 21b–22, which proclaim the doom of the Persian Empire without pronouncing its name.[26]

---

26 It should perhaps be mentioned in this respect that there is a debate on the extent to which vv. 21b–22 reflect or directly refer to particular realities of their historical context. Some scholars emphasize the formulaic and stereotypical character of the images used in vv. 21b–22, and these observations may lead them to deny or minimize the specific relationship of these verses to the time of Zerubbabel's activity, or to the specific historical context of the Persian domination in general (Kessler 2002, 223–226; Koopmans 2017, 279–283; cf. also Reventlow 1993, 30). However, at the time of their composition, these verses could hardly have been perceived as a random catalogue of eschatological images without specific socio-political potential. To take one example, in the context of the *pax persica* the overthrow of the "throne of kingdoms" announced in v. 22 must have had a strong empire-critical aspect, regardless of whether it stems from Zerubbabel's time or later (cf. already Meyers and Meyers 1988, 67; Lux 2009, 249). In fact, the relationship of these verses to imperial power is even more specific, since here the

In v. 23, YHWH first promises to Zerubbabel to "take" him. With God as the subject, the verb לקח often designates appointment into an office, a service, etc.[27] With this meaning, the verb also appears with reference to David, whom YHWH took from the pasture in order to make him prince over Israel (2 Sam 7:8; similarly Ps 78:70). Rose (2000, 217–218, 241–243) argues that in some of the passages where God "takes" somebody (e.g., Israel to be his people in Exod 6:7), the emphasis is more on the privileged relationship and protection than appointment into an office, and he then interprets the word in this way also in Hag 2:23. However, at least some of the passages that Rose refers to in support of his case are inappropriate, since the verb לקח is used in them with a more literal meaning as part of a certain image.[28] In general, I cannot escape the impression that Rose strains the argument in order to avoid a political interpretation of Haggai's last oracle. The verb לקח is followed in Hag 2:23 by the verb שים, which also often expresses appointment into an office (Exod 1:11, etc.[29]). The sequence לקח – שים in the sense of "taking" somebody and appointing him into a function for a task appears also in Josh 8:12; 1 Sam 8:11; Ezek 19:5 (cf. Ezek 17:5). In Hag 2:23, this meaning of the verbs clearly ensues from the context, and I will thus come back to it below, after commenting on the phrase "make you like a seal."[30]

At the end of v. 23aα, the sequence of verbs describing YHWH's future actions is interrupted by an enlarged address of Zerubbabel and a new formula of YHWH's saying. The addressee's name is accompanied by the patronym "son of Shealtiel" yet, unlike in Hag 1:1, 14; 2:2, 21, not his function of governor. This corresponds well to the message of vv. 21b–23. After the breakdown of the current political order (vv. 21b–22), Zerubbabel's elevation will lead to the restoration of the Davidic dynasty in Judah. In this context, the patronym emphasizes Zerubbabel's dynastic legitimacy, and designating Zerubbabel as a Persian gov-

---

biblical text subversively works with images taken over from the Persian royal ideology attested in the inscriptions and visual monuments of Darius I (Rückl, forthcoming).
27 See, e.g., Amos 7:15. Wolff 1986, 83; Rose 2000, 216–217; Kessler 2002, 227; Hallaschka 2011, 112.
28 E.g., 2 Sam 22:17 = Ps 18:17: "He sent from on high, he took me (יקחני); he drew me out of many waters." Similarly Deut 4:20; Hos 11:3.
29 Cf. Kessler 2002, 229.
30 Cf. Kessler's pertinent observation that v. 23 contains several terms (e.g., "servant," "choose") that in various passages of the Hebrew Bible are used in connection with very important concepts, yet it would be mistaken to treat these terms individually and then assume that all nuances linked to them in other passages may be connoted in our text (Kessler 2002, 226–227).

ernor in connection with the re-establishment of the Judean monarchy would make no sense after the fall of the empire.³¹

Instead of mentioning Zerubbabel's function in the Persian administration, YHWH addresses Zerubbabel as his servant. The title "my [i.e., YHWH's] servant" is given to several important characters in the Hebrew Bible, among them David.³² As observed by H. Ringgren (2003, 394), whenever David is designated as YHWH's servant, "the context almost always involves election and the perpetual continuation of the dynasty." Although it cannot be assumed with certainty that the author and intended readers of Hag 2:23 knew at least some of these texts, their number suggests that the ascription of the title to Zerubbabel in Haggai had royal and perhaps also Davidic connotations.³³ The notion of the king as a deity's privileged servant is widespread across countries and centuries in the ancient Near East.

YHWH will make Zerubbabel "like a seal." The word חותם is sometimes translated as "signet ring" (ESV, NJB, etc.) in light of Jer 22:24, where the king Jehoiakin is depicted as a seal on YHWH's right hand. However, without this connection, it would not be apparent from Hag 2:23 alone that it refers to a seal on a ring. The extensive discussion on the meaning of the simile used in Hag 2:23 has been nicely summarized by Kessler.³⁴ As Kessler shows, the crucial question is which aspect of the seal is used in the image: 1) according to some scholars, the basis of the simile is the intimate and exclusive relationship between the seal and its owner; 2) others believe that the seal is the symbol of authority; and 3) according to still others the point is that a subordinate person who receives the seal from a superior person receives the right to represent him.

In Jer 22:24, the image no doubt expresses the proximity of the signet ring and its owner – even if Jehoiakin is (or were) the signet ring on God's hand, YHWH will tear him off. Despite the a priori proximity of the Judean king to YHWH, Jehoiakin will be sent into exile and never return (vv. 25–27). The intimate relationship to and the preciousness of a beloved person is expressed by the seal image also in Song 8:6 ("Set me as a seal upon your heart, as a seal upon your arm"). In contrast to this, and due to the brevity of the expression,

---

31 See also Hallaschka 2011, 109, 114; Leuenberger 2015, 245.
32 Second Samuel 7:5, 8 = 1 Chr 17:4, 7; 1 Kgs 11:13; 14:8; 2 Kgs 19:34; Ps 89:4; Ezek 34:23; 37:24–25 – in Ezekiel, David probably designates a future Davidic king; cf. also 2 Sam 3:18; 1 Kgs 11:32, 34; 2 Kgs 19:34 = Isa 37:35; 2 Kgs 20:6; 2 Chr 6:42; Pss 18:1; 36:1; 78:70; 89:21; 132:10; 144:10; Jer 33:21–22, 26. On the usage of the title with other characters, see Kessler 2002, 228–229.
33 See, e.g., Leuenberger 2015, 245–247.
34 Kessler 2002, 230, with references to the proponents of various solutions.

in Hag 2:23 the meaning of the image is not clear from the verse alone. Since there is no evidence that "making as a seal" alone functioned in ancient Hebrew as a generally comprehensible metaphor of a certain act, and since Hag 2:23 deals with Jehoiakin's grandson who is concerned by the last part of the oracle against Jehoiakin in Jer 22:24–30, according to which none of Jehoiakin's posterity will sit on the Judean throne and rule (v. 30), it is quite probable that the phrase "I will make you like a seal" is elliptic precisely because it alludes to the image used in Jer 22:24.[35] I thus support a variant of the first type of interpretation: the image of Zerubbabel made like a seal expresses the proximity to God into which Jehoiakin's grandson will be introduced, because this is the meaning that the image of the signet ring on YHWH's hand has in Jer 22:24. The essential point is, however, that in Jeremiah's text this proximity ensues from Jehoiakin's royal function (which he is being divested of). Therefore, Hag 2:23 most likely proclaims nothing less than restoration of the Davidic monarchy (at the same time, the meaning of the seal as representative of its owner may be connoted here as well). The other statements in the verse must be understood in connection with this meaning of 2:23aβ; e.g., the verb לקח most likely means here a separation and authorization for a certain office, and the term "my servant" no doubt has royal connotations in this context.

The same certainly holds true for the substantiation of Zerubbabel's elevation by YHWH's election. In the Hebrew Bible, various entities – individuals, collectives, or a place – can be divinely elected.[36] However, it is again noteworthy that the individual whose election is mentioned most often is David (2 Sam 6:21; 1 Kgs 8:44; 11:34; 1 Chr 28:4; 2 Chr 6:6; Pss 78:70; 89:4). And although it is disputable whether the author of Hag 2:23 or his first readers could know some of the abovementioned texts, it is quite likely that in the given context Zerubbabel's election has royal and Davidic connotations.[37]

Divine election was ascribed to many kings of the ancient Near East, while it had a special importance for those rulers who did not assume power smoothly

---

[35] Understanding Hag 2:23aβ as a kind of "answer" to Jer 22:24 is largely accepted; see, e.g., Kessler 2002, 230–231; Redditt 2014, 439–440; Hallaschka 2011, 116; Leuenberger 2016, 248–249. For the elliptic nature of the proclamation "I will make you like a seal," cf. Meyers and Meyers 1988, 69, according to whom the expression is an ellipsis for "I set you as a signet on my finger/hand." The connection between Hag 2:23 and Jer 22:24 is questioned by Pomykala 1995, 49, and Goswell 2010, 82.
[36] See Rose 2000, 212–213, for a detailed overview.
[37] Davidic and dynastic connotations in v. 23 as a whole are disputed by Pomykala 1995, 45–53. He may be right that the verse does not presuppose the concept of the dynastic promise, but this does not exclude that the oracle legitimizes Zerubbabel as a descendant of the Davidic dynasty by referring to Davidic traditions.

from the position of a crown prince. This was also the case for Darius I, who says of himself in DSf § 3c that Ahura Mazda chose him from the whole earth.[38] In many other places Darius depicts his election for kingship using different vocabulary, such as when he states that Ahura Mazda bestowed the kingship on him. An interesting situation occurs at the beginning of the Behistun inscription, where on the one hand Darius affirms to be from the royal dynasty of Achaemenids, yet on the other hand he also says that he is king by the favor of Ahura Mazda (DB §§ 1–5).

There should be little surprise that divine election figures in a text that legitimizes Zerubbabel, whose accession to throne – if it would happen – would not be entirely standard either. Despite his origin from the family that reigned in preexilic Judah, Zerubbabel would have become king following a period when the Judean monarchy did not exist, and his father was not a king.

What would the Davidic restoration involve according to Hag 2:23? As already mentioned, there is a tendency in recent scholarship to downplay the concrete political significance of the verse or the whole oracle in vv. 20–23. On the one hand, according to some scholars, the verse announces that Zerubbabel will become an "eschatological ruler" or messiah.[39] This interpretation does not depoliticize the text entirely but removes the oracle's fulfillment from normal human history. However, despite the grandiose dimensions of the announced future (especially if we read v. 23 together with v. 21b–22), there is no reason to assume that the first addressees of the oracle would not have construed the Davidic restoration as an event taking place in normal historical time.

Other scholars have emphasized the oracle's allusive character. According to J. Kessler, the author of v. 23 intentionally describes Zerubbabel's future in vague terms. This author did not seek to ascribe to Zerubbabel a concrete political status or to announce the establishment of a particular socio-political organization in Judah but rather to express general hope for the community. Zerubbabel, who as a member of the Davidic family is related to a glorious past, is a *persönlicher Hoffnungsträger*.[40] An extreme position of this kind is defended by W. H. Rose, who affirms that "it is safe to conclude that there is no reason to assume" that Hag 2:23 "would necessarily imply a change of his [i.e. Zerubbabel's] position." According to Rose, the prophet only promises to Zerubbabel divine protection, thanks to which he will not share the fate of the overthrown

---

[38] The division into paragraphs in the Persian texts corresponds to Kent (1953).
[39] E.g., Meyers and Meyers 1988, 69–70.
[40] Kessler 2002, 237–239; cf. also Wolff 1986, 85–86, from whom Kessler takes over the German term.

political actors.⁴¹ Haggai's last oracle is read in a very similar way also by G. Goswell (2010).

Rose and Goswell are so clearly mistaken that instead of entering into a detailed discussion with their strained arguments, I will only make a methodological remark. It is fundamentally misleading to disqualify relatively probable and broadly accepted conclusions by pointing out that the interpreted text does not state the idea in question "explicitly." Particularly when the issue is the interpretation of prophetic texts, which for various reasons often use figurative language, such an argument has no weight at all. This is even more so if, after this kind of critique, a scholar suggests a reading which is not expressed in the text "explicitly" either, and when explaining individual textual elements he is constantly forced to reject the traditional interpretation as *unnecessary* and to defend his own reading as *possible*.

However, it is true that Haggai's last oracle is somewhat allusive and vague. In both parts of the oracle, this may in part be due to some fear of Persian power. Yet, as regards the part that directly concerns Zerubbabel, Kessler's explanation has something to it. On the one hand, the biblical author proclaims the imminent fall of the Persian Empire and the restoration of Davidic rule. On the other hand, some vagueness in the terms used makes it easier to connect the oracle with the contemporary situation, in which Zerubbabel may already be depicted as YHWH's chosen leader but not yet called a king.

From a different angle, the political ambition of Haggai's last oracle is reduced by the interpretation that tries to perceive behind v. 23 political expectations that would be concrete but "realistic." According to some scholars, the verse expresses the hope that the province of Yehud will gain the status of a vassal kingdom within the Persian Empire under the dynastic leadership of the Davidide Zerubbabel and his descendants (Leuenberger 2015, 247). However, this "sober" interpretation of v. 23 is impossible if the promise to Zerubbabel is read on the same level as the previous two verses, which proclaim the breakdown of the current political world order. As will be shown at the end of this section, there are no convincing grounds for the literary-critical excision of vv. 21b–22.

Haggai's idea of Zerubbabel's leadership should also be inferred from how the last oracle is articulated with the rest of the book or the supposed primitive collection of Haggai's oracles. The book's chief theme is unquestionably the rebuilding of the temple in Jerusalem.⁴² According to the dates given in Hag

---

41 Rose 2000, 241–242; for the whole argumentation, see pp. 208–243.
42 To be sure, the name of the site is never mentioned in the book, but it makes little sense to question the basic supposition that the concerned temple is that of Jerusalem.

2:10, 20, the last oracle was proclaimed on the day of the foundation of the temple, referred to in the penultimate oracle (2:10–19). As noted above and demonstrated in detail below, the dates are, at least formally, part of the redactional framework, and their reliability is thus questionable. Nevertheless, the motival connection between the book's last two oracles is palpable.

In the ancient Near East, temple building was most often a royal prerogative.[43] In preexilic Judah, the Davidides' care for the sanctuary in Jerusalem also played an important role in their royal ideology. According to the books of Samuel and Kings, David acquired a place where the future temple would be erected (2 Sam 24), Solomon built it (1 Kgs 5:16–7:51), and other kings initiated its reconstructions (Ahaz, 2 Kgs 16:10–18; Hezekiah, 2 Kgs 18:4, 16; Josiah, 2 Kgs 23). A tight connection between the Jerusalem temple and the Davidic kingship is perhaps the most conspicuous in Ps 132, wherein YHWH's favor granted to David and to the dynasty is a reward for the king's merits in establishing the sanctuary, and at the same time the dynasty is guaranteed by YHWH's residing in Zion. In this respect, Ps 132 probably reflects well the Judean royal ideology, even if the text's current form with the explicit reference to the conditional character of the Davidic kingship in v. 12 can hardly be preexilic (Rückl 2016, 142–146).

Apparently, however, at some point after 586 BCE, the Davidic kingship's close connection to the temple was judged by some to be potentially harmful to the dynasty's interests. As I tried to show in detail elsewhere, the author of 2 Sam 7 endeavored to break the traditional connection between the temple and kingship (Rückl 2016; similarly also Oswald 2008, 17–105). Nathan's oracle, for one thing, denies the importance of the temple for the dynastic promise, and secondly it rejects the notion of the temple as YHWH's place to dwell. The origin of 2 Sam 7 can be imagined in two historical contexts. First, it might have been written during the Neo-Babylonian period, after 586 BCE. If so, the purpose of the connection between the dynastic promise and the polemic against the traditional role of the temple in royal ideology would be an attempt to maintain (or promote) the promise after the fall of the temple. However, 2 Sam 7 could also stem from that part of the Persian period when the temple of Jerusalem was restored, but the Davidides could not derive their legitimacy from it since the cult and the temple were understood as the domain of priests under the auspices of Persian rule.

Like 2 Sam 7, Haggai defends the program of the Davidic restoration. Yet, contrary to 2 Sam 7, Haggai perpetuates and reconstitutes the traditional, "natu-

---

[43] Schaudig 2010, 142–143; see also, e.g., Keel 1997, 269–280.

ral" relationship between the Davidic kingship and the Jerusalem temple. Historically, the temple was indeed most likely founded under Zerubbabel's leadership. This is suggested by Zech 4:9 ("The hands of Zerubbabel have laid the foundation of this house; his hands shall also complete it"), where Zerubbabel's merits for beginning the temple's reconstruction seem to be stressed against other actors involved in the restoration of Judean society in the early Persian period. Correspondingly, as will be argued below, the invitation in Hag 2:4 to courageously build the temple was originally addressed to Zerubbabel together with "all the people of the land," and not to the high priest Joshua, whose name was added by the author of the redactional framework. Given the importance that the care for the Jerusalem temple had in the preexilic Judean royal ideology, the act of the temple foundation carried out by the Davidide Zerubbabel must have itself connoted a certain restoration of preexilic conditions. In Haggai, the importance of the temple foundation for Zerubbabel's legitimation is enhanced by being juxtaposed with the proclamation of Zerubbabel's elevation described in terms that echo preexilic Judean royal ideology.

The grandiose character of the imminent Davidic restoration would be even more pronounced in the primitive collection of Haggai's oracles if, as it was argued above, vv. 3–9* originally followed vv. 21b–23. After the destruction of the current political world order (i.e., the Persian Empire), the Davidic dynasty will return to power and restore the monarchy, with the rebuilt temple of Jerusalem in its political center. Into this center the nations of the world will bring their riches.

The influx of wealth into the political and/or religious center is a topos of ancient Near Eastern literature. As demonstrated already by M. Weinfeld (1983, 93–115), various Mesopotamian texts since the beginning of the second millennium BCE have depicted foreigners or their kings bringing tribute, gifts, and taxes either to a great king or an important sanctuary located in a political center. Similar concepts of a world-dominating king or the world's sanctuary appear also in biblical literature.

An example of this motif from the Neo-Babylonian period may be found in Nebuchadnezzar II's inscription describing the king's various building activities in Babylon and Borsippa (no. 15 in Langdon 1905). Here, Nebuchadnezzar first describes his election by Marduk and his conquests of distant countries, stating at this occasion that he offered to Marduk in Babylon "silver and gold, [...] whatsoever has a value, [...] rich presents"[44] from the dominated territories. A similar motif is Nebuchadnezzar's summoning of the empire's nations to build the Ete-

---

44 Langdon 1905, 118–126; cf. also the end of the inscription, 140–141.

menanki temple (Langdon 1905, 148–151). In the Persian period, already the Cyrus cylinder states that "all the kings who sit upon thrones throughout the world, from the Upper Sea to the Lower Sea, who live in the di[stricts far-off], the kings of the West, who live in tents, all of them brought their heavy tribute"[45] to Cyrus in Babylon.

However, the idea of a *multinational* empire supported by the individual nations sending their gifts to the empire's centre acquired an essential role in Persian imperial ideology, as we know it from the inscriptions and visual monuments of Darius I and other kings after him.[46] The motif of lands (or their inhabitants) bringing tribute appears already in § 7 of the Behistun inscription, which Darius commanded to be distributed in translations throughout the empire and whose Aramaic version thus could have been known to Haggai himself as well as to a scribe composing a collection of his oracles or later authors/redactors of the book. The importance of this motif in Darius's royal propaganda is confirmed by its appearance in his other inscriptions (DPe § 2; DNa § 3; DSe § 3; cf. also XPh § 3). In DSf 3f–k, similarly to Nebuchadnezzar's mentioned inscription, Darius presents a list of nations who brought material for and participated in the construction of the king's palace in Susa. Nations bringing gifts to a Persian king are also depicted on a relief on the eastern staircase of the Apadana palace in Persepolis.

In Hebrew literature, the motif of a world-dominating king appears already in the eighth/seventh century BCE, when some of its formulations common in Neo-Assyrian texts are received in the court of Jerusalem and ascribed to the king of Judah, as is attested, for example, by Ps 2.[47] The motif of the nations and/or their riches flowing to Zion appears several times in prophetic books (Isa 2:1–5 // Mic 4:1–5; Isa 18:7; 49:22–23; 60–61; Joel 4:11–17; Zech 8:20–23).[48] However, it is often difficult to date these texts with precision. Haggai 2:7–9 seems to be especially close to Isa 60, which has led some scholars to propose a literary relationship between these texts.[49] It seems more probable, however, that from a certain point in time we should simply reckon with a widespread discourse on the "pilgrimage of nations" (Leuenberger 2015, 173). Given the emphasis put on the multinational character of the empire in Persian royal ideolo-

---

[45] Lines 28–30; the translation by M. Cogan is from Hallo 2003, 315.
[46] Koch 1996, 147–151, 197–202, and *passim*.
[47] For a thorough list of parallels between Ps 2 and Neo-Assyrian prophecies, see Hilber 2005, 90–95. On the dating of the psalm, see Otto 2002, with further references. However, cf. Salo 2017, 82–91, who dates the psalm to the early Persian period.
[48] A much longer list is adduced by Weinfeld 1983, 110–114.
[49] Both directions of dependence have been suggested; see Leuenberger 2015, 173, for a detailed comparison and further references.

gy, expressed, for example, by the image of the nations' presents flowing into the political center (which, of course, is religiously motivated),[50] it may be surmised that the discourse of the "pilgrimage of nations" in the Hebrew Bible is a repercussion of Persian propaganda.

The oracle in Hag 2:3–9 closes with YHWH's promise that he will give peace "in this place." The expression "in this place" (ובמקום הזה) is probably used for its vagueness – the focus of the peace gift is the temple in the capacity of YHWH's dwelling-place, yet the peace concerns a space much larger than the temple building itself, no matter whether the author thought of the peace of Jerusalem, Yehud or the whole world, newly organized around the temple of Jerusalem. Again, the connection between the motif of peace and the arrangement of the empire around a religious-political center appears also in Mesopotamian texts.[51] On the other hand, as suggested by Jer 14:13, the proclamation of peace to Jerusalem (whose name goes unmentioned in both verses and is only alluded to by the word שלום) probably is a traditional motif of Judean prophecy.[52] In Hag 2:3b the proclamation of the peace gift "in this place" is somewhat unexpected, since there was no reference to a situation of war in the preceding verses. Therefore, similarly to v. 6 with its "once more," this verse makes better sense after vv. 21b–23, where a fratricidal war is mentioned as part of the collapse of the current political order.

To conclude, the combination of vv. 21–23 and 3–9* constitutes a traditional complex of motifs, adapted for the situation of Yehud in the early Persian period. The restoration of the Davidide Zerubbabel is linked to the rebuilding of the temple and the victory over enemies; YHWH, who will dwell in the temple, is about to bless not only the reigning Davidide, but also the people and the "place" organized around the center defined by the dynasty and the temple. The influx of the nations' wealth into the religious-political center implies some form of the nations' subjugation. The author of vv. 21–23 and 3–9* thus apparently imagined the restored Judean kingdom to a large extent after the Persian model as a multinational empire, with its symbolic-political center being more cultic in character than was the case with the prototype (similarly Lux 2009, 249). Haggai proclaims the restoration of the Davidic monarchy, yet the nations' gifts are depicted as flowing into the temple. A shift of the community's focus from the throne to the temple can be observed also in other biblical texts from the Persian period, most prominently in the priestly texts of the Pentateuch and in Ezekiel. Similarly to what may be observed in Haggai, the central Yahwistic

---

50 Koch 1996, 163–164.
51 Cf., e.g., Langdon 1950, 88–89, 170–171.
52 Cf. already Beuken 1967, 61–62.

sanctuary functions in P as the center of the cult of the whole world (Nihan and Römer 2009, 170–172), although in the latter case the aspect of the material support provided to the cult by the foreign nations is absent.

The expectations of the author of Hag 2:21b–23 may be labelled "unrealistic," and it is difficult to imagine that they were shared by Zerubbabel, who probably would have been a rational political practitioner. Therefore, the book's last oracle probably does not reflect an anti-Persian insurrection led by Zerubbabel. Does this mean that the oracle as a whole or at least the most grandiose predictions in vv. 21b–22 should be considered late and secondary?

J. Wöhrle ascribes vv. 6–8, 21b–22 to a redaction affecting a preliminary stage of the book of the Twelve at the turn of the fifth/fourth centuries.[53] Therefore, even the author of this redaction would formulate his hopes "against all appearance" (Wöhrle 2008, 171), and his view would be unrealistic. Still, it seems somewhat problematic to connect vv. 6–8, 21b–22 with the historical Haggai or another author writing in Zerubbabel's time. Could somebody writing in this period and perhaps even close to real power in Yehud have held such utopian expectations? At first glance, it is easier to attribute these verses to an unknown anonymous scribe from the turn of the fifth/fourth centuries. On the other hand, however, it seems incomprehensible why this scribe would have associated the breakdown of the political world order (i.e. the Persian Empire) with Zerubbabel, who would have long been dead by this scribe's time. In so doing, the scribe would emphasize that the older prediction in v. 23 did not come true, and he would also present as unfulfilled the very prediction he introduced into the text in vv. 21b–22!

According to M. Hallaschka (2011, 116–120), the entire last oracle is an addition from the Hellenistic period. Hallaschka believes that this text already presupposes the connection of Haggai and Zechariah, yet he substantiates this claim exclusively by the common occurrence of individual words in Hag 2:20–23 and Zech 1–6,[54] which I do not find very convincing. In Hallaschka's view, the universal judgment of nations with cosmic dimensions reflects Alexander the Great's conquest of the Persian Empire and the wars of the Diadochi.[55] Hence, Zerubbabel is supposed to function in the text as a cipher for the restoration of the Davidic line, a role for which he was presumably predestined by his

---

53 For an overall description of this redaction, see Wöhrle 2008, 139–171. Verse 22 was ascribed to a redaction of the book of the Twelve already by Nogalski 1993, 229–237.
54 Cf. already Nogalski, 1993, 51–52, 232.
55 Cf. Leuenberger 2012, 165–166, who thinks that the situation of chaos, which constitutes the background of the universal judgment of nations, was characteristic especially for the western part of the Persian Empire already during the last century of its existence.

being, according to the biblical witness, instrumental in the restoration of the temple and at the same time the last Davidide holding a political function in Judah. In support of his interpretation, Hallaschka mentions other late texts having an interest in Zerubbabel (Ezra 1–6; 1 Esd 4:13, 5–6; Sir 49:11; Matt 1:12–13; Luke 3:27; Josephus, A.J. XI). However, in none of these texts does Zerubbabel appear as a cipher for a future Davidic "messiah," which is even more striking in view of the fact that the existence of Hag 2:20–23 could have led to such an understanding of Zerubbabel. In Hag 2:20–23 itself nothing suggests that Zerubbabel should be construed as a metaphor, and Hallaschka seems to be forced into this reading by his late dating of the text. The method of the author of such an addition would not be very appropriate to his supposed intentions. He would not indicate in any way that in his text Zerubbabel's character should be understood figuratively; moreover, he would have inserted his text into a literary work that spoke of Zerubbabel as a historical character, which would further impede the text's reception intended by him. All in all, the supposed author of the addition would have set up his prophecy to be interpreted as failed. Therefore, instead of speculating on the motives of such a clumsy scribe, Hag 2:21b–23 should be considered one of those clearly unfulfilled oracles in the Hebrew Bible that, precisely for that reason, have a good chance of being authentic prophecies.

3 Zerubbabel and Joshua as Recipients of Haggai's Oracles

I have argued so far that the primitive form of Haggai's oracles proposed an order in Judah that to a significant extent would be in accord with Judean pre-exilic royal ideology. The Davidic dynasty should again appear at the head of Judah, with their now worldwide power being legitimated by YHWH's dwelling in the Jerusalem temple. Correspondingly, Zerubbabel's right to rule has been legitimated by his leading role in the rebuilding of the temple.

This image stands in some tension with Hag 1:1, 12, 14; 2:2, 4, where Joshua the high priest is mentioned as an addressee of Haggai's oracles together with Zerubbabel. These references to Joshua most likely did not belong to the primitive layer of Haggai's prophecies but instead stem from the author of the narrative framework.

A redactional seam between the framework and the primitive collection is particularly visible at the beginning of the book. Haggai 1:1–3 contains two formulae of YHWH's word (vv. 1, 3) and one messenger formula (v. 2), which seems rather redundant (Leuenberger 2015, 104, 112). More importantly, the introduction to the first oracle looks clumsy because of the way it distributes the text between the voice of an anonymous narrator and that of the prophet. In v. 1, the narrator introduces the prophetic saying by a word formula according to which "YHWH's word came by the hand of Haggai the prophet to Zerubbabel the son of Shealtiel, governor of Judah, and to Joshua the son of Jehozadak, the high priest." In v. 2, the oracle itself begins with a messenger formula followed – somewhat surprisingly – by an affirmation of the people. However, it is not unusual for a prophetic disputation oracle to begin with a quotation of the position that is going to be refuted (cf., e.g., Jer 33:23–26; Ezek 33:23–29).[56] The impression of incoherence is only created in v. 3, where it is again the narrator who speaks, introducing an answer to the people's statement by a new word formula, as if the people's affirmation would not be part of the prophetic speech but a line in a dialogue between the prophet and the people reproduced by the narrator. Apart from this clumsiness and redundancy, there is a tension between the addressees mentioned in Hag 1:1 and the addressees implied by the oracle itself. While the oracle, i.e., vv. 2, 4–11, addresses "this people," whose speech is quoted in v. 2, the word formula in v. 1 presents Zerubbabel and Joshua as the addressees.

All these problems are easily explained by the diachronic distinction between the oracle and the redactional framework. The oracle contained in vv. 2, 4–11* has been made part of a *narrative* about Haggai's prophesying and the reaction it provoked in Judeans and their leaders. The redactor took advantage of the latently dialogical nature of the "disputation word," transforming it into a depiction of a dialogue between the prophet and the people. However, this shift was not carried out completely. The redactor has left the first line, uttered by the people (v. 2bβ), in the original form of a quotation contained in God's speech introduced by the messenger formula. After that, however, the narrator's voice reappears and introduces YHWH's answer (vv. 4–11) by a new word formula (v. 3), which creates the impression of a dialogue. The narrative depiction of the interaction of the prophet and the people then continues in vv. 12–14. To sum up, as regards vv. 1–3, v. 2 is part of the older oracle, while vv. 1 and 3 belong to the redactional framework.[57]

---

[56] On the genre of the prophetic disputation word, see Graffy 1984.
[57] So also Steck 1971, 359–362; Graffy 1984, 98–99; Wolff 1986, 16; Reventlow 1993, 6, 9, 11; Wöhrle 2006, 288–290; Leuenberger 2015, 103–104, 117. Other scholars suggested that also v. 2 belongs to the secondary framework or that v. 3 is earlier than v. 2 (Elliger 1982, 86; Beuken 1967, 29–30; Hallaschka 2011, 42–45). This seems unconvincing. Verse 4 makes more sense as the continuation of v. 2 than as the beginning of an oracle.

The references to both Zerubbabel and Joshua in 1:1, 12, 14 are clearly part of the redactional framework. The situation is more complicated with these leaders' appearance in 2:2, 4, where it belongs formally to the oracle itself. However, the list of the addressees in v. 2 – Zerubbabel the son of Shealtiel, governor of Judah, Joshua the son of Jehozadak, the high priest, and all the rest of the people – is in nearly total agreement with the lists in 1:12, 14 (the only differences being that Zerubbabel's function is absent from v. 12, and both vv. 12 and 14 lack the word "all" before "the rest of the people"). For that reason, 2:2 is generally considered to be the redactor's work as well.[58]

Verse 4 features again all three actors of the temple rebuilding – Zerubbabel, Joshua, and the people – each of them called upon to be strong. There are differences in the way they are addressed. While Zerubbabel is addressed only by his name, Joshua's name is accompanied by his patronym and the function of the high priest; the people is called "all the people of the land" (כל עם הארץ). While the short address of Zerubbabel fits well within the context of a prophetic oracle, the long address of Joshua seems somewhat awkward here, especially next to Zerubbabel's short address. The references to Zerubbabel and the people have two common features: both are addressed differently than in the narrative framework, and with both of them the appeal to be strong is followed by the formula of YHWH's saying. In contrast, Joshua is addressed in the same way as in the framework, with his patronym and title, and the command to him is not followed by the prophetic formula. All of this suggests that Joshua was inserted into the oracle by the author of the framework.[59] This means that originally Joshua did not figure in Haggai's oracles at all and has been introduced into the book by the author of the redactional framework.

There is thus a clear difference between the oracles and the framework: In the former, the Judeans building the temple are led by Zerubbabel, and this activity in turn legitimates his leading position; in the latter, the temple building activity is depicted as led by Zerubbabel and Joshua.

This conclusion brings to mind some topoi of the research on Judean leadership in "postexilic" times. According to many scholars, during the Persian peri-

---

[58] Reventlow 1993, 19; Wöhrle 2006, 291; Hallaschka 2011, 62, 75 (with further references); Leuenberger 2015, 152–153, 158. Admittedly, without v. 2 the oracle would begin in v. 3 without any introduction or reference to its addressees. On the other hand, an introduction is missing even if we start with v. 2, so that either way we must suppose that in the original collection the oracle was preceded by a word formula (which now appears in v. 1) or an analogue of it.
[59] So also Wolff 1986, 53, 58; Wöhrle 2006, 291–292; Leuenberger 2015, 153, 163. Hallaschka (2011, 63–64) believes that vv. 4, 5aβb are more recent than the narrative framework (while he correctly considers v. 5aα to be a very late gloss). However, his literary-critical argumentation is based on extremely subtle criteria and thus not very convincing.

od the high priest rose to a more powerful position in comparison with the one he had in the Judean monarchy.[60] Moreover, it is also widely believed that several texts of the Hebrew Bible, most notably Zech 4:1–7, 10b–14 and 6:9–15, contain some concept of a "diarchy," according to which the community should be led by one civic (perhaps Davidic) and one priestly leader. The development of this idea might be linked with the activity of Zerubbabel and Joshua.[61] However, during the past two decades some scholars have subjected this image to sharp criticism. According to D. Rooke, for instance, sources from throughout the "postexilic" period are remarkably consistent in presenting the high priest as a cultic figure, whose "responsibilities remain[ed] confined to the cultic matters as was the case before the Exile" (Rooke 2000, 328). In agreement with this, Rooke (2000, 125–151) argues that neither in Haggai nor Zech 1–8 do we find unequivocal evidence for a project of civil-religious diarchic leadership that would reckon with an increase in the high priest's (civil) power.

To my mind, the general situation in the sources is more complex, yet their thorough discussion would lead us too far from the topic of the present study. Rooke (2000, 127–135) is right when she points out that all of the references to Joshua in the editorial framework of Haggai occur in the context of the temple rebuilding. On the other hand, she is not *entirely* right in stating that this context is "a natural and inevitable area of concern for the high priest" (Rooke 2000, 135).

As already mentioned, in the ancient Near East, temple building was most often a royal prerogative, and during the existence of the Judean monarchy the Davidides' care for the sanctuary in Jerusalem probably played an important role in their royal ideology. In agreement with this, the chief priests of the Jerusalem temple are described in Kings as firmly subordinated to the kings, whose instructions they follow precisely in the realm of the cult and temple repairs (2 Kgs 12:5–17; 16:10–18; 22:3–23:25).[62] We have also seen that in the primitive collection of Haggai's oracles, temple building was in Zerubbabel's purview, thereby continuing to be closely linked with (the restoration of) Davidic power. Therefore, when Haggai's redactional framework construes Joshua and Zerubbabel as two characters leading the temple restoration, it is a development which may be of some significance. The rebuilding of a temple often has a legitimating function for a king's rule, and we have seen that it indeed served to legitimate Zerubbabel's authority in the primitive collection of Haggai's oracles.

---

60 See already Wellhausen 1885, 419–422, 494; for further references, see Rooke 2000, 1–4.
61 E.g., Tollington 1993, 175–179; for further references, see Rose 2000, 66.
62 On this image, see Rooke 2000, 73–76.

The portrayal of Joshua as having a leading position in the process of the temple restoration thus probably had some legitimating potential as well.

Unfortunately, it is difficult to know what further consequences this depiction of Joshua's leading position would have had for the status of the high priest according to the author of Haggai's framework, and in which ways the redactor's project corresponded or not to realities of the early Persian period. Nevertheless, it is possible to assume that in the situation where some actors of the discourse endeavored to redefine the Judean community as essentially cultic – as we may observe above all in the Priestly texts of the Pentateuch (Nihan and Römer 2009, 168–172) –, such ideas of a kind of "diarchy," as vague and utopian they may have been, could contribute to an increase in at least some kind of soft power for the high priest.

Bibliography

Ackroyd, Peter R. 1951/52. "Studies in the Book of Haggai." *JJS* 2:163–176; *JJS* 3:1–13.
Ackroyd, Peter R. 1956. "Some Interpretative Glosses in the Book of Haggai." *JJS* 7:163–167.
Barthélemy, Dominique. 1992. *Critique textuelle de l'Ancien Testament. Vol 3: Ezéchiel, Daniel et les 12 Prophètes*. OBO 50/3. Fribourg: Academic Press.
Ben Zvi, Ehud. 2003. "The Prophetic Book: A Key Form of Prophetic Literature." In *The Changing Face of Form Criticism for the Twenty-First Century*, edited by Marvin A. Sweeney and Ehud Ben Zvi, 276–297. Grand Rapids: Eerdmans.
Ben Zvi, Ehud. 2009. "The Concept of Prophetic Books and Its Historical Setting." In *The Production of Prophecy: Constructing Prophecy and Prophets in Yehud*, edited by Diana V. Edelman and Ehud Ben Zvi, 73–95. BWo. London and Oakville: Equinox.
Beuken, Willem A. M. 1967. *Haggai-Sacharja 1–8: Studien zur Überlieferungsgeschichte der frühnachexilischen Prophetie*. SSN 10. Assen: Van Gorcum.
DeQueker, Luc. 1993. "Darius the Persian and the Reconstruction of the Jewish Temple in Jerusalem (Ezra 4,24)." In *Ritual and Sacrifice in the Ancient Near East: Proceedings of the International Conference Organized by the Katholieke Universiteit Leuven from the 17th to the 20th of April 1991*, edited by Jan Quaegebeur, 67–92. OLA 55. Leuven: Peeters.
Edelman, Diana. 2005. *The Origins of the "Second" Temple: Persian Imperial Policy and the Rebuilding of Jerusalem*. London and Oakville: Equinox.
Elliger, Karl. 1982. *Das Buch der zwölf Kleinen Propheten. Vol. 2: Die Propheten Nahum, Habakuk, Zephanja, Haggai, Sacharja, Maleachi*. 8th edition. ATD 25/2. Göttingen: Vandenhoeck & Ruprecht.
Fishbane, Michael. 1988. *Biblical Interpretation in Ancient Israel*. 2nd edition. Oxford: Clarendon Press.
Goswell, Greg. 2010. "The Fate and Future of Zerubbabel in the Prophecy of Haggai." *Bib.* 91:77–90.
Grabbe, Lester L. 1998. *Ezra-Nehemiah*. OTR. London: Routledge.
Graffy, Adrian. 1984. *A Prophet Confronts His People: The Disputation Speech in the Prophets*. AnBib 104. Rome: Biblical Institute Press.

Hallaschka, Martin. 2011. *Haggai und Sacharja 1–8: Eine redaktionsgeschichtliche Untersuchung*. BZAW 411. Berlin and New York: de Gruyter.

Hallaschka, Martin. 2012. "From Cores to Corpus: Considering the Formation of Haggai and Zechariah 1–8." In *Perspectives on the Formation of the Book of the Twelve: Methodological Foundations – Redactional Processes – Historical Insights*, edited by Rainer Albertz, James D. Nogalski, and Jakob Wöhrle, 171–189. BZAW 433. Berlin and Boston: de Gruyter.

Hallo, William W. 2003. *The Context of Scripture. Vol. 2: Monumental Inscriptions from the Biblical World*. Leiden and Boston: Brill.

Hilber, John W. 2005. *Cultic Prophecy in the Psalms*. BZAW 352. Berlin and New York: de Gruyter.

Keel, Othmar. 1997. *The Symbolism of the Biblical World: Ancient Near Eastern Iconography and the Book of Psalms*, translated by J. Hallett. Winona Lake: Eisenbrauns.

Keil, Carl Friedrich. 1878. *The Twelve Minor Prophets. Vol. 2: Nahum, Habakkuk, Zephaniah, Haggai, Zechariah, Malachi*. K&D. Edinburgh: Bloomsbury T&T Clark.

Kent, Roland G. 1953. *Old Persian: Grammar, Texts and Lexicon*. AOS 33. New Haven: American Oriental Society.

Kessler, John. 2002. *The Book of Haggai: Prophecy and Society in Early Persian Yehud*. VTSup 91. Leiden, Boston, and Cologne: Brill.

Koch, Klaus. 1996. "Weltordnung und Reichsidee im alten Iran und ihre Auswirkungen auf die Provinz Jehud." In *Reichsidee und Reichsorganisation im Perserreich*, edited by Peter Frei and Klaus Koch, 133–337. OBO 55. Fribourg and Göttingen: Academic Press and Vandenhoeck & Ruprecht.

Koopmans, William T. 2017. *Haggai*. HCOT. Leuven, Paris, and Bristol: Peeters.

Krata, Reinhard Gregor. 2004. "Serubbabel und Joschua." In *Das Judentum Im Zehalter des Zweiten Tempels: Kleine Schriften I*, 79–92. FAT 42. Tübingen: Mohr Siebeck.

Langdon, Stephen. 1905. *Building Inscriptions of the Neo-Babylonian Empire. Part 1: Nabopolassar and Nebuchadnezzar*. Paris: Leroux.

Leuenberger, Martin. 2012. "Time and Situational Reference in the Book of Haggai: On Religious- and Theological-Historical Contextualizations of Redactional Processes." In *Perspectives on the Formation of the Book of the Twelve: Methodological Foundations – Redactional Processes – Historical Insights*, edited by Rainer Albertz, James D. Nogalski, and Jakob Wöhrle, 157–169. BZAW 433. Berlin and Boston: de Gruyter.

Leuenberger, Martin. 2015. *Haggai*. HThKAT. Freiburg i. Br.: Herder.

Lux, Rüdiger. 2009. "'Wir wollen mit euch gehen …': Überlegungen zur Völkertheologie Haggais und Sacharjas." In *Prophetie und Zweiter Tempel: Studien zu Haggai und Sacharja*, 241–265. FAT 65. Tübingen: Mohr Siebeck.

Mason, Rex A. 1977. "The Purpose of the 'Editorial Framework' of the Book of Haggai." *VT* 27:413–421.

Meyers, Carol L., and Eric Meyers. 1988. *Haggai, Zechariah 1–8: A New Translation with Introduction and Commentary*. AB 25b. Garden City: Doubleday.

Nihan, Christophe, and Thomas Römer. 2009. "Le débat actuel sur la formation du Pentateuque." In *Introduction à l'Ancien Testament*, edited by Thomas Römer, Jean-Daniel Macchi, and Christophe Nihan, 158–184. 2nd edition. MdB 49. Geneva: Labor et Fides.

Nogalski, James. 1993. *Literary Precursors to the Book of the Twelve*. BZAW 217. Berlin: de Gruyter.

Olmstead, Albert T. 1944. "Tattenai, Governor of 'Across the River.'" *JNES* 3:46.

Oswald, Wolfgang. 2008. *Nathan der Prophet: Eine Untersuchung zu 2Samuel 7 und 12 und 1Könige 1*. AThANT 94. Zurich: TVZ.

Otto, Eckart. 2002. "Politische Theologie in den Königspsalmen zwischen Ägypten und Assyrien: Die Herscherlegitimation in den Psalmen 2 und 18 in ihren altorientalischen Kontexten." In *„Mein Sohn bist du" (Ps 2,7): Studien zu den Königspsalmen*, edited by Eckart Otto and Erich Zenger, 33–65. SBS 192. Stuttgart: Katholisches Bibelwerk.

Pomykala, Kenneth E. 1995. *The Davidic Dynasty Tradition in Early Judaism: Its History and Significance for Messianism*. EJIL 7. Atlanta: Scholars Press.

Redditt, Paul L. 2014. "Prophecy and the Monarchy in Haggai and Zechariah." *CBQ* 76:436–449.

Reventlow, Henning Graf. 1993. *Die Propheten Haggai, Sacharja und Maleachi*. 9th edition. ATD 25/2. Göttingen: Vandenhoeck & Ruprecht.

Ringgren, Helmer, Udo Rüterswörden, and Horacio Simian-Yofre. 2003. "עָבַד 'ābad." *TDOT* 10:376–405.

Rooke, Deborah W. 2000. *Zadok's Heirs: The Role and Development of the High Priesthood in Ancient Israel*. OTM. Oxford: Oxford University Press.

Rose, Wolter H. 2000. *Zemah and Zerubbabel: Messianic Expectations in the Early Postexilic Period*. JSOTSup 304. Sheffield: Sheffield Academic Press.

Rückl, Jan. 2016. *A Sure House: Studies on the Dynastic Promise to David in the Books of Samuel and Kings*. OBO 281. Fribourg and Göttingen: Academic Press and Vandenhoeck & Ruprecht.

Rückl, Jan. 2018. *Ageus: Budování chrámu v Judsku perské doby*. Český ekumenický komentář ke Starému zákonu 37. Prague: Centrum biblických studií AV ČR a UK v Praze, in collaboration with Česká biblická společnost.

Rückl, Jan. Forthcoming. "Haggai as an Old Book."

Rückl, Jan. Forthcoming. "'I Will Shake the Heavens and the Earth': Haggai 2:21f. and the Persian Imperial Ideology."

Rudolph, Wilhelm. 1976. *Haggai – Sacharja 1–8 – Sacharja 9–14 – Maleachi: Mit einer Zeittafel von Alfred Jepsen*. KAT XIII/4. Gütersloh: Gütersloher Verlagshaus.

Salo, Reettakaisa Sofia. 2017. *Die judäische Königsideologie im Kontext der Nachbarkulturen: Untersuchungen zu den Königspsalmen 2, 18, 20, 21, 45 und 72*. ORA 25. Tübingen: Mohr Siebeck.

Schaudig, Hanspeter. 2010. "The Restoration of Temples in the Neo- and Late Babylonian Periods: A Royal Prerogative as the Setting for Political Argument." In *From the Foundations to the Crenellations: Essays on Temple Building in the Ancient Near East and Hebrew Bible*, edited by Mark J. Boda and Jamie Novotny, 141–164. AOAT 366. Münster: Ugarit-Verlag.

Steck, Odil Hannes. 1971. "Zu Haggai 1 2–11." *ZAW* 83:355–379.

Tollington, Janet E. 1993. *Tradition and Innovation in Haggai and Zechariah 1–8*. JSOTSup 150. Sheffield: JSOT Press.

Weinfeld, Moshe. 1983. "Zion and Jerusalem as Religious and Political Capital: Ideology and Utopia." In *The Poet and the Historian: Essays in Literary and Historical Biblical Criticism*, edited by Richard Elliott Friedman, 75–115. HSS 26. Chico: Scholars Press.

Weiser, Artur. 1963. *Einleitung in das Alte Testament*. 5th edition. Berlin: Evangelische Verlagsanstalt.

Wellhausen, Julius. 1963. *Die kleinen Propheten*. 4th edition. Berlin: de Gruyter.

Wellhausen, Julius. 1885. *Prolegomena to the History of Israel: With a Reprint of the Article "Israel" from the "Encyclopaedia Britannica"*, translated by J. Sutherland Black and A. Menzies. Edinburgh: Black.

Wöhrle, Jakob. 2006. *Die frühen Sammlungen des Zwölfprophetenbuches: Entstehung und Komposition*. BZAW 360. Berlin and New York: de Gruyter.

Wöhrle, Jakob. 2008. *Der Abschluss des Zwölfprophetenbuches: Buchübergreifende Redaktionsprozesse in den späten Sammlungen*. BZAW 389. Berlin and New York: de Gruyter.

Wolff, Hans Walter. 1986. *Dodekapropheton. Vol. 6: Haggai*. BK.AT 14/6. Neukirchen-Vluyn: Neukirchener Verlag.

Martin Schott
Messianism in Transition: Zech 9:9–10 between First and Second Zechariah

1 Introduction: A Provocative Concept of Leadership

The last messianic promise in the Book of the Twelve, Zech 9:9–10, comprises a rather peculiar concept of leadership. It presents a royal leader without royal power: A saved (נושע) and humble king riding on a mere donkey. Consequently, these verses have met with mixed reactions throughout the history of their reception.

The Old Greek translation of Zechariah, which probably dates to the time of the Hasmonean kingdom, eliminates all the aspects of the Hebrew text which convey the impression of a passive or weak king (van der Kooij 2003; Pola 2009; Eidsvåg 2016, 161–184): Instead of being saved (נושע), the king becomes a saviour (σῴζων). Instead of God (והכרתי), the king himself destroys the enemy's weaponry (καὶ ἐξολεθρεύσει). Instead of proclaiming peace to the nations (ודבר שלום לגוים), the king receives tribute: "wealth and peace from the nations" (καὶ πλῆθος καὶ εἰρήνη ἐξ ἐθνῶν).[1] In the Babylonian Talmud, likewise, the Persian King Shapur I articulates his contempt for the Jewish messiah and his donkey by offering him his horse (bSan 98a): "You say that the Messiah will come upon a donkey: I will rather send him a white horse of mine."[2]

The humble king is not only despised by Greek translators and later Persian colleagues; he is also ignored by the wider literary context of the book of Zecha-

---

[1] The Greek translator may have read the Hebrew ורב ושלום מהגוים instead of ודבר שלום לגוים (van der Kooij 2003, 59). The modification is based on transposition and substitution of similar-looking Hebrew consonants – an accepted exegetical device in rabbinic literature as well as in the Septuagint. For πλῆθος in the sense of "wealth," see Zech 14:14.
[2] The Talmud addresses this problem in an original manner by referring to the book of Daniel: Dan 7:13 describes "one like a son of man" as appearing on the clouds of heaven, which creates a much more impressive image than a king on a donkey. Both means of transportation, the fast clouds of heaven and the slow donkey, represent two mutually exclusive options for the rabbis. Their realization depends on certain conditions, as explained in the Talmud: "If they (the Israelites) have merit, then (he will come) with the clouds of the sky, if they do not have merit, (he will come) humble and riding on a donkey" (bSan 98a). Therefore, the future appearance of the Messiah rests on the present behavior of his people. His appearance on a donkey would be a punishment rather than a reason to rejoice.

riah, which does not mention him again. He has no part in the fight over Jerusalem in the last days depicted in Zech 12–14. Quite to the contrary, the last chapter of the book, Zech 14, ends with a vision of YHWH becoming king over the entire earth (Zech 14:9). No space seems to be left for a human leader, not even for a humble one.

Both the messianic concept behind this provocatively weak royal leader and its compositional function within the rather theocratic context require an exegetical explanation, which this article aims to provide.[3]

2 The King on a Donkey in Relation to Traditional Royal Ideology

The nature of the eschatological king in relation to traditional royal ideology is debated: Does he represent the classical image of an ideal monarch (e.g., Reventlow 1993, 96) or rather a "counter-image" to traditional monarchy (e.g., Wöhrle 2008, 176)? The following observations suggest a differentiated answer.

Zechariah 9:9 opens with a call for Zion's attention: "Rejoice aloud, O Daughter Zion, shout, O Daughter Jerusalem! Behold, *your* king is coming to you." The phrase "your king" (מלכך) insinuates a certain familiarity with the king. Indeed, the following statements on his nature (v. 9) and his task (v. 10) combine at least some traditional aspects of ancient Near Eastern and Judean royal ideology concerning the king's nature and his task.

1. The king's nature (v. 9): He is just (צדיק), saved (נושע) and humble (עני). It can be taken for granted that justice is the main duty of a king in ancient Near Eastern cultures (cf. Maul 1998).[4] As a matter of course, the king of Zechariah is "just." Similarly, the passive participle נושע ("saved") does not surprise in an ancient Near Eastern context: A just king surely benefits from the military support of his divine saviors. Their help is often presented as the most crucial factor in battle (Weippert 1972, 483; Oded 1992, 21–24). Even humility is a feature which perfectly suits a king (contra Willi-Plein 2007, 163). Towards the God who saved him, it would be the only appropriate attitude. Assyrian and Babylonian kings could call themselves humble before their gods in order to stress their proximity to them: "[I]t is certainly true that ancient kings did boast of their humility" (Millard 1990, 49).

---

[3] The following considerations are based on my Ph.D. (Schott 2019).
[4] For the Hebrew Bible, compare Jer 22:3, 15; Ps 72:2; Prov 16:13 and the eschatological expectations in Isa 9:7; 11:4; Jer 23:5.

2. The king's task (v. 10): He brings peace to the defeated nations and rules over the entire world. The first part of the verse explains how God "saves" (v. 9: נוֹשָׁע) the king:[5] He frees his kingdom from the enemy's forces.[6] The king is saved from hostile horses and chariots (v. 10) precisely because he himself rejects symbols of power like these (v. 9). The breaking of the bow is a typical ancient Near Eastern image for the defeat of an enemy (Keel 1977, 169; Weippert 1972, 467). The parallelism "And the bow of war will be cut off / and he will proclaim peace to the nations" indicates that also the broken bow belongs to the nations (and not to Israel) and symbolizes their broken military power (contra Boda 2016, 572). Otherwise, one would need to explain why the nations should obey a king who disarmed his own people. Furthermore, it is a common motif in ancient royal ideology that the royal task of bringing peace and justice – far from being limited to the king's own people – stretches over the whole world (Oded 1992, 104). This global dimension was even adopted by a small kingdom like Judah as the royal Psalm 72 shows (Zenger 2002, 81–82).[7] Zechariah 9:10 cites this Psalm almost literally: "from sea to sea, from the river to the ends of the earth" (Ps 72:8).

Undeniably, Zech 9:9–10 draws heavily on traditional royal ideology. However, the author restricts himself to aspects which stress the passiveness of the king and his dependence on God.[8] This results in a very peculiar picture, which denies the king any active participation in the establishment of his reign. God alone subjects the nations to the king's rule by destroying their weaponry, beginning with the horses and wagons which threat Jerusalem and Ephraim and ending with the bow of war in general. The king is left with the word of peace, probably a peace offer, to the defeated enemies. He is a man of the word, not a man of the sword.[9]

---

[5] As an explanation of the participle נוֹשָׁע, v. 10aα would perfectly fit in its context. Since both verses (Zech 9:9–10) can be read as divine speech (cf. Zeph 3:14–15; Zech 2:14), the first-person singular in v. 10 cannot be taken as evidence for a redactional insertion (contra Reventlow 1993, 96).

[6] The pair "horses and chariots" usually symbolizes the strength of foreign powers (e.g., Ps 46:19; Ezek 39:9–10; Hos 2:20).

[7] It is still a matter of debate whether the respective verses in Ps 72 are part of the basic layer or whether they belong to a postmonarchic stratum. However, Ps 2:8 also supports the thesis that the global dimension of the king's reign was an integral part of Judean royal ideology (Zenger 2002, 81–82).

[8] Especially if one reads Zechariah in the light of Ps 72, which portrays the king as judge and savior of the humble and poor, the king in Zechariah (being himself saved and humble) no longer seems so distinctively royal.

[9] This portrayal of the king comes very close to the self-depiction of the pious (the ṣaddiqim) in the Psalms, who in their prayers adopt the words of King David as their own. In respect to

Zechariah 9:9–10 stands at the high point of a postmonarchic theological development which increasingly considers human and divine power as mutually exclusive (cf. Isa 9:6b; 11:4). The king declines a symbol for the coming salvation: Salvation comes with him, not through him.

One question remains to be answered: How does the king's mount – his donkey – fit into the overall picture?[10] Scholars often understand the donkey as the classical royal mount per se: "It is the steed of the upper classes and the sign of royal dignity" (Levin 2003, 298). Martin Noth (1956, 333) referred to a text from the Mari Archives (ARM VI, 76, 20–25): The governor Baḫdi-Lim writes to his king Zimri-Lim and gives a piece of advice concerning the proper means of transportation in public: The king "should not ride on horses" but rather "on a cart with donkeys" in order "to honour his kingship."

Nevertheless, given the age of this letter (eighteenth century BCE), its value as a witness for the royal nature of the donkey in biblical times is questionable. It was written about 1500 years before Second Zechariah, 1000 years before the emergence of the Israelite kingdom and still a few centuries before the domestication of the horse. With the invention of two-wheeled chariots and the development of horse-riding techniques during the second half of the second millennium BCE, the donkey rapidly lost its economic and military significance and thereby its symbolic reputation. In its place, the horse became the new symbol of kingship (Limet 1995, 41).

Textual and iconographic evidence from the first millennium BCE attest to the horse as the new royal animal. The Jebel Barkal Stela (fifteenth century BCE), for instance, preserves an Egyptian record of the battle of Megiddo (Zakovitch 2004, 136). Pharaoh Thutmosis III grants safe conduct to his defeated enemies. The chiefs were forced to leave on donkeys because he had taken their horses and chariots as tribute: "Then My Majesty ordered that they be granted passage to their towns. They all went on donkeys, since I had taken their horses." Furthermore, Assyrian art depicts kings on horses while fighting in battle or hunting lions, wild donkeys, or bulls. In fact, they never appear on a donkey, which

---

the sinner they count themselves as righteous, in respect to the haughty they regard themselves as humble (e.g., Ps 18:28), facing the bow of their enemies (Pss 11:2; 37:14–15) they long for divine salvation (e.g., Ps 37:39). Certainly, they would have recognized the king on the donkey as one of their own.

10 The author stresses the importance of the king's mount by listing all the known Hebrew terms for the domesticated donkey (Way 2010): חמור is the usual term for a donkey, which is not necessarily gender specific. עיר designates the full-grown, male stallion. בן אתון (lit. "the offspring of a female donkey") does not refer to the age but once again to the species: It is not a horse, it is not a mule, which would be much more precious, it is a mere donkey. Contra Way (2010), who stresses the royal dignity of the donkey.

instead seems to be the typical mount of women and children (Clutton-Brock 1992, 85, 92, 94).

The biblical traditions emerged only after this transformation process had come to an end and does not form an exception to the general image: The "Hebrew tradition strongly associates horse ownership with statehood and the power of the king" (Cantrell 2011, 40). The ban on horses and chariots due to their alleged foreign origin in the deuteronomistic law of the king (Deut 17:16) only proves that horses and chariots had been a common phenomenon during the monarchic period (Perlitt 1995, 242). The deuteronomistic condemnation of the kings who trust in human instead of divine power consequently leads to the condemnation of their horses as symbols of their royal hubris.

As a result, the donkey might have been a reliable and respected assistant in daily life, probably even at the king's court, but it was by no means suitable for military or symbolic purposes. Thus, the donkey further underscores that the saved and humble king exclusively depends on divine salvation. He is humble because he rejects the typical symbol of royal power: the horse.[11]

3 The Motif of the King on a Donkey and its Literary Context

3.1 Zechariah 9:9–10 and First Zechariah: A Summary of Messianic Hope

There are good reasons to challenge the old consensus that Zech 9–14 emerged independently of Zech 1–8 (cf. Gonzalez 2013). Pivotal aspects of the oracular material in Zech 1–8 – such as the return of the exiles, the judgment on the nations, and the question of leadership – find a proper continuation (and reinterpretation) in Zech 9:1–11:3. Especially the messianic promise of Zech 9:9–10 fits well within the Haggai-Zechariah corpus. The announcement of the king coming to his residence in Zech 9:9 repeats almost verbatim the announcement of God coming to his temple in Zech 2:14 (Stead 2009, 263–264; Gonzalez 2013, 14–15; Boda 2016, 563).

---

11 The parallelism "Humble and riding on a donkey / on a stallion, offspring of a jenny" further underscores this interpretation. It is carefully balanced: Every part consists of exactly thirteen consonants. By means of this syntactic structure, the author makes clear that riding on a donkey is the material expression of humility.

Zech 2:14: רני ושמחי בת ציון כי הנני בא
Shout and be glad, Daughter Zion. For I am coming [...]
Zech 9:9: גילי מאד בת ציון הריעי בת ירושלם הנה מלכך יבוא לך
Rejoice greatly, Daughter Zion! Shout, Daughter Jerusalem! See, your king comes to you [...]

Thus, Zech 9:9 shifts the focus from the rebuilding of the temple to the establishment of messianic kingship. This literary allusion is accompanied by some conceptual analogies concerning the role of human leadership: The promise for Zerubbabel in Hag 2:20–23 differentiates between the defeat of the hostile powers by God and the appointment of the human leader, who plays no active military role in the establishment of his reign. Likewise, the divine messenger in Zech 4:6 encourages Zerubbabel with the words: "Not by might nor by power, but by my spirit." Even the restriction to a royal figure in Zech 9:9–10 without even mentioning the High Priest is not surprising within the book of Zechariah: The presumably late verses Zech 3:6 and Zech 6:12 degrade the High Priest to a mere placeholder for the future Davidic *zemah* (Hallaschka 2011, 319).

Naturally, Zech 9:9–10 also adds some new aspects to the royal image: For the first (and last) time, the book of Zechariah explicitly calls a Judean leader "king," a term which Haggai and Zech 1–8 reserve for the Persian king (Hag 1:1; 2:1; Zech 7:1). This may point to a changed political reality – the downfall of the Persian Empire – which may have stirred messianic hopes. As a result, the leader's task shifts from domestic affairs (the building of the temple, Zech 4:6–10) to international diplomacy: the establishment (or rather proclamation) of worldwide peace (Zech 9:10). In contrast to Zerubbabel, the king is not concerned with priestly responsibilities or accompanied by a priestly colleague.

In a synchronic sense, therefore, Zech 9:9–10 represent a kind of messianic culmination of the Haggai-Zechariah corpus. In a diachronic sense, Zech 9:9–10 could well have functioned as a former conclusion of the two books. Of course, this far-reaching thesis would require further explanation (cf. Schott 2019). In the context of this article, two general and preliminary observations must suffice: (1) The promise in Zech 9:9–10 probably constitutes the literary-historical core of Zech 9–10. It stands out from its context by its poetic structure and by its thematic focus on a human leader. At the same time, it cannot be removed from its context without leaving a gap. Whereas the two messianic verses could well stand on their own, all the other sections of Zechariah 9 depend syntactically or at least conceptually on Zech 9:9–10,[12] addressing the cir-

---

[12] The defeat of the neighboring nations in Zech 9:1–8 creates a power vacuum, which only Zech 9:9–10 fills. Zechariah 9:11 has a second-person feminine singular addressee and thus presupposes the introduction of Zion in Zech 9:9. An alternative option could be to attach Zech

cumstances under which the king's reign will be realized. (2) As a former conclusion of the book, Zech 9:9–10 would fill a striking gap within Zech 7–8. In their present shape, these last chapters of First Zechariah function as a summary of the book's prophetic hope, especially of the oracular material between the night visions (cf. Stead 2009, 230; Assis 2010, 1–26; Boda 2003a, 402–405; Tiemeyer 2016, 230–238). Yet they lack any reference to human leadership, even though this is a prominent topic in Haggai and Zechariah.

To sum up, Zech 9:9–10 could have functioned as an earlier conclusion to First Zechariah and, by extension, as the starting point for Second Zechariah, motivating further expansions in the latter part of the book.

3.2 Zechariah 9:9–10 and Second Zechariah: The Gradual Rejection of Messianic Hope

In their present shape, Zech 9–14 consist of two main sections, Zech 9:1–11:3 and Zech 12:1–14:21, which share some common ground. They both envisage the coming of a king – human or divine – who will reign over the whole world from his residence in Jerusalem (Zech 9:9–10 and Zech 14:9). His reign will guarantee peace with the nations and protection for Jerusalem. A time of war will pave the way to his enthronement.

On the whole, the differences between Zech 9:1–11:3 and Zech 12:1–14:21 outweigh their similarities.[13] The hopes of Zech 9:1–11:3 are optimistic and rather restorative in nature: The texts expect a human leader who will rule the reunited kingdom of Judah and Ephraim, to which the scattered Israelites will return. The expectations of Zech 12–14, in contrast, have pessimistic overtones and convey a rather transformational view of the future. They concentrate the eschatological events onto one single day – the day of YHWH. It is the day of Jerusalem's final salvation, the day of the ultimate defeat of the nations, and the day of God's enthronement as king over the whole world (Zech 14:9). These

---

9:14–17 to Zech 9:1 (Wöhrle 2008, 127), which would result in a theophany from the north. However, apart from the geographic direction, the linkage between the two Aramaean placenames (Hadrach and Damascus) and the mythical holy mountain in the north remains rather loose. Furthermore, in Zech 9:14 YHWH does not appear from the north, but "in the storms of the south" (בסערות תימן).

13 See among others Ollenburger 1996, 742: "However, it seems clear enough that there is a conflict between the future as restoration, envisioned in chaps. 9–10, and the utopia envisioned in chaps. 12 and 14. And it may be that the nature of that conflict is reflected in chaps. 11–13."

chapters do not mention an earthly king and are silent about the north as part of a united monarchy. In addition, Jerusalem will be seriously threatened. According to Zech 14:1–2, it will even be conquered by its enemies.

How should a reader respond to these differences? The so-called shepherd allegory in Zech 11:4–17 gives an answer by forming a bridge between the two diverging eschatological visions. The genre and meaning of the cryptic chapter are still a matter of debate.[14] In its present shape, it conveys a kind of twofold prophetic sign act, which looks back to the failure of a good shepherd (Zech 11:4–14) – probably the prophet himself (cf. Gonzalez 2013, 33–35) – and ahead to the rise of a bad shepherd (Zech 11:15–17). As such, it enacts God's judgment on his people, who rejected their shepherd and with him their God. Leaving the controversial questions aside, the acts performed by the shepherd's instruments clearly mark the essential points of transition between Zech 9:1–11:3 and Zech 12–14 (Boda 2003b, 290–291):[15] The good shepherd breaks his stave "Favor" (Zech 11:10) to break God's covenant with the nations. As a result, the nations attack Jerusalem. Then, he breaks his stave "Union" to break the brotherhood between Judah and Israel (Zech 11:14). As a result, Jerusalem is left alone in the war against the nations without the support of its northern allies.

Regarding the question of leadership, the second sign act in Zech 11:15–16 is of special importance. YHWH commissions the prophet to take the implements of a worthless shepherd: He enacts the rise of a shepherd who disgraces his profession by neglecting and even killing his sheep. This threatening announcement draws on the hopes for a Davidic ruler in Ezek 34:23 and completely reverses them. Ezekiel 34:23 reads: "Then I will set over them one shepherd, My servant David." And Zechariah objects by using similar vocabulary: "For I am about to raise up on earth a shepherd who will not care [...]." In the light of this allusion, the bad shepherd can be described as an "anti-messiah" (Rudolph 1976, 211: "a kind of precursor of the antichrist" ["eine Art Vorläufer des Antichrist"]). His announcement equals the rejection of an eschatological Davidic leader and transitions the reader from the messianic hope of Zech 9:9–10 to the eschatology of Zech 14.

---

14 Scholarly opinions considerably diverge even on the most basic questions about the time reference of the chapter, the character of the shepherd, and the genre of the text: Does the text depict past or future events? Does the protagonist act as a good or an evil shepherd? Does the speaker reflect on his own experience as a leader in a metaphorical or even allegorical report or does he represent God's actions as a shepherd on behalf of his flock in a (fictional) sign-act?

15 Contra Petterson 2010, 243, who denies any discontinuities within Zech 9–14: "Zechariah 9 establishes the broad outline of this program, with Yahweh coming to reestablish a kingdom like David's. [...] Zechariah 10–14 then 'telescopes' different themes."

These compositional observations bear two consequences for the understanding of Second Zechariah as a whole. (1) In a synchronic sense: When read from the perspective of Zech 11, the hopes expressed in Zech 9:1–11:3 become preliminary, whereas Zech 12–14 illustrate the ultimate fate of Jerusalem and the nations. The progression from a human king in Zech 9 via the rejection of the Davidic king in Zech 11 to a divine king in Zech 14 shows that the divine kingship in Zech 14 is meant in exclusive terms. In its present shape, Second Zechariah is characterized by a non-messianic or even anti-messianic attitude (cf. Redditt 1989, 635; contra Boda 2016, 766; Petterson 2010, 243).[16] (2) In a diachronic sense: Whereas the development of Zech 9–14 certainly is much more complicated – neither Zech 9:1–11:3 nor Zech 12–14 form a homogeneous unity[17] –, one essential assumption can hardly be denied: Zech 9:1–11:3 must have been written before the last chapters of the book. They do not convey the slightest notion of the crisis which Zech 11:4–17 depicts and which Zech 12–14 try to overcome.[18]

4 The Motif of the King on a Donkey and its Historical Background

Despite recent objections (e.g., Redditt 2012; Boda 2016, 31–37), the bulk of the material in Zech 9–10 clearly originates from the Hellenistic period. The following characteristics support this assumption: The missing reference to the Persians and the predominant language of warfare in comparison to First Zechariah point to a changed political reality (Gonzalez 2013, 7–8). Zechariah 9:13 considers the sons of Greece as the *sole* adversary of the sons of Zion (Stade 1881–1882, 275–290; Gonzalez 2013, 19–20). Their defeat is the last step to the messianic reign. The anachronistic reference to Assyria and Egypt as two mili-

---

16 On the antithetical relationship between Zech 9:9–10 and Zech 11:15–16, see Wöhrle 2008, 180. Wöhrle understands Zech 9:9–10 as a later objection to Zech 11:15–16. Yet the compositional progression described above may point to the opposite interpretation of this connection.
17 Cf. the detailed redaction-critical observations in Redditt 2012; Wöhrle 2008, 67–138, which prove that the classical "block model" should be supplemented by a more differentiated "layer model."
18 See Stade 1881–1882, 94, who nevertheless takes a holistic approach: "Sonach müssen zwischen c. 9.10 einerseits und c. 11–14 andererseits Ereignisse liegen, welche Deuterozacharja davon überzeugten, daß nunmehr bestimmte Zukunftserwartungen ihre Berechtigung verloren hätten, daß nunmehr an deren Stelle andere getreten seien."

tary powers in Zech 10:11 may function as cipher for the Seleucid and Ptolemaic empires in the third century BCE (Stade 1881–1882, 290–296).

Whereas the promise in Zech 9:9–10 lacks any clear reference to its historical context, it could easily be read against a Hellenistic background: While Haggai and First Zechariah still reserve the term "king" for the Persian kings, Zech 9:9–10 announces its own Judaean king as the only king of the world. This shift may indicate a rejection of contemporary (foreign) leadership. Indeed, the peculiar picture of the pious and weak king would form a fitting counter-image to Hellenistic royal ideology. On the famous Alexander sarcophagus, which influenced later Hellenistic royal iconography, the king appears as a warrior on his horse (Demandt 2009, 152–153; Brinkmann et al. 2013, 181–187). Ptolemy I *Soter* already bore the title "savior," which associates the human king with divine saviors (Zimmermann 2001, 752) and sharply contrasts the "saved" king of Zechariah. Whereas the horse of the Hellenistic warrior king embodies his military power, the donkey of the Jewish king embodies his dependency on his God, who remains the actual savior.

5 Conclusion: From Messianism towards a Theocratic Eschatology

In ancient Near Eastern and Judean royal ideology, human and divine leadership formed a self-evident unity, which became questionable after the demise of the Judean monarchy. The book of Zechariah testifies to a theological development that tries to cope with the absence of the Judaean king. During this process, royal power is redefined in eschatological terms (Hag 2:20–23; Zech 3:6; 6:12), problematized as rival to divine power (9:9–10), eventually rejected (11:15–16), and replaced by a mere theocratic eschatology (14:9).

Zechariah 9:9–10 stands at the turning point of this development: It still uses classical royal language but omits the typical attributes and symbols of power, which results in a monarchy minus the military. Still, the promise does not represent a kind of pacifist utopia, but rather expresses sober realism: After the hopes for the restoration of the monarchy remained unfulfilled throughout the Persian period, the redactors could not imagine the establishment of a worldwide Judaean reign without supernatural intervention. The promise assigns the sword to God and leaves the king with the word of peace. The future king is reduced to a mere symbol of the coming salvation.

Later redactors even relinquish this symbol and restrict themselves to a sheerly theocratic vision of the future. Instead of a restoration of the old monarchy, they expect a radical transformation of the world and its inhabitants on the day of the Lord, which leads to the universal kingdom of YHWH: "And YHWH will be king over the whole earth. On that day YHWH will be one, and his name one" (Zech 14:9).

Bibliography

Assis, Elie. 2010. "Zechariah 8 as Revision and Digest of Zechariah 1–7." *JHS* 10: Article 15.
Brinkmann, Vinzenz, Ulrike Koch-Brinkmann, and Heinrich Piening. 2013. "Der Alexandersarkophag." In *Alexander der Große: Herrscher der Welt*, edited by Rupert Gebhard, Ellen Rehm, and Harald Schulze, 181–187. Darmstadt: Zabern.
Boda, Mark J. 2003a. "From Fasts to Feasts: The Literary Function of Zechariah 7–8." *CBQ* 65:390–407.
Boda, Mark J. 2003b. "Reading Between the Lines: Zechariah 11.4–16 in its Literary Contexts." In *Bringing out the Treasure: Inner Biblical Allusion in Zechariah 9–14*, edited by Mark J. Boda and Michael H. Floyd, 277–291. London and New York: Bloomsbury T&T Clark.
Boda, Mark J. 2016. *The Book of Zechariah*. NICOT. Grand Rapids: Eerdmans.
Cantrell, Deborah O'Daniel. 2011. *The Horsemen of Israel: Horses and Chariotry in Monarchic Israel*. History, Archaeology, and Culture of the Levant 1. Winona Lake: Eisenbrauns.
Clutton-Brock, Juliet. 1992. *A History of the Horse and the Donkey in Human Societies*. Cambridge: Harvard University Press.
Demandt, Alexander. 2009. *Alexander der Große: Leben und Legende*. Munich: Beck.
Eidsvåg, Gunnar Magnus. 2016. *The Old Greek Translation of Zechariah*. VTSup 170. Leiden: Brill.
Hallaschka, Martin. 2011. *Haggai und Sacharja 1–8: Eine redaktionsgeschichtliche Untersuchung*. BZAW 411. Berlin and New York: de Gruyter.
Gonzalez, Hervé. 2013. "Zechariah 9–14 and the Continuation of Zechariah during the Ptolemaic Period." *JHS* 13: Article 9.
Keel, Othmar. 1977. "Der Bogen als Herrschaftssymbol: Einige unveröffentlichte Skarabäen aus Ägypten und Israel zum Thema 'Jagd und Krieg.'" *ZDPV* 93:141–177.
van der Kooij, Arie. 2003. "The Septuagint of Zechariah as Witness to an Early Interpretation of the Book." In *The Book of Zechariah and Its Influence*, edited by Christopher M. Tuckett, 53–64. Aldershot: Ashgate.
Levin, Christoph. 2013. "The Poor in the Old Testament: Some Observations." In *Re-Reading the Scriptures: Essays on the Literary History of the Old Testament*, edited by Christoph Levin, 281–300. Tübingen: Mohr Siebeck.
Limet, Henri. 1995. "Évolution dans l'utilisation des équidés dans le Proche-Orient ancien." In *Le cheval et les autres équidés: aspects de l'histoire de leur insertion dans les activités humaines*, edited by Liliane Bodson, 31–45. Liège: Université de Liège.
Maul, Stefan M. 1998. "Der assyrische König – Hüter der Weltordnung." In *Gerechtigkeit: Richten und Retten in der abendländischen Tradition und ihren altorientalischen Ursprüngen*, edited by Jan Assmann et al., 65–77. Munich: Wilhelm Fink.
Millard, Alan Ralph. 1990. "The Homeland of Zakkur." *Sem.* 39:47–52.
Noth, Martin. 1956. "Remarks on the Sixth Volume of Mari Texts." *JSSt* 1:322–333.

Oded, Bustenay. 1992. *War, Peace and Empire: Justifications for War in Assyrian Royal Inscriptions*. Wiesbaden: Reichert.

Ollenburger, Ben C. 1996. "The Book of Zechariah." *NIB* 7:735–840.

Perlitt, Lothar. 1995. "Der Staatsgedanke im Deuteronomium." In *Allein mit dem Wort: Theologische Studien*, edited by Hermann Spieckermann, 236–248. Göttingen: Vandenhoeck & Ruprecht.

Petterson, Anthony R. 2010. "The Shape of the Davidic Hope across the Book of the Twelve." *JSOT* 35:225–246.

Pola, Thomas. 2009. "Sach 9,9–17^{LXX} – Indiz für die Entstehung des griechischen Dodekaprophetons im makkabäischen Jerusalem?" In *La Septante en Allemagne et en France: Septuaginta Deutsch und Bible d'Alexandrie*, edited by Wolfang Kraus and Olivier Munnich, 238–251. OBO 238. Fribourg and Göttingen: Academic Press and Vandenhoeck & Ruprecht.

Redditt, Paul L. 1989. "Israel's Shepherds: Hope and Pessimism in Zechariah 9–14." *CBQ* 51:631–642.

Redditt, Paul L. 2012. *Zechariah 9–14*. IECOT. Stuttgart: Kohlhammer.

Reventlow, Henning Graf. 1993. *Die Propheten Haggai, Sacharja und Maleachi*. 9th edition. ATD 25/2. Göttingen: Vandenhoeck & Ruprecht.

Rudolph, Wilhlem. 1976. *Haggai – Sacharja 1–8 – Sacharja 9–14 – Maleachi: Mit einer Zeittafel von Alfred Jepsen*. KAT XIII/4. Gütersloh: Gütersloher Verlagshaus.

Schott, Martin. 2019. *Sacharja 9–14: Eine kompositionsgeschichtliche Analyse*. BZAW 521. Berlin and Boston: de Gruyter.

Stade, Bernhard. 1881–1882. "Deuterozacharja: Eine kritische Studie: Teil I–III." *ZAW* 1:1–96 and *ZAW* 2:151–172, 275–309.

Stead, Michael R. 2009. *The Intertextuality of Zechariah 1–8*. LHB 506. London and New York: Bloomsbury T&T Clark.

Tiemeyer, Lena-Sofia. 2016. *Zechariah's Vision Report and Its Earliest Interpreters: A Redaction-Critical Study of Zechariah 1–8*. LHB 626. London and New York: Bloomsbury T&T Clark.

Way, Kenneth C. 2010. "Donkey Domain: Zechariah 9:9 and Lexical Semantics." *JBL* 129:105–114.

Weippert, Manfred. 1972. "Heiliger Krieg in Israel und Assyrien: Kritische Anmerkungen zu Gerhard von Rads Konzept des 'Heiligen Krieges im Alten Israel.'" *ZAW* 84:460–493.

Willi-Plein, Ina. 2007. *Haggai, Sacharja, Maleachi*. ZBK.AT 24/4. Zurich: TVZ.

Wöhrle, Jakob. 2008. *Der Abschluss des Zwölfprophetenbuches: Buchübergreifende Redaktionsprozesse in den späten Sammlungen*. BZAW 389. Berlin and New York: de Gruyter.

Zakovitch, Yair. 2004. *"Who Proclaims Peace, Who Brings Good Tidings": Seven Visions of Jerusalem's Peace*. Haifa: University of Haifa Press [Hebrew].

Zenger, Erich. 2002. "'Es sollen sich niederwerfen vor ihm alle Könige' (Ps 72,11): Redaktionsgeschichtliche Beobachtungen zu Psalm 72 und zum Programm des messianischen Psalters Ps 2–89." In *„Mein Sohn bist du" (Ps 2,7): Studien zu den Königspsalmen*, edited by Eckhard Otto and Erich Zenger, 66–93. SBS 192. Stuttgart: Katholisches Bibelwerk.

Zimmermann, Klaus. 2001. "Soter." *DNP* 11:752–753. Stuttgart: Metzler.

Hervé Gonzalez
Zechariah 9–14 and the Transformations of Judean Royal Ideology during the Early Hellenistic Period

This essay is concerned with the concept of royal leadership in Zech 9–14, and in particular how the monarchy and the royal house are envisaged in the utopian future that these prophetic materials depict. While the book of Zechariah clearly emphasizes the importance of the cult of Jerusalem – legitimizing its rebirth at the start of Persian period –, biblical scholars have long discussed to what extent the book could be read as a messianic text which also announces the restoration of the local monarchy and Davidic kingship in particular. Within this book, chs. 9–14 stand out as being particularly relevant to the study of royal leadership, since they arguably develop a more explicit discourse concerning the future of local kingship and the royal family than is evident in the earlier chapters.[1] This discourse on royal leadership is especially visible in Zech 9:9–10 and Zech 12:1–13:1.[2] Zechariah 9:9–10 explicitly announces the installation of a king (מלך) in Jerusalem – a major innovation compared to Zech 1–8, where the only leader given the title of "king" is the Persian emperor Darius (7:1).[3]

---

[1] The greater importance attributed to the future of local kingship and the Davidic dynasty in Zech 9–14 than in Zech 1–8 did not go unnoticed by the authors of the New Testament, who often refer to Zech 9–14 to develop their messianic ideas; see, e.g., Duguid 1995, 276–280; Boda and Porter 2005, 215–254; Liebengood 2014.
[2] Other passages, such as those dealing with shepherd motif (in 10:1–3a, ch. 11, and 13:7–9), or Zech 14, which insist on divine kingship (only), are also part of Zech 9–14's discourse on royal leadership. Due to space limitations, and because these passages deal less explicitly with royal leadership or the royal family, they will not be the focus of this study. However, some references to these passages will be made to provide at least a general idea of how they fit with the interpretation defended here.
[3] Cf. Rose 2012, 219–222. Neither Zerubbabel nor Ṣemaḥ are explicitly presented as "king" in Zech 1–8. This observation is overlooked especially by C. L. Meyers and E. M. Meyers, who emphasize continuity between Zech 9:9–10 and Zech 1–8 (Meyers and Meyers 1995, 210–212;

Note: I am thankful to Julia Rhyder who proofread a first version of this text, and helped to improve with relevant suggestions. Comments by Christophe Nihan and Jan Rückl have also been particularly helpful to improve the argument. Stephen Germany also attentively proofread the English. Of course, the responsibility for the ideas, and possible errors, is my own. A last introductory comment concerns Martin Schott's recent book on Zech 9–14 (2020), which appeared just before the publication of the present volume; unfortunately, the inputs of his new analysis could not be included in this essay.

Zechariah 12:1–13:1, for its part, refers no less than five times to "the house of David" (בֵּית דָּוִיד), which is again innovative, considering that David is never mentioned in chs. 1–8, and even Zerubbabel is not explicitly presented as a Davidide in these earlier chapters.[4]

Yet despite the importance of Zech 9:9–10 and Zech 12:1–13:1 in negotiating the future of local kingship and of the royal family in the book, the meaning of these passages and their relationship to each other remains debated.[5] A. R. Petterson (2009) recently argued that all of Zech 9–14 consistently supports the future restoration of the Davidic monarchy. This reading is not new, with several predecessors especially in the sixties, with the study of P. Lamarche (1961), and in the nineties, with the studies of A. Laato (1992, 260–301; 1997, 208–218) and I. Duguid (1995).[6] Other scholars, while also assuming a consistent discourse within Zech 9–14, have defended opposite positions. Following a suggestion of R. Mason ([1973] 2003), D. L. Petersen (1995) reads Zech 9:9–10 and Zech 12:1–13:1 together not as texts that announce the return of kingship but rather that democratize royal privileges, a reading which has been further defended by A. Leske (2000; see also Pomykala 1995, 112–125). Others, like J. Becker (1980, 72–73), or more recently W. H. Rose (2012) and G. Goswell (2016), have argued that Zech 9–14 is consistent in announcing divine kingship only.[7]

Building on a different line of thought already advanced by various scholars during the late nineteenth and twentieth century (see already Wellhausen 1963, esp. 189 and 199; Elliger 1951; Rudolph 1976) and further developed in recent

---

Meyers 1996, 134–136). Despite some elements of continuity (especially with Zech 2:14–16), Zech 9:9–10 departs from chs. 1–8 in explicitly depicting the installation in Jerusalem of a human king, using the term מֶלֶךְ.

4 This is made clear only in the (rather late) genealogy of 1 Chr 3:19. To be sure, the name Ṣemaḥ has Davidic associations (cf. Jer 23:5; 33:15), but the book of Zechariah does not clearly identify Zerubbabel with Ṣemaḥ. As a result, some scholars doubt the Davidic origins of Zerubbabel (e.g., Pomykala 1995, 120 n. 222).

5 See, e.g., the presentation of different positions in Petterson 2009, 13–45.

6 In the sixties, see also Amsler 1963, 58–61; or Chary 1969, 139–141, who, despite thinking that Zech 9–14 brings together various materials, sees in Zech 9–14 "une œuvre unifiée, toute centrée sur le messie" (p. 141; note that Chary's view was more nuanced in 1955, 229–230); see also Seybold 1972. In the nineties, see also Cook 1993, esp. 459–466; 1995, 133, 137–138. See also, somewhat differently, Lacocque 1988, esp. 156, who considers that the notion of a suffering servant, similar to that of Deutero-Isaiah, is present in the two passages and in the rest of Zech 9–14; see also Mason 1998, 351–357 in a similar direction. For more references, see Petterson 2009, 36–40.

7 They follow an orientation already visible in Hanson 1973 and 1979, who heavily emphasizes the role of YHWH (the divine warrior) throughout the whole of chs. 9–14. See also Ulrich 2010, who considers that the king of Zech 9:9–10 and the pierced one in Zech 12:10 are both YHWH (who can "incarnate").

research (see esp. Floyd 2000; Sweeney 2000; Redditt 2008; 2012; Boda 2003; 2016),[8] the present essay will substantiate the view that Zech 9:9–10 and Zech 12:1–13:1 actually contain markedly different notions of royal leadership, which in turn present a significant re-interpretation of traditional concepts of monarchic power. I hope to show that looking for a consistent discourse in these chapters does not help in identifying and explaining the peculiar language and ideas of both passages, even if they are not disconnected and interact with each other in a rather complex manner. A differentiated approach helps to explain why opposite views have resulted from attempting to reconstruct a consistent discourse throughout Zech 9–14: scholars who presuppose consistency throughout these chapters focus on the notion of leadership in one passage, and then try to find a similar notion in the other passage; depending on which text is prioritized, the reconstructed consistent discourse will be radically different.[9]

---

8 See esp. Rudolph 1976, 215: "Hier dagegen in der zweiten Hälfte des Sacharjabuchs stehen zwei *Zukunft*serwartungen nebeneinander, die sich gegenseitig ausschließen. Das einzige Verbindungsglied ist die Verknüpfung mit Jes 53 (עָנִי 9,9). Aber während dieser durch Jahwe gerettet wird (נוֹשָׁע), folgt die zweite Konzeption dem Vorbild des Ebed-Jahwe bis zu dessen Tod." M. H. Floyd (2000, 464–467) sees in Zech 9:9–10 a future king realizing the Davidic ideal, but he considers that Zech 12 "makes it possible for leaders of the Davidic descent to resume a role of special importance, but not the same kind of role that they played in preexilic times" (Floyd 2000, 523; see also 511–514). M. A. Sweeney (2000) reads Zech 9:9–10 (and more broadly Zech 9) as referring positively to the Persian king, and then Zech 10–14 as opposing Persian rule. P. L. Redditt (2008; 2012a) considers that Zech 11–14 challenges the hopes presented in Zech 9–10. M. J. Boda (2016, 648–655, 707–708; 2017, 72–78) differentiates Zech 9–10 and Zech 12–14 and argues for an ideological change in the text that is introduced by the woe oracles of ch. 11; he sees this change connected to the end of Zerubbabel's political activity. See also Collins 1995, 31–33, who differentiates the ideology of Zech 9 and Zech 12. Meyers and Meyers (1993; 1995) and Meyers (1996) have a more nuanced but also ambiguous position. They see different emphases in the two texts, noting in particular that Zech 9:9–10 is closer to the ideology of Zech 1–8 than Zech 12–13 is. Hence, the former text could have the function of linking the material of Second Zechariah to Zech 1–8 (Meyers 1996, 135–136). Nonetheless, both texts would have compatible, basically consistent views on a transhistorical future hope for a restored Davidic kingdom, which remains more or less muted.

9 See, e.g., Becker (1980, 72–73), who reads Zech 9:9–10 on the basis of the rest of Zech 9–14: "In the broader context (Zechariah 9–14) there is no reference to an actual king to be found; rather, the kingship of Yhwh is emphasized (14:9 ff., 16–17)." See also Leske 2000, 665: "In this study I propose to demonstrate that when contextual considerations and the assumption that the author or redactor saw these chapters as an integral whole are taken into account, the 'king' in Zech 9:9 should not be interpreted as a future messianic Davidide." The first half of Leske's article is dedicated to (non-)messianic notions in other biblical texts such as Isa 40–66 and Chronicles and their relationship to Zech 9–14, serving to prepare the reader to accept that Zech 9:9 has a similar view. However, such an argument should primarily be based on the analysis of the text in question (Zech 9) rather than on other texts.

This essay will first explore each of the two notions of leadership in Zech 9:9–10 and Zech 12:1–13:1, showing how they both revise traditional royal ideology in their own ways. While Zech 9:9–10 envisions a *royal* leadership which is deprived of military power, Zech 12:1–13:1 attributes a *collective* form of leadership to the "house of David," restricted essentially to the city of Jerusalem and to military and ritual domains. Finally, I will propose that these differences can be explained in light of a series of socio-political changes in the early Hellenistic period.

1 The King of Jerusalem in Zechariah 9:9–10: A Utopia of Political Independence and Peace on a Large Levantine Territory

In the form of a call to Jerusalem to rejoice – which echoes in the book the call to rejoice for the installation of YHWH in Jerusalem in Zech 2:14–16,[10] the announcement in Zech 9:9–10 of the installation of a king in Jerusalem is set within the larger context of the restoration described in Zech 9, which particularly emphasizes territorial possession in the Levant, as we will see. This notion of restoration is then further developed in ch. 10, with a similar territorial emphasis.[11] In this context, v. 9 not only announces the joyful arrival of the king to Jerusalem, but it specifically depicts his qualities and attributes: righteous (צדיק), saved (נושע), humble (עני), and riding a donkey. Verse 10 then focuses on his rule, during which YHWH will cut off the instruments of war (chariot, horse, and bow) from Jerusalem and Ephraim, and the king will guarantee peace and rule over a large territory including especially the Levant.

⁹ גילי מאד בת ציון הריעי בת ירושלם
הנה מלכך יבוא לך צדיק ונושע הוא
עני ורכב על חמור ועל עיר בן אתנות
¹⁰ והכרתי רכב מאפרים וסוס מירושלם
ונכרתה קשת מלחמה ודבר שלום לגוים
ומשלו מים עד ים ומנהר עד אפסי ארץ

---

10 See, e.g., Mason 1976, 229–230; [1973] 2003, 30–31; Laato 1992, 294; Petersen 1995, 57–58; Nurmela 1996, 214–217; Tai 1996, 45–47; Lee 2015, 93–99.
11 The main rupture in the text takes place with the woe oracles of ch. 11; see section 3 below.

⁹ Rejoice greatly, daughter of Zion! Shout, daughter of Jerusalem!
Behold, your king is coming to you; he is righteous and saved,
humble and riding on a donkey, on a pure-bred jackass.
¹⁰ I will cut off the chariot from Ephraim, and the horse from Jerusalem,
and the battle bow will be cut off. He will speak peace to the nations,
and his dominion will be from sea to sea and from the river to the ends of the earth.

Scholars differ in their understanding of Zech 9:9–10, especially regarding the meaning of the royal figure.[12] This question was discussed in antiquity, as evidenced in particular by the ancient Greek version, which emphasizes the active role of the king in the military. He is a "savior" (σῴζων) instead of "saved" in the MT, and he himself (in contrast to YHWH in the MT) cuts off the war instruments from the land (see also the Peshitta). Thus, while the MT describes actions of both YHWH and the king (see also the Vulgate), the LXX has a simplifying reading, which harmonizes the two verses focusing only on the king and his actions with a more classic, military royal ideology.[13] As recently argued by G. M. Eidsvåg (2016, 160–184), the LXX reading is most probably secondary, and it is best understood as a revision from the Hasmonean period, emphasizing the king's military role at a time when Judean kingship was being reestablished and strengthened through military activity. Hence, it appears that a rather complex text reflected in the MT has provoked various interpretations, trying in particular to simplify it, as is the case up to the present.

While most scholars propose plain messianic or royal interpretations,[14] others understand that the king is God himself, pointing out especially the literary context of the passage. As emphasized especially by P. D. Hanson, Becker, Leske, Rose, and Goswell,[15] YHWH is the protagonist in the rest of Zech 9, performing royal actions, especially war. Also, the previous unit ends in v. 8 by depicting his presence at "his house." Therefore, in vv. 9–10, it could seem logi-

---

12 Here, it would be too long to enumerate the various interpretations of Zech 9:9–10 in past research. For a brief overview see, e.g., Mason [1973] 2003, 29–30.
13 Cf., e.g., Saebø 1969, 51–53; Barthélemy 1992, 976–977; Laato 1992, 269; Wöhrle 2008, 177 n. 17; *pace*, recently, Wolters (2014, 278–280), who still emends the Hebrew text based on the LXX (see also the Peshitta and the Vulgate); he argues in favor of the term מושיע, "saving" or "savior" (see already in this direction, e.g., Sellin 1930, 550; Nowack 1922, 374–375).
14 E.g., Wellhausen 1963, 189; Mitchell 1912, 272–277; Elliger 1951, 139–141; Ringgren 1952, 138–139; Rudolph 1976, 177–182; Smith 1984, 254–257; Lacocque 1988, 154–157; Redditt 1995, 109, 114–115; Collins 1995, 32; Meyers 1996, 134–136, who speaks about "the quiescent, though triumphal, tone of the messianic oracle" (p. 134); Willi-Plein 2007, 161–164; Wöhrle 2008, 173–189; Lee 2015, 92–117.
15 Hanson 1973, 37–59; 1979, 292–324; Becker 1980, 72–73, who also insists that YHWH is the one acting in v. 10a (MT); Leske 2000, 671; Rose 2012, 226–228; Goswell 2016.

cal that the king entering in Jerusalem would be YHWH, especially since literary parallels in Zech 2:14–16 and Zeph 3:14–17 announce the divine arrival in Zion.[16] This reading would also be consistent with the ending of the book in Zech 14, which insists on YHWH as the king over all the earth (vv. 9 and 16–17; cf. Rose 2012, 228–229; Goswell 2016, 8–9). Hence, Hanson, for instance, has proposed reading Zech 9 as a hymn which celebrates the mighty deeds of the divine warrior, drawing on an ancient ritual pattern of the conflict myth that he reconstructs.[17]

However, such a conclusion, mainly based on contextual observations, does not match the fact that the depiction of the king in vv. 9–10 is quite peculiar, not very apt for a divine figure. In particular, the terms נוֹשָׁע ("saved") and עָנִי ("humble"), as well as the king's arrival on a donkey, do not suggest a divine identification. In addition, the Masoretic (and the Vulgate) reading of v. 10 – more difficult than the LXX reading – differentiates the actions of the king from those of YHWH and thus does not support identifying the two figures. While the beginning of v. 10 (MT) has a divine speech in the first person, in which YHWH announces that he will cut off the instruments of war from the land, the end of the verse uses the third person to depict the king proclaiming peace to the nations and ruling over a large territory.

Recently, Goswell (2016), following especially Rose (2012), has dedicated an entire article to argue that Zech 9:9–10 is compatible with a theocratic reading. According to him, the Niphal participle נוֹשָׁע could be translated with a reflexive or resultative meaning ("victorious") rather than a passive one ("saved"). In light of various texts – especially from the Psalms – which describe the salvation or the exaltation of the afflicted, the humble, or the poor, Goswell interprets the term עָנִי as referring to someone who is "set to be exalted"; he also points to the related term עֲנָוָה, which is used in Ps 18:36 to refer to the humility or the gentleness of God helping the king, and in Ps 45:5 to refer to a royal virtue. Hence, according to Goswell, the king of Zech 9:9–10 is not passive, and his humility actually anticipates his glory. Goswell further argues that an anthropomorphic depiction of YHWH riding a donkey is possible, especially in light of Zech 14:4, which also has an anthropomorphic description of YHWH standing on the Mount of Olives. Regarding the changes of persons in the text,

---

[16] See esp. Rose 2012, 229–231; Goswell 2016, 8–10, 12–13; cf. Mason [1973] 2003, 32–34; Petersen 1995, 57–58; Leske 2000, 671.
[17] Hanson 1973, 37–59; 1979, 292–324. Note that Hanson actually does not exclude the presence of a royal agent in Zech 9: "[W]ithout any sense of contradiction the divine king and his anointed ruler are together celebrated, a fluidity running throughout the royal psalms of the OT" (Hanson 1973, 51; cf. Hanson 1979, 320); *pace* Larkin 1994, 74.

which apparently refers to YHWH and the king as distinct persons, Goswell argues that this is only a stylistic device, which does not exclude reading the text as referring to YHWH only (cf. Rose 2012, 227–228). Goswell also notes that the depiction of the king's territory in v. 10 – quoting the royal Psalm 72 (v. 8) – has clear Davidic connotations, but he argues that this language, which originally describes the Davidic kingdom, is reapplied to the dominion of the divine king. Goswell supports his interpretation by arguing that a Davidic king is completely absent from the literary context of the passage.

While Goswell's argument is aimed at showing that a theocratic interpretation of Zech 9:9–10 is possible, he does not explain why the depiction of the king is so peculiar. More cautious, K. J. A. Larkin argues against Hanson that the coming king is not the divine warrior, but she still suggests that he is God, in the form of "a humble king, comparable to the Servant"[18] (in Deutero-Isaiah). Petersen also thinks that Zech 9 does not refer to "the return of a real or ideal Davidide" (Petersen 1995, 59, and see 56–60). Underscoring that the king shares similar attributes with the deity, such as righteousness and victory, Petersen also speaks about a "divine king" (Petersen 1995, 58), but his character is actually entirely redefined, especially by the term עני, "humble." Based on Zeph 3:12 and Deutero-Isaiah (esp. Isa 49:13; 51:21; 54:11; cf. 53:4), and following a suggestion of Mason ([1973] 2003, 42–45), Petersen considers that this term has a corporate connotation and concludes that the king personifies "those who exercise rule in the community" (Petersen 1995, 58), with a similar collective presentation of kingship found in Isa 55:1–5. In a similar line of argument, Leske (2000) interprets the king as corresponding to the Servant of Deutero-Isaiah, who represents "God's faithful people" (665 and passim). In light of Zech 12, Leske more specifically identifies this figure with the people of Judah, which is in conflict with Jerusalemite leadership.

These readings try to make sense of the central role of YHWH in Zech 9 on the one hand, and of the peculiar depiction of the humble king on the other hand. However, interpreting the king as a divine or a collective figure creates other difficulties that require arguing – somewhat counterintuitively – that we should not read the text literally, but rather in light of notions found in other texts, either within the book of Zechariah (e.g., Zech 2 or 14) or outside it (e.g., Deutero-Isaiah). With most scholars, I agree that the text should rather be read literally: YHWH, the mighty protagonist of the passage, installs his humble hu-

---

18 Larkin 1994, 76, and see more generally 70–77; see also Becker 1980, 72–73. Ulrich (2010, esp. 261, 264) also interprets the king of Zech 9:9–10 as YHWH himself (or his "incarnate" form), but he does so on the basis of Zech 12:10, which he reads as referring to the piercing of YHWH himself.

man king in Jerusalem. As the changes in person in the MT (and the Vulgate) suggest, YHWH and the king are two distinct figures who have different, complementary roles. When understood this way, the humility of the king as well as the absence of any reference to his actions in the literary context of the passage are actually consistent with the strong emphasis on YHWH's actions throughout the whole section. The specific terminology depicting the king supports this reading. Elsewhere in the Hebrew Bible, YHWH is never the subject of a Niphal form of the verb ישע – best translated with a passive meaning[19] – and the adjective עני never applies to him, always to humans. And never is YHWH depicted as riding a donkey; donkey riders are always humans in the Hebrew Bible (see, e.g., Willi-Plein 2007, 163–164).[20] It is true that YHWH can be described with the adjective צדיק (Exod 9:27; Deut 32:4; Jer 12:1; Isa 45:21; Pss 7:12; 11:7; 116:5; 119:137; 129:4; 145:17; Lam 1:18), but it should also be observed that in the vast majority of biblical occurrences (more than 180) this term refers to humans. In addition, scholars who try to explain this terminology – especially the king's humility and righteousness – in light of the Suffering Servant of Deutero-Isaiah[21] tend to overlook important differences between the two figures. In particular, the Suffering Servant is not described as a king (מלך), nor is he associated with the rule over a specific territory; and contrary to the Suffering Servant, no specific pain is attributed to the king in Zech 9. Thus, it should not come as a surprise that, except for the term צדיק (cf. 53:11), the terminology used in the two depictions is not the same.[22]

I would argue, rather, that the specific traits of the king in Zech 9:9–10 are best understood in light of psalmic terminology and ideology, which revises traditional royal ideology so as to emphasize the king's vulnerability and piety

---

19 Especially in light of the LXX which has an active meaning (σῴζων), the Niphal participle נושע is sometimes translated as "victorious" rather than "saved" (see, e.g., Hanson 1979, 294; Petersen 1995, 55; Goswell 2016, 14–15). Although being saved can be associated with victory, this translation already somewhat changes the meaning of the Hebrew term, over-interpreting it. It is probably not by chance that, despite the possible association with victory, a Niphal form of ישע never applies to YHWH in the Hebrew Bible.
20 The fact that the type of donkey (חמור) is quite precisely specified in Zech 9:9 – "a purebred jackass" עיר בן אתנות; cf. Way 2010; 2011, 162–170; see also n. 32 below) – seems to confirm that the king belongs to the human realm.
21 Cf. מענה in Isa 53:4, נענה in 53:7, צדיק in 53:11; see Mitchell 1912, 273; Lamarche 1961, 131–134 (and more generally up to p. 147); Baldwin 1972, 165; Mason [1973] 2003, 35–37, 41–45; 1976, 236; 1998, 354–355; Petersen 1995, 58–59; Larkin 1994, 73–76.
22 The Suffering Servant is not described with term עני but with the related terms מענה and נענה (Isa 53:4, 7). Although the notion of salvation is important in Deutero-Isaiah, the root ישע is not used in the depiction of the Suffering Servant. In addition, the motif of the donkey has no parallel in Deutero-Isaiah.

towards YHWH.²³ Although the connection to the Psalms is sometimes noted,²⁴ the extent to which it serves to re-signify ancient royal ideology needs to be discussed further. It is indeed striking that the terms צדיק and עני as well as the verb ישע are particularly central in the Psalms, where they are regularly used to describe the dependency of the individual on divine protection: the individual is called עני or צדיק, and he relies on and expects the divine intervention saving him (verb ישע) from a critical situation and bringing him his reward.²⁵ In addition, since many of the individual Psalms are attributed to king David, the humble or just individual expecting divine salvation is none other than the king himself, who serves as a model of piety for the community. Indeed, while ancient royal Psalms traditionally praise the king's power and glory, the increasing attribution of individual prayers to king David during the Second Temple period – a process attested by manuscript evidence²⁶ – creates a different picture of the king, that of a vulnerable individual, entirely dependent on YHWH for his protection. This revision of traditional royal ideology is explicit,

---

23 The possible connections between Zech 9 and Isa 53 can actually be explained by a similar influence of the psalmic ideology that developed during the Second Temple period and influenced the development of prophetic literature.
24 Mason [1973] 2003, 35–42; 1976, 236; Hanson 1973, 57–58; 1979, 304–308; Larkin 1994, 72–76; Duguid 1995, 266–267; Collins 2003.
25 The Psalms contain more than one third of the biblical occurrences of the verb ישע, which appears at least once in almost half of the Psalms. The salvation almost exclusively comes from YHWH, and David is the individual *par excellence* saved from his enemies by YHWH. The Psalms also contain more than one third of the biblical occurrences of the term עני (see also, the related adjective ענו as well as the verb ענה); the term refers to the individual who is in a situation of distress and in need of the divine help and who is the object of divine salvation (e.g., Pss 12:6; 18:28; 35:7). As for the term צדיק, scholars rightly insist that justice (צדקה) is a central notion in the traditional royal ideology (see, e.g., Mason 1998, 354, referring to Ps 72:1). Still, elsewhere in the Bible, the use of the specific term צדיק to qualify a human ruler is found almost exclusively in psalmic literature (including the hymnic text of 2 Sam 23:3), referring to David, the psalmist (see also Jer 23:5, where it describes a "legitimate offspring," צמח צדיק, and 1 Sam 24:18, referring to David). Otherwise, the term largely applies to all kinds of individuals or groups, as the importance of this term in wisdom literature makes clear. The Psalms contain more than one fourth of the biblical occurrences of the term צדיק. The righteous person of the Psalms, which is best represented by David, is both the individual who acts according to justice and depends on divine justice for his deliverance and reward (e.g., Pss 37:29, 39; 58:12; 112:4; 118:15, 20; 140:14).
26 A greater number of Psalms are attributed to David in the Targum than in the MT, and even more in the LXX (see also the Peshitta); Qumran evidence, especially 11QPsᵃ, reflects an effort to rearrange and to "Davidize" the Psalter. This process also impacted the formation of the Masoretic Psalter, as is suggested, for instance, by the fact that some Psalms are attributed to David in the MT but not in the LXX (see MT Pss 122 and 124); see, e.g., Auwers 2000, 135–159; Dorival 2005; Ramantswana 2011.

for instance, in Ps 33, which criticizes royal military might, insisting that "a king is not saved (נוֹשָׁע) by the greatness of the army" (v. 16a) or that "the (war) horse is a vain means of salvation" (v. 17a), in order to emphasize divine protection instead.[27] Several other passages in the Psalms also stress the idea that deliverance does not come from military power and weapons (chariot, horse, sword, or bow; Pss 20:8; 44:4–8).

Similarly, Zech 9:9–10 uses aspects of traditional royal ideology, quoting in particular the royal Psalm 72 (v. 8) on the great extent of the royal dominion (v. 10b),[28] but it also re-signifies traditional royal ideology to insist on the kings' vulnerability and his dependency on YHWH, following the terminology and ideology of the psalms of the individual.[29] Alongside Ps 33:16, Zech 9:9 is the only passage in the Hebrew Bible that applies the Niphal participle נוֹשָׁע to a king (cf. 2 Sam 22:4 // Ps 18:4; see, e.g., Mason [1973] 2003, 36; Wöhrle 2008, 177 n. 17), and YHWH's destruction of the instruments of war in Zech 9:10 indicates their uselessness, not unlike the notion found in Pss 20:8; 44:4–8. In MT Zech 9:9–10 (and in the Vulgate), the king's dependence on YHWH's protection is also made clear by the fact that it is not the king but YHWH who cuts off the instruments of war (chariot, horse, and war bow). This notion of the destruction of the instruments of war by YHWH is found in several prophetic as well as psalmic texts, insisting on the vulnerability, the weakening or the destruction of human groups by YHWH (Jer 49:35; 51:21; Hos 1:5; Nah 2:4; Mic 5:9; Ps 37:15), announcing the end of war and a time of peace (Hos 2:20; Ps 46:10; cf. Isa 2:4 // Mic 4:3; Ezek 39:9–10), or emphasizing divine protection against enemy attack (Ps 76:4, 7). It thus appears that whole depiction of the king and his reign in

---

[27] To be sure, royal piety and dependency on the deity were also aspects found in the traditional royal ideology from the monarchic period. Nonetheless, in post-monarchic times, theses aspects seem to receive greater importance, strengthened by a critique of royal military activities and power (cf., e.g., Deut 17:16; 1 Sam 8:10–11; Ps 33:16–17).

[28] The literal quotation of Ps 72:8 in Zech 9:10, which is the longest biblical quotation in Zech 9–14, clearly indicates the strong influence of the Psalms on Zech 9:9–10. The choice of the royal Psalm 72 is probably due to its strategic place in the Psalms (or a precursor of the book), closing an ancient collection of Davidic prayers (cf. Ps 72:20).

[29] Note, for instance, that the royal Ps 72 mentions the humble (עָנִי, vv. 2, 4, 12) and the righteous (צַדִּיק, v. 7), who are also saved (using the verb יָשַׁע, vv. 4, 13). However, in this royal psalm, contrary to Zech 9:9, the humble and the righteous are not the king, and the king actually saves them. In Zech 9:9–10, as in individual prayers attributed to David in the Psalms, the king takes on the role of the humble and righteous individual in need of divine salvation, so as to exemplify dependency and piety towards YHWH; cf. Duguid 1995, 266–267; Collins 2003, 37–39; Boda 2017, 74.

Zech 9:9–10 underscores the king's dependence on YHWH, using especially terms and notions that are central in the Psalms.³⁰

Such an emphasis on the king's vulnerability and dependence suggests that he does not engage in war. Instead, YHWH is the one who fights on his behalf and cuts off the instruments of war.³¹ This interpretation is supported by v. 10, which specifies the main function of the king, i.e., to "speak peace to the nations" (ודבר שלום לגוים). In addition, it best explains why the king enters Jerusalem on a donkey. Especially in the context of a military engagement, we would expect the king to ride on a horse, an animal that almost always serves as a vehicle for war in Zech 9–14.³² However, the king's association with the

---

30 Note, for instance, that the call to rejoice addressed to Jerusalem/Zion at the start of v. 9 also uses psalmic terminology, which evokes the happy consequences of the divine salvation (esp. the verbs גיל and רוע, Hiphil; cf. Sweeney 2000, 663; Collins 2003, 32–34). The close relationship of a prophetic text to psalmic traditions should not come as a surprise, especially since in early Judaism hymns could be considered as prophecy (see, e.g., in Chronicles, or see the presence of oracles in Psalms, e.g., Ps 110:1) and David could be viewed as a prophet (see, e.g., 11QPs 27:11; Acts 2:29; Sifre to Deut 1:1), cf., e.g., Ramantswana 2011, 451–453. Several hymns have also been included in the Prophets, especially in the Twelve (see Jon 2, Nah 1, or Hab 3), and some Psalms are even attributed to Haggai and Zechariah in the LXX (Pss 146–148); as with Isaiah and the Twelve, the Qumran community also wrote *Pesharim* on the Psalms.

31 The military forces suppressed by YHWH are primarily foreign ones, as suggested by the references to the chariot and the horse (I owe this observation to Jan Rückl), but the text seems to envision more broadly the suppression all kind of military forces, both foreign and Judean, in order to emphasize peace.

32 Cf. Zech 9:10; 10:3b, 5; 12:4; 14:15. It has often been emphasized that the donkey can be a royal animal (see, e.g., Lipiński 1970, 51–52; Rudolph 1976, 180; Mason 1998, 355; Goswell 2016, 16–17; see, however, Leske 2000, 672–673), but since the horse can also be a royal animal (see, e.g., Jer 22:4), this observation alone does not explain why the donkey is mentioned in Zech 9:9. It is difficult not to see a connection between the arrival of the king in Jerusalem on a donkey in v. 9 and the cutting off of the horses from Jerusalem, together with other instruments of war, in v. 10. It appears that vv. 9–10 oppose the royal donkey to the warlike horse; cf. Baldwin 1972, 165–166; Mason [1973] 2003, 38–39; Lacocque 1988, 155; Duguid 1995, 268; Willi-Plein 2007, 163–164; Wöhrle 2008, 176–177 n. 15; Nogalski 2011, 907; Wolters 2014, 281. Following a suggestion of G. von Rad ([1966] 1984, 222–223), and with special reference to the enthronement of Solomon in 1 Kgs 1:34–35, 39–40 (cf. 2 Sam 13:29; 18:9), Goswell (2016, 16–17) reads Zech 9:9 as an allusion to an ancient tradition about the king on his way to be enthroned (cf., e.g., Ringgren 1956, 37). This is an interesting suggestion, but since in 1 Kgs 1 Salomon is described as riding on a mule (פרדה, vv. 33, 38, 44; cf. פרד in 2 Sam 13:29; 18:9) rather than a donkey, it does not explain the specific depiction of the king in Zech 9:9, riding "on a donkey, on a pure-bred jackass" (על חמור ועל עיר בן אתנות). Most probably, this precise depiction of the donkey aims at strengthening an opposition with the war horse, making clear that the royal donkey is a pure-bred, i.e., not at all a hybrid with horse blood; cf. Lipiński

donkey makes good sense in light of the following verse, which announces YHWH's suppression of the instruments of war, including the horse. In this context, it appears that the king is all but a military leader. Scholars have also observed the striking absence of the king in the rest of the section, chs. 9–10, which describes YHWH's and Israel's battle against the enemy in different ways. According to traditional ANE royal ideology, we would also expect the king to be the main fighting figure in the war, especially in the twice-mentioned battle fought by Israel/Judah, first in Zech 9:11–17 and then again in ch. 10. Instead, it can be observed that the battle in Zech 9:13–15 depicts YHWH as a storm-god warrior with specific traits of a war leader who directly commands his troops (Judah, Ephraim, and Jerusalem), without any need of a human intermediary.³³ In contrast, the war depiction in ch. 10 refers to human, Judean military leadership and power; in particular, v. 4 uses four images: the "corner" (פנה), the "peg" (יתד), the "bow of war" (קשת מלחמה), and "all oppressors/overseers together" (כל נוגש יחדו). However, the connotations of this verse are collective, as the last image makes clear ("*all* oppressors *together*"). And contrary to what has sometimes been argued especially for the first two images, this verse does not contain any specific royal or messianic element.³⁴ For instance, even if

---

1970, 52; Rudolph 1976, 178; Leske 2000, 672–673; Willi-Plein 2007, 163; Way 2010; 2011, 162–170; Wolters 2014, 280–281.

33 See in v. 13 how YHWH uses his people in war as his personal weapons (as his bow and his sword). See also the depiction of YHWH blowing the horn, an instrument that can be used for sending military signals (see, e.g., 1 Sam 13:3; Josh 6:1–21; Judg 3:27; 6:34; 7:18–22; Jer 51:27). Such anthropomorphic depictions are innovative within the Hebrew Bible and serve to depict YHWH as a concrete war leader, commanding his troops directly, without any need of a human leader. For a more developed argument on this point, see Gonzalez 2019.

34 See, e.g., the discussion in Wolters 2014, 316–325; *pace*, e.g., Otzen 1964, 143–145; Mason [1973] 2003, 79–84; Meyers and Meyers 1993, 200–202; 1995, 212–225; Duguid 1995, 270–272. These commentators tend to agree that the last two images, the war bow and the oppressor, do not contain any particular royal or messianic element (but see Mason [1973] 2003, 82, with rather weak arguments on the war bow). Nonetheless, they try to interpret the corner and the peg as royal images, even if they often admit that their royal association is not clear-cut. In order to do so, they need first to understand the term פנה as meaning "cornerstone" (cf. Isa 28:16; Jer 51:26; Ps 118:22; Job 38:6) and then to interpret this meaning in light of Ps 118:22 as having royal or messianic connotations. They also read the term יתד, "peg," in light of Isa 22:23–25, where it applies to Eliakim, a high officer of the royal, Davidic court (Ezra 9:8 is sometimes brought as corroborating evidence, but this text is far from clear in this regard). However, in all the passages where פנה can be translated as "cornerstone," the term is associated in one way or another with the term אבן, "stone"; and this latter term – and the stone image more generally – is absent in Zech 10. Therefore, the term פנה in Zech 10:4 is best read as a metaphorical designation for a "chief" or a "leader" of a group, as is also the case in Judg 20:2; 1 Sam 14:38, and Isa 19:13, which refer especially to non-royal leaders. Despite its singular form in Zech 10:4, the term most probably serves as collective designation, similarly to the

Petterson assumes that the king of Zech 9:9–10 should be included among the leaders mentioned in Zech 10:4, he admits that this verse does not describe any king at war.[35] In assuming the presence of the king despite the fact that Zech 10:4 does not mention him, not only is Petterson's methodology problematic because it seeks to harmonize two different passages (Zech 10:4 with Zech 9:9–10), but it misses a central point in Zech 9–10, which is that *the future, ideal king is a peaceful one who does not fight*.[36]

But why announce a king if this figure is deprived of any military role, a central function of the king in traditional ancient Near Eastern royal ideology? We will come back to this question in the last section of this essay, which will deal with socio-historical aspects. For now, it is important to observe that the announcement of a local king in Jerusalem is consistent with the emphasis on territorial and political independence, which is visible throughout the whole of chs. 9–10. To be sure, scholars differ in their interpretations of the place of Zech 9:9–10 in these chapters and sometimes argue that it is secondary.[37] Especially

---

term נגוש at the end of verse, which is a collective singular. Regarding the second term, יתד, it can be used as an image of power, authority, or stability, but the sole evidence that points to royal associations (Isa 22:23–25) precisely applies this term to a person who is neither a king, nor even a Davidide. Duguid is right in pointing out that the Targum has an explicit messianic reading of Zech 10:4, but messianic (over-)interpretation is a well-known characteristic of the prophetic Targums, which says more about the Aramaic translation and its historical context (roughly the first centuries CE) than about the Hebrew text when it was composed; see, e.g., Levey 1974; Chilton 1999, esp. 138–144. Duguid also argues that, similarly to Ezek 34, Zech 10 announces a judgment against the shepherds (see v. 3a) in order to envisage a new shepherd, a royal figure that would be presented in v. 4. Duguid may be correct that Zech 10:3 alludes to Ezek 34, but this allusion does not continue in v. 4. On the contrary, instead of announcing a new Davidic "shepherd" as Ezek 34 does, Zech 10:4 changes the image, referring rather to the corner, the peg, the battle bow, and the overseer, which are absent in Ezek 34 (cf. Tigchelaar 1996, 99). In addition, as Duguid (1995, 272–273) himself emphasizes, and as is generally recognized, the pro-David oracle of Ezek 34 is reversed in Zech 11 (esp. vv. 15–16); see also n. 99 below. Hence, the least that can be said is that a royal or messianic reading of Zech 10:4 is not the simplest one.

35 See Petterson 2009, 166: "it is therefore not clear that any of these three metaphors were used because of earlier associations with the house of David"; see then p. 210: "While none of these metaphors is clearly Davidic, the wider context and background make it almost certain that the Davidic shepherd-king is to be included among these leaders."

36 Cf., e.g., Collins and Collins 2008, 46. Note in this regard that the notion of a "messianic" figure fighting or bringing salvation is actually rare in prophetic literature, Mic 5:1–5 being an exception. Such a role is rather attributed to YHWH, while his representative is in charge of administrating the new order brought by the divine intervention; see Nihan 2017.

37 See already Nowack 1922, 374; Elliger 1951, 139; Rudolph 1976, 178; Mason [1973] 2003, 28; Nogalski 1993, 217–229; Wöhrle 2008, 69–83, 174–189.

because I think that the absence of the king from the war scenes of Zech 9 is consistent with his peaceful role, I rather read Zech 9 as a quite unified passage, which has later been expanded with ch. 10.[38] Be that as it may, it can be argued that Zech 9:9–10 clearly participates in promoting an ideal that is developed throughout the whole of chs. 9–10: that of *Israel enjoying political independence on a large Levantine territory* (cf., e.g., Nogalski 1993, 226). This political and territorial aspect actually binds the different units of Zech 9–10 together and is therefore central for the interpretation of the passage.

Chapter 9 begins by describing in vv. 1–8 the divine conquest of the Levant – Syria, Phoenicia and Philistia (cf., e.g., Lee 2015, 63–91). This first scene ends in an original way by emphasizing the integration of Canaanite groups (Philistines) into Israel (vv. 6b–7, cf. v. 1), as well as YHWH's protection of his people from his "house" (ביתי) – most probably within the book of Zechariah, the Jerusalem temple – which will prevent the oppressor (נגש) to pass (v. 8). Hence, this divine conquest of the Levant forms a fitting introduction to the subsequent announcement of the installation of the king in Jerusalem, who will rule over a very large territory including the whole Levant, as v. 10 – quoting Ps 72:8 – makes clear.[39]

In the following scenes of Zech 9 and 10, the idea of the political independence of Israel is further emphasized through another theme, namely, that of Israel's war to free the land from foreign oppression. Zechariah 9:11–17 and ch. 10 both describe the battle of Judah and Ephraim against their enemies.[40]

---

38 On the secondary character of ch. 10, see, e.g., Hanson 1979, 325–334; Steck 1991, 35–37; Tigchelaar 1996, 89–109; Kunz 1998, 45–60; cf. Redditt 2012a, 24, 69–72.

39 As is often noted, the depiction of the territory at the end of v. 10, quoting Ps 72:8, might have cosmic connotations: "from sea to sea, and from the river to the end of [the] earth/land" (מים עד ים ומנהר עד אפסי ארץ); see, e.g., Meyers and Meyers 1993, 137–138. However, this depiction is not purely mythical. Meyers and Meyers refer to Northwest Semitic traditions to argue that the river alluded to is a mythical one, but it most probably refers to the Euphrates, such as in Exod 23:31; see also Gen 15:18; Deut 1:7; 11:24; Josh 1:4; 1 Kgs 4:1, 4 (cf. Mitchell 1912, 275; Redditt 1995, 114–115). In light of the territorial description in these passages, and especially after vv. 1–8, which focus on the Levantine nations, Zech 9:10 most probably refers to a Levantine territory, envisaged very broadly.

40 Zechariah 10:1–3a stands out in chs. 9–10, displaying a more negative perspective that envisages a judgment against the "shepherds" (הרעים) and the "billy goats" (העתודים). It is quite probably redactional. It serves as a transition between the two versions of the war in chs. 9 and 10, preparing at the same time the negative depictions of the community and its leaders (presented as "shepherds") in ch. 11 and 13:7–9; see in a similar direction, e.g., Elliger 1951, 144–145; Rudolph 1976, 189–192, and Larkin 1994, 86–91, who distinguish Zech 10,1–2; Redditt 2012a, 24, 70–72; 2012b, 216–218, distinguishing vv. 2–3a; Kunz 1998, 47–50, and Wöhrle 2008, 76–77, 128–131, distinguishing vv. 1–3a (although the latter considers these verses as preceding their surrounding context).

While these texts differ in their emphasis, especially as ch. 10 distinguishes the crucial role of Judah in the battle (vv. 3b–5), both chapters conclude the battle with a description of Israel enjoying the possession of the land. Especially Zech 10 insists that the numerous sons of Ephraim will return and dwell in a land that will be as large as to include the Lebanon and the Gilead (vv. 6–12). In addition, Zech 9 provides more details about the context of the battle. In particular, vv. 11–12 set the scene in Jerusalem, which is described as a "stronghold" (בצרון),[41] and v. 13 explicitly mentions the enemies threatening the city of Jerusalem: the "sons of Yavan," i.e., the Greeks.[42] Overall, the battle descriptions in chs. 9 and 10 illustrate well the emphasis of Zech 9:8 on YHWH's protection over his people, and especially over Jerusalem, against a foreign threat.

In sum, by announcing a local ruler controlling the whole Levant, Zech 9:9–10 exemplifies the ideal of political independence of the land developed throughout chs. 9–10. As a result, and as most scholars agree, Zech 9:9–10 is best read as announcing the return of kingship in Jerusalem, using elements of royal ideology that are traditionally associated with the Davidic dynasty. In particular, the notion of a king ruling from Jerusalem over a large Levantine territory and enjoying a close relationship to YHWH is reminiscent of Davidic rule, especially as portrayed in royal Psalms (and in the historiographical traditions). Nonetheless, the traditional role of the king is significantly revised according to later psalmic ideology, which emphasizes the king's vulnerability and his complete dependence on YHWH for his protection and salvation. As a result, the king of Zech 9:9–10 appears like the vulnerable David of the psalms of the individual, who seeks the salvation of YHWH in times of danger. Even if this figure marks the political and territorial independence of Israel, he is also deprived of any military role. Instead of leading the war, he will be the guarantor of peace in the Levant and will serve as an example of piety and reliance on YHWH.

Finally, it should also be observed that, despite the passage's strong relationship to the Psalms, which further associates the king of Zech 9 with a Davidic figure, the main point of the text is not about the Davidic lineage of the future

---

41 Wolters (2014, 284–287) proposes to read the term בצרון, a *hapax legomenon*, as a synonym of בצרה "(sheep)fold," while most commentators read it as has synonym of מבצר, "stronghold" (see, e.g., Rudolph 1976, 183; Redditt 2012a, 34, 45; Boda 2016, 574–575, 580–581). The latter meaning is supported by all the ancient versions.

42 Hanson (1979, 297–298) has been influential in arguing on metrical grounds that this mention of the Greeks is a later gloss; see, e.g., Redditt 1995, 96–97. However, the poetry of Zech 9 is all but metrically regular. In addition, this specification is central for the text, since otherwise there would be two descriptions of the battle in Zech 9 and 10 with no identification of the enemy.

king. Contrary to texts like Isa 11:1; Jer 23:5; Ezek 37:24–25, or Mic 5:1, Zech 9:9–10 does not provide any explicit reference to the Davidic origins of the ruler, such that, strictly speaking, this king could have a different lineage.[43] The writers of this passage possibly had a Davidic king in mind, but they did not choose to emphasize this aspect, privileging other characteristics such as the roles of maintaining peace in the Levant and exemplifying piety towards YHWH.

2 The House of David in Zech 12:1–13:1: A Utopia of a Ritualized Jerusalemite Community

In contrast to Zech 9:9–10, Zech 12:1–13:1 explicitly refers to the "house of David" no less than five times (12:7, 8, 10, 12 and 13:1), and sometimes with highly positive connotations (see esp. v. 8). Observing this, and pointing out connections between chs. 9–10 and 12 – or more broadly between all the units of Zech 9–14 –, some scholars associate the house of David in Zech 12:1–13:1 with the king of Zech 9:9–10 and conclude that both passages aim at announcing some form of restoration of Davidic kingship.[44] If Zech 9–14 had a consistent discourse on this matter, this could be a fair conclusion. However, while Zech 9 and Zech 12:1–13:1 might refer to the same event (see, e.g, Petterson 2009, 221–222), these scholars rule out from the start the possibility that the various depictions of the same battle in these chapters could nevertheless present diverging views on particular aspects[45] – a hypothesis which explains well why there are

---

43 Cf. Chary 1955, 229; Rudolph 1976, 179; Pomykala 1995, 125 n. 246. This is how Sweeney (2000, 664), for instance, can go as far as to identify the king of Zech 9 with Darius I. This is also a reason why attributing Zech 9:9–10 and the ancient core of Mic 5:1–5* to the same level of redaction in the Twelve falls short; *pace* Wöhrle 2008, 173–189; Redditt 2008, 77–78.

44 See esp. Lamarche 1961, esp. 105–123; Seybold 1972, 107–109; Lacocque 1988, esp. 156; Laato 1992, 190–194; 1997, 216–218; Petterson 2009, 213–242.

45 See Petterson 2009, 222: "In each cycle there is a focus on a different aspect of this final-day battle that will usher in Yahweh's kingdom, but all the time building on and developing what has gone before, rather than negating or modifying it." Clearly, Petterson regards Zechariah as a completely coherent book, written or redacted by one author, Zechariah himself (cf. pp. 3–4); see also p. 246, where Petterson assumes "that the final redactor sought to produce a coherent presentation throughout the work." The problem with this assumption is that it is somewhat arbitrary, excluding that "the final redactor" could also have produced a work containing a complex and plural discourse on the future of the house of David, especially if he was dealing with material from diverse origins. In addition, the notion of a "final redactor" is perhaps too simple, as if the text remained fixed from the time of its composition. Rather, textual and redaction criticism point to more complex processes of interpretative textual transmission during the Second Temple period.

no less than four scenarios of the same battle in chs. 9–14 (see, e.g., Ellul 1981). Especially when dealing with a prophetic book, we cannot a priori assume a consistent discourse throughout the whole book. Most prophetic books were reworked in the course of their transmission during the Second Temple period, showing clear signs of reinterpretation, with new meanings being introduced secondarily.[46] Hence, we should not only look for continuity between Zech 9:9–10 and Zech 12:1–13:1; we should also be open to the idea that these two passages might present different discourses on the royal house, even if they share close connections.

In its present form, Zech 12:1–13:1 opens a new section in chs. 9–14 (see the superscription in v. 1) by presenting another scenario of war that is parallel to that of Zech 9–10. Again, Jerusalem is threatened by foreign attack and Judeans fight for the defense of the city. At some points the parallel is not only thematic but also terminological; for instance the verb גנן, "to protect," quite rare in the Hebrew Bible,[47] is used in Zech 9:15 and 12:6 to describe the protection of YHWH for his people during the battle.[48] Thus, Petterson (2009, 221–222) is most probably correct in arguing that Zech 12 describes anew the war of Jerusalem against foreign aggression that is already depicted in Zech 9–10, with new insights on the event. There are, however, also significant differences. A major structural difference concerns the outcome of the war. While both chs. 9 and 10 conclude their war descriptions emphasizing the possession of the land (see esp. Zech 9:16–17; 10:6–12), the war scene of Zech 12:1–13:1 ends with a depiction of a great ritual mourning by the community over a pierced figure (12:10–13:1). We will come back to this point below.

Another major difference is the identification of the enemy. While the enemy in Zech 9 is specifically identified as the "sons of Yavan," the enemies in

---

46 Especially for the books of Jeremiah and Ezekiel, this process is well attested by manuscript evidence; for references and discussion, see Gonzalez 2021, 294–300.

47 Elsewhere, it is used in 2 Kgs 19:34; 20:6 // Isa 37:35; 38:6, and also Isa 31:5, also to describe the divine protection over Jerusalem; Boda 2016, 708.

48 See also: the enemy's consumption (אכל) by fire (אש) in 12:6; cf. 9:4 (and see the warlike consumption, אכל, in 9:15); the use of the verbs נכה (Hiphil), "to smite," with divine subject (12:4; cf. 9:4; 10:11), and שים, "to set," with warlike associations, with divine subject and with Jerusalem (12:2–3; cf. 9:13) and Judah (12:6; cf. 10:3) as the object; the images of stone (אבן) in a martial context (12:3; cf. 9:15, 16); the opposition to war horses (12:4; cf. 9:10); the use of the term אלוף, "chieftain," associated with Judah (12:5, 6; cf. 9:7); the victory presented as resulting from the action of YHWH who "saves" (ישע Hiphil) his people (12:7; cf. 9:16; 10:6); YHWH called אלהיהם, "their God," in 12:5, a suffixed form which appears only 9:16 and 10:6 within the book of Zechariah. Note also that the similar titles in 12:1 and 9:1, both starting with the sequence משא דבר יהוה (elsewhere in the Hebrew Bible only in Mal 1:1), also strengthen the parallel between the two chapters.

Zech 12 are broadly presented as "all the peoples round about" (כל העמים סביב, v. 2) or "all the nations of the land/earth" (כל גויי הארץ, v. 3). This presentation seems to include a large number of nations, with a special focus on the neighboring ones, i.e., the Levantine nations. This new accent not only differs from Zech 9–10 insofar as these chapters specifically target the Greeks as the enemy (9:13) but also insofar as the divine conquest leads to the inclusion (after judgment and purification) of the Levantine nations within the territory of Israel that is protected by YHWH (see esp. 9:1, 7, 10; cf. 10:10b). In addition, while Judah plays a specific role in the deliverance of Jerusalem in Zech 12 – as is also the case in Zech 9–10 (cf. 9:13; 10:3b–5) –, Ephraim is no longer mentioned (and this remains the case up to the end of the book), as commentators often observe (e.g., Redditt 2012a, 17; Boda 2016, 24). In fact, the text can even been read as implying that Ephraim belongs to the neighboring nations that attack Jerusalem. These differences highlight a major change between the war scenarios of Zech 9–10 and Zech 12. While Zech 9–10 announces the unity of all Israel and more broadly the entire Levant under the rule of the ideal king of Jerusalem, the restoration in Zech 12 is essentially focused on the city of Jerusalem, with Judah being the only group associated with Jerusalem.

As a matter of fact, even the role of Judah is ambiguous. Commentators debate whether or not Judah belongs to the enemies of Jerusalem at the beginning of the war. The unclarity of Zech 12:2b, in particular, has provoked opposite interpretations from antiquity until the present. Some scholars understand that Judah is also attacked in the siege against Jerusalem, as the parallel syntax "against Judah" (על יהודה) and "against Jerusalem" (על ירושלם) suggests;[49] this reading is supported by the Septuagint and the Peshitta. Others understand that Judah fights "in the siege against Jerusalem" (יהיה במצור על ירושלם) as the end of the verse suggests,[50] and this reading is supported by the Vulgate and Targum. Note, however, that the reading of the Targum is more nuanced, making clear that Judah is forced by the nations to participate in the attack against Jerusalem. This interpretation corresponds well to the ambiguity of the formulation, which suggests that Judah is both victim and assailant (see also Wolters 2014, 405–406).[51] In addition, understanding that Judah is, in one way

---

[49] See, e.g., Hanson 1979, 355, 357 (but see pp. 361–362); Redditt 1995, 129; Willi-Plein 2007, 191; Petterson 2009, 216; Boda 2016, 697 and 701; cf. Mitchell 1912, 321–322; Rudolph 1976, 216–217.
[50] Cf. Zech 14:14; e.g., Larkin 1994, 145, 147–148; Pomykala 1995, 116; Wöhrle 2008, 99–100. Others, like Petersen (1995, 112), are reluctant to take any stand.
[51] Perhaps the ambiguity comes from a secondary modification of the verse in one direction or the other; see, e.g., Elliger 1951, 156; Saebø 1969, 271; Pomykala 1995, 116, and Wöhrle 2008, 99–100, who argue that the preposition על, "against," before Judah is secondary; see differently Otzen 1964, 262, reading ערי, "the cities [of Judah]" instead of על.

or another, involved in the siege against Jerusalem explains why Judah is specifically mentioned among the nations in vv. 2–3 and v. 4. And in this perspective, v. 5, which presents the chieftains of Judah acknowledging that the inhabitants of Jerusalem have YHWH on their side,[52] makes sense as indicating the moment when Judah stops opposing Jerusalem. It is indeed only after this acknowledgment that Judah is depicted in vv. 6–7 as fighting against the assaulting nations.

Be that as it may, there is no simple relationship between Judah and Jerusalem in Zech 12:1–13:1 – at least in its current form –, as v. 7 makes clear when stating that "YHWH will save the tents of Judah first so that the glory of the house of David and the glory of the inhabitants of Jerusalem will not be high above Judah." This verse not only emphasizes the distinction of Judah vis-à-vis Jerusalem, but it also presents Judah as a group deserving no less honor than the Jerusalemite elites and population do, suggesting thereby some sort of competitive relationship between Judah and Jerusalem.[53] And finally, once the fight is over, Judah is no longer mentioned in chs. 12–13, especially in the great mourning that takes place after the war; apparently this ritual mainly concerns Jerusalem and its elites (see below).

Therefore, as the texts now stands, it makes clear that Judah is distinct from Jerusalem, and also that Judah is (or at least becomes at some point during the war) an ally of Jerusalem, one that deserves considerable honor, similarly to Jerusalem. Such clarification of the role and status of Judah vis-à-vis Jerusalem is a sign that these aspects were unclear or complex, perhaps a matter of de-

---

52 The syntax of v. 5b is not clear and has provoked textual changes from antiquity up to the present. As it stands, the MT (supported by the Vulgate) can be read: "My strength (is that) the inhabitants of Jerusalem (are) in YHWH Ṣeba'ôt their God" (אמצה לי ישבי ירושלם ביהוה צבאות אלהיהם). The text is often slightly emended, לי ישבי being read into one word, לישבי, as does the Targum (see, e.g., Rudolph 1976, 217; Meyers and Meyers 1993, 323–324; Larkin 1994, 148; Boda 2016, 704). Hence the text would read: "The strength of the inhabitants of Jerusalem (is) in YHWH Ṣeba'ôt their God." Another proposed emendation is: אם צהלו [...] ישבי ירושלים, "If only the inhabitants of Jerusalem would raise a shout for YHWH of Hosts their God!" (see Hanson 1979, 357); and other more speculative emendations have also been proposed (see Otzen 1964, 187: לבם אמצה [...]; Rudolph 1976, 217: אמצה אם [...]). The Greek text reads at the start of the sentence a form of the verb מצא, "find" (εὑρήσομεν ἑαυτοῖς [...]; "we will find out that the inhabitants of Jerusalem are in YHWH almighty their God"); this is also the case of Targum, but with a slightly different reading: "salvation has been found by the inhabitants of Jerusalem in the presence of YHWH Ṣeba'ôt their God." Despite these diverse readings, note that all versions emphasize the relationship of the inhabitants of Jerusalem to YHWH, "their God," which is the important point made by the Judean leaders (*pace* Hanson's and Rudolph's emendations).

53 Cf. Reventlow 1993, 116; Pomykala 1995, 116–117; Nogalski 2011, 948–949.

bate, when Zech 12 was composed. Hanson (1979, 354–368) interpreted the relationship between Judah and Jerusalem in Zech 12 in terms of a social conflict between two parties; he identifies a visionary party, corresponding to Judah in Zech 12, opposed to a hierocratic party (Jerusalem). This identification of opposing parties is quite conjectural, and Hanson's reading of Zech 12 as reflecting a social conflict also fails to convince because the text insists that Judah will, at least eventually, help Jerusalem in its fight against the nations. Hanson's sociological interpretation is problematic, but some of his observations on Zech 12 remain correct, especially the fact that the text clearly distinguishes between Jerusalem and Judah, and it envisages their relationship as involving some kind of rivalry.

Another type of explanation for the complex relationship between Jerusalem and Judah in Zech 12:1–13:1 takes a redactional approach. Various reconstructions of the text's literary history have been proposed, but most of them consider that the text was initially more (or even solely) focused on Jerusalem. The presence of Judah in the battle would have been added or secondarily strengthened.[54] This hypothesis explains well why Judah is mentioned sepa-

---

54 Among the scholars envisaging a complex and progressive literary development of the passage, many consider that Judah was absent in the text's ancient core; see Plöger 1962, 102–103, 116–117, identifying this core in vv. 2a, 3a, 4abβ*, 9–14; Rudolph 1976, 216–225, who identifies a similar core (vv. 1b, 2a, 3a, 4a, and 9–14) and believes Judah was introduced and given a prominent role with the addition of vv. 4bα–8 in the Maccabean period (see also Lutz 1968, esp. 11–21, pointing to a brief core in vv. 2a, 3a, 4a, and Saebø 1969, 267–274, with only an original *Kernwort* in vv. 3–4a). Recently, Biberger 2010, 307–310, identifies the *Grundschicht* in vv. 2a, 3a, 6b, revised with the addition of vv. 3b, 4a, 9–14 as well as 13:1; at this stage, Judah was still absent from the text, and it is only later with the addition of vv. 2b, 4a, and 6a, and even later vv. 5, 7, and 8, that Judah was introduced and its role was developed. Other scholars consider that Judah was already mentioned in the text's ancient core, especially in v. 5 and/or v. 6, but its place and role have been secondarily emphasized. Elliger (1951, 156–162) sees this core in vv. 1–2a, 3a, 4a, 5, 6b and 12:9–13:1, with Judah being mentioned originally in v. 5 only. According to Redditt (1995, 128), the original source (vv. 1–2a [perhaps with 2b], 3–4a, 5, and 8–9) already mentioned Judah in v. 5 and perhaps also in v. 2b; its role in war has been further stressed by a pro-Judahite revision in vv. 4b, 6–7; more recently, Redditt (2012a, 25, 102–104; 2012b, esp. 217–218) has also argued that the final redactor of Zech 9–14 has inserted vv. 7–8 to bridge the first part of ch. 12 with Zech 12:10–13:1. Willi-Plein (2007, 192–203) also thinks that the original composition (vv. 2–4a, 5–6, 9–11) already mentioned Judah in v. 2 and v. 5, but also in v. 6; the significance of its role has been further emphasized with the additions of vv. 4b and 7–8. Wöhrle's hypothesis (2008, 95–106) differs in including v. 4 within the text's ancient core (vv. 1–6*). According to Wöhrle, Judah was already mentioned in v. 2*, 4, and 6aα (but not v. 5). However, according to Wöhrle, the original role of Judah was not a positive one. Judah was first depicted as an enemy fighting with the nations against Jerusalem; it is only secondarily, with the additions of v. 6aβb and vv. 5, 7–8 (as well as על before יהודה in v. 2b), that Judah would have been turned into an ally of Jerusalem against the nations. From this

rately from Jerusalem in v. 2 as well as in v. 4, and that in the latter verse, the reference to the divine protection over Judah interrupts the announcement of the divine judgment over the nations.⁵⁵ And although this is less clear, v. 7 (with or without v. 8), and perhaps also v. 5 and v. 6, may well have been added in order to insist on the place and the role of Judah in the military protection of Jerusalem. This is a tempting hypothesis, which, if true, further supports the understanding that the text is fundamentally dealing with the fate of the city of Jerusalem, which is opposed to all the surrounding peoples. In this context, Judah's place and role are all but clear, to the point that Judah could be envisaged as belonging to the enemies. Hence the text, possibly secondarily, clarifies that Judah will support Jerusalem, at least before the end of the fight. Such a need for clarifying – secondarily or not – that Judah is or becomes Jerusalem's ally strengthens the difference between Judah and Jerusalem. It confirms that, even if Judah enjoys a special place and role (being Jerusalem's unique ally) in the text as it now stands, Judah nonetheless remains clearly distinct from Jerusalem, to the point that it can be treated more generally as one of the peoples of the land surrounding the city (albeit being a very close one).⁵⁶

Regardless of the precise process of composition of Zech 12:1–13:1, the ideological difference with Zech 9–10 is clear. While in Zech 9(–10) Jerusalem is the

---

overview, we can conclude that the verses that have the most chances to be secondary in Zech 12:1–13:1 (setting aside the double introduction in v. 1) are precisely the ones which emphasize the (rather positive) place and role of Judah during the battle, especially v. 4b (see also, e.g., Mitchell 1912, 323) and vv. 7(–8) – two verses that are written as a prophetic speech instead of a divine speech as in the surrounding context –, but perhaps also v. 2b, v. 5, and v. 6(a).
55 In fact, the two parallel phrases in the same verse בתמהון כל סוס אכה ("I will smite every horse with panic") and וכל סוס העמים אכה בעורון ("I will smite every horse of the peoples with blindness") may well indicate that the scribal technique of *Wiederaufnahme* has been used to introduce new material in the verse, especially pertaining to the role of Judah in the war.
56 *Pace*, e.g., Mason [1973] 2003, 148–153, who, despite acknowledging the possibility of a complex compositional process in Zech 12, overlooks the distinction between Jerusalem and Judah in the text. It is true that, in their current form, vv. 2–7 insist on a close relationship between Jerusalem and Judah. But this particular emphasis at least implies that both entities are distinct and that their relationship is not necessarily a close one – hence the need to specify it. The distinction between the "inhabitants of Jerusalem" and Judah should not come as a surprise, especially in light of historiographic and prophetic texts dealing with the monarchic period in particular but not exclusively; see 2 Kgs 23:2; Isa 5:3; 22:21; Jer 4:4; 11:2, 9, 12; 17:25; 18:11; 32:32; 35:13, 17; 36:31; Song 1:4; Dan 9:7; 2 Chr 20:15, 18, 20; 21:13; 32:33; 33:9; 34:9, 30; 35:18; see also the distinction between the city and "people of the country" (עם הארץ) in 2 Kgs 11:20; 24:14; 25:3). Although both belong to the kingdom of Judah, Jerusalem and Judah are two distinct entities that are united by the monarchy. However, as I will argue, the monarchy is absent in Zech 12.

center of a large territory, including not only Judah but also Ephraim and the entire Levant, the city stands basically alone in Zech 12:1–13:1, with Judah being the sole possible ally, which nonetheless remains somewhat distinct and separated from the city. In sum, Jerusalem functions primarily by itself in chs. 12–13; it is *no longer a territorial center*, to the point that even its relationship to Judah is a matter of discussion. This point is also confirmed by the fact that, unlike Zech 9–10, Zech 12:1–13:1 does not contain any emphasis on land possession after the war (nor before). Instead, the war leads to a great mourning over a pierced figure.

As I mentioned above, the house of David plays an important role in these chapters. This is especially the case in the battle and the subsequent rituals. Zechariah 12:8 goes as far as to state that, during the battle, under the protection of YHWH, "the stumbling one among the inhabitants of Jerusalem will be on that day like David, and the house of David will be like a divine being, like the messenger of YHWH before them."[57] Such a comparison of the house of David to a divine being, or even to God depending on how one translates כאלהים, could have been perceived as theologically problematic in antiquity. The LXX theologically smoothes out the text by reading "like the house of God" (ὡς οἶκος θεοῦ), and the Targum rather compares the house David to princes (כרברבין). Also, the additional comparison at the end of the verse, "like the messenger of YHWH before them" (כמלאך יהוה לפניהם), is often considered as a corrective theological gloss aiming at interpreting the first comparison (כאלהים) in way that avoids comparing the house of David to YHWH himself.[58] These possible attempts to slightly downplay the comparison are actually a sign of the prestigious status and the significant role of the house of David in the battle of ch. 12.

The importance of the house of David in Zech 12:8 has led several commentators to interpret this verse as announcing the restoration of the royal dynasty.[59] To be sure, as Petersen (1995, 119) emphasizes, Zech 12:8 is close to traditional royal ideology that presents the king as the son of the deity (see esp.

---

[57] Verse 8aβb: והיה הנכשל בהם ביום ההוא כדויד ובית דויד כאלהים כמלאך יהוה לפניהם.
[58] See, e.g., Elliger 1951, 164; Deissler 1988, 306; Lacocque 1988, 188; Reventlow 1993, 116; Mason 1998, 357; Nogalski 2011, 950.
[59] See Mitchell 1912, 326 ("hopes of the restoration of the dynasty"); Horst 1964, 255 (speaking about the ancient hope of a "Messias aus dem Davidischen Stamm"); Lamarche 1961, esp. 122, 151, 153, 156 ("un messianisme dynastique"); Amsler 1963, 60–61; Seybold 1972, 108 ("Hoffnung auf eine *Wiederkunft des goldenen davidischen Zeitalters*") and p. 109 (reading Zech 12:7-8 together with Zech 9:9–10); Laato 1992, 294 ("the fulfillment of hopes for the reestablishment of the Davidic dynasty"); Cook 1993, 461–462; 1995, 138 ("a millennial Davidic reign"; "an end-time Davidic ruler"); Petterson 2009, 218–224 (insisting on the connections between chs. 9 and 12 in order to envisage a Davidic king in Zech 12:8); Wolters 2014, 411 (following Petterson and reading in Zech 12:8 "a very bold affirmation of the continuing Davidic hopes").

Ps 2:7) or even calls him "god" (אלהים, Ps 45:7).[60] Also, even if it might be secondary, the expression "messenger of YHWH" recalls the expression "messenger of god" (מלאך [ה]אלוהים) which is sometimes applied to David in the books of Samuel in order to underscore his authority and righteousness (1 Sam 29:9; 2 Sam 14:17, 20; 19:28).[61] And in any case, this expression also seems to compare the house of David to a heavenly being (Elliger 1951, 164). In the martial context of Zech 12, the "messenger of YHWH" has the specific function of defending and delivering Jerusalem, as is also the case in the siege of Jerusalem in 2 Kgs 19:35 // Isa 37:36. He is similar to the "messenger of God" (מלאך האלהים) in Exod 14:19, who also goes "before" (לפני) the people of YHWH and protects them against the enemy.[62] Hence, while v. 8 underscores the strength that YHWH will give to the inhabitants of Jerusalem during the battle, it also emphasizes the crucial role of the house of David, which will lead the Jerusalemites to victory.[63]

A similar hierarchy could also be implied in vv. 7 and 10 as well as 13:1 (MT), where the house of David is always mentioned before the inhabitants of Jerusalem. In addition, the clan of the house of David (משפחת בית דויד, v. 12) is also the first mentioned in the short list of clans that will participate in the great ritual mourning over the pierced one after the battle. Also note that the Greek text of Zech 13:1 is entirely focused on the house of David. While the MT

---

60 *Pace*, in particular, Pomykala 1995, 121–123, who goes too far when stating: "Nowhere in the text of Zech 12:2–13:1 is there reference to the terminology and imagery associated with the davidic dynasty tradition" (p. 123).
61 Cf. Lamarche 1961, 77; Amsler 1963, 28, 60; Seybold 1972, 107–108; Rudolph 1976, 223; Smith 1984, 275; Petersen 1995, 118–120; Boda 2007, 123; 2016, 709. Leske (2000, 676) proposes a counterintuitive reading of Zech 12:8, critical towards the House of David, because he tries to read Zech 12 as a text which is consistently favorable to Judah vis-à-vis the Jerusalemites and the Davidides.
62 Cf. Mitchell 1912, 326; Lamarche 1961, 77. See also Judg 2:1–5, with the expression מלאך יהוה; the messenger of YHWH in Zech 12 is also similar to the commander of the army of YHWH (שר צבא יהוה) in Josh 5:14–15, fighting for Israel. As such, the relationship of the inhabitants of Jerusalem with the house of David is comparable to the relationship of Gideon with the messenger of YHWH (מלאך יהוה) in Josh 6: despite his military weakness, Gideon is ensured that he will have victory over the Midianites because the messenger of YHWH will be with him (Judg 6:15–16); cf. Smith 1984, 275.
63 This conclusion is further emphasized when v. 8 is read in light of v. 5. It implies that the strength of the inhabitants of Jerusalem comes from YHWH through the house of David, which will be like a heavenly being or messenger. Even Hanson (1979, 364–365), who considers Zech 12 to be composed by a visionary group opposed to the hierocratic Jerusalemite elites, is forced to recognize that v. 8 is quite positive regarding the Davidides and Jerusalemites; hence, he considers vv. 8–9 as belonging to a later hierocratic revision of a text which basically reflects the ideology of the visionary group – a rather complex reconstruction (see also Smith 1984, 276).

announces purity and prosperity for the house of David and the inhabitants of Jerusalem through the opening of a spring (מָקוֹר), the Greek text, which presupposes מָקוֹם (τόπος, "place") instead of מָקוֹר ("spring"), is quite shorter, indicating only that "every place shall be open for the house of David"; it does not contain any further indication, neither about the inhabitants of Jerusalem nor about purity.[64] In the Greek version, therefore, the focus of the verse seems to be on the free access to the temple for the house of David, or perhaps on its territorial possession, rather than on the purification of all the Jerusalemites (MT). The fact that the Greek reading is shorter is a possible indication of its greater antiquity compared to the MT's reading.[65] At the same time, the term מָקוֹם presupposed by the Greek text is perhaps a misreading or an interpretation of an original מָקוֹר, "spring."[66] It is possible, therefore, that a more ancient text mentioned a "spring" open to the house of David (only).[67] This could already be an allusion to purification, but more probably the term מָקוֹר was used here in its metaphorical meaning of "posterity" (see Ps 68:26; cf. Hos 13:15; Prov 5:18; Deut 33:28). This reading fits well with the collective designation of the "house of David" (בֵּית דָּוִיד; see below), as well as with the reference to the clan of the house of Nathan in v. 12, immediately following the mention of the clan of the house of David. As several commentators have argued, this clan could well be a Davidic clan, associated to Nathan, son of David (cf. 2 Sam 5:14; 1 Chr 3:5; 14:4; cf. Luke 3:31), in the same way that the clan of the Shimeites mentioned immediately after the clan of the house of Levi in v. 13 probably refers to a Levitical clan (Shimei being son of Gershom, son of Levi).[68] Hence, Zech 12:12–

---

[64] The Greek version reads: ἐν τῇ ἡμέρᾳ ἐκείνῃ ἔσται πᾶς τόπος διανοιγόμενος ἐν τῷ οἴκῳ Δαυιδ.

[65] Also, the reference to inhabitants of Jerusalem in the MT is best explained as a contextual harmonization with the rest of ch. 12, which consistently associated the house of David with the inhabitants of Jerusalem (vv. 7, 8, 10).

[66] Indeed, the LXX also displays an exegetical tendency, visible in the addition of the word πᾶς, "every/all," that has no corresponding term in the MT. This small interpretative (supplementing) change is perhaps due to the misreading of מָקוֹר, "spring," as מָקוֹם, "place," so as to clarify which "place" is referred to (i.e., "every place") when מָקוֹר is mistakenly read as מָקוֹם.

[67] The shorter, more ancient form of the verse than in the MT could have read: "On that day, a spring shall be open for the house of David" (יהיה ביום ההוא נפתח מקור לבית דויד).

[68] See, e.g., Meyers and Meyers 1993, 346–348; Biberger 2010, 288; Redditt 2012a, 112; Boda 2016, 719–720; 2017, 77–78. On the Shimeites, see the identical expression משפחת השמעי in Num 3:21; cf. Exod 6:17; Num 3:18; 1 Chr 6:2; 23:6–11. Other individuals called Shimei are mentioned in the Bible, but they do not represent clans. Regarding the clan of the house of Nathan, another possibility would be that Zech 12:12 refers to a clan associated with the figure of Nathan the prophet by the time of David; see in this direction Ulrich 2010, who reads the clans of Zech 12:12–14 as referring to the time of David and Salomon; however, this suggestion does not explain well the mention of Levi.

14 apparently insists on the lineage of the houses of David and Levi (cf. Boda 2017, 76–78), and it is quite possible that an ancient form of 13:1 further emphasized the posterity of David, and thus, its continuation and the future importance of his house.[69] This notion would be quite similar to that of Jer 33:14–26, which also insists on Davidic posterity and its significance, together with the Levitical line (see especially v. 22).[70] In any case, the LXX shows that Zech 12:1–13:1 could be read in antiquity with a greater emphasis on the significance of the house of David, in association with cult, territory, or (more probably) posterity.

Hence, it appears that the house of David is given a form of leadership with military as well as ritual functions. These roles contrast with the depiction of the king in Zech 9:9–10, who has no military function[71] and inaugurates a time of prosperity instead of leading a ritual mourning. Plus, what is striking in Zech 12:1–13:1 is that the text never explicitly announces a king nor even some kind of individual leadership, contrary to Zech 9:9–10. Indeed, even if we accept that the text is concerned with the posterity of the clan of David, no particular figure from this clan is singled out (contrary to Jer 33:14–26). Should we conclude, therefore, as for instance Cook (1993, 462) does, that "This emphasis on the house of David in ch. 12 hints at the hope for a Davidic king, although this is not explicit"?[72] A central problem with this line of interpretation is that it does not explain why the text is not explicit in announcing a Davidic king.

---

69 This reading would make good sense if some groups were still claiming to be royal descendants at the time of the composition of the text. First Chronicles 3 attests a concern for the continuation of the Davidic line until well into the Persian period (and even in the early Hellenistic period according to the LXX); the Davidic genealogy of Jesus in Matt 1 and Luke 3 even reaches the Roman period; see already in this direction Mitchell 1912, 326; Sellin 1930, 572–573; Plöger 1962, 104–105; Rudolph 1976, 223; cf. Rückl 2016, 230; and note that even in Medieval times, some Jews were claiming to be Davidic descendants, see Franklin 2012; *pace* the allegorical interpretations of the house of David, such as Chary 1969, 199 ("il faut l'entendre comme désignant les chefs en général, la classe dirigeante plutôt que la famille davidique proprement dite").
70 Jeremiah 33:14–26 revises the promise of a Davidic king in Jer 23:5–6 in a way that emphasizes the continuation and the fecundity of the clans of David and Levi (see esp. v. 22). Note that both Zech 12:1–13:1 and Jer 33:14–26 could well date from the early Hellenistic period; on the former, see the argument below; on the latter (absent in the LXX), see, e.g., Lange 2012 and other references with the discussion in Gonzalez 2021, 295–297.
71 In this sense, the military role of the house of David in Zech 12 is closer to the role of the Judean leaders during the battle in Zech 10:4–5.
72 Somewhat differently, see also Smith 1984, who, despite acknowledging that "[n]o personal Messiah is singled out in this passage" (p. 276), still postulates the presence of a specific individual leader: "The house of David, probably represented by a prince or a governor, would regain its leadership role" (p. 275).

As W. Nowack (1922, 392) already observed, the particularity of Zech 12–13 is to use consistently and exclusively the collective designation "house of David," בית דויד, with no mention of an individual royal leader.[73] In addition, the "house of David" is consistently associated to the "inhabitant(s) of Jerusalem" (י[ו]שב[י] ירושלם) – in Zech 12:7, 8, 10 and 13:1 (MT), the only exception being in the Greek text of the latter verse. It is all the more remarkable that the two expressions never appear together in the Hebrew Bible. Thus, an important point of the passage is to insist on the close relationship between the house of David and the city of Jerusalem. Although this specific accent sounds rather traditional, it makes good sense in a context where Judah is distinguished from Jerusalem. It implies that the authority of the house of David is basically restricted to Jerusalem and does not extend beyond it over the region of Judah.

This is especially clear in the military domain. Although in the present form of the text v. 8 insists on the preeminence of the house David and the inhabitants of Jerusalem during the battle, v. 7 makes clear that the role of Judah at war is no less important and honorific.[74] In the ritual domain, one may wonder whether the authority of the house of David could extend more largely than

---

[73] See also Wellhausen 1963, 199 ("einen Einzelnen David, einen König giebt es nicht mehr"); Mitchell 1912, 241; Chary 1954, 230 ("Elle [= la Maison de David] reste une entitée collective indéterminée"); Pomykala 1995, 117–120, adding several arguments in favor of collective representation of the house of David in Zech 12:1–13:1 (see p. 121: "nothing is asserted about an individual"); Willi-Plein 2007, 198 ("Vorausgesetzt ist also für Jerusalem nicht ein davidischer König, wohl aber eine Gruppe von Funktionsträgern, die sich genealogisch auf die Davidslinie zurückführen"); Rose 2012, 223–224 ("we are not dealing with an individual, but with a collective: the 'house of David'").

[74] The literary relationship between v. 7 and v. 8 is disputed. Based especially on formal grounds, several scholars think that they both belong to a single addition to the text: they are both written as a prophetic speech instead of divine speech as in the surrounding context; see, e.g., Elliger 1951, 158; Willi-Plein 2007, 194, 198–199; Wöhrle 2008, 101–102; Redditt 2012a, 25, 102–104; 2012b, esp. 217–218. At the same time, their content reflects different orientations. While v. 7 insists on the significance of Judah, v. 8 emphasizes the importance of the Jerusalemites and the Davidides more particularly. It is true that these ideological accents are not mutually exclusive, such that we cannot exclude that they come from a single scribe, but they are nonetheless quite distinct. Since the text has probably been revised with a stronger Judean orientation (see above), it is tempting to think that v. 7 is part of this revising process, aiming in particular at counterbalancing the preeminence of Jerusalem emphasized in v. 8; cf. Saebø 1969, 273–274; Lutz 1968, 13; Rudolph 1976, 222–223 (arguing that v. 7 was originally located after v. 8); Biberger 2010, 310; *pace* Hanson 1979, 364–365, who think that v. 8 revises vv. 1–7, and Smith 1984, 276. Given its form (a prophetic speech), the latter verse could also be secondary, but note that its content fits quite well with the Jerusalemite focus of the core of the passage. Especially within a section like Zech 9–14 which is inspired by various traditions and literary forms, a purely formal change does not necessarily imply a different scribe (cf. Mitchell 1912, 324–325, arguing against the secondary character of vv. 7–8).

Jerusalem. The great mourning led by the Davidides might not only include Jerusalemite clans but also Judean clans, as the mention of the land (הארץ) that will mourn (v. 12) and the phrase "all the remaining clans" (כל המשפחות הנשארות, v. 14) suggest (Boda 2016, 711). Still, the ritual is explicitly associated with Jerusalem and its population, but never with Judah (cf. Leske 2000, 677). In v. 10, the mourning is introduced by the outpouring of a "spirit of grace and supplication over the house of David and over the inhabitant of Jerusalem" and it is also specifically located in Jerusalem in v. 11. In addition, this ritual leads in 13:1 to an improved situation for the house of David and, in the MT, the inhabitants of Jerusalem, without any mention of Judean clans. Therefore, even if this ritual might include Judean clans, we can conclude that it mainly concerns the city of Jerusalem.

The fact that the house of David is basically deprived from any authority outside Jerusalem is consistent with the distinction between Jerusalem and Judah in Zech 12:1–13:1. Contrary to the situation in Zech 9–10, Jerusalem is not the center of a specific territory. Logically, therefore, the house of David is not given any territorial rule (contrary to Zech 9:10 especially) – although in 13:1 the Greek (mis)reading "place" (presupposing מקום) instead of "spring" (מקור) might add a territorial dimension. And in this context, the absence of an individual figure of domination, such as a king, does not come as a surprise. The house of David is given *a collective form of leadership which is basically restricted to the city of Jerusalem and which includes especially military and ritual roles; but it is not given any other political role, royal in particular.*[75]

Defending a messianic reading of Zech 12, several scholars emphasize that the text actually does mention an individual figure who plays an important role: the pierced one in v. 10, for whom the community will greatly mourn after the battle, clan by clan, and men and women separately (12:11–14).[76] In addition,

---

[75] To some extent, the limitation of the authority of the house of David can be compared to the restricted role attributed to the Davidic "prince" (נשיא) in Ezek 40–48, a section that avoids referring to a "king" (מלך, contrary to Ezek 37:22, 24). In Ezek 40–48, however, this leadership is not collective but rather individual, and with a greater ritual authority over all Israel. Laato also proposes a connection between Zech 9–14 and Ezekiel, especially chs. 40–48, which limit the role of the "prince": both texts display a criticism against the royal house. However, Laato (1992, 281–283, 294, 300) still believes that "[w]hile the Zadokite party modified the Ezekelian vision in Ezek 40–48 by restricting the role of the *nāśî'* in the cult, the religious group which is responsible for Zech 9–14 remained loyal to the Zecharianic (i.e. Ezekelian) messianic hopes concerning the coming righteous Messiah as we have seen in Zech 9:9–10" (p. 282). He fails to see how Zech 9–14 also transforms traditional royal ideology.

[76] See esp. Lamarche 1961, 115–157; Chary 1969, 140–141, 200–207; Rudolph 1976, 223–224; Reventlow 1993, 117; Duguid 1995, 275–276; Laato 1992, 290–294; 1997, 217; Petterson 2009, esp. 237–245. In general, these scholars interpret the pierced one in Zech 12:10 as being the

they emphasize the royal traits of this figure. The expression "in the valley of Megiddo" (בבקעת מגדו[ן]) is found elsewhere in the Hebrew Bible only in 2 Chr 35 (v. 22), which depicts the battle that led to the death of king Josiah, mortally wounded by an arrow. Also, this text highlights the lament composed by Jeremiah for the king's death, a well-known and influential lament among funeral

---

("good") shepherd of Zech 11:4–14 (in conflict with his flock), and/or the shepherd struck by the sword in Zech 13:9. This identification is not impossible, but it should also be observed that the three passages have different images and associations. In Zech 11:4–14, the prophet-shepherd is not struck. Both Zech 12:10 and 13:9 have the image of a central figure who is pierced or struck by the sword, but Zech 12:10 does not use the shepherd motif, and the consequences of this event are not exactly the same in the two texts. In Zech 12:10–13:1, it leads to a great mourning of the community and, in the MT – but not in the LXX (see above) –, purification through spring water in Jerusalem. In Zech 13:7–9, the striking of the shepherd leads to a drastic judgment on the flock, followed by purification through fire. By contrast, some scholars do not envisage a specific individual in Zech 12:10. For instance, Sweeney (2000, 689–691) reads "what they have pierced" in v. 10 as referring to those who are slain among the nations. Against this view, note that YHWH participates actively in killing the assailants (v. 9), so that this is hardly the reason for the penitential attitude of the community. According to Floyd (2000, 524–525, 528), Zech 12:10 refers more broadly to the battle casualties in both camps of the war. However, the description does not mention any Judean or Jerusalemite wounded, and it rather emphasizes the exceptional strength of Judah and Jerusalem as well as the assistance of YHWH during the battle (vv. 4–9). Other scholars propose collective interpretations of the pierced figure. Mitchell (1912, 331) understands it as the "godly persons who have perished by violence," similarly to the Suffering Servant of Isa 53 who represents the community. Hanson also follows this direction in arguing in light of passages in Trito-Isaiah (e.g., 57:13; 66:5–16) that the visionary group behind Zech 12 identifies itself with the victim (Hanson 1979, 365–366, cf. pp. 66–67; see also Mason [1973] 2003, 161–165). Leske (2000) and Lacocque (1988, 190–192) have a similar reading, identifying this group more broadly with the population of Judah oppressed by the Jerusalemites. Zechariah 12 may have conceptual similarities with Isa 53, but this interpretation is mainly based on texts from Isaiah rather than on Zech 12, the latter giving no particular indication in favor of a collective meaning (cf. Larkin 1994, 167–169; Stiglmair 1994, 56–57; cf. Balwin 1972, 194, emphasizing that Zech 12 does not identify the pierced one with the Suffering Servant). On the contrary, the literary context suggests the piercing of an individual (see esp. 11:17; 13:3, 9). Although the reference to the "only" (יחיד) and "firstborn" (בכור) son in v. 11 are images that serve to emphasize the idea of a great loss (cf. Sweeney 2000, 688), they tend to support reading a reference to the death of an individual. In this sense, the interpretation of Petersen (1995, 121), which envisages a child sacrifice during the war, similarly to the one in 2 Kgs 3:27, is closer to the text, albeit perhaps too literal, since the two terms do not aim at describing directly the dead but rather the magnitude of the mourning. See below n. 84 against the interpretation of YHWH as being the one figuratively "pierced." Although I argue in favor of the pierced one as being an individual, I will not comment here on past identifications of the pierced one with historical figures (see a list already in Mitchell 1912, 330–331, or Chary 1969, 202–203), which are as numerous as they are speculative (cf. Wöhrle 2008, 104 n. 124). I rather understand the pierced one as a figure combining royal and prophetic traits (see below).

singers, both male and female, which would have been preserved through writing (v. 25).[77] Hence, it is quite possible that Zech 12:11 alludes to the mourning for the death of Josiah, as the Peshitta and the Targum make explicit, and especially as the context emphasizes the importance of the house of David.[78]

On this basis, and given that Zech 9 announces the restoration of monarchy, scholars like Laato (1992, 290–294) or Petterson (2009, esp. 237–239) conclude that Zech 12 also announces a future king or Messiah. However, these scholars overlook the text's central point regarding this particular figure: he is clearly *deceased*.[79] As a result, he can play no active role in the leadership of the community into the future. In marked contrast to Zech 9 which envisages an ideal royal leader in the future, Zech 12 insists that the ideal individual leader of the community will firmly belong in the past.[80] This notion is consistent with the

---

[77] Cf., e.g., Mitchell 1912, 331–332; Duguid 1995, 275–276; see also, e.g., Baldwin 1972, 193, or Sweeney 2000, 689–691 even if they do not interpret the pierced one as a royal figure.
[78] Cf. Laato 1992, 291, 293–294; Petterson 2009, 233–234.
[79] Cf. Mason [1973] 2003, 161; Rudolph 1976, 160, 213–215, 223–224; Larkin 1994, 169.
[80] Cf. Mitchell 1912, 330; Biberger 2010, 287. Laato (1992), who emphasizes that the death of the pierced one in the valley of Megiddo (Zech 12:10) alludes to king Josiah, goes as far as to speak about a "Josiah Redivivus" (e.g., p. 296). However, the possible allusion to Josiah in Zech 12:10 precisely serves to recall and emphasize the death of a royal figure rather than his new coming to life. In order to maintain an active messianic figure after the war, Laato (1992, 300) also suggests that the reinvigoration of the Davidic house described in Zech 12:8 could be a consequence of the outpouring of the spirit in Zech 12:10–13:1; see also Lamarche 1961, 122, 156, who admits that the text does not speak about the resurrection of the Messiah, but he still suggests that Zech 12:8 could perhaps envisage a form of resurrection of the Davidic dynasty. However, the mourning over the pierced one is clearly set after the war, contrary to the positive depiction of the house of David in Zech 12:8 (see the announcement of the end of the battle in v. 9). The suggestion of Otzen 1964, 180–182, that Zech 12:10 refers to a cultic ritual of death and resurrection is too far-fetched, and in any case, the text does mention any resurrection of the pierced one. Duguid is more subtle in defending a messianic perspective in Zech 10–14, suggesting that the announcement of the death of the bad shepherd in Zech 11:17, together with the allusions to Ezek 34 and Jer 23 in Zech 11 (and 10:3), can imply that YHWH will provide a new Davidic king: "The last word is not judgment upon God's people but woe to the worthless shepherd (v. 17), which brings with it at least the hope that a return to the promises of Ezekiel 34 and Jeremiah 23 is possible" (Duguid 1995, 273–274). However, Duguid overlooks what he himself argues: the promises of Ezek 34 and Jer 23 are reversed in Zech 11 (see p. 273), and the "Messiah" is pierced in Zech 12:10 and 13:9 (pp. 275–276). Similarly, Boda (2017, 76, and more generally 76–78) notes the text's emphasis on the continuation of the Davidic and Levitical lines as well as "consistent echoes to key Davidic prophecies from Jeremiah and Ezekiel" in Zech 11. On this basis, he suggests that, despite a change of perspective in Zech 11–14 compared to Zech 9–10, the hope for a renewed Davidic kingship is not abandoned in Zech 11–14. In doing so, Boda overlooks how Zech 11 reverses ancient Davidic promises (as he demonstrates himself in Boda 2003, 284–287), and that Zech 12 does not mention any king nor an individual active leader, referring rather collectively to clans (in this respect, Zech 12

following war scene in ch. 14, which never speaks about a future human king.[81] The influence of this leader on the community can continue, but only through his memory, which will be recalled by means of ritual commemoration. This aspect is especially clear in the description of the great ritual mourning for the pierced one, which gathers the community clan by clan (vv. 12–14). The commemoration of the past leader brings together and ritually organizes the community. Hence, rather than envisaging the community being united under the leadership of an individual royal figure, the text emphasizes that the community will be united via ritual practice that commemorates past leadership.[82]

In addition, the pierced one not only has royal traits, but also prophetic ones, as Meyers and Meyers (1993, 338–349) argue. To be sure, both aspects are not antithetical, but scholars who defend messianic ideas in Zech 12 generally

---

seems to depart from Jer 33). Also, in identifying the shepherd of Zech 11:4–14 with a Davidic descendant, Boda (2003, 286–288) overplays the relationship to Ezek 34 and 37, introducing an idea that is not stated – at least explicitly – in Zech 11. In general, scholars who read Zech 12:1–13:1 as a messianic text seem to be influenced by the Christian view on the death of the Messiah (cf. John 19:37), which sees it as temporary only (see for instance Lamarche 1961, 156, speaking about resurrection, or Petterson 2009, 226, on Christian interpretation). Petterson argues that there are also messianic readings of this passage in the Jewish tradition, especially concerning the Messiah son of Joseph/Ephraim (2009, 226–227; cf., e.g., Gordon 2003). However, even in this Jewish interpretation, the Messiah dies and cannot be active anymore. His death can be interpreted as preparing the arrival of another Messiah (son of David), but in any case, Zech 12–14 never refers to a scenario of this kind; this clearly reflects a later interpretation. Instead of a new leader, Zech 12 emphasizes the loss of a leader.

81 *Pace* Petterson 2009, 237–245, who argues that the emphasis on the kingship of YHWH in Zech 14:9, 16–17 implies the presence of a human king in Jerusalem; p. 245: "Rather than seeing the hope for a coming Davidic king being eclipsed by the hope for Yahweh to be the king, ch. 14 continues to hold out a strong hope for a future king in the line of David by portraying the outcome and fruit of his death"; see also Chary 1969, 141, on Zech 14: "Dans le plan actuel, cette action est comprise comme l'œuvre du messie, bien que celui-ci n'apparaisse plus et que l'action interne du chapitre soit menée par Yahweh seul." Petterson and Chary are right in not *a priori* opposing divine and human kingship. Yet, not only do they not explain why Zech 14 would not be explicit about human kingship, but they also completely overlook a central aspect of Zech 12:1–13:1 (as well as in Zech 13:7–9): the sole (human) individual leader is deceased, and the text never announces his replacement by another figure except YHWH.

82 The importance given to the memory of past leadership is also visible in the names of the clans, which refer to ancient figures, especially David and Levi. The fact that the clan of the house of Levi and the clan of Shimeites – most probably a small Levitical clan (see above) – are specially mentioned further stresses the importance of cultic rituals in addition to the significance of the royal house; note, however, that the Syriac tradition does not mention the clan of the house of Levi. The specific (and unexpected) mention of Shimeites, a secondary clan which, unlike the other clans, is not presented as a "house" (בית), could perhaps reflect the identity of the group that developed Zech 9–14; cf. Gonzalez 2017, 70.

overlook this important dimension of the text. The piercing (verb דקר), as well as the mourning it provokes, similar to the one for the death of a unique or firstborn child (Zech 12:10), recall the piercing of prophets by their own parents announced in the following section with the same rare verb דקר (Zech 13:3). Also, the mourning of Hadad Rimmôn in Zech 12:11 could well allude to prophetic rituals. Most commentators nowadays understand that it refers to fertility rituals for the Syrian storm god Hadad who was also called *Rammānu*, "the thunderer," vocalized *Rimmôn* in Hebrew, as 2 Kgs 5:18 attests (see Greenfield 1999, 381).[83] First Kings 18 similarly describes penitential rituals of fertility associated with prophets of the storm-god Baal on Mount Carmel, which is close to the valley of Megiddo. Moreover, not unlike the false prophets of Zech 13:6 who have injuries (מכות), the prophets of Baal in 1 Kgs 18 are presented as harming themselves with swords and spears (v. 28). Zechariah 12–13 therefore opposes the death of the pierced one and the mourning it will provoke (Zech 12:10–14) to the death of the false prophets and their penitential rituals (Zech 13:2–6). Thereby, the text suggests that the pierced figure is, contrary to the prophets mentioned in Zech 13:2–6, a true prophet of YHWH. This reading explains well the use of the first person pronoun to refer to the pierced one in the context of a divine speech (והביטו אלי, "they will look at *me*"). It is quite possible that the text mixes here divine and prophetic voices, as is also the case in Zech 11 (see vv. 10 and 13), the idea being that YHWH can be identified with his prophet.[84] Also, the prophetic dimension of the pierced one is consistent with the

---

83 Cf., e.g., Mason [1973] 2003, 165–166; Lacocque 1988, 184, 190; Meyers and Meyers 1993, 343; Stiglmair 1994, 454–455. The interpretation of Hadad Rimmôn as a place name is still sometimes defended (see Petterson 2009, 233; cf., e.g., Rudolph 1976, 224–225), but this interpretation tries to bypass the problem of the mention of a Canaanite deity. It is difficult to believe that scribes would have written such a name without noticing that the passage could be read as referring to a lamentation for a fertility god – a tradition they most probably knew (cf. 1 Kgs 18; 2 Kgs 5:18). Also, the emendations that have been proposed to make Zech 12:11 theologically less problematic (e.g., Delcor 1953, 67–72) are conjectural and do not really explain how such a reading could have developed and could have been preserved (as Delcor 1953, 72, himself acknowledges; see also against Delcor's emendation Hoftijzer 1953, and Baldwin 1972, 193).

84 Commentators have often proposed reading the first person pronoun in אלי as a third person, אליו (see already Stade 1881, 34, or Redditt 2012a, 106–107), a reading which is already attested in antiquity (see, e.g., the Lucianic text or John 19:37), and which facilitates interpretation; others simply remove the personal pronoun (אל, see, e.g., Elliger 1951, 156; Pomykala 1995, 117); see also the different readings of this verse listed by Deissler 1998, 50–52. However, the first person pronoun in the MT is supported by the main witnesses (LXX, Peshitta, Targum, Vulgate) and it is the most difficult reading; cf. Delcor 1951a, 192; Saebø 1969, 96–102; Rudolph 1976, 116–118; Deissler 1998, 54. Hence, the pierced one can only be YHWH or a representative that is identified with him. Some scholars hold the view that the piercing is a figurative one, directly against YHWH; in particular, Delcor (1951a) reads the verb דקר in v. 10 similarly to the

presentation of the community receiving YHWH's spirit of grace and supplication (v. 10; cf. v. 1b). Hence, the death of the pierced one can be interpreted as the loss of a leader that has not only royal traits but also prophetic ones.[85] As such, the text can be read as announcing that at some point after the sayings of Zechariah, royal as well as prophetic leadership will belong to the past; and it is memory alone that will allow this past leadership to be present within the community, especially through ritual commemoration.[86]

---

synonym verb חלל in Ezek 36:23, which says that the name of YHWH has been profaned; see in a similar direction Gaide 1968, 119–120; Otzen 1964, 178–179; Becker 1980, 72–73; Stiglmair 1994; Larkin 1994, 162–170 envisaging "a figure strongly identified with God, perhaps a kingly/ divine figure" [170]; Boda 2016, 716–717. Although some connections can be observed between Ezek 36 and Zech 12–13 (see also Larkin 1994, 161–163), this metaphorical reading is problematic because, *pace* Delcor's argument (1951a, esp. 193), the root דקר always has a clear physical connotation (even when hunger is involved, as in Lam 4:9); and when Prov 12:18 compares rash words with "piercings by sword" (כמדקרות חרב), the comparison works precisely because of the plain physical meaning of the root. Hence, on the contrary, it can be argued that the verb דקר is used in Zech 12:10 to leave no doubt about the reference to a physical piercing (cf. Mitchell 1912, 330; Lacocque 1988, 190; Meyers and Meyers 1993, 337–340; Duguid 1995, 276; see also Hoftijtzer 1953, 407–408). The immediate context of Zech 12:10 also confirms this literal meaning, especially as Zech 13:3 describes the piercing of a false prophet with the same verb (cf. also Zech 11:17; 13:9). In addition, it is the name of YHWH which is profaned in Ezek 36:23, contrary to Zech 12:10, where it is YHWH or his representative – despite later midrashim which introduce the idea of the divine name. Hence, Zech 12:10 most probably refers to the piercing of one of YHWH's representatives, especially if the verse switches from divine to prophetic speech.

85 Note that, by changing the prophet into a shepherd, Zech 11 already combines the prophetic and royal roles. To a certain extent, these different aspects of the pierced one can be compared to the various traits of the figure of the Servant in Deutero-Isaiah, who can also take on a royal dimension (e.g., in 44:26–28) and a prophetic one (e.g., in ch. 50) – I thank Christophe Nihan for this observation. This is why scholars have proposed prophetic as well as royal interpretations of this figure; see for instance the different interpretations presented already by Coppens 1974, 70–72. While the royal traits that the high priest acquires in post-monarchic traditions have often been observed (see, e.g., Nihan and Rhyder 2018 on Aaron's vestments in Exod 28), a similar phenomenon apparently also influenced the construction of prophetic figures in the absence of local monarchy – something which deserves further investigation.

86 I have proposed along these lines that the text could more specifically refer to the death of the prophet Zechariah, to whom the oracles of Zech 9–14 are attributed (at least in the present of form of the book), so as to illustrate the end of YHWH's prophets after the death of Zechariah (cf. Zech 13:2–6, and see also 1:5; Malachi is rather an original figure, a divine messenger pointing also to an end of classical prophecy) and also the persecution of the prophets of YHWH – a tradition that developed during the Second Temple period (cf. 1 Kgs 19:10; 2 Chr 24:19–21; Matt 5:12; Acts 7:52). Note that the phrase "they will look at me whom they pierced" seems to mix the divine voice with the prophetic voice which, in the context of the book, is the voice of Zechariah (Gonzalez 2013, 32–35). In that case, the reference to the death of the prophet Zechariah, using royal associations, would serve to emphasize that the time of the

To summarize, Zech 12:1–13:1 proposes a radically different concept of royal leadership than Zech 9–10. For Zech 9, the role of an individual royal figure remains essential in order to guarantee the independence of all Israel on a large Levantine territory, maintain peace on earth and exemplify Yahwistic piety. Zechariah 12–13, by contrast, envisages the collective leadership of the house of David in specific domains, especially the military and ritual ones, and in an area that is basically restricted to the city of Jerusalem. When it comes to the idea of an individual who might lead the community, Zech 12:1–13:1 only refers to a leader with both royal and prophetic traits, who will be located in the past, and whose commemoration will serve to unify and ritually organize the community. These different concepts of leadership correspond to different ways of envisaging the community. Zechariah 9–10 presents a large and inclusive community – including especially Jerusalem, Judah and Ephraim, but also more broadly the Levantine nations – that will be politically independent on a large territory with Jerusalem as its capital city. Instead, Zech 12:1–13:1 has a limited community which basically corresponds to the city of Jerusalem and which is primarily focused on ritual practice. In the latter passage, the absence of a future king is consistent with the absence of territory belonging to Jerusalem; even Judah remains somewhat apart from the city.

3 The Utopia of Political Independence and its Revision during the Early Hellenistic Period

In the present form of the book of Zechariah, Zech 12:1–13:1 marginalizes the ideal painted in Zech 9–10, one of territorial possession and political independence under the leadership of a royal figure in Jerusalem. Although Zech 12:1–13:1 envisages some form of restoration for the house of David, especially with prominent military and ritual roles, it also limits the sphere of authority of the house of David, and it depicts the restored community as being united through ritual and commemoration of past leadership rather than under the rule of a royal leader.

---

kings and the prophets will come to an end after Zechariah, who represents the last classical prophet, will die in a way that recalls the death of the last good king, Josiah. In any case, in addition to alluding to past royal leadership, the great mourning in Zech 12:10–14 also seems to develop the traditions (well attested in ancient Judaism) of the persecution of YHWH's prophets and of the end of classical prophecy in order to emphasize the authority of the past prophets, the importance of their memory, and indirectly also the authority of prophetic literature which preserves their memory.

As several scholars have argued, the change of perspective in the book between Zech 9–10 and Zech 12(–14) is supported by the negative images in Zech 11.[87] This chapter contains images that play with the shepherd-flock metaphor and clearly depart from the utopian restoration in Zech 9–10:
- While Zech 9:16–17 and 10:7–10 emphasize fertility in the land, Zech 11:1–3 announces upheaval, fire, and drought.
- While YHWH takes care of his flock in Zech 9:16 and 10:3b, Zech 11:4–14 describe the flock as doomed to slaughter (צאן ההרגה, vv. 4, 7); the flock is even abandoned and cursed by the prophet-shepherd who has been commissioned by YHWH (vv. 8–9).
- While in Zech 9:1–10 the Levant is unified, pacified, and protected by YHWH following his conquest, Zech 11:6 announces war involving kings; and the divine covenant with the nations is broken (11:10).
- While Zech 9–10 articulates the close relationship between Judah and Ephraim (9:10, 13) and envisages the successful gathering of all Israel in its land (9:11–12; 10:6–12; cf. 9:1b), Zech 11 announces conflicts in the land (v. 6) and also within the flock (v. 9b), and v. 13 explicitly articulates the division between Judah and Israel.
- While Zech 9:9–10 envisages a pious and peaceful ruler, Zech 11:15–16 announces a bad shepherd that will abuse the flock.

The interpretation of Zech 11 has been discussed extensively,[88] and limitations of space prevent me from entering into further detail here. The important point is that the ideal promoted in Zech 9–10, that of an Israel united in a large, fertile territory, free from foreign oppression and politically independent, is completely opposed by the negative depictions and oracles of ch. 11.[89] Petterson (2009,

---

[87] See esp. Rudolph 1976, 161–162, 241–243; Steck 1991, 37–39; Willi-Plein 2007, 190–191; Foster 2007, 752–753; Wenzel 2011, 226–230, 270–274; Redditt 2012a, 78–79, 87, 91–92; Boda 2003, 288–291; 2016, 654.
[88] See a review of earlier interpretations in Foster 2007, 736–743.
[89] This reversal in ch. 11 is already anticipated within Zech 9–10 by Zech 10:1–3a, which recalls the drama of the exile and also announces a punitive intervention of YHWH using the shepherd-flock imagery; cf. Elliger 1951, 134, 144–145; Tigchelaar 1996, 92–94; Kunz 1998, 47–50; Boda 2003, 290; 2017; Redditt 2012a, 24–25, 70–72. Wöhrle 2008, 85–86, also considers this passage as having a special relationship with ch. 11*, but he attributes it to his *Grundschicht* of Deutero-Zechariah: Zech 9:1aα; 10:1–3a; 11:1–5, 7, 8b, 9–17; 12:1a; 13:7–9. While Wöhrle convincingly argues that the passages against the shepherds in Zech 9–14 belong to a single literary layer, the fact that in the present form of the text they anticipate and help to structure important ideological changes in Zech 12–14 *vis-à-vis* Zech 9–10 rather suggests that this layer is secondary, at least later than Zech 9–10* (and possibly also than Zech 12:1–13:1*).

171–191), following Meyers and Meyers (1993, esp. 300–303), argues that ch. 11 does not contradict earlier hopes because it mainly refers to dramatic situations in Israel's past, especially the divisions between Judah and Israel after Solomon as well as the Babylonian destruction and exile. Meyers and Meyers and Petterson are probably correct that Zech 11 contains allusions to past situations, but not all the dramas depicted in ch. 11 refer to the past only, as they recognize it themselves in the case of vv. 15–16. And even granting their hypothesis, the question would remain: Why allude to and insist on the dramatic past after having announced a glorious future? In Zech 11, the function of alluding to dramas in the past is not to say that they are over and only belong to the past. Even Petterson as well as Meyers and Meyers, who interpret Zech 11:4–14 as a retrospective on the history of Israel, admit that this retrospective is connected to the present and the immediate future of the community, since they consider that it has the function of explaining the crisis that the community endures before its great restoration.[90] Hence, while Zech 11 might allude to past dramas, the function of such an allusion is to suggest that further dramas may well happen again to the community; recalling a dramatic past serves to envision a dramatic future.[91] Note that Zech 9–10 also contains allusion to the past. However, the past which is alluded to is a different, quite positive one, corresponding to the positive future envisaged: Zech 9:10, which quotes the royal Psalm 72, alludes to the ancient Davidic kingdom, as mentioned above; Zech 9:11–12 seems to allude to the return of the exiles during the Persian period in order to promote the continuation of this return;[92] or Zech 10:8 alludes to a past in which the sons of Ephraim were numerous so as to announce their great number in the future.[93] Hence, while both Zech 9–10 and Zech 11 allude to the past, the past situations they recall are very distinct, because they envisage the future in quite different ways.

In addition, it has been observed that although Zech 11 and Zech 12:1–13:1 have quite distinct perspectives, the ideal announced in the latter fits more with the doom oracles of ch. 11 than Zech 9–10 does.[94] The fact that Ephraim or

---

[90] See, e.g., Meyers and Meyers 1993, 300: "this narrative derives its creative momentum from the prophet's looking to the past in light of its present."
[91] See, e.g., Duguid 1995, 280: "Those who fail to learn from past history of Israel will be doomed to repeat it."
[92] See the formulation with the perfect form שלחתי in v. 11, "I have set free," referring to the past, most probably the early Persian return from exile. It is followed in v. 12 by an imperative form שובו, "return," switching to a near future.
[93] The past situation probably refers to Josh 17:14–18; see the literary parallel between Zech 10:10 and Josh 17:16 emphasizing the lack of space; cf. Lee 2015, 220–222; Boda 2016, 631–632.
[94] Rudolph 1976, 161–162, 242–243; Steck 1991, 37–39; Boda 2003, 290–291; 2016, 25; Redditt 2012a, 93–94.

Joseph is no longer mentioned in chs. 12–14 is consistent with the division between Israel and Judah announced in 11:14. Also, the attack by all the nations against Jerusalem in chs. 12 (and 14) makes sense in light of the rupture of the divine covenant with the nations in 11:10. In addition, the absence of the notion of a large territory depending on Jerusalem as well as the absence of an ideal human king in Zech 12(–14) and the emphasis on the loss of an ideal leader (12:10–14) correspond well with the announcement of bad shepherds in Zech 11 (see esp. vv. 4–5 and 15–16). As such, Zech 11 prepares the change of ideal promoted in Zech 12–14, an ideal which, contrary to Zech 9–10, no longer emphasizes territorial possession and political independence centered around Jerusalem, but rather ritual aspects in Jerusalem.

In past research, this change of ideal – when observed – has been explained in terms of the use of different sources by a redactor, or successive additions and revisions in Zech 9–14 or the book of Zechariah. Perhaps a redactor used different sources (see esp. Redditt 1994, 673–675; 2012a, 20–26, 147–149), but it remains unclear why he would have done so, especially in a way that clearly displays different perspectives. In addition, this hypothesis does not explain the terminological and thematic connections between the different sources nor the origin of these sources (see Gonzalez 2015, 124–126, on Redditt's model). The model of successive additions and revisions, which considers that chs. 9–14 (and the book of Zechariah more broadly) has been progressively composed and revised under different circumstances, best explains both the differences and the connections between the different passages. Many scholars consider that this process spanned more or less a century, within the Persian or the early Hellenistic period.[95] Interestingly, even scholars who try to defend the idea that Zech 9–14 could have been composed by a single person (Zechariah in particular) argue that some time has passed between the composition of the two passages, and social or political circumstances have changed (Curtis 2006, esp. 277–280; Wenzel 2011, esp. 271–272; Meyers 1996 somehow suggests it).

Hence, it is quite probable that at some point in the compositional history of the book of Zechariah the addition of Zech 12:1–13:1* served to revise utopian ideas found in chs. 9–10, marginalizing the earlier ideal of political independence in a large territory under the leadership of a royal figure in Jerusalem. This revision is rather nuanced, however, since it maintains some continuity with the traditional royal ideology, envisaging some form of restoration for the house of David, with significant military and ritual roles; yet, at the same time, the addition limits the sphere of authority of the house of David, deselecting

---

[95] Mitchell 1912, 251–259; Rudolph 1976, 161–164; Plöger 1962, 99–117; Gese 1973, 41–43; Hanson 1979, 280–401; Steck 1991, 25–111; Boda 2016, 23–37; see also Redditt 2012a, 26–29.

the territorial and royal ideal so as to focus instead on local rituals and the commemoration of past leadership. These nuances can only be observed by accepting that chs. 9–14 form a complex literary ensemble rather than trying to harmonize the different notions they contain.

Several hypotheses have been proposed to shed light on the circumstances that provoked this revision. Some scholars have emphasized the social location of the group developing Zech 9–14, whose opposition to the leaders in Jerusalem and especially the temple authorities would have grown over time. Plöger (1962) and Hanson (1979), who were particularly interested in the origins of apocalyptic literature, have pioneered this approach, and although they have been significantly (and rightly) criticized,[96] the model of a social conflict has been quite influential until today, adapted in various ways.[97] Limitations of space prevent me from discussing this model and its recent adaptations. In general, this line of explanation remains quite speculative in the way it identifies the groups in conflicts and the nature of the conflict. In particular, reading Zech 9–14 as reflecting the opposition of a dissident group against the temple overinterprets the literary evidence, and it does not help to explain why Zech 9–14 has been added to chs. 1–8, which support the Jerusalem temple and its cult (Cook 1995, 123–165; Gonzalez 2017). In addition, while these scholars emphasize the religious aspect of a conflict, the socioeconomic and political dimensions of this supposed conflict remain quite obscure.[98]

Another kind of explanation emphasizes historical changes, especially political ones. This line of interpretation is supported by the importance of the shepherd motif in Zech 9–14, especially in ch. 11. Several scholars consider that the exploitation of the flock and the bad shepherds this chapter announces should be connected, in way or another, to foreign domination, especially Persian or Hellenistic rule (see the discussion and references below). This line of political interpretation is also supported by the fact that the oracle about the bad shepherd in Zech 11:14–16 even reverses the oracle of Ezek 34 announcing the coming of an ideal shepherd, as many scholars have observed.[99]

---

96 See Carroll 1979; Cook 1995; Meyers and Meyers 1993, 56; Gonzalez 2017.
97 See Mason [1973] 2003, esp. 204–208; Lutz 1968, esp. 205–212; Redditt 1989, 632; 1994; 2012a, esp. 149–150; see also Curtis 2006 (esp. 229–230, 273–280), who, despite attributing the whole book of Zechariah to the prophet and his group, insists on a significant change in their social location, being increasingly marginalized and separated from the institutional center, the temple. Curtis is followed by Wenzel 2011, esp. 271–272. See the discussion in Gonzalez 2017, 30–33.
98 Also, the supposed apocalyptic character of Zech 9–14 has been contested, see, e.g., Tigchelaar 1996, esp. 242–265; Biberger 2010, esp. 386–389; Redditt 2012a, 150–152.
99 See, e.g., Rudolph 1976, 210; Duguid 1995, 268–275; Redditt, 2012a, 90–91; Wolters 2014, 392; Boda 2003, 284–287; 2016, 650–652; Nihan and Gonzalez 2018, 111–113.

In the last decades, the study of O. H. Steck (1991) represents the most detailed attempt to date the different phases of composition of Zech 9–14 according to the political context (see already in a similar direction Mitchell 1912, 251–259; Rudolph 1976, 161–164). Steck's arguments are based on a relative chronology of the latest revisions to the book of Isaiah and the book of the Twelve, as well as a historical interpretation of each revision (esp. pp. 73–91). Steck follows scholars like K. Elliger (1950) and M. Delcor (1951b) who argued that Zech 9:1–8 alludes to Alexander's conquest in the Levant. He dates Zech 9:1–10:2 to the time of Alexander and Zech 10:3–11:3 to the years that almost immediately followed (320–315). The following phase is the addition of Zech 11:4–13:9, which Steck dates to 311–302/1, that is, after the battle of Gaza and the capture of Jerusalem by Ptolemy. Steck is aware that a historical interpretation of this passage remains quite speculative but nonetheless tries to associate details of the text with (his knowledge of) historical events, especially concerning the relationship between Judea and Samaria. In particular, he follows O. Plöger (1962, 105–106) in his proposal that the pierced one could be Joshua, murdered by his brother the high priest Johanan, and he interprets the shepherd mentioned in Zech 13:7 as Manasseh, who was the brother of the high priest Jaddua, and who, according to Josephus, became the first high priest of the newly built Gerizim temple through the help of Sanballat (A.J. XI.297–312).

Steck's reconstruction is stimulating in its attempt to correlate the compositional stages of Zech 9–14 with political history. However, a criticism that can be made is that it is too focused on specific historical events, which are not necessarily well reflected in the text, and about which we often lack information. Also, the identification of specific individuals behind the figures of the text has led to countless historical interpretations, so that Steck's defense of Plöger's identification of the pierced one raises suspicion more than it convinces.[100] Given the many speculations that the historical approach to Zech 9–14 has engendered, scholars nowadays tend to be more cautious (cf., e.g., Redditt 2012a, 26–28), and some even think that a historical interpretation of this text is a sterile, out of date enterprise. Nonetheless, scholars still continue presupposing a historical context, especially an early Persian one, even when they do

---

[100] Against Steck, it can be argued in particular that the Gerizim temple was not built in the early Hellenistic period but earlier in the Persian period, as more recent archaeological evidence demonstrates (see esp. Magen 2008, 97–137, 167–180). In addition, the date of the possible capture of Jerusalem by Ptolemy I is uncertain (see, e.g., Grabbe 2008, 281–283), a more likely date being that of 311 BCE, finding support in the Satrap Stele in particular (see discussion and arguments in Gonzalez and Mendoza forthcoming).

not argue for it.¹⁰¹ A strong tendency that has developed in recent decades has been to favor a (rather early) Persian context for the composition of Zech 9–14, as if this would be less speculative, given that the first part of the book refers to this context. However, opting for an early Persian context is no less speculative than opting for a late Persian or early Hellenistic one.¹⁰² Indeed, the *terminus ad quem* is given by the (late) second-century BCE manuscripts from Qumran (esp. 4QXII^a and 4QXII^b).¹⁰³ Moreover, references to the early Persian period in the first part of the book only suggest that the second part does not predate this context; it does not provide any sure setting. Contrary to what is sometimes believed, the *terminus a quo* is not necessarily the most probable date of composition. The book of Daniel also refers to the Persian period, but it is clearly Hellenistic in its present form; and, note that, contrary to Dan 7–12, Zech 9–14 does not explicitly refer to Persian times.

Sweeney (2000, 677–678) considers that Zech 9:9–10 refers to Darius I, who "initially supported the reconstruction of the Temple and thereby offered prospect of peace and restoration to Jerusalem and Judah. But Darius suffered a series of revolts from within the empire against his rule and several major defeats in his wars against the Greeks that would call the stability and continuity of Persian rule into question" (Sweeney 2000, 657). Sweeney refers to these difficulties in Darius' rule to explain the change of perspective in the rest of

---

101 For instance, Smith believes that "any attempt to find a specific historical setting for the materials in Zech 9–14 will end in failure" (1984, 249). Nonetheless, Smith – quite influenced by Hanson – still dates the text to the early Persian period (e.g., 1984, 252).
102 Linguistic analysis has also been used to date Zech 9–14 to the (early) Persian period, emphasizing some degree of continuity with Classical Biblical Hebrew and differences with the language of books that have later forms of Biblical Hebrew (esp. Esther, Daniel, Ezra, Nehemiah, and Chronicles); see esp. Hill 1982; Shin 2007; 2016. However, this approach is no less interpretative than a socio-historical approach, especially since we lack information on the date of both the texts and the linguistic features they use. Linguistic difference can be due to various factors (region, sociolect, idiolect, style, transmission, etc.), so that identifying when it reflects a chronological gap is an enterprise that is more complex than is often been assumed; see, e.g., Rezetko and Young 2014. And linguistic proximity does not necessarily imply a similar historical context. In particular, we should pay more attention to the conservative character of biblical prophecy – visible for instance in the numerous mutual influences and borrowings among prophetic books –, which is stronger than in texts like Esther, Daniel, Ezra, Nehemiah and Chronicles. Hence, we should not expect prophetic books to display strong linguistic variation, even if they belonged to different historical contexts, nor should we expect a similar language as in the books that have late forms of Biblical Hebrew, even if they are contemporaneous. For a more developed argument, see Gonzalez 2021, 297–302.
103 In light of this observation, the dating of parts of Zech 9–14 to Maccabean or Hasmonean times – as proposed, e.g., by Treves 1963, and more recently Stiglmair 1994, 455–456, or Kunz 1998, esp. 371 – appears highly improbable.

Zech 9–14, particularly visible in the more negative depiction of the shepherd passages (Zech 10:1–2; 11; 13:7–9). He also cautiously suggests that the mourning in Zech 12 "may be motivated by the potential loss of Zerubbabel in the course of the Temple reconstruction but the reader must keep in mind that conclusive evidence for the 'killing' or 'disappearance' of Zerubbabel is lacking" (Sweeney 2000, 690). Sweeney's interpretation of the king in Zech 9:9–10 as referring to Darius is problematic because this king is installed in Jerusalem. And contrary to chs. 1–8 (1:1, 7; 7:1), chs. 9–14 do not refer explicitly to Persian rule. In addition, to support his interpretation, Sweeney attributes the conquest of the Levant in Zech 9:1–8 to the king, while the text attributes it to YHWH, and Sweeney overlooks the anti-military character of this king. Furthermore, in order to explain the change from a positive to a negative view of Darius' rule, Sweeney refers to problems in his reign, insisting especially on the revolts at the outset of his reign (see, e.g., 677–678). However, the fact that these problems already happen at the start of Darius' reign does not help explaining the initial positive presentation of the king in Zech 9. Also, we do not know the impact of these events in the region of Judah, for which no revolt is attested; and the fate of Zerubbabel is a matter of scholarly speculation.

Boda's explanation appears more convincing. He points to a waning of the influence of the Davidides in the early Persian period that would have provoked the revision of the ideal Davidic rule in Zech 9:9–10 to a restoration without any human king in Zech 12–14.[104] Zechariah 11:4–16 in particular would reflect the "possible collusion between the temple and the Persians in the demise of political influence for the Davidic line" (Boda 2016, 653). While the good shepherd who resigns in vv. 4–14 could be Zerubbabel, the bad shepherd in vv. 15–16 could be Elnathan, husband of Shelomith, daughter of Zerubbabel. This interpretation of Zech 11 is also quite speculative, especially because our knowledge of the role of the Davidides in the early Persian period, and especially their possible troubles, is extremely limited. In particular, Boda's interpretation relies on an unprovenanced collection of bullae and two seals, whose authenticity has raised doubts among specialists.[105] Still, we know that, at least at some

---

[104] See Boda 2016, 654: "The rhetorical shift signaled by this central passage in 11:4–16 reveals the significant impact of the demise of the Davidic line in the Persian period. It necessitates the more severe approach to restoration described in the day of Yahweh oracles found in Zech 12–14, in which Yahweh will emerge as king. These oracles highlight Yahweh's actions to purify the people and royal line, and even the nations."
[105] The collection has been published by Avigad 1976; this material has for instance not been included in the reference work on Judean stamp impression from the Persian and Hellenistic periods, Lipschits and Vanderhooft 2011 (see p. 1 n. 1 and p. 6). Note also that Lemaire's hypothesis that identifies the name ḥnnh, found on bullae and impressions on store jars from the

point in the Persian period, Judean governors were not necessarily Davidides, so that a waning influence of the Davidides could be a possible explanation for the change of perspective in Zech 9–14.

This explanation is also proposed by Meyers and Meyers (1993, 15–29, 349–360) who, despite their tendency to harmonize somewhat the notions in chs. 9 and 12 (and 14), add other socio-political aspects in the fifth century to explain the revision of royal ideology in ch. 12 (and also in ch. 9), such as: the impact of the Greek rebellion against the Persian Empire; the increasing Persian control over the Levant; demographic and economic problems in the region; and also – on a different level – the influence of critical traditions concerning the monarchy (in deuteronomistic and prophetic literature) and the notion that traditional prophecy was reaching its end. Meyers and Meyers' approach, which broadens the scope of the socio-political context, is probably the safest one for the historical interpretation of Zech 9–14 (see esp. Meyers and Meyers 1993, 15–29, 351–359; see also similarly Petersen 1995, 3–23). Rather than speculating on the impact of some specific individuals or events – about which our knowledge is often quite scarce – it is methodologically more sound to read the text's main ideas in light of a larger socio-political context where they best fit. This approach is all the more fitting for a text which has a strong political element (esp. the martial and pastoral themes).

I am not convinced, however, that the early Persian period well explains the text's main emphases. Following a classical hypothesis in historical-critical scholarship (especially since Stade 1882), I have already argued in previous studies that the early Hellenistic period is the socio-historical context that best helps us to understand the political, socio-economic, and cultic troubles depicted in these chapters, especially when compared to the first part of the book, chs. 1–8 (Gonzalez 2013; 2017; 2021, 306–316).[106] In particular, the political instability reflected by the emphasis on the attack of Jerusalem by other nations, a theme which is absent in Zech 1–8, is best read in a context when Levantine cities were indeed besieged by large armies. While this kind of event remained rare during the Persian period – the main exception being the quashing of the

---

Persian period, with the biblical Hananiah son of Zerubbabel should not be followed (1 Chr 3:19; see Lemaire 1977, 130; an identification followed, for instance, by Edelman 2005, 26–30). Not only is the *yod* of the theonym absent in the epigraphic evidence, but the same name has also been found on other Yehud stamp impression from Tel Harasim and Babylon, written with the *scriptio plene*: ḥnwnh; see Naveh 1996, 44–47 (I thank Benjamin Sass for this reference); thus, the name should rather be read Hanunah, and Naveh even understands it as a feminine name.

106 See in a similar direction Albertz 1994, 566–570; Floyd 2000, 452–457, 508–511; Nogalski 2011, 808–810.

Sidonian revolt in the middle fourth century –, political instability increased significantly in the Levant in the early Hellenistic period, with important Levantine cities such as Tyre, Gaza, and Samaria being attacked more than once in the late fourth and third centuries BCE. Also, the Greeks in Zech 9:11–17 are depicted as threatening Jerusalem, and their defeat leads Israel to take possession of the land (vv. 16–17; cf. 10:6–12) and to enjoy political independence (cf. 9:9–10). Contrary to an idea that has gained wide acceptance,[107] this depiction does not allude to the Greco-Persian wars of the early fifth century BCE, which did not happen in the Levant but in the Aegean; and the text is not written to support the Persian Empire in these conflicts (unlike in Zech 1–8, Persia is never mentioned in Zech 9–14) but to promote an ideal of political independence (cf. Nogalski 1993, 225–226). By contrast, the depiction of the Greeks corresponds well with the early Hellenistic period, when they are militarily present in the southern Levant and can represent a threat to Jerusalem; they dominate the region and are the main obstacle to political independence.

Here, I would like to go further in arguing that the change of perspective that can be observed in Zech 9–14 can be explained in light of the main sociopolitical changes of the early Hellenistic period, especially from a time of great political instability under the Diadochi to a time of relative political stabilization and consolidation of the Ptolemaic administration in the southern Levant during the third century BCE. The socio-historical interpretation I propose has affinities to the way Steck understands the progressive development of Zech 9–14 in the early Hellenistic period. Nonetheless, it is more cautious in relating the text's depictions to the historical context, taking into consideration the text's utopian character and interpreting it mainly in light of central aspects of the socio-political context rather than specific historical events.

In Zech 9–10, the utopian ideal of political independence under a peaceful royal leader that unites the whole Levant can be read as reacting to the high political instability which characterized the very first decades of the Hellenistic period.[108] With Alexander's conquest and then during the incessant wars of

---

[107] See esp. Meyers and Meyers 1993, 15–29, 147–149, 174; Petersen 1995, 9–11, 18–21, 63; Sweeney 2000, 565–566; Curtis 2006, 174–177; 2012, 196–201.

[108] For a similar dating, see esp. Elliger 1951, 134; Steck 1991, 35–37, 73–80. This hypothesis is supported by the probable allusion to Alexander's conquest of the Levant; see esp. Elliger 1950, Delcor 1951b, Willi-Plein 2010, and the discussion in Gonzalez 2021, 310–315. The function of this allusion is to credit YHWH for the military exploits of Alexander, and to emphasize that YHWH is in control of international political changes, especially the fall of the Persian Empire and the arrival of the Greeks. Note also that Zech 9–10 is probably not a homogenous composition, especially as ch. 10 revises the battle scene of ch. 9; see the reference in n. 38 above. Although I consider ch. 10 as slightly later than ch. 9, I treat them together here because, as I showed, they reflect a similar territorial ideology. To be a bit more precise, the

the Diadochi that followed his death, not only were important Levantine cities regularly destroyed, but control over the region switched several times: first from Darius to Alexander, and then from one Diadoch to another, possibly no less than five times, especially between Ptolemy and Antigonos (see, e.g., Grabbe 2008, 278–281, 286–287; Gonzalez and Mendoza 2020). None of them was able to stably control the Levant, which was eventually divided into two parts, to be ruled by the Ptolemaic and the Seleucid Empires. This high instability of Hellenistic rule at that time explains the notion in Zech 9–10 of a new local rule associated with the military defeat of the Greeks in the Levant.[109] Apocalyptic literature, which started developing at that time, also emphasizes the end of Hellenistic rule, leading to an ideal order.[110] In Zech 9, this utopian order has an ideal king who serves as a counter-model to the first Hellenistic rulers.[111] He brings exactly what these rulers could not offer: peace and political stability in the world; territorial unity and integrity of the whole Levant; and Yahwistic piety. In particular, it can be observed how the ideal king in Zech 9 reinterprets traditional Judean royal ideology in a way that echoes important aspects of Hellenistic royal ideology. To some extent, the king's entry in Jerusalem in Zech 9:9–10 can be compared to the ceremonial entries in cities performed by the Hellenistic rulers.[112] Royal parades through cities took place on various occa-

---

addition of Zech 10:3b–12 – which particularly emphasizes the importance of Judah in the fight against the enemies and the massive return of the sons of Ephraim to the land – can be understood in light of the destructions and the population changes that affected Samaria and its region during the wars of the Diadochi; see Gonzalez and Mendoza 2020. Despite what scholars often assume, changes in Samaria were more significant by the time of the wars of the Diadochi than under Alexander. Judah (and Jerusalem) was less affected by the Diadochi wars than Samaria, so that it could secondarily be changed into the main combatant, who would help Ephraim, more significantly affected by the military and territorial policies of the first Hellenistic rulers, to regain possession of its land.

109 Critical ideas and forms of opposition to Hellenistic domination could have appeared very quickly after Alexander's conquests, as the revolt of Samaria against Alexander in 331 BCE indicates (see, e.g., Grabbe 2008, 276–278; Gonzalez and Mendoza 2020, 171–193). Although 1 Macc 1:1–9 is a late Hellenistic text, it clearly attests the negative perception of the first Hellenistic rulers within Judean tradition.

110 This kind of literary development opposing Hellenistic rule is visible not only in the Judean culture but also in other cultures of the Near East; see, e.g., Collins 1975. Note, however, that the notion of an ideal order is not alien to Hellenistic royal ideology, and that the Near Eastern literature that resists Hellenistic rule seems to subvert this notion (see n. 114 below).

111 Note that, similarly to Zech 9–10, Egyptian apocalyptic texts from the Hellenistic period, such as the Oracle of the Potter, also announce an ideal ruler who is not presented as an agent bringing salvation through battle, but rather as a symbol of the new era ushered in by divine intervention; see Quack 2002, 271–272; Koenen 1968, 180–182; 2002, 164–183.

112 On these ceremonial entries, see Strootman 2007, 289–325. Strootman describes this kind of ceremony as "consisting of three stages: an official welcome before the main gate, a ceremo-

sions, such as a festival or, typically, after a military victory. On these occasions, the king could parade with his best attributes and impressive armies, so as to display military and economic power, and he was acclaimed by the local population. These parades served to present the king as the liberator and protector, the only one able to bring peace and prosperity to the world thanks to his great military strength.[113] The king also demonstrated his piety by concluding his parade at the main sanctuary of the city, where he would offer a sacrifice to the local deity. Zechariah 9:9–10 echoes such practices of ceremonial entry into a city, but with a major change: the king's entrance into Jerusalem is not as a war leader exhibiting his military strength and economic power, and claiming to be the pious liberator, protector and guarantor of peace, but as a humble king deprived of military force, whose piety makes him entirely dependent on YHWH for his own protection.[114] In addition to revising traditional royal ideology so as

---

nial passage of the king along the city's main artery, and offerings by the king in the principal sanctuary" (Strootman 2007, 289).

113 Such ideology is also clearly visible in the regnal title "Soter" (savior) chosen by Ptolemy I. It should be observed that the notion of an ideal and peaceful order is not only a central theme in late prophetic texts such as Zech 9 or apocalyptic literature, but also in Hellenistic royal ideology (see also, e.g., Theocritus' *Idyll* XVII); cf. Strootman 2007, 289–347, 355–356. Zechariah 9, however, subverts Hellenistic royal ideology by implying that the peaceful order will not be brought by the king's military strength, but by YHWH who will install his peaceful and demilitarized king.

114 In particular, the description of the king in Zech 9 as "saved" opposes the ideology of the Hellenistic king as savior, and more specifically the regnal title "Soter" of Ptolemy I; cf. Kunz 1998, 229–239. In addition, the king's arrival on a donkey rather than a horse can be read as an implicit criticism of the military power of the first Hellenistic rulers. Following the example of Alexander riding his well-renown horse Bucephalus (and also Alexander's father Philip II of Macedonia, presented on coins on a horse or a chariot), these rulers used the horse as an instrument of war and as a symbol of their power; cf., e.g., Hyland 2003, 145–163 (on horses in Alexander's armies), or Iossif 2012, 78–82 (on horses in Seleucid ideology). Alexander and the Diadochi after him also significantly increased the importance of the cavalry in their armies, which served as a crucial element in their military strategy (cf. Polybius III 117.5); Scheuble-Reiter 2014; Fisher-Bovet 2014, 123–133. In Zech 9:10, the emphasis on the destruction of the instrument of war, and especially the war chariot and the horse, together with the bow, may well respond to the importance of the cavalry in the Hellenistic armies. Moreover, the king's qualification as עני, "humble" or "poor," contrasts with the Hellenistic kings' display of economic power through parades or through other practices, such as euergetism, that developed in the early Hellenistic period. Finally, despite being centered on the Levant, the territorial rule of the ideal in Zech 9 also has cosmic connotations (see, e.g., Meyers and Meyers 1993, 136–138; Boda 2016, 572–574) which can echo the claim of universal dominion by Alexander and his successors (see Hauben 2014; Meeus 2014; Strootman 2014). Zechariah 9, however, attributes the dominion over the Levant and beyond to the king of Jerusalem instead of a Hellenistic ruler.

to implicitly criticize Hellenistic rule, the additions of chs. 9–10 helped to read the ancient scroll of Zechariah in the sense that the allusions to a future local ruler in Zech 1–8* will reach their fulfillment only after the end of Persian domination, at a time when Jerusalem will be in conflict against the Greeks, and will eventually overcome them thanks to a great divine intervention.[115]

Zechariah 12, by contrast, does not envisage a change of political power with a new local ruler allowing Israel (and more broadly the Levant) to be politically independent; rather, it focuses on the organization and the rituals of the local Jerusalemite community, under divine protection. I would like to suggest that this new perspective in the book (leaving aside the question of political independence) reflects the stabilization of Hellenistic power in the Levant during the third century BCE. By the end of the reign of the Diadochi in the early third century, political power no longer switched from one hand to another, and the rhythm of war decreased in the Levant (despite the Syrian wars of the third and early second centuries). The Ptolemies and Seleucids progressively developed the local administration of their provinces, essentially aiming at the maximum exploitation of their resources, in a context of competition between empires.[116] This stabilization of political power, making its collapse harder to conceive, may have provoked the revision of the restoration depicted in Zech 9–10 which we witness in Zech 12. No longer is the ideal of political independence emphasized; instead, together with divine protection, the rituals in Jerusalem and the commemoration of past leaders are stressed. Jerusalem is no longer

---

115 To some extent, this utopian development on political independence in Zech 9–10, dating to the very early Hellenistic period, can be compared to ideas of political independence that scholars often identify in texts from the early Persian period in Haggai (esp. 2:20–23) and Zech 1–8 (esp. 6:9–15); see, e.g., the contribution of Jan Rückl in this volume. The resonance with previous ideas of political independence from the early Persian period might be one of the reasons for the enlargement of the scroll of Zechariah with chs. 9–10. It has even been proposed that these texts in Haggai and Zech 1–8 have grown out of a context of political instability, especially due to the revolts in the Persian Empire in the early years of the reign of Darius I; see in particular Waterman 1954; Bickerman 1981, 19–41; Blenkinsopp 1996, 202–203; Meyers 1996, 127–128 (on Haggai 2:20–23); Albertz 2013, 125–126. Although this historical interpretation is debated (see already Ackroyd 1958, or see the discussion in Grabbe 2004, 279–282) and should certainly be qualified (see the recent historical assessment of Rückl 2018, 43–54, 200–211), it is not impossible that some elements of political instability also facilitated the composition of such texts. In any case, it should also be noted that the political instability was much higher in the Levant during the early Hellenistic period, and the ideal of political independence is more clearly affirmed in Zech 9–10 than in Zech 1–8.
116 See, e.g., the new settlement pattern of the region of Samaria in the 3rd century BCE, probably due – among other reasons – to Ptolemaic policies aiming at improving the agricultural exploitation of the territory; Gonzalez and Mendoza 2020, 211–220.

envisaged as a territorial and political center, but rather as a cultic site for the local community.[117] This presentation of Jerusalem indirectly validates the ritual function of the local temple. As such, in revising the ideal of Zech 9–10, the scribes developing the scroll of Zechariah maintained continuity with the previous oracles contained in the book. Similarly to Zech 1–8, which reflects political concerns (see esp. Zech 6:9–15) but whose main emphasis deals with the restoration of the temple and its cult, Zech 9–14 eventually accentuates the community rituals more than the restoration of the monarchy.

This hypothesis, which associates the change of ideal in Zech 9–14 with the stabilization of the new foreign domination, makes sense in light of ch. 11, which prepare for this change in the text by announcing division, exploitation, and bad leadership. This is not the place to interpret this chapter in detail. While most of the recent studies try to interpret the dramas it forecasts in light of the Persian domination over Judah,[118] I have argued elsewhere (Gonzalez 2017, 47–62) that the specific type of economic exploitation that Zech 11:4–14 depicts (unparalleled in the Hebrew Bible), involving a complex and multileveled network of agents (buyers, sellers, shepherds, and merchants), corresponds well with the administrative and tax policies that developed in the southern Levant under Ptolemaic rule.[119] The Ptolemies intensified and diversified tax collection, involving local elites at various levels of the administration (in a way that did not favor the economic interests of the temple).[120]

Overall, it appears that Zech 9–14 reflects the main socio-political changes of the early Hellenistic period, in particular the strong political instability of the first decades, and the progressive installation and strengthening of the Ptolemaic administration in the southern Levant during the third century BCE. Utopian images of military victory, territorial possession, political independence and kingship could be developed in a context when the new domination was still unstable, but with its progressive stabilization, they had to be revised, integrating a more dystopian perspective (see esp. Zech 11).

---

117 Note that the political role of Jerusalem within the region of Judah probably decreased during the 3rd century BCE compared to the Persian period. The office of provincial governor disappeared at some point, and some non-Jerusalemite elites, such as the Tobiads, enjoyed a growing importance in the administration of the region. Numismatic evidence suggests that the Jerusalem temple progressively lost political importance, to the point that the mint in Jerusalem closed during the 3rd century BCE; see Grabbe 2008, 291–297; Gonzalez 2017, 52–60.
118 See esp. Sweeney 2000, 675–683; Foster 2007; Redditt 2012a, 80–88; Boda 2003, 287–288; 2016, 652–653.
119 See in a similar direction Mitchell 1912, 303–308; Gese 1973, 43; Albertz 1994, 568–569 and 665 n. 33; Floyd 2000, 487.
120 See, e.g., Grabbe 2008, 166–170, 208–213, 291–297; 2011.

4 Conclusion

The book of Zechariah attests the variety of uses and transformations of the traditional Judean royal ideology under foreign domination in the negotiation of concepts of leadership. In light of the analysis of Zech 9:9–10 and 12:1–13:1 offered here, and the clear differences which can be observed between them, scholars should resist the urge to apply single schemes across these texts, as if there were only one discourse on leadership within them. Zechariah 9–14 not only reveal the capacity of ancient scribes to radically re-signify traditional concepts such as royal leadership; these chapters also show that such concepts could be re-envisaged in a variety of ways, in accordance with different historical contingencies. They also suggest that a concern for individual leadership could be revised with a notion of collective leadership for some specific domains, especially military and rituals ones. In addition, they attest to the role that the memory of past leaders could play in shaping the community. Thus, the book of Zechariah provides valuable evidence for the multifaceted and complex ways in which royal leadership could be negotiated and re-negotiated in the scribal practices. This evidence also suggests that during the Second Temple period, the ideal of a local royal leader remained secondary to the project of building a community centered on the ritual of the main local institution, the Jerusalem temple.

Bibliography

Ackroyd, Peter R. 1958. "Two Old Testament Historical Problems of the Early Persian Period." *JNES* 17:13–27.

Albertz, Rainer. 1994. *A History of Israelite Religion in the Old Testament Period. Vol. 2: From the Exile to the Maccabees*. London: SCM Press.

Albertz, Rainer. 2013. *Israel in Exile: The History and Literature of the Sixth Century B.C.E.*, translated by David Green. Atlanta: SBL Press.

Amsler, Samuel. 1963. *David, roi et messie: La tradition davidique dans l'Ancien Testament*. CahT 49. Neuchâtel: Delachaux & Niestlé.

Auwers, Jean-Marie. 2000. *La composition littéraire du Psautier: Un état de la question*. CahRB 46. Paris: Gabalda.

Avigad, Nahman. 1976. *Bullae and Seals from a Post-Exilic Judean Archive*. Qedem 4. Jerusalem: The Institute of Archaeology of The Hebrew University of Jerusalem.

Baldwin, Joyce G. 1972. *Haggai, Zechariah, Malachi: An Introduction and Commentary*. London: Tyndale Press.

Barthélemy, Dominique. 1992. *Critique textuelle de l'Ancien Testament. Vol. 3: Ezéchiel, Daniel et les 12 Prophètes*. OBO 50/3. Fribourg: Academic Press.

Becker, Joachim. 1980. *Messianic Expectations in the Old Testament*. Edinburgh: Bloomsbury T&T Clark.

Biberger, Bernd. 2010. *Endgültiges Heil innerhalb von Geschichte und Gegenwart: Zukunftskonzeptionen in Ez 38–39, Joel 1–4 und Sach 12–14*. BBB 161. Göttingen: Vandenhoeck & Ruprecht.

Bickerman, Elias J. 1981. "En marge de l'écriture." *RB* 88:19–41.

Blenkinsopp, Joseph. 1996. *A History of Prophecy in Israel*. Rev. and en. edition. Louisville: Westminster John Knox Press.

Boda, Mark J. 2003. "Reading Between the Lines: Zechariah 11.4–16 in Its Literary Contexts." In *Bringing Out the Treasure: Inner Biblical Allusion in Zechariah 9–14*, edited by Mark J. Boda and Michael H. Floyd, 277–291. London and New York: Sheffield Academic Press.

Boda, Mark J. 2007. "Messengers of Hope in Haggai–Malachi." *JSOT* 32:113–131.

Boda, Mark J. 2016. *The Book of Zechariah*. NICOT. Grand Rapids: Eerdmans.

Boda, Mark J. 2017. "Inner Biblical Allusions in the Shepherd Units of Zechariah 9–14." In *Exploring Zechariah. Vol. 2: The Development of Zechariah and Its Role Within the Twelve*, edited by Mark J. Boda, 169–182. ANEM 16. Atlanta: SBL Press.

Boda, Mark J., and Stanley E. Porter. 2005. "Intertextuality to the Third Degree: Prophecy in Zech 9–14 and the Passion of Christ." In *Traduire la Bible Hébraïque: De la Septante à la Nouvelle Bible Segond*, edited by Robert David and Manuel M. Jinbashian, 215–254. Montréal: Mediaspaul.

Caroll, Robert P. 1979. "Twilight of Prophecy or Dawn of Apocalyptic?" *JSOT* 14:3–35.

Chary, Théophane. 1955. *Les prophètes et le culte à partir de l'exil*. BT.B 3. Paris and Tournay: Desclée.

Chary, Théophane. 1969. *Aggée-Zacharie-Malachie*. SB. Paris: Gabalda.

Chilton, Bruce. 1999. "The Targumim and Judaism of the First Century." In *Judaism in Late Antiquity. Part Three: Where We Stand: Issues and Debates in Ancient Jerusalem*. Vol 2, edited by Jacob Neusner and Alan J. Avery-Peck, 115–150. Leiden, Boston, and Cologne: Brill.

Collins, Adela Yabro, and John J. Collins. 2008. *King and Messiah as Son of God: Divine, Human, and Angelic Messianic Figures in Biblical and Related Literature*. Grand Rapids: Eerdmans.

Collins, John J. 1975. "Jewish Apocalyptic Against Its Hellenistic Near Eastern Environment." *BASOR* 220: 27–36.

Collins, John J. 1995. *The Scepter and the Star: The Messiahs of the Dead Sea Scrolls and Other Ancient Literature*. ABRL. New York: Doubleday.

Collins, Terry. 2003. "The Literary Contexts of Zech 9:9." In *The Book of Zechariah and Its Influence*, edited by Christopher Tuckett, 29–40. Hampshire and Burlington: Ashgate.

Coppens, Joseph. 1974. *Le Messianisme et sa relève prophétique: Les anticipations vétérotestamentaires. Leur accomplissement en Jésus*. BEThL 38. Gembloux: J. Duculot.

Cook, Stephen L. 1993. "The Metamorphosis of a Shepherd: The Tradition History of Zechariah 11:17 + 13:7–9." *CBQ* 55:453–466.

Cook, Stephen L. 1995. *Prophecy & Apocalypticism: The Postexilic Social Setting*. Minneapolis: Fortress Press.

Curtis, Byron G. 2006. *Up the Steep and Stony Road: The Book of Zechariah in Social Location Trajectory Analysis*. SBLABib 25. Atlanta: SBL Press.

Curtis, Byron G. 2012. "The Mas'ot Triptych and the Date of Zechariah 9–14." In *Perspectives on the Formation of the Book of the Twelve: Methodological Foundations – Redactional Processes – Historical Insights*, edited by Rainer Albertz, James Nogalski, and Jakob Wöhrle, 196–201. BZAW 433. Berlin and Boston: de Gruyter.

Deissler, Alfons. 1988. *Zwölf Propheten III: Zefanja, Haggai, Sacharja, Maleachi*. NEB 21. Würzburg: Echter Verlag.

Deissler, Alfons. 1998. "Sach 12,10 – die grosse crux interpretum." In *Ich bewirke das Heil und erschaffe das Unheil (Jesaja 45,7): Studien zur Botschaft der Propheten*, edited by Friedrich Diedrich and Bernd Willmes, 49–60. FB 88. Würzburg: Echter Verlag.

Delcor, Mathias. 1951a. "Un problème de critique textuelle et d'exégèse. Zach XII, 10: Et aspicient ad me quem confixerunt." *RB* 58:189–199.

Delcor, Mathias. 1951b. "Les allusions à Alexandre le Grand dans Zach IX 1–8." *VT* 1:110–124.

Delcor, Mathias. 1953. "Deux passages difficiles: Zach XII 11 et XI 13." *VT* 3:67–77.

Dorival, Gilles. 2005. "Les titres des Psaumes en hébreu et en grec: les écarts quantitatifs." In *L'Écrit et l'Esprit: Études d'histoire du texte et de théologie biblique en hommage à Adrian Schenker*, edited by Dieter Böhler, Innocent Himbaza, and Philippe Hugo, 58–70. OBO 214. Fribourg: Academic Press.

Duguid, Iain. 1995. "Messianic Themes in Zechariah 9–14." In *The Lord's Anointed: Interpretation of Old Testament Messianic Texts*, edited by Philip E. Satterthwaite, Richard S. Hess, and Gordon J. Wenham, 265–280. Carlisle: Paternoster.

Edelman, Diana V. 2005. *The Origins of the "Second Temple": Persian Imperial Policy and the Rebuilding of Jerusalem*. BWo. London and Oakville: Equinox.

Eidsvåg, Gunnar M. 2016. *The Old Greek Translation of Zechariah*. VTSup 170. Leiden and Boston: Brill.

Elliger, Karl. 1950. "Ein Zeugnis aus der jüdischen Gemeinde im Alexanderjahr 332 v. Chr." *ZAW* 62:63–115.

Elliger, Karl. 1951. *Das Buch der zwölf Kleinen Propheten. Vol. 2: Die Propheten Nahum, Habakuk, Zephanja, Haggai, Sacharja, Maleachi*. 2nd edition. ATD 25/2. Göttingen: Vandenhoeck & Ruprecht.

Ellul, Danielle. 1981. "Variations sur le thème de la guerre sainte dans le Deutéro-Zacharie." *ETR* 56:55–71.

Fischer-Bovet, Christelle. 2014. *Army and Society in Ptolemaic Egypt*. Armies of the Ancient World. Cambridge: Cambridge University Press.

Floyd, Michael H. 2000. *Minor Prophets: Part 2*. FOTL 22. Grand Rapids: Eerdmans.

Foster, Robert L. 2007. "Shepherds, Sticks, and Social Destabilization: A Fresh Look at Zechariah 11:4–17." *JBL* 126:735–753.

Franklin, Arnold E. 2012. *Noble House: Jewish Descendants of King David in the Medieval Islamic East*. Philadelphia: University of Pennsylvania Press.

Gese, Hartmut. 1973. "Anfang und Ende der Apokalyptik, dargestellt am Sacharjabuch." *ZThK* 70:20–49.

Gonzalez, Hervé. 2013. "Zechariah 9–14 and the Continuation of Zechariah during the Ptolemaic Period." *JHS* 13: Article 9.

Gonzalez, Hervé. 2015. "Review of Zechariah 9–14, International Exegetical Commentary on the Old Testament (IECOT)." *WO* 45:122–128.

Gonzalez, Hervé. 2017. "Zacharie 9–14 et le temple de Jérusalem: Observations sur le milieu de production d'un texte prophétique tardif." *Judaïsme Ancien – Ancient Judaism* 5:23–77.

Gonzalez, Hervé. 2019. "Le dieu de l'orage en chef de guerre: une représentation traditionnelle de YHWH réinterprétée contre la domination hellénistique (Zacharie 9,14)." In *Représenter hommes et dieux dans le Proche-Orient ancien et dans la Bible: Actes du colloque organisé par le Collège de France, Paris, les 5 et 6 mai 2015*, edited by Thomas Römer, Hervé Gonzalez, and Lionel Marti, 212–254. OBO 287. Leuven: Peeters.

Gonzalez, Hervé. 2021. "No Prophetic Texts from the Hellenistic Period? Methodological, Philological, and Historical Observations on the Writing of Prophecy in Early Hellenistic Judea." In *Times of Transition: Judea in the Early Hellenistic Period* edited by Sylvie Honigman, Oded Lipschits, and Christophe Nihan, 293–340. Mosaics: Studies on Ancient Israel. Tel Aviv and University Park: The Institute of Archaeology of Tel Aviv University and Penn State University/Eisenbrauns.

Gonzalez, Hervé, and Marc Mendoza. 2020. "'What Have the Macedonians Ever Done for Us?' A Reassessment of the Changes in Samaria by the Start of the Hellenistic Period." In *Yahwistic Diversity and the Hebrew Bible: Tracing Perspectives of Group Identity from Judah, Samaria, and Diaspora in Biblical Traditions*, edited by Benedikt Hensel, Dany Nocquet, and Bartosz Adamczwesky, 169–229. FAT/2 120. Tübingen: Mohr Siebeck.

Gordon, Robert P. 2003. "The Ephraimite Messiah and Targum(s) Zechariah 12:10." In *Reading from Right to Left: Essays on the Hebrew Bible in Honour of David J. A. Clines*, edited by J. Cheryl Exum and Hugh G. M. Williamson, 184–195. JSOTSup 373. London: Sheffield Academic Press.

Goswell, Gregory. 2016. "A Theocratic Reading of Zechariah 9:9." *BBR* 26:7–19.

Grabbe, Lester L. 2004. *A History of the Jews and Judaism in the Second Temple Period. Vol. 1: Yehud: A History of the Persian Province of Judah.* LSTS 47. London et al.: Bloomsbury T&T Clark.

Grabbe, Lester L. 2008. *A History of the Jews and Judaism in the Second Temple Period. Vol. 2: The Coming of the Greeks: The Early Hellenistic Period (335–175 BCE).* LSTS 68. London et al.: Bloomsbury T&T Clark.

Grabbe, Lester L. 2011. "Hyparchs, Oikonomoi and Mafiosi: The Governance of Judah in the Ptolemaic period." In *Judah Between East and West: The Transition from Persian to Greek Rule (400–200 BCE)*, edited by Oded Lipschits and Lester L. Grabbe, 70–90. London: Bloomsbury T&T Clark.

Greenfield, Jonas C. 1999. "Hadad הדד." *DDD* 377–382.

Gressmann, Hugo. 1929. *Der Messias*. FRLANT 43. Göttingen: Vandenhoeck & Ruprecht.

Hanson, Paul D. 1973. "Zechariah 9 and the Recapitulation of an Ancient Ritual Pattern." *JBL* 92:37–59.

Hanson, Paul D. 1979. *The Dawn of Apocalyptic: The Historical and Sociological Roots of Jewish Apocalyptic Eschatology*. 2nd rev. edition. Minneapolis: Fortress Press.

Hauben, Hans. 2014. "Ptolemy's Grand Tour." In *The Age of the Successors and the Creation of the Hellenistic Kingdoms (323–276 B.C.)*, edited by Hans Hauben and Alexander Meeus, 235–261. StHell 53. Leuven: Peeters.

Hill, Andrew E. 1982. "Dating Second Zechariah: A Linguistic Reexamination." *HAR* 6:105–134.

Hoftijzer, Jean. 1953. "A propos d'une interprétation récente de deux passages difficiles: Zach. xii 11 et Zach. xi 13." *VT* 3:407–409.

Horst, Friedrich. 1964. *Die Zwölf kleinen Propheten: Nahum bis Maleachi*. 3rd edition. HKAT 14. Tübingen: Mohr Siebeck.

Hyland, Ann. 2003. *The Horse in the Ancient World*. Stroud: Sutton.

Iossif, Panagiotis P. 2012. "Les 'cornes' des Séleucides: vers une divinisation 'discrète.'" *Cahiers des études anciennes* 49:43–147.

Koenen, Ludwig. 1968. "Die Prophezeiungen des 'Töpfers.'" *ZPE* 2:178–209.

Koenen, Ludwig. 2002. "Die Apologie des Töpfers an König Amenophis oder das Töpferorakel." In *Apokalyptik und Ägypten: Eine kritische Analyse der relevanten Texte aus dem griechisch-römischen Ägypten*, edited by Andreas Blasius and Bernd U. Schipper, 139–187. OLA 107. Leuven: Peeters.
Kunz, Andreas. 1998. *Ablehnung des Krieges: Untersuchungen zu Sacharja 9 und 10*. HBS 17. Freiburg i. Br.: Herder.
Laato, Antii. 1992. *Josiah and David Redivivus: The Historical Josiah and the Messianic Expectations of Exilic and Postexilic Times*. CBOT 33. Stockholm: Almqvist & Wiksell International.
Laato, Antii. 1997. *A Star is Rising: The Historical Development of the Old Testament Royal Ideology and the Rise of Jewish Messianic Expectations*. University of South Florida International Studies in Christianity and Judaism 5. Atlanta: Scholars Press.
Lacocque, André. 1988. "Zacharie 9–14." In *Aggée, Zacharie, Malachie*, edited by Samuel Amsler, André Lacocque, and René Vuilleumier, 127–216. 2nd rev. edition. CAT 11c. Geneva: Labor et Fides.
Lamarche, Paul. 1961. *Zacharie IX–XIV: Structure littéraire et messianisme*. EBib. Paris: Gabalda.
Lange, Armin. 2012. "The Covenant with the Levites (Jer 33:21) in the Proto-Masoretic Text of Jeremiah in Light of the Dead Sea Scrolls." In *"Go Out and Study the Land" (Judges 18:2): Archaeological, Historical and Textual Studies in Honor of Hanan Eshel*, edited by Aren M. Maeir, Jodi Magness, and Lawrence H. Schiffman, 95–116. Leiden and Boston: Brill.
Larkin, Katrina J. A. 1994. *The Eschatology of Second Zechariah: A Study of the Formation of a Mantological Wisdom Anthology*. CBET 6. Kampen: Pharos.
Lee, Suk Yee. 2015. *An Intertextual Analysis of Zechariah 9–10: The Earlier Restoration Expectations of Second Zechariah*. LHBOTS 599. New York: Bloomsbury T&T Clark.
Lemaire, André. 1977. "Review of Nahman Avigad, Bullae and Seals from a Post-Exilic Judean Archive." *Syria* 54:129–131.
Leske, Adrian. 2000. "Context and Meaning of Zechariah 9:9." *CBQ* 62:663–678.
Levey, Samson H. 1974. *The Messiah: An Aramaic Interpretation: The Messianic Exegesis of the Targum*. New York: Ktav Publishing House.
Liebengood, Kelly D. 2014. *The Eschatology of 1 Peter Considering the Influence of Zechariah 9–14*. MSSNTS 157. Cambridge and New York: Cambridge University Press.
Lipiński, Edward. 1970. "Recherches sur le livre de Zacharie." *VT* 20:25–55.
Lipschits, Oded, and David Vanderhooft. 2011. *The Yehud Stamp Impressions: A Corpus of Inscribed Impressions from the Persian and Hellenistic Periods in Judah*. Winona Lake: Eisenbrauns.
Lutz, Hanns-Martin. 1968. *Jahwe, Jerusalem und die Völker: Zur Vorgeschichte von Sach 12,1–8 und 14,1–5*. WMANT 27. Neukirchen-Vluyn: Neukirchener Verlag.
Magen, Yitzhak. 2008. *A Temple City. Vol. 2: Mount Gerizim Excavations*. JSP 8. Jerusalem: Israel Antiquities Authority.
Mason, Rex. 1976. "The Relation of Zech 9–14 to Proto-Zechariah." *ZAW* 88:227–239.
Mason, Rex. 1998. "The Messiah in the Postexilic Old Testament Literature." In *King and Messiah in Israel and the Ancient Near East: Proceedings of the Oxford Old Testament Seminar*, edited by John Day, 338–364. JSOTSup 210. Sheffield: Sheffield Academic Press.
Mason, Rex. [1973] 2003. "The Use of Earlier Biblical Material in Zechariah 9–14: A Study in Inner Biblical Exegesis." In *Bringing Out the Treasure: Inner Biblical Allusion in*

Zechariah 9–14, edited by Mark J. Boda and Michael Floyd, 1–208. JSOTSup 370. London and New York: Sheffield Academic Press.

Meeus, Alexander. 2014. "The Territorial Ambitions of Ptolemy I." In *The Age of the Successors and the Creation of the Hellenistic Kingdoms (323–276 B.C.)*, edited by Hans Hauben and Alexander Meeus, 263–306. StHell 53. Leuven: Peeters.

Meyers, Carol L., and Eric M. Meyers. 1985. *Haggai, Zechariah 1–8: A New Translation with Introduction and Commentary*. AB 25B. Garden City: Doubleday.

Meyers, Carol L., and Eric M. Meyers. 1993. *Zechariah 9–14: A New Translation with Introduction and Commentary*. AB 25B. New York et al.: Doubleday.

Meyers, Carol L., and Eric M. Meyers. 1995. "The Future Fortunes of the House of David: Evidence of Second Zechariah." In *Fortunate the Eyes that See: Essays in Honor of David Noel Freedman in Celebration of His Seventieth Birthday*, edited by Astrid Beck, 127–142. Grand Rapids: Eerdmans.

Meyers, Eric M. 1996. "Messianism in First and Second Zechariah and the End of Biblical Prophecy." In *"Go to the Land I will Show You": Studies in Honor of Dwight W. Young*, edited by Joseph E. Coleson and Victor H. Matthews. AVO 4. Winona Lake: Eisenbrauns.

Mitchell, Hinckley G. T. 1912. *A Critical and Exegetical Commentary on Haggai and Zechariah*. ICC. Edinburgh: Bloomsbury T&T Clark.

Naveh, Joseph. 1996. "Gleanings of Some Pottery Inscriptions." *IEJ* 46:44–51.

Nihan, Christophe. 2017. "Utopies royales et origines du messianisme dans la Bible hébraïque." In *Encyclopédie des messianismes juifs dans l'Antiquité*, edited by David Hamidović, Xavier Levieils, and Christophe Mézange, 13–82. BToSt 33. Leuven: Peeters.

Nihan, Christophe, and Hervé Gonzalez. 2018. "Competing Attitudes toward Samaria in Chronicles and Second Zechariah." In *The Bible, Qumran and the Samaritans*, edited by Magnar Kartveit and Gary N. Knoppers, 93–114. Studia Samaritana 10. Berlin and Boston: de Gruyter.

Nihan, Christophe, and Julia Rhyder. 2018. "Aaron's Vestments in Exodus 28 and Priestly Leadership." In *Debating Authority: Concepts of Leadership in the Pentateuch and the Former Prophets*, edited by Katharina Pyschny and Sarah Schulz, 45–67. BZAW 507. Berlin and Boston: de Gruyter.

Nogalski, James D. 1993. *Redactional Processes in the Book of the Twelve*. BZAW 218. Berlin and New York: de Gruyter.

Nogalski, James D. 2011. *The Book of the Twelve: Micah–Malachi*. Smyth & Helwys Bible Commentary. Macon: Smyth & Helwys.

Nowack, Wihlem. 1922. *Die kleinen Propheten*. 3rd rev. edition. HK III/4. Göttingen: Vandenhoeck & Ruprecht.

Nurmela, Risto. 1996. *Prophets in Dialogue: Inner-Biblical Allusions in Zechariah 1–8 and 9–14*. Åbo: Åbo Akademi University Press.

Otzen, Benedikt. 1964. *Studien über Deuterosacharia*. Copenhagen: Prostant apud Munksgaard.

Petersen, David L. 1995. *Zechariah 9–14 and Malachi: A Commentary*. OTL. Louisville: SCM Press.

Petterson, Anthony R. 2009. *Behold Your King: The Hope for the House of David in the Book of Zechariah*. LHBOTS 513. London: Bloomsbury Academic.

Petterson, Anthony. 2010. "The Shape of the Davidic Hope Across the Book of the Twelve." *JSOT* 35:226–246.

Plöger, Otto. 1962. *Theokratie und Eschatologie*. 2nd rev. edition. WMANT 2. Neukirchen-Vluyn: Neukirchener Verlag.

Pomykala, Kenneth. 1995. *The Davidic Dynasty Tradition in Early Judaism: Its History and Significance for Messianism*. SBLEJL 7. Atlanta: Scholars Press.
Quack, Joachim F. 2002. "Ein neuer prophetischer Text aus Tebtynis (Papyrus Carlsberg 39te9 + Papyrus PSI inv. D. 17 + Papyrus Tebtynis Tait 13 vs.)." In *Apokalyptik und Ägypten: Eine kritische Analyse der relevanten Texte aus dem griechisch-römischen Ägypten*, edited by Andreas Blasius and Bernd U. Schipper, 253–274. OLA 107. Leuven: Peeters.
Rad, Gerhard von. [1966] 1984. "The Royal Ritual in Judah." In *The Problem of the Hexateuch and Other Essays*, 222–231. London: SCM Press.
Ramantswana, Hulisani. 2011. "David of the Psalters: MT Psalter, LXX Psalter and 11QPs^a Psalter." *OTE* 24:431–463.
Redditt, Paul L. 1989. "Israel's Shepherds: Hope and Pessimism in Zechariah 9–14." *CBQ* 51:631–642.
Redditt, Paul L. 1993. "The Two Shepherds in Zechariah 11:4–11." *CBQ* 55:676–686.
Redditt, Paul L. 1994. "Nehemiah's First Mission and the Date of Zechariah 9–14." *CBQ* 56:664–678.
Redditt, Paul L. 1995. *Haggai, Zechariah and Malachi*. NCBC. London: Marshall Pickering.
Redditt, Paul L. 2008. "The King in Haggai-Zechariah 1–8 and the Book of the Twelve." In *Tradition in Transition: Haggai and Zechariah 1–8 in the Trajectory of the Hebrew Theology*, edited by Mark J. Boda and Michael H. Floyd, 305–332. LHBOTS 475. New York: Bloomsbury T&T Clark.
Redditt, Paul L. 2012a. *Zechariah 9–14*. IECOT. Stuttgart: Kohlhammer.
Redditt, Paul L. 2012b. "Redactional Connectors in Zechariah 9–14." In *Perspectives on the Formation of the Book of the Twelve: Methodological Foundations – Redactional Processes – Historical Insights*, edited by Rainer Albertz, James Nogalski, and Jakob Wöhrle, 207–222. BZAW 433. Berlin and Boston: de Gruyter.
Reventlow, Henning Graf. 1993. *Die Propheten Haggai, Sacharja und Maleachi*. 9th edition. ATD 25/2. Göttingen: Vandenhoeck & Ruprecht.
Ringgren, Helmer. 1952. "King und Messias." *ZAW* 64:120–147.
Ringgren, Helmer. 1956. *The Messiah in the Old Testament*. SBT 18. London: SCM Press.
Rose, Wolter H. 2012. "Zechariah and the Ambiguity of Kingship in Postexilic Israel." In *Let Us Go Up to Zion: Essays in Honour of H. G. M. Williamson on the Occasion of His Sixty-Fifth Birthday*, edited by Iain Provain and Mark J. Boda, 219–231. VTSup 153. Leiden: Brill.
Rückl, Jan. 2016. *A Sure House: Studies on the Dynastic Promise to David in the Books of Samuel and Kings*. OBO 281. Fribourg: Academic Press.
Rückl, Jan. 2018. *Ageus: Budování chrámu v Judsku perské doby*. Český ekumenický komentář ke Starému zákonu 37. Prague: Centrum biblických studií AV ČR a UK v Praze, in collaboration with Česká biblická společnost.
Rudolph, Wilhlem. 1976. *Haggai – Sacharja 1–8 – Sacharja 9–14 – Maleachi: Mit einer Zeittafel von Alfred Jepsen*. KAT XIII/4. Gütersloh: Gütersloher Verlagshaus.
Rezetko, Robert, and Ian Young. 2014. *Historical Linguistics and Biblical Hebrew: Steps Toward an Integrated Approach*. ANEM 9. Atlanta: SBL.
Sæbø, Magne. 1969. *Sacharja 9–14: Untersuchungen von Text und Form*. WMANT 34. Neukirchen-Vluyn: Neukirchener Verlag.
Scheuble-Reiter, Sandra. 2014. "Zur Organisation und Rolle der Reiterei in den Diadochenheeren: Vom Heer Alexanders des Großen zum Heer Ptolemaios' I." In *The

Age of the Successors and the Creation of the Hellenistic Kingdoms (323–276 B.C.), edited by Hans Hauben and Alexander Meeus, 475–500. StHell 53. Leuven: Peeters.

Schott, Martin. 2019. *Sacharja 9–14: Eine kompositionsgeschichtliche Analyse*. BZAW 521. Berlin and Boston: de Gruyter.

Sellin, Ernst. 1930. *Das Zwölfprophetenbuch. Zweite Hälfte: Nahum–Maleachi*. 3rd rev. edition. KAT XII/2. Leipzig: A. Deichertsche Verlagsbuchhandlung D. Werner Scholl.

Seybold, Klaus. 1972. "Spätprophetische Hoffnungen auf die Wiederkunft des davidischen Zeitalters in Sach. 9–14." *Judaica* 29:99–111.

Shin, Seoung-Yun. 2007. *A Lexical Study on the Language of Haggai-Zechariah-Malachi and Its Place in the History of Biblical Hebrew*. Jerusalem: The Hebrew University of Jerusalem.

Shin, Seoung-Yun. 2016. "A Diachronic Study of the Language of Haggai, Zechariah, and Malachi." *JBL* 135:265–281.

Smith, Ralph L. 1984. *Micah–Malachi*. WBC 32. Waco: Word Books.

Stade, Bernhardt. 1881. "Deuterozacharja: Eine kritische Studie. I. Theil." *ZAW* 1:1–96.

Stade, Bernhardt. 1882. "Deuterozacharja: Ein kritische Studie. III. Theil. Die Za 9 ff. enthaltenen Beziehungen auf die weltgeschichtliche Lage". ZAW 2:275–309.

Steck, Odil Hannes. 1991. *Der Abschluss der Prophetie im Alten Testament: Ein Versuch zur Frage der Vorgeschichte des Kanons*. BThS 17. Neukirchen-Vluyn: Neukirchener Verlag.

Stiglmair, Arnold. 1994. "Der Durchbohrte – Ein Versuch zu Sach 12." *ZKT* 116:451–456.

Strootman, Rudolf. 2007. *The Hellenistic Royal Court: Court Culture, Ceremonial and Ideology in Greece, Egypt and Near East, 336–30 BCE*. Ph.D. diss., Utrecht University.

Strootman, Rudolf. 2014. "'Men to Whose Rapacity Neither Sea Nor Mountain Sets a Limit.' The Aims of the Diadochs." In *The Age of the Successors and the Creation of the Hellenistic Kingdoms (323–276 B.C.)*, edited by Hans Hauben and Alexander Meeus, 308–322. StHell 53. Leuven: Peeters.

Sweeney, Marvin A. 2000. *The Twelve Prophets*. Vol. 2. Berit Olam. Collegeville: Liturgical Press.

Tai, Nicholas H. F. 1996. *Prophetie als Schriftauslegung in Sacharja 9–14: Traditions- und kompositionsgeschichtliche Studien*. CThM 17. Stuttgart: Calwer.

Tigchelaar, Eibert J. C. 1996. *Prophets of Old and the Day of the End: Zechariah, the Book of the Watchers and Apocalyptic*. OTS 35. Leiden: Brill.

Treves, Marco. 1963. "Conjectures Concerning the Date and Authorship of Zechariah IX–XIV." *VT* 13:196–207.

Ulrich, Dean R. 2010. "Two Offices, Four Officers, or One Sordid Event in Zechariah 12:10–14?" *WTJ* 72:251–265.

Waterman, Leroy. 1954. "The Camouflaged Purge of Three Messianic Conspirators." *JNES* 13:73–78.

Way, Kenneth C. 2010. "Donkey Domain: Zechariah 9:9 and Lexical Semantics." *JBL* 129/1:105–114.

Way, Kenneth C. 2011. *Donkeys in the Biblical World: Ceremony and Symbol*. HACL 2. Winona Lake: Eisenbrauns.

Willi-Plein, Ina. 1974. *Prophetie am Ende: Untersuchungen zu Sacharja 9–14*. BBB 42. Cologne: P. Hanstein.

Willi-Plein, Ina. 2007. *Haggai, Sacharja, Maleachi*. ZBK.AT 24/4. Zurich: TVZ.

Willi-Plein, Ina. 2010. "Prophetie und Weltgeschichte: Zur Einbettung von Sach 9,1–8 in die Geschichte Israels." In *Geschichte Israels und deuteronomistisches Geschichtsdenken*, edited by Peter Mommer and Andreas Scherer, 301–315. AOAT 380. Münster: Ugarit-Verlag.

Willi-Plein, Ina. 2014. *Deuterosacharja*. BK.AT XIV/7.2.1. Neukirchen-Vluyn: Neukirchener Verlag.

Wellhausen, Julius. 1963. *Die Kleinen Propheten, übersetzt und erklärt*. 4th edition. Berlin: de Gruyter.

Wenzel, Heiko. 2011. *Reading Zechariah with Zechariah 1:1–6 as the Introduction to the Entire Book*. CBET 59. Leuven, Paris, and Walpole: Peeters.

Winnicki, Jan K. 1989. "Militäroperationen von Ptolemaios I. und Seleukos I. in Syrien in den Jahren 312–311 v. Chr. (I)." *AncSoc* 20:55–92.

Winnicki, Jan K. 1991. "Militäroperationen von Ptolemaios I. und Seleukos I. in Syrien in den Jahren 312–311 v. Chr. (II)." *AncSoc* 22:147–202.

Wolters, Al. 2014. *Zechariah*. HCOT. Leuven, Paris, and Walpole: Peeters.

Wöhrle, Jakob. 2008. *Der Abschluss des Zwölfprophetenbuches: Buchübergreifende Redaktionsprozesse in den späten Sammlungen*. BZAW 389. Berlin and New York: de Gruyter.

III: **Concepts of Leadership in Chronistic Literature**

Anna Maria Bortz
Conflicting Roles of Leadership in the Temple Building Account of Ezra 1–6

1 Introduction

The temple building account of Ezra 1–6, which recounts the story from the Edict of Cyrus to the rebuilding of the temple in Jerusalem, presents itself as a collection of different texts and documents that have been composed into a more or less coherent narrative. A reading of these first six chapters discloses the many different authorities that play a part in the restoration of the community and the construction of the temple. At the same time, the reader faces the problem of putting all of the authorities and protagonists of this early restoration period into a reasonable chronological order. This paper attempts to shed some light on the nature and function of the multiple restoration traditions that have been integrated into this temple building account.

Ezra 1–6 can be subdivided roughly into a Hebrew part, which comprises the first three chapters of the book,[1] and an Aramaic part starting with Ezra 4:8.[2] The Aramaic part can be further subdivided into two sections: Ezra 4 and Ezra 5–6. In Ezra 4, the reader is presented with the correspondence of Artaxerxes which, due to its setting *after* the reign of Darius and its focus on the rebuilding of the city instead of the temple, seems strangely out of place. For these reasons, it has been suggested that (this self-contained passage of) Ezra 4 is a later insertion bridging the time between the beginning of the temple restoration under Cyrus as portrayed in Ezra 1 and its completion under Darius (cf. Kratz 2000, 66; Rothenbusch 2012, 58; Grätz 2009, 260–262; 2006, 405, 414–

---

[1] For the view that the first three chapters of Ezra are distinct from the rest of the book, see also Fried 2012, 25, who describes Ezra 1–3 as a prologue. Gunneweg 1985, 94 speaks of Ezra 1–3 as the first scene of the first act.
[2] The actual Hebrew passages of Ezra 1–6 comprise Ezra 1:1–4:7 and Ezra 6:19–22. The fact that the change in language does not adhere to the traditional chapter divisions nor to the "document limits" (cf. Ezra 4:23–24) has often been noted. While the Hebrew verses in Ezra 6:19–22 can be explained as a secondary frame that adds a short note about the Passover festival, Ezra 4:1–7 and 4:23–24 call for a more nuanced explanation. In any case, Ezra 4:1 marks the beginning of a new passage and at the same time serves as a literary joint to the following correspondence of Artaxerxes. Kidner [1979] 2009, 53 notes: "From this point onwards right to the end of Nehemiah there is conflict." Cf. also Halpern 1990, 111; Blenkinsopp 1988, 42.

416).³ The question of the scope and function of this insertion would require a discussion of its own. Thus, due to limitations of space, I will not discuss Ezra 4 in my remarks on the conflicting roles of leadership.

In Ezra 5–6, we are then presented with the so-called Aramaic Chronicle. These two chapters deal with questions of legitimacy of the temple rebuilding during the time of Darius. At the same time, they refer back to the so-called Edict of Cyrus, which had supposedly guaranteed the return of the exiles and the rebuilding of the temple (2 Chr 36:22–23 // Ezra 1:1–4). With respect to their content, Ezra 5–6 are closely related to the Hebrew chapters Ezra 1–3.

2 Leadership in the "Aramaic Chronicle" (Ezra 5–6)

There seems to be a consensus that the oldest parts of Ezra 1–6 lie somewhere within chapters 5–6, the so-called Aramaic Chronicle, which can be considered an independent and more or less self-contained passage (cf. Kratz 2000, 57; 2013, 164; Williamson 2004, 257; Pakkala 2004, 3; Grätz 2006, 417–419; Rothenbusch 2012, 86). Here, at first glance the question of leadership seems to be answered unequivocally: During the time of Darius I, which is contemporaneous with the time of Zerubbabel and Joshua as well as of Haggai and Zechariah (Ezra 5:1–2), the temple is being built and completed. Here, we are presented with information that corresponds to what we know from the prophetic books of Haggai and Zechariah. Upon closer investigation, however, we find that different concepts of leadership show through. For not only Darius but also one of his predecessors, Cyrus, plays a role, together with the otherwise unknown Sheshbazzar as well as the elders of the Jews.

It has been debated whether Ezra 5:1–6:18 can be considered a unified narrative.⁴ As will be discussed further below, inconsistencies in content suggest that an earlier version of the Aramaic Chronicle has been gradually expanded.

---

3 Ezra 4:1–5 (Hebrew) and 4:24 (Aramaic) can thus be considered literary joints that facilitate the insertion of the correspondence between Ezra 3 and Ezra 5. That Ezra 4 is a self-contained unit can be shown by looking at 1 Esdras, where the entire passage has been moved to a new context in 1 Esd 2:15–25.

4 It has been suggested that 5:1–5 are a later insertion or introduction to the actual source; cf. Kratz 2000, 57–59, Gunneweg 1985, 95–96; Williamson 2004, 261–262. Furthermore, certain inconsistencies point to a secondary Aramaic frame in Ezra 6:16–18; cf. Kratz 2000, 59–60; Rothenbusch 2012, 84–85. Grätz (2014, 220) suggests that an earlier version of the Aramaic Chronicle can be found in Ezra 5:3–6:14aα, 15.

The text probably experienced literary growth due to its later connection with Ezra 1–3 and Ezra 4. It can also not be ruled out that in this process an earlier beginning was lost and/or that we have here a fragment taken from another context. While the precise literary growth of Ezra 5–6 remains elusive in certain respects, there is reason to assume that Ezra 5:1–2 as well as parts of Ezra 6:14*, 16–19 belong to a narrative framework that has been extended and adjusted to fit its new context.[5] It is problematic, however, to reconstruct the original beginning of the actual Aramaic source that has been embedded in Ezra 5–6. In any case, Ezra 5:3 cannot be an absolute beginning, since it refers to certain people mentioned previously (וכן אמרין להם).

2.1 Ezra 5:3–15* – The King, the Governor, and the Council of Elders

If for a moment, however, we leave aside the first two introductory verses of Ezra 5, which provide a dating and setting for the events that follow, we plunge right into the story. In v. 3 the conflict begins. The builders of the temple are asked about the legitimacy of the building project by Tattenai, the governor of "Beyond the River" (עבר־נהרה), and other officials. The matter is brought before Darius, and we are then presented with an account of the elders of the Jews which states that already Cyrus had given the order to rebuild the temple and that he had appointed a governor with the name of Sheshbazzar (Ezra 5:14). Sheshbazzar's task was to return the temple vessels (which Nebuchadnezzar had taken) to Jerusalem and to lay the temple foundations. The reproduction of the so-called Edict of Cyrus in Ezra 5 is matched by a supposedly official docu-

---

5 Ezra 6:14 is unusually long, and the basic message that the temple has been completed is repeated in v. 15. In this way, v. 15 seems to refer back to the elders named in v. 14 and not to the Persian officials in v. 13. While v. 15 presents us with an actual date of the completion and therefore seems to belong to the original narrative framework of the story, v. 14aβb might be a later insertion adding further information concerning the protagonists of the restoration and at the same time bridging the time gap between Cyrus and Darius. The mention of Artaxerxes even seems to suggest that the insertion already knew a composition that included Ezra 4. Thus, an earlier ending might be found in Ezra 6:14aα, 15 (ושבי יהודיא בנין ושיציא ביתה דנה); cf. Grätz 2014, 220. On the evaluation of Ezra 5:1–2 as a later addition, see Willi 1995, 66 ("Dieser ganze Passus, der die Bücher Hag und Sach aufnimmt und in kürzester Form wiedergibt, ist aber redaktionell nach 4,24 eingefügt und erscheint als Motivation zur Wiederaufnahme des sistierten Baus") and Rothenbusch 2012, 84, who regards Ezra 5:3 as a "formaler Neueinsatz." See also 2.2 below.

ment quoted later in Ezra 6:3–5, although there the appointment of a governor is not mentioned.⁶

The idea that the building of the temple had already started with Cyrus as presented in Ezra 5:16 might reflect a shared tradition with the messianic hope that (years earlier) Deutero-Isaiah had voiced upon the appearance of this Persian king on the global scene: According to Isa 44:28 YHWH awakes the Persian king Cyrus as the anointed one who initiates the temple building.⁷ Unique to the book of Ezra is the character of Sheshbazzar, a man with a Babylonian name, appointed as local leader, i.e., as governor (פחה). At the beginning of the restoration, he functions as an intermediary between the king and the local people.

Interestingly, however, in the setting of Ezra 5–6 the building process of the temple had been continued until (or just started during?) the time of Darius I, who is the one to renew the decree of Cyrus (Ezra 6). With him, further antagonists and protagonists enter the scene: the governor of "Beyond the River," Tattenai, Shetar-Bosnai, and other Persian officials, who question the building project and the elders of the Jews as local leaders, who try to justify it. While these Persian officials are at first introduced as opponents (Ezra 5:3–17), they later become supporters of the restoration project (Ezra 6:13). So, according to Ezra 5:3–6:13, (14*,) 15, during the reign of Darius, the Council of the Elders seems to be the local authority, corresponding and negotiating with the Persian officials (cf. Grätz 2006).

The text therefore preserves a tradition that has three official groups involved in the process of restoration: the king(s), the governors/Persian officials as intermediaries, and the elders as local leaders. While Cyrus and his appointed governor Sheshbazzar had been in charge of the early building project, it was now continued under the leadership of the elders of the community (later supported by the Persian officials) during the time of Darius. The idea that the temple building was initiated by Cyrus, however, does not correspond to what we read in the prophetic books of Haggai-Zechariah. Here, the foundation of the temple is laid during the reign of Darius. The dating of the building process to the reign of Cyrus is most likely explained by the phenomenon that the begin-

---

6 This is not the place to discuss the actual content and authenticity of this decree, which is also cited in 2 Chr 36:22–23 and Ezra 1:1–4. Yet it can be said that in all three cases certain phrases and the inherent theological agenda point towards a piece of tradition from which no authentic or original source can be reconstructed with certainty. Cf. Bedford 2001, 180–181; Rothenbusch 2012, 109–110; Grabbe 1998, 130–131, 2006, 541–563; Willi 1995, 47–58; Grätz 2015, 132.

7 This verse is probably a later addition to the older Cyrus oracles and reflects the idea that the Persian kings accompanied and provided for the Judean restoration; cf. Kratz 1991, 88–90; Grätz 2015, 133.

ning of the Persian hegemony was considered the beginning of a new period of deliverance. Cyrus, as the first king of the Achaemenid Empire, was thus made responsible for the epitome of the restoration: the laying of the temple foundations (cf. Kratz 1991, 88–90; Willi 1995, 47–50; Grätz 2014, 221–222).

The Aramaic Chronicle probably knew that the actual rebuilding of the temple did not begin until Darius I but wanted to preserve Deutero-Isaiah's tradition. Ezra 5:16 therefore already seems to conflate these two traditions. The main focus, however, is on the Persian king Darius, his Persian officials, and the elders of the community in Jerusalem. Grätz (2006) has shown that this Council of the Elders reflects a particular agenda of the Aramaic Chronicle, which seems to retroject the Hellenistic (Ptolemaic) γερουσία/πρεσβύτεροι attested in texts such as A.J. XII.138 or 2 Macc 11:27–33 into Persian times (Grätz 2006, 420). It is therefore reasonable to assume authorship by someone associated with this body of elders, a group that is described as loyal to the state and closely affiliated to the temple (cf. Grätz 2006, 421). At the same time, this description bears witness to a concept of leadership during the restoration that differs significantly from what we know from other biblical texts.

2.2 Ezra 5:1–2; 6:14 – Dual Leadership and the Haggai-Zechariah Tradition

The first two verses of the Aramaic Chronicle, however, suggest another scenario. If we begin reading the temple building account in Ezra 5:1–2, we get a very different impression of the leading participants in the building project: here, Haggai and Zechariah and correspondingly Joshua and Zerubbabel appear on the scene. Following Haggai-Zechariah, one must assume that Zerubbabel, Joshua, and the two prophets were the prominent leaders of the restoration during the time of Darius (cf. Hag 1:1, 12, 14; 2:2, 4, 21, 23; Zech 3; 4:7–10; 6:9–15).[8] Yet it is striking that they appear only briefly in the Aramaic Chronicle. The two prophets are mentioned only in Ezra 5:1, [2]; 6:14, both of which frame the actual story. Likewise, Zerubbabel and Joshua are named only in the introductory verse Ezra 5:2, where they are said to initiate the rebuilding process. But unlike in the books of Haggai and Zechariah, where Zerubbabel and Joshua are presented with their full titles – זרבבל בן־שאלתיאל פחת יהודה ואל־יהושע בן־יהוצדק הכהן הגדול (Hag 1:1) – in the book of Ezra they are introduced by fili-

---

8 Contrary to Isa 44:28, in Haggai-Zechariah the beginning of the temple building is set in the time of Darius – about twenty years later. Haggai-Zechariah, however, seem to reflect an older tradition (see n. 9 below).

ation only. No mention is made of any administrative or religious titles. Zerubbabel in Ezra 5, unlike Sheshbazzar, thus does not appear as a governor. Nevertheless, it is obvious that here the text of Ezra knows this prophetic tradition (cf. Willi 1995, 66).

From Ezra 5:3 on, neither Zerubbabel nor Joshua play a role in the following account. Here, we can detect the competing role of the elders beginning in Ezra 5:5. Kratz (2000, 59–60) has noted that both Zerubbabel and Joshua, who appear only in v. 2, as well as Haggai and Zechariah, who frame the narrative in 5:1 and 6:14, could be a later insertion in the text. As Grätz (2006, 407–408) has pointed out, the question in v. 3 "Who gave you a decree to build this house, and to finish this wall?" addressed to Zerubbabel and Joshua (Ezra 5:2) is repeated almost verbatim in v. 9, where it is instead addressed to the elders, who from then on play a crucial role in the restoration. The conspicuously long passage in Ezra 6:14 that then includes Haggai and Zechariah in the process of completion of the temple building appears to be an even later addition (cf. Grätz 2006, 414). It is therefore likely that the two prophets and the diarchic leadership of Zerubbabel and Joshua have been added later, probably with the aim of including this older prophetic tradition.[9]

It is interesting, however, that Ezra 5 does not simply adopt the prophetic tradition; it also changes the focus. While the prophetic books attribute a great part of the restoration to the dual leadership of Joshua and Zerubbabel, the additions in the Aramaic Chronicle (Ezra 5:1–2; 6:14) suggest that the focus is more on the role of the two prophets, who are said to accompany the building process. This is emphasized three times (Ezra 5:1–2; 6:14) whereas Zerubbabel and Joshua are mentioned only briefly (cf. Williamson 2004, 261). The fact that both appear without official titles in Ezra 5–6 even seems to conceal the diarchic principle of secular and religious leadership. Indeed, without the information from Haggai and Zechariah, we would not know that Zerubbabel and Joshua are associated with the offices of governor and high priest, respectively. It is possible that the triad of king, Persian officials, and elders did not leave room for other forms of leadership in this account of the restoration.

Hence, an earlier version of the Aramaic Chronicle probably did not know or mention the dual leadership of Zerubbabel and Joshua or the prophetic pair of Haggai and Zechariah. They came onto the scene only later, although they are most likely part of an older tradition. The new focus on prophetic agency thereby matches the prominent role that the prophetic tradition takes in the

---

9 It is likely that Ezra knows and uses information from the books of Haggai-Zechariah and not vice versa; see already Noth 1957, 145 as well as Kratz 1991, 88–90, 2000, 59–60; Hallaschka 2011, 133 n. 776.

temple building account of Ezra 1–6 as a whole (cf. Edelman 2009, 47–59; Grätz 2015, 129, 134–135). Thus, with these additions, prophetic leadership comes into focus, while the diarchic leadership of Zerubbabel and Joshua does not play a very important role.

3 Leadership in the Composition of Ezra 1–3

To complicate things further, we must now consider Ezra 1–3, which can be read as a Hebrew prologue to the Aramaic chapters of Ezra 5–6, redirecting the reader and providing additional information. This prologue begins with the Edict of Cyrus, which gives the exiles permission to return and to rebuild the temple (Ezra 1), and ends with the laying of the temple foundations and the building process (Ezra 3), where Ezra 5 then picks up.[10]

Ezra 1–3 can thus be taken as a largely unified narrative. Although Ezra 2 is often separated from Ezra 1 and/or Ezra 3, it can be shown that the composition of Ezra 1–3 serves as a prologue for Ezra 5–6 by adhering to a specific pattern which is also inherent in the exodus narrative. It displays a fixed set of motifs – *exodus, census, and offerings for the construction or maintenance of the sanctuary* – that is also found in Exodus and Numbers.[11] In doing so, it places two crucial events in Israel's history in parallel – the exodus from Egypt and the

---

10 See also n. 2 above. It seems to be a consensus that Ezra 4* is a later insertion. At the same time, Ezra 1–3 can of course not be attached to Ezra 5–6 without (chronological) problems. Yet, the ending in Ezra 3:13, which describes the noise of the people accompanying the building process, seems to correspond to the situation in Ezra 5:3, where the Persian officials come to visit. Thus, Ezra 5 picks up where Ezra 3 leaves off: with the building of the temple during the reign of Darius. Yet, again, we cannot rule out that Ezra 5:3 might have had a different beginning that was lost during the composition process.
11 The census of God's people is an integral part of the exodus narrative: After the exodus from Egypt, upon arrival at the Sinai, and after crossing the desert for forty years the people of Israel are registered. This procedure is mentioned several times: first, in Exod 30:11–16 and 38:24–26 without presenting an actual list of people; in Num 1–4; 26 it is then taken up again and elaborated on. Just as in the books of Exodus and Numbers, the mustering process in Ezra 2 is connected to an exodus (cf. Ezra 1) – not from Egypt, but from Babylon. After a period of transition, having overcome hardships and life-threatening experiences, the people are counted in the books of Exodus and Numbers as well as in Ezra. These censuses after the exodus can be understood as a kind of stocktaking before God (cf. Exod 12:37; 30; Num 1; 26; Ezra 2). In each case, exodus and census are followed by donations made for the construction of the temple or the inauguration of the cult – in Exod and Num for the priestly sanctuary (Exod 30:11–16; 38:25–26; Num 7:2 and possibly Num 31:48–52), in Ezra for the Second Temple (Ezra 2:68–69), which is then built in Ezra 3 and Ezra 5–6, respectively. Cf. also Bortz 2018, 204–226.

return of the exiles from Babylonia. The people that are building the temple are allowed to do so not only because Cyrus or Darius – as instruments of YHWH – gave them permission to, but because they are God's chosen people that have – once again – been led back to the Promised Land by YHWH. They are the "one and only" legitimate Israel that re-establishes the "true cult." Ezra 1–3 therefore portrays a (new) exodus from Babylonia as setting or "prehistory" for what happens in Ezra 5–6. In this way, the prologue sets a new framework for the narrative in Ezra 5–6.

3.1 A New Triad: The Heads of the Ancestral Houses, the Priests, and the Levites

Ezra 1 begins with the Edict of Cyrus and thus follows the Aramaic Chronicle in attributing the return and rebuilding of the temple to this Persian king. As has often been pointed out, Ezra 5–6 served as a literary source for Ezra 1.[12] Yet Ezra 1 now shifts the focus from the question of the legitimacy of rebuilding the temple to details of the return and the role of Cyrus as an instrument of YHWH. Here too, Sheshbazzar is entrusted with the return of the temple vessels. Just as in Ezra 5, we have the two actors Cyrus and Sheshbazzar.

Two striking differences, however, must be noted: unlike Ezra 5, Ezra 1 makes no mention of Sheshbazzar laying the temple foundations. Furthermore, Sheshbazzar here is not called פחה ("governor") but rather הנשיא ליהודה ("prince of Judah"), an archaizing title reminiscent of the נשיאם in the book of Numbers (Num 2:3–30; 7; 34:18–28) – perhaps a reference to the exodus – as well as the future נשיא as the leader of Judah (cf. Ezek 44:3; 45:7–8, etc.) (cf. Williamson 1985, 18; Grätz 2006, 417; Edelman 2005, 178–179). In any case, Ezra 1 does not use the actual administrative title. Yet what Ezra 1 and 5–6 have in common is that they attribute the initiative and responsibility for the temple rebuilding (and thus the beginning of the *Heilszeit*) to Cyrus, a tradition that goes back to (the redaction of) Deutero-Isaiah (Isa 44:28). In Deutero-Isaiah we also already find the return from Babylonia to Judah portrayed as a second exodus (cf., e.g., Kiesow 1979). Hence, as has often been noted, Ezra 1 seems to rely closely on this prophetic tradition (Willi 1995, 55; Blenkinsopp 1988, 16; 2008, 308; Williamson 1985, 16; Fried 2015, 28–30).

---

12 Cf. e.g. Kratz 2000, 57: "Esr 1 setzt in Erzählung um, was die Ältesten der Juden gegenüber der persischen Behörde in 5,13–16 zu ihrer Rechtfertigung vorbringen und die Entdeckung des Kyrosedikts unter Darius in 5,17–6,5 ans Licht bringt." See also Noth 1957, 145; Gunneweg 1985, 49; Halpern 1990, 88–89; Willi 1995, 51–52; Rothenbusch 2012, 108–109; Grätz 2006, 416–417.

In addition to the leaders already mentioned in Ezra 5, we have yet another group of actors that is introduced in v. 5: the heads of the ancestral houses,[13] the priests, and the Levites. This triad of actors reappears not only throughout Ezra 1–3 (e.g., Ezra 2:70; 3:12) but also in the narrative framework that has been added to the Aramaic Chronicle in Ezra 6:16–19.

Ezra 2 then presents an elaborate list of the אנשי עם ישראל that were now returning to Jerusalem and Judah. Yet we do not know the exact time of the return – was it under Cyrus, or Cambyses, or Darius? This chapter somehow serves as a transition from the time of Cyrus and Sheshbazzar to a time when Zerubbabel and Joshua were active (cf. Ezra 3:2, 8) – twenty years later.

This list of returnees is preceded by yet another short list of "those they came with" (Ezra 2:2a). First Esdras 5:8 clearly understood these to be the chiefs leading the return by adding τῶν προηγουμένων αὐτῶν. Yet the apposition אשר־באו עם־ in Ezra 2:2a seems only loosely connected to the introductory verse of Ezra 2:1. At the same time, many of these listed names seem to belong to "prominent individuals but whose activities seem to lie in a different context (Nehemiah, Ezra?, Mordecai, Bilshan, Bigvai?)" (Grabbe 1998, 14). Hence Ezra 2:2a appears to be a later addition that gathers all kinds of important leading figures and authorities at the time of the restoration to ensure that all of them had participated in the return (cf. also Bortz 2018, 114–117). Yet, except for Zerubbabel and Joshua, none of them plays a role in the following narrative. Rather, we have a group of returnees listed according to their ancestral houses[14] as well as priests, Levites, and other cultic personnel. The structure of the list ("the men of the people of Israel" and the cultic personnel) is then taken up again in Ezra 2:70, where all of them are said to settle in Jerusalem and Judah. The list itself as well as v. 70 thereby also seem to follow the underlying structure of the triad *heads of ancestral houses, priests, and Levites*, with the exception that some additional groups of the *clerus minor* have been added.[15]

---

13 See n. 14 below.
14 The list is captioned with the phrase אנשי עם ישראל. The listing of the people according to the pattern בני + PN suggests that we are here dealing with the ראשי האבות named in Ezra 1:5. This list should be read as a short form of ראשי בית האבות; cf. Gunneweg 1985, 45; Williamson 1985, 15; Blenkinsopp 1988, 77. It is unclear how to classify the sociological division of "a father's house" during the postexilic period in view of other terms like משפחה or שבט. In any case, the term denotes a subdivision of the people of Israel. The ראשי האבות thus seem to serve as the representatives of this postexilic community. Cf. also Rothenbusch 2012, 381–386; Karrer 2001, 88.
15 The literary unity of Ezra 2:70 has been a matter of debate; cf. Williamson 1985, 272–273. Due to the striking order in which the groups are enumerated, it can be suggested that the verse originally only contained the groups of the priests, the Levites, and the people; cf. Gunneweg 1985, 68–69; Williamson 1985, 273; Karrer 2001, 85 n. 53; Bortz 2018, 143–144.

What remains enigmatic is the (probably Persian) loanword התרשתא in Ezra 2:63.[16] The returning priests that were not able to trace their ancestry in the register were not permitted to participate in the cult by the so-called *Tirshata*. It is unclear whether here we are dealing with a personal name or a title,[17] although the article suggests the latter. Since the term is only rarely attested in the Hebrew Bible[18] and nowhere else, we cannot say whether it describes a specific office and, if so, which tasks this office would have comprised. In any case, it is interesting that in a context where the focus seems to be on personal names (esp. Ezra 1–3; 5:1–2; cf. the long list of names in Ezra 2) and not on official titles, the person behind התרשתא remains anonymous.

Zerubbabel and Joshua then appear on the scene in Ezra 3:2, 8 – and only here (except for the later addition in 2:2 and the reference to Joshua in 3:9[19]). As in Ezra 5:2 they are introduced by filiation only; no mention is made of the titles פחה or הכהן הגדול. Furthermore, especially when it comes to the temple building scene, they appear among others – (again) the triad of priests, Levites, and other returnees (cf. Ezra 3:8). Just as in Ezra 5–6, their leading role does not seem to be as prominent in this text as in Haggai-Zechariah.

Interestingly, when it comes to the question of who laid the temple foundations, Ezra 3 leaves us in the dark. Ezra 3:10 attributes this action to anonymous builders (ויסדו הבנים את־היכל יהוה) accompanied by the priests, the Levites, and the people (cf. Ezra 3:8). Thus, at the most important moment of the temple restoration – the laying of the foundations – the text remains vague. We simply do not know who these בנים were. But we do know that – unlike Ezra 5:16 – the text does not explicitly attribute this task to Sheshbazzar or Zerubbabel (cf. Hag 1:14; Zech 4:9–10). The actual builders remain just as unknown as the ones in Ezra 5:4 (גבריא די־דנה בינא בנין). Hence, while the text seems to know and make use of the prophetic tradition in Haggai-Zechariah (cf. Ezra 3:6 // Hag 2:8; Ezra 3:8 // Hag 1:12, 14; Ezra 3:12 // Hag 2:3), it does not adopt its concept of leadership. The focus of Ezra 1–3 is on the people, priests, and Levites as whole.

---

16 The meaning of the presumably Persian loanword התרשתא remains unclear. The translation as "excellency" found in older literature (cf. Scheftelowitz 1901, 93–94) cannot, however, be upheld; cf. In der Smitten 1971, 620. For an overview, see Williamson 1985, 27.
17 It might be possible to view the term as a corruption of the Persian personal name Tiridata (*Tiri* as the Persian astral goddess + *dāta* "law"), which is also attested in Nippur in the fifth century BCE (cf. Dandamaev and Lukonin 1989, 340). Yet the use of the definite article in התרשתא would contradict this assumption.
18 The name is attested elsewhere only in Neh 7:65, 69; 8:9; 10:2. In the latter two verses, it is associated with the person of Nehemiah. The scarcity of the evidence, however, does not permit us to associate the term Tirshata with the office of the governor (פחה).
19 Probably also a later addition; cf. Bortz 2018, 162–166.

3.2 Conflating Leadership

Ezra 1–3 thus presents a compromise of different traditions. It combines the tradition of the Aramaic Chronicle in Ezra 5–6, which it seems to rewrite, as well as the prophetic traditions of Deutero-Isaiah and Haggai-Zechariah. In this way, the Hebrew prologue – similarly to the addition of the leaders in Ezra 2:2a – gathers all the leaders of the early restoration that seem to have been associated with the rebuilding of the temple.

However, Ezra 1–3 is not a simple amalgamation of different traditions but has its own theological or ideological agenda. It correlates information gathered from different traditions into a coherent (but in parts blurry) restoration narrative. This prologue does not tell us who exactly laid the temple foundations or during whose reign (Cyrus or Darius?) this happened; rather, it emphasizes that this happened as part of a new exodus and a new *Heilszeit*.

Following the tradition of Haggai-Zechariah, Ezra 3 associates Zerubbabel and Joshua with the building of the temple and therefore with the time of Darius (yet whom the text chooses not to name). This tradition might even later have been added to Ezra 5:1–2. Contrary to Zech 4:9–10, the laying of the temple foundation is not attributed to Zerubbabel, although it is also not attributed to Sheshbazzar.

At the same time, the prologue of Ezra 1–3 suggests that the *Heilszeit* and therefore the beginning of the restoration and the temple building must have begun – as in Deutero-Isaiah – with Cyrus. He therefore is the only king named. So, even where the text follows the Haggai-Zechariah tradition, Cyrus (and with him the beginning of Persian supremacy) remains the main reference point.

Significantly, in most cases the text leaves out the official titles and designations of the people participating in the temple building project. It is striking that Ezra 1–3 does not use the official designation פחה – neither for Sheshbazzar nor for Zerubbabel. Sheshbazzar is called נשיא, reminiscent of the נשאים of the first exodus (Num 2; 7). Zerubbabel remains without a title. So, the text seems to intentionally avoid the administrative term פחה as well as a precise dating. And whereas Cyrus (as the only available king legitimized through the tradition of Deutero-Isaiah) initiates the temple building, the actual builders seem to be the people. Similarly, the person and function of the *Tirshata* in Ezra 2:63, probably known to the ancient audience, remains enigmatic to us. In Ezra 1–3, the structures and hierarchies of leadership during this period of the restoration are kept obscure.

It appears that this prologue, unlike the narrative of 1 Esdras, which focuses on the dual leadership of the Persian king and a Judean leader for each period of the restoration (Cyrus/Sheshbazzar, Darius/Zerubbabel and Artaxerxes/Ezra; cf. Honigman 2011, 196), does not want to focus on any individual "great" personality but rather wants to embed all of the important figures associated with the temple building into a glorious early phase of restoration that followed a second exodus and therefore epitomizes the beginning of the new *Heilszeit*. Sheshbazzar plays a role in the return of the temple vessels, as do Zerubbabel and Joshua in the temple building. But the focus of these first chapters lies rather on the list at the heart of this prologue: the returnees.

With this, the leadership during the time of the restoration is transferred to the triad of the *(heads of the) people of Israel*, *the priests*, and *the Levites*, under which all the other leaders can be subsumed. This triad takes a lead in the restoration and plays an important role throughout Ezra 1–3 as well as Ezra 6:16–19. These are the people of the second exodus who have been freed and chosen again by YHWH and are now contributing to the rebuilding of his temple. Thus, the Hebrew prologue to the following Aramaic Chronicle sets the focus on the returnees as a whole – the community of the "true Israel" and the primary protagonists of the early restoration.

4 Conclusion

To sum up, Ezra 1–6 does not give us unequivocal information about the leading figures during the early phase of the restoration. As a multilayered literary unit that imagines this new beginning after the exile from a Hellenistic perspective, it becomes clear that each passage has its own ideological and theological interests in presenting these historic events. We find different traditions and motifs interwoven and placed within a composite narrative.

Ezra 5–6 originally attribute the leadership of the Judean restoration to Cyrus and Sheshbazzar as well as the elders. Perhaps only with the addition of the prologue in Ezra 1–3 do Haggai and Zechariah as well as Zerubbabel and Joshua appear on the scene. Yet unlike 1 Esdras, which focuses on the hero Zerubbabel in its retelling of the Ezra narrative, in Ezra 1–6 the characters of Sheshbazzar, Zerubbabel, and Joshua remain vague and flat, since the focus is now on the people as a whole, the "true Israel" of the second exodus. The elders of the Jews in Ezra 5–6 and the heads of the ancestral houses in Ezra 1–3 can thereby easily be associated.

The close connection of the *people (heads of ancestral houses)*, *priests*, and *Levites* as well as the focus on the temple and the reference to the exodus tradition suggest a priestly agenda behind the reworked unit of Ezra 1–6. The use of the prophetic tradition also seems to point to authorship closely associated with the temple. Yet, somewhat unexpectedly, Ezra 1–3 does not show any trace of an Aaronide or Zadokite lineage, a tradition that is prominently represented elsewhere in the postexilic books of Ezra-Nehemiah and Chronicles (cf., e.g., the genealogy of Ezra in Ezra 7:1–5; 8) (cf. Schunck 2009, 214–215; Dahm 2003, 32–44). Ezra 1–6 here seems to have preserved an alternative tradition.[20] At the same time, the positive portrayal and the idealization of the Persian kings as promotors of the Judean restoration seems to suggest a composition that already looks back on the Persian hegemony (see also Davies 1996, 160). The authors therefore might be drawing an idealized picture of a king that contrasted with their experience of Hellenistic rule.

Given the role of Gedaliah in Mizpa (2 Kgs 25:22–24; Jer 40:5, 7, 11; 41:2) and the external evidence of the sixth to fourth centuries BCE (seal impressions, the Elephantine papyri, etc.), the office of a פחה, a governorship of Yehud, can very well be assumed (cf. Kratz 2004, 93–106; Grätz 2008, 175; Avigad 1976, 6–7; Stern 1982, 202–213; Lemaire 2002, 213–216). It is therefore not too far-fetched to associate Sheshbazzar (at the time of Cyrus) as well as Zerubbabel (at the time of Darius) with this office according to biblical tradition (cf. Kratz 2004, 105; Grabbe 2004, 141–142). Yet it is evident that the temple building account in Ezra 1–6 does not provide us with reliable information as to what role these leaders actually played. The text has its own agenda of putting the focus on the returnees as a whole. But as prominent figures of the restoration, Cyrus and Sheshbazzar, Darius and Zerubbabel (and Joshua) as well as the two prophets Haggai and Zechariah have found a place in the collective memory of the people. It therefore comes as no surprise that Ezra 1–6 brings all of these figures together.

Bibliography

Avigad, Nahman. 1976. *Bullae and Seals from a Post-Exilic Judean Archive*. Qedem 4. Jerusalem: Hebrew University.
Bedford, Peter R. 2001. *Temple Restoration in Early Achaemenid Judah*. JSJ.S 65. Leiden: Brill.
Blenkinsopp, Joseph. 1988. *Ezra-Nehemiah: A Commentary*. OTL. Philadelphia: Westminster Press.
Blenkinsopp, Joseph. 2008. "Ezra-Nehemiah: Unity or Disunity?" In *Unity and Disunity in Ezra-Nehemiah: Redaction, Rhetoric, and Reader*, edited by Mark J. Boda and Paul L. Reditt, 306–314. HBM 17. Sheffield: Sheffield Phoenix Press.
Bortz, Anna M. 2018. *Identität und Kontinuität: Form und Funktion der Rückkehrerliste Esr 2*. BZAW 512. Berlin and Boston: de Gruyter.

---

[20] Dahm (2003, 40) suggests that existing priestly lineages were most likely subsumed under the Aaronide-Zadokite lineage as part of a late editing of the Hebrew Bible. Similarly, MacDonald (2015) assumes that the sons of Zadok were a "late innovation in the biblical texts" (p. 147) and "the result of textual exegesis" during Hellenistic times (p. 148). So either Ezra 1–6 did not know of that tradition or it intentionally presents an alternative one.

Dahm, Ulrike. 2003. *Opferkult und Priestertum in Alt-Israel: Ein kultur- und religionswissenschaftlicher Beitrag.* BZAW 327. Berlin and New York: de Gruyter.
Dandamaev, Muchammed A., and Vladimir G. Lukonin. 1989. *The Culture and Social Institutions of Ancient Iran.* Cambridge et al.: Cambridge University Press.
Davies, Philip R. 1996. "Scenes from the Early History of Judaism." In *The Triumph of Elohim: From Yahwisms to Judaisms*, edited by Diana V. Edelman, 145–182. Grand Rapids: Eerdmans.
Edelman, Diana V. 2005. *The Origins of the "Second Temple": Persian Imperial Policy and the Rebuilding of Jerusalem.* London and Oakville: Equinox.
Edelman, Diana V. 2009. "Ezra 1–6 as Idealized Past." In *A Palimpsest: Rhetoric, Ideology, Stylistics, and Language Relating to Persian Israel*, edited by Ehud Ben Zvi, 47–59. PHSC 5. Piscataway: Gorgias Press.
Fried, Lisbeth S. 2012. "Ezra's Use of Documents in the Context of Hellenistic Rules of Rhetoric." In *New Perspectives on Ezra-Nehemiah: History and Historiography, Text, Literature, and Interpretation*, edited by Isaac Kalimi, 11–26. Winona Lake: Eisenbrauns.
Fried, Lisbeth S. 2015. *Ezra: A Commentary.* Sheffield: Sheffield Phoenix Press.
Grabbe, Lester L. 1998. *Ezra-Nehemiah.* London and New York: Routledge.
Grabbe, Lester L. 2004. *A History of the Jews and Judaism in the Second Temple Period. Vol. 1: Yehud: A History of the Persian Province of Judah.* LSTS 47. London et al.: Bloomsbury T&T Clark.
Grabbe, Lester L. 2006. "The 'Persian Documents' in the Book of Ezra: Are They Authentic?" In *Judah and the Judeans in the Persian Period*, edited by Oded Lipschits and Manfred Oeming, 531–570. Winona Lake: Eisenbrauns.
Grätz, Sebastian. 2006. "Die Aramäische Chronik des Esrabuches und die Rolle der Ältesten in Esr 5–6*." *ZAW* 118:405–422.
Grätz, Sebastian. 2008. "Zu einem Essay von Albrecht Alt: Die Rolle Samarias bei der Entstehung des Judentums." In *Kontexte: Biografische und forschungsgeschichtliche Schnittpunkte der alttestamentlichen Wissenschaft*, edited by Thomas Wagner et al., 171–184. Neukirchen-Vluyn: Neukirchener Verlag.
Grätz, Sebastian. 2009. "Verweigerte Kommunikation? Das Verhältnis zwischen Samaria und Juda in der persischen Zeit im Spiegel der Bücher Esra und Nehemia." In *Kommunikation über Grenzen: Kongressband des XIII. Europäischen Kongresses für Theologie. 21.–25. September 2008 in Wien*, edited by Friedrich Schweitzer, 252–268. VWGTh 33. Gütersloh: Gütersloher Verlagshaus.
Grätz, Sebastian. 2014. "Chronologie im Esrabuch: Erwägungen zu Aufbau und Inhalt von Esra 1–6." In *Nichts Neues unter der Sonne? Zeitvorstellungen im Alten Testament*, edited by Jens Kotjatko-Reeb et al., 213–225. BZAW 450. Berlin and New York: de Gruyter.
Grätz, Sebastian. 2015. "Bund und Erwählung in Esra-Nehemia." In *Covenant and Election in Exilic and Post-Exilic Judaism*, edited by Nathan MacDonald, 123–137. FAT II/79. Tübingen: Mohr Siebeck.
Gunneweg, Antonius H. J. 1985. *Esra: Mit einer Zeittafel von A. Jepsen.* KAT XIX/1. Gütersloh: Gütersloher Verlagshaus.
Hallaschka, Martin. 2011. *Haggai und Sacharja 1–8: Eine redaktionsgeschichtliche Untersuchung.* BZAW 411. Berlin and New York: de Gruyter.
Halpern, Baruch. 1990. "A Historiographic Commentary on Ezra 1–6: Achronological Narrative and Dual Chronology in Israelite Historiography." In *The Hebrew Bible and Its*

Interpreters, edited by William H. Propp et al., 81–142. Biblical and Judaic Studies from the University of California, San Diego 1. Winona Lake: Eisenbrauns.

Honigman, Sylvie. 2011. "Cyclical Time and Catalogues: The Construction of Meaning in 1 Esdras." In *Was 1 Esdras First? An Investigation into the Priority and Nature of 1 Esdras*, edited by Lisbeth Fried, 191–208. SBL 7. Atlanta: SBL Press.

In der Smitten, Wilhelm T. 1971. "Der Tischātā' in Ezra-Nehemia." *VT* 21:618–620.

Karrer, Christiane. 2001. *Ringen um die Verfassung Judas: Eine Studie zu den theologisch-politischen Vorstellungen im Esra-Nehemia-Buch*. BZAW 308. Berlin and New York: de Gruyter.

Kidner, Derek. [1979] 2009. *Ezra and Nehemiah: An Introduction and Commentary*. TOTC 12. Nottingham: Inter-Varsity-Press.

Kiesow, Klaus. 1979. *Exodustexte im Jesajabuch: Literarkritische und motivgeschichtliche Analysen*. OBO 24. Fribourg and Göttingen: Academic Press and Vandenhoeck & Ruprecht.

Kratz, Reinhard G. 1991. *Kyros im Deuterojesaja-Buch: Redaktionsgeschichtliche Untersuchungen zu Entstehung und Theologie von Jes 40–55*. FAT 1. Tübingen: Mohr Siebeck.

Kratz, Reinhard G. 2000. *Die Komposition der erzählenden Bücher des Alten Testaments: Grundwissen der Bibelkritik*. UTB 2157. Göttingen: Vandenhoeck & Ruprecht.

Kratz, Reinhard G. 2004. "Statthalter, Hohepriester und Schreiber im perserzeitlichen Juda." In *Das Judentum im Zeitalter des Zweiten Tempels*, edited by Reinhard G. Kratz, 93–119. FAT 42. Tübingen: Mohr Siebeck.

Kratz, Reinhard G. 2013. *Historisches und biblisches Israel: Drei Überblicke zum Alten Testament*. Tübingen: Mohr Siebeck.

Lemaire, André. 2002. "Das Achämenidische Juda und seine Nachbarn im Lichte der Epigraphie." In *Religion und Religionskontakte im Zeitalter der Achämeniden*, edited by Reinhard G. Kratz, 210–230. VWGTh 22. Gütersloh: Gütersloher Verlagshaus.

MacDonald, Nathan. 2015. *Priestly Rule: Polemic and Biblical Interpretation in Ezekiel 44*. BZAW 476. Berlin and Boston: de Gruyter.

Noth, Martin. [1943] 1957. *Überlieferungsgeschichtliche Studien: Die sammelnden und bearbeitenden Geschichtswerke im Alten Testament*. 2nd edition. Tübingen: Max Niemeyer.

Pakkala, Juha. 2004. *Ezra the Scribe: The Development of Ezra 7–10 and Nehemiah 8*. BZAW 347. Berlin and New York: de Gruyter.

Rothenbusch, Ralf. 2012. *"... abgesondert zur Tora Gottes hin": Ethnisch-religiöse Identitäten im Esra/Nehemiabuch*. HBS 70. Freiburg i. Br.: Herder.

Scheftelowitz, Isidor. 1901. *Arisches im Alten Testament*. Vol I. Diss. Königsberg.

Schunck, Klaus-Dietrich. 2009. *Nehemia*. BK.AT XXIII/2. Neukirchen-Vluyn: Neukirchener Verlag.

Stern, Ephraim. 1982. *Material Culture of the Land of the Bible in the Persian Period 538–332 B.C.* Warminster: Aris & Phillips.

Willi, Thomas. 1995. *Juda – Jehud – Israel: Studien zum Selbstverständnis des Judentums in persischer Zeit*. FAT 12. Tübingen: Mohr Siebeck.

Williamson, Hugh G. M. 1985. *Ezra, Nehemiah*. WBC 16. Dallas: Word Books.

Williamson, Hugh G. M. 2004. *Studies in Persian Period History and Historiography*. FAT 38. Tübingen: Mohr Siebeck.

Bob Becking
Was Ezra a Persian or a Yehudite Leader?

1 What Kind of Leader Was Ezra?

In the last several decades, much attention has been given to the nature of Nehemiah's leadership, especially in the context of American Evangelical churches (see, e.g., White 1986; McKenna 2005; Maciariello 2003, 397–407; Patton 2007, 8–14). For reasons unknown, Ezra has not received as much attention. A few suggestions, however, have been given by Tamara Cohn Eskenazi, Eric Coggins, and in the recent commentary of Shepherd and Wright. Eskenazi (1988, 136–144) characterizes Ezra's role in the narrative as that of a "self-effacing teacher of the Torah." Coggins (2012, 33–51) stresses Ezra's spiritual leadership which he shares with Nehemiah, but unlike Nehemiah, Ezra is not afraid of surrounding himself with those of greater ability. Shepherd and Wright (2018, 188–211) classify his leadership as "patrimonial," derived from and based on the power of the Persian overlord. These three voices indicate the tension between Torah-based leadership and Persian commands that I would like to discuss in this paper. Unfortunately, the Persian administration did not organize a dossier on Ezra in which the deeds and doings are listed together with a set of official documents describing his task. This implies that the question of the nature of Ezra's leadership must be answered by a detour through the (often difficult) biblical material.

This detour is necessary, since the books of Ezra and Nehemiah do not contain straightforward historical information, even though they present themselves as "historical narratives." A closer reading reveals that both books should be treated as literary texts communicating a set of values through the guise of historical events. This is not the place, however, for a detailed treatment of this topic (for further discussion, see Grabbe 1980; Eskenazi 1988, 136–144; Davies 2018, 114–124; Becking 2018; Andersson 2019, 87–105).

2 How Many Ezras?

2.1 Ezra 7–10 vs Nehemiah 8

The character Ezra is mentioned in Ezra 7–10 as well as in Neh 8. A first reading of the texts makes clear that he is cast in the role of one of the leaders of the postexilic community. This prima facie clear observation masks a problem:

What is the narrative connection between the two texts? Is the Ezra from Ezra 7–10 the same person as the Ezra in Neh 8 (on a narrative as well as on a historical level)? Many scholars adhere to the idea of an Ezra memoir, which assumes that Neh 8 would originally have been situated between Ezra 7–8 and 9–10. With this supposed memoir, Ezra would have accounted for his deeds and doings (see, e.g., Williamson 1983, 1–30, but also Myers 1965, xlviii–lii; Clines 1984, 6–8; Williamson 1985, xxviii–xxxii; Pakkala 2006, 17–24; Throntveit 1992, 8–10; Blenkinsopp 2009, 44–85; Willi 2012; Grabbe 2015, 100–101; Shepherd and Wright 2018, 5). These scholars would answer the question of the identity of the two Ezras positively. I do not regard Neh 8 as a part of the Ezra memoir for the following reasons (for further discussion, see Becking 2018):

(a) Nehemiah 8 does not contain a first-person singular report on Ezra, which is uncommon for a memoir.
(b) Nehemiah 8 perfectly fits the narrative context of Neh 8–12. These chapters describe how the identity and the security of the community in Jerusalem is safeguarded not only by the wall around the city (see Neh 3–4); rather, the (re)building of the community should be based also on an internal defense: obedience to the divine Torah. This is the theme of Neh 8–12. The reading of the Torah by Ezra fits perfectly into this theme.
(c) The motif of "mixed marriages" is absent in Neh 8–12. It would thus be surprising to find Neh 8 within the Ezra narrative, in which this theme is overwhelmingly present.

In sum: Nehemiah 8 should not be regarded as an erratic block or as a section of Ezra that has been wrongly placed in Nehemiah by an inattentive copyist.

This raises, however, the question of the relationship between "Ezra" in Neh 8 and "Ezra" in Ezra 7–10. Are they the same person, who would then have lived a relatively long time? Are they two different persons with the same name? That would be very surprising in view of the scarcity of the name Ezra.[1] Most probably, there is something else at stake. Before I can answer these questions, I have to consider my third argument.

I have argued elsewhere that Ezra 7–10 is a pseudepigraphic text based on a minor character from the book of Nehemiah. In Neh 8, Ezra is in a subordinate role in which he is presented as instrumental in the reapplication of the Torah of Moses. This subordinate role is the starting point for all of the other traditions on Ezra: Ezra 7–10; 1 Esdras; *4 Ezra*; the *Greek Apocalypse of Ezra*; the *Vision of Ezra*; and the *Questions of Ezra*. In these traditions, Ezra's role extended to a teacher

---

[1] In the Hebrew Bible, the name *"èzrā"* does not occur outside the books of Ezra and Nehemiah; the variant spelling ʿèzrāh is attested in 1 Chr 4:17.

of Israel and a rabbi *avant la lettre* (see Fried 2014). The first stage on this trajectory are the last four chapters in the book of Ezra. This text functioned as a pamphlet indicating the identity of those Judeans who were permitted to celebrate in the renewed temple cult around 400 BCE.[2] The narrative on the rebuilding of the temple (Ezra 3–6; fictional as well) was placed in front of this pamphlet. The narrative in Ezra 7–10 might better be understood as a reflection of the period of seven years of punishment in which the cult could continue, but in a defiled temple and under strict rules. The so-called Artaxerxes *firman* (Ezra 7:11–28) should be regarded as a later addition by a redactor writing in Hellenistic times.[3] This implies that we have to reckon with three literary "Ezra" figures:
- Ezra A, a character in Neh 8;
- Ezra B, in the story in Ezra 7–10*;
- Ezra C, in the Artaxerxes *firman*.

2.2 Two Connected Roles

In Neh 8, Ezra A is cast in the role of a priest and co-worker of Nehemiah. Ezra's public reading of (parts of the) Torah stirred up the minds of the community, which led to the reintroduction of the Feast of Tabernacles (Neh 8:13–18 [ET 8:14–19]).

In Ezra 7–10, Ezra B is a scribe who was sent on a mission by the Persian king Artaxerxes, but construed by the narrator as someone under the divine guidance of the God of Israel. In the description of Ezra's fictional mission, the narrator focuses on two aspects: first, the essential role of the Levites in the construction of cult and community (Ezra 8), and second, the so-called "mixed marriage crisis" (9–10).[4] The latter occupies the bulk of the text. In Ezra 9–10,

---

[2] The argument for this position is based on the Bagoses story (Josephus, A.J. XI.297–301) in connection with the observation by Rainer Albertz on a shift in the correspondence between Yedoniah and Bagoas on the rebuilding of the temple of Yahô in Elephantine after its destruction by a coalition of the priests of Khnum and the wicked Widranga. The first letter was sent to the political and religious leadership, both in Jerusalem and Samaria. The second request was no longer sent to both Jerusalem and Samaria, indicating a problem in leadership (see Becking 2011, 217–233).
[3] The argument of Grätz (2004) is convincing.
[4] The issue of "mixed marriages" should be seen as an element in a larger conflict (see, e.g., Karrer 2001, 67–127; Grabbe 2004, 313–316; Blenkinsopp 2009, 117–159; Southwood 2011, 46–59; 2012; Rom-Shiloni 2013, 33–47; Moffat 2013; Shepherd and Wright 2018, 40–48). In my view, the conflict had no ethnic dimensions. The text argues against the intermarriage of the returning exiles with the descendants of those who remained in the land and was thus an intra-Judahite and not an inter-ethnic issue (see Becking 2009, 31–49).

Ezra is portrayed as a pious man with strict views concerning the interpretation of the moral code of the Torah. Although he at times shows empathy with "others and outsiders," overall he aims at a fenced-off and purified community. His implementation of this form of religion is adopted by the vast majority of the "returnees."

These two roles do not overlap completely. Nevertheless, there is a clear connection between the two. Both Ezra A and Ezra B are leading figures who inspired by the regulations of the Torah are helping the community to pass the threshold of a new phase in its existence.

3 Ezra in Weberian Terms

3.1 Max Weber

By the end of his life, the German sociologist Max Weber proposed the concept of charismatic leadership (Weber 1980). In this type of leadership, authority is based on the charisma of the leader. It stands in contrast to two other types of leadership. Judicial leadership is based on laws, societal codes, and generally accepted arrangements within a society. (Western) democracy is a clear example: The president of Finland derives his authority from the Finnish law codes. The other type is traditional leadership in which the authority is not based on rational-legal deliberations but on the past performance of elite families in kingdoms (kings, sultans, sheikhs, elders), gentry, and some family-owned companies. This inherited form of meritocracy is fading away in modern society. The person bearing the charisma occupies a leadership position through charismatic rule that gives him or her a specific kind of authority that often generates acceptance and mass obedience. Trust in the charismatic leader is based on the perception that he or she articulates what is seen as wrong in a society or community and then fulfills the collective hopes to correct these wrongs. The authority of the leader is based on unique personality traits, which lead to a high identification of the adherents with the goals and views of the charismatic leader. Given this identification, it can motivate the leaders to extraordinary achievements or actions.

Weber's ideas have been elaborated by Rainer Lepsius (1993, 95–118). Lepsius theorized that the rise of a charismatic leader is connected with a specific situation within a society or a community. In societies there are – alongside periods of prosperity and general well-being – phases in which there is a momentum that can be labelled as latently and/or manifestly charismatic. In latent situations, a fundamental lack of orientation permeates the society. In such a situation, a charismatic leader is sometimes able to articulate the problems in a clear voice and hence to offer a new and steadfast orientation to change the situation into a more explicit call for charismatic leadership. The charisma of the leader often has a religious dimension: either the leader or his/her direct followers claim an element of divine mission. The language describing the acts of the charismatic leader is often apocalyptic – bad times that will be substituted by good times; misleading leaders versus those who really understand what the people need, connected with a "now or never" sense of urgency. The success of a charismatic leader depends on the strength of his personality and on the degree to which he is able to raise public support for his views.

Weber's ideas have influenced biblical scholars (see Holstein 1975, 159–179; Rodd 1981, 95–106), especially in the interpretation of leaders like Moses (e.g., Weisman 1977, 399–411; Frevel 2014, 261–287; 2018, 89–114) or the judges (Yoder 2015).

3.2 Ezra A in Weberian Terms

What kind of leader was Ezra in Weberian terms? As for Ezra A – the co-worker in Neh 8 – only a few elements might hint at him being a charismatic leader.

(1) Within the narrative sequence of the book of Nehemiah, the situation in Jerusalem was far from ideal. The devastation of the city and the carrying away of the temple vessels – symbols of the divine presence – had shocked the basic confidence of the community. Their orientation laid in ruins. This is articulated in the desperate cry of Hanani to Nehemiah: "The remnant there in the province who survived the captivity is in great distress and reproach, and the wall of Jerusalem is broken down and its gates are burned with fire" (Neh 1:3).

The question arises which event – or chain of events – is referred to by this picture. Many scholars connect the image given by Hanani with a specific event in Judean history: either the destruction by Nebuchadnezzar (Fensham 1982, 151–152), or the destruction referred to in Ezra 4:23 (see Williamson 1983, 166–172; Shepherd and Wright 2018, 48–50). Becker (1990, 61–62) claims that the author had no specific time frame in mind. The use of the participle $m^e por\grave{e}ṣ\grave{e}t$ indicates, in my opinion, an ongoing situation. In other words, the desolate state of the city as a result of the Babylonian conquest is a continuous situation (see also Myers 1965, 94–95). The picture is later repeated by Nehemiah when speaking to the Persian king: "Let the king live forever. Why should my face not be sad when the city, the place of the tombs of my fathers, lies desolate and its gates have been consumed by fire?" (Neh 2:3).

Both texts indicate a latent charismatic situation. The problems surrounding the rebuilding of the wall by Nehemiah only make the situation more urgent.

(2) After reading sections from the Torah, Ezra quite quickly gained public support for his views. They listened to him, understood the explanations, had a great festive meal, and accepted the celebration of the Feast of Tabernacles (Neh 8).

Before making a conclusion, other elements in the narrative, however, need to be taken into consideration.

(a) Ezra's authority is derived from the authority of Nehemiah, who was the main leader in the process of rebuilding the city and community.
(b) Ezra's authority is also derived from the fact that he is a priest (Neh 8:2). This could be regarded as an element of traditional leadership, since priests had a hereditary position of control over the cult and divination.
(c) Ezra does not act out of his own initiative. Although Neh 8 is silent about the nature of the hierarchy between Nehemiah and Ezra, they both derive their authority from the imperial court that had approved Nehemiah's mission. In other words, Ezra also has elements of a judicial leadership.

In sum, Ezra A cannot be classified as a leader who fits completely into one category. His leadership is multidimensional.

3.3 Ezra B in Weberian Terms

Could the same be said about Ezra B? The answer is not readily evident. Some elements hint in the direction of a positive answer, while others do not. The narrative in Ezra 7–10* assumes a latent charismatic situation. These chapters focus on the lack of Levites for the cult in Jerusalem (Ezra 8:15–30) as well as a situation of marriages with "strange women" that corrupted the purity of the community (Ezra 9:1–5). The core of Ezra's sermon-like prayer (Ezra 9:6–15) is an articulation of the fundamental lack of moral orientation:

> And now, our God, what shall we say after this?
> For we have forsaken your commandments,
> that you had commanded by your servants, the prophets, saying,
> "The land which you are entering to possess is an unclean land with the uncleanness of the peoples of the lands, with their abominations which have filled it from end to end with their impurity.
> So now do not give your daughters to their sons nor take their daughters for your sons, and never seek their peace or their prosperity, that you may be strong and eat the goods of the land and leave as an inheritance to your sons forever."

> After all that has come upon us for our evil deeds and our great guilt, since you, our God, has spared despite our iniquities and has given us an escaped remnant as this. (Ezra 9:10–13)

In the narrative development of Ezra 7–10*, this prayer occupies a key functional place (see also Eskenazi 1988, 60–77; Shepherd and Wright 2018, 45). Since the textual unit refers back to previous elements in the story (the mentioned crisis) and anticipates forthcoming measures (the dissolution of marriages), the prayer is instrumental in seeking a way out of this crisis. Besides, it is fundamental as the basis of the author's desired community. Hogewood (2006, 69–82) has shown that the prayer has a clear performative power: The words of Ezra encourage the community to act. This explains the absence of a request addressed to the deity. The prayer ends with two questions for the implied audience ("Should we again break your commandments and intermingle with the peoples who commit these abominations? Would you not be angry with us to the point of destruction, until there is no remnant nor any who escape?"; Ezra 9:14) and with a doxology praising YHWH ("O, YHWH, God of Israel, you are righteous, for we have been left an escaped remnant, as on this day; behold, we are before you in our guilt, for no one can stand before you because of this"; Ezra 9:15).

With his sermon-like prayer, Ezra B is able to raise public support for the harsh measures he is about to implement: the dissolution of marriages that, although based on texts known from Deut 7, nevertheless stand in contrast to the treatment the moral code of the Hebrew Bible prefers for the widow and the needy (see, e.g., Otto 1994, 47–67; Gnuse 2015, 18–27; Unterman 2017, 41–84). In fact, Ezra B is demonizing the "strange women" and casting them in the role of scapegoats to be blamed for the misery of the times (Janzen 2002). The strategy of scapegoating the other remains to this day an element in the rhetoric of charismatic leaders appealing to the apocalyptic sense of "us against them; good versus bad." Reading the narrative, however, shows traces of the other aspects of leadership. When Ezra is introduced in the story, his pedigree is given (Ezra 7:1b–5), connecting him to Aaron over seventeen generations. The genealogy is related to that of 1 Chr 5:27–41 (6:1–15). The historical accuracy of this genealogy can hardly be seen with any certainty. Abisua, Bukki, Uzzi, Zerachiah, Merajot, Azariah, Amariah, Achitub, and Seraiah are not mentioned in priestly roles outside of Chronicles, Ezra, and Nehemiah. Hilkiah is possibly identical with Hilkiah the high priest named in 2 Kgs 22. More important, however, is to note that this long family tree functions as an argument of authority.[5] Ezra is present-

---

5 On the function of genealogies in the Hebrew Bible, see Wilson 1977; VanderKam 2004, 45–46; Löwisch 2015.

ed as a descendant in a priestly line dating back to Mosaic times. He is thus bestowed with the authority of a traditional leader. In addition to this, his leadership is confirmed by two factors that cast him in the role of a judicial leader. His authority is based on the initiative of the Persian king Artaxerxes, although the king disappears from the story after Ezra 8:1. The other aspect of his judicial authority is indicated by the fact that Ezra appropriates the moral and legal code of ancient Israel in solving the problem of "mixed marriages." A clear example can be found in Ezra 9:10–11: "For we have forsaken your commandments, that you had commanded by your servants, the prophets, saying [...]." Then follows an anthology of commandments with intertextual relations with Deut 7:1–3; 11:8; 23:6; Lev 18:24–30. Note that Moses is implicitly seen as a prophet (see also Deut 34:10; Luke 9:33; Quran 7:103–117). However, as Blenkinsopp (1989, 173–179) has rightly pointed out, the ban in Deuteronomy applies to both sexes, while the narrator of Ezra limits himself to marriages with strange women (see also Moffat 2013, 79–80). This appropriation of the tradition could also be construed as an element of charismatic leadership. Charismatic leaders tend to present their re-arrangements of the tradition as the original tradition.[6]

I will round off this section by stating that the leadership of Ezra B, like Ezra A, cannot be classified in one single dimension. Unlike Ezra A, he is not dependent on the leadership of Nehemiah.[7]

4 Ezra and the Principal-Agent Theory (and Problem)

So far, an answer to the pivotal question of this paper has not been given. The analysis of the leadership of Ezra A and B in a Weberian discourse only showed that in the judicial dimension of Ezra's leadership, both "Ezras" were seen as supported by God and king. Both the Israelite moral code and the Persian initiative drove their actions.

In order to get a clearer picture of the dynamics of this twofold influence, I will look at the principal-agent theory as it has been developed by economists. This theory describes the dynamics between a principal and an agent.[8] The ba-

---

[6] Compare, for instance, the rhetoric of the Dutch populist Geert Wilders on the Judeo-Christian roots of Western society.
[7] Ezra C will not be discussed in this paper.
[8] See Rees 1985a, 3–26; 1985b, 75–97. There is a multitude of publications discussing the value of the theory in all aspects of human life and behaviour, see, e.g., Schulze, Lubatkin, and Dino 2003, 473–490; Roach 2016, 28–35; Basak 2017, 41–60.

sic idea is quite simple: The principal gives an order to the agent (a farmer asks a lad to milk a cow; a joiner asks an apprentice to put up a fence; a school director asks a teacher to give a lesson, up to more complicated tasks). In order to smoothen the process, a reward is given in the form of a payment. Things are, however, not as easy and predictable in more complex situations, especially in cases of asymmetric information: when the agent has to fulfill various tasks or when the agent – being an expert in the field – has an advantage by knowing more about things like the specifics of a production process or the dynamics of the grass-root situation in a community.

Sometimes the interests of the principal and the agent do not align with each other and may be in conflict. In all such cases, an agent is in a position to negotiate better conditions: more time for the job, better wages, etc. The principal has to reflect and consider to which degree he can accept the claims and the demands of the agent. Next to that, the principal has to deliberate in what way he can control the results of a process he knows hardly anything about. Econometrists have constructed a formula by which a principal can weigh the risks of giving an assignment in a complex situation: $w = a + b(e + x + gy)$.[9]

Looking at the relationship between Ezra and Artaxerxes through this lens, a few observations can be made.

- The Persian Empire is a complex entity.[10]
- The king has relatively little knowledge about the political situation and the social-religious framework in the province of Yehud.
- In view of Egypt's determination to regain its independence, the king is in need of a strong and trustworthy buffer state without social unrest.[11]
- As a skilled scribe, Ezra is a good candidate to perform the order of Artaxerxes:
  - Ezra A is presented as a scribe and a priest who had the knowledge to read and explain the Torah of Moses in a new and still uncertain situation (Neh 8:1–12).

---

9 w (wage) is equal to a (the base salary) plus b (the intensity of incentives provided to the employee) times the sum of three terms: e (unobserved employee effort) plus x (unobserved exogenous effects on outcomes) plus the product of g (the weight given to observed exogenous effects on outcomes) and y (observed exogenous effects on outcomes). b is the slope of the relationship between compensation and outcomes. See Rees 1985, 2:75–97; Guesnerie and Laffont 1984, 329–369.
10 See, e.g., Wiesehöfer 1994; Briant 1996.
11 During the fifth century BCE, Egypt was almost constantly trying to throw off the Persian yoke. On Persian border-politics, see Hoglund 1992; Fantalkin and Tal 2006, 167–197; Faust 2018, 34–59.

- Ezra B is presented as follows: "He was a scribe skilled in the law of Moses, which YHWH, the God of Israel had given" (Ezra 7:6).

  In the traditional Judean and Israelite society, a writer was someone who employed or commissioned documents or, commissioned by the temple, composed, drafted, collected or copied documents. In emerging Judaism, the *sofēr* gradually turned into a scribe whose business was the interpretation of the Torah. From the perspective of Persian rulers, a *sofēr* was to be compared with a high court-official, a "chancellor." The Hebrew word *māhîr*, "skilled," refers to a trained craftsman, see also Ps 45:2; Prov 22:29; Isa 16:5 and the Aramaic cognate in *Ahiqar* 1:1 (Blenkinsopp 1989, 137–138; Heltzer and Avishur 2002, 217–222; Fried 2015, 297). The expression *māhîr b^{e}tôrat mośe* indicates that he was skilled, both in copying and editing the old law traditions and also in applying them to the situation of his own days (Jagersma 2012, 116–122).

- The gifts by the king can be construed as a reward to stimulate Ezra B to perform: "The king gave him all he requested because the hand of YHWH his God was upon him" (Ezra 7:6).

  Within the discourse of the principal agent-theory, this gift by the king can be construed as the outcome of the negotiations between Artaxerxes and Ezra B on $w = a + b(e + x + gy)$.

In other words, Ezra B can easily be seen as an agent to fulfill the task commissioned by the principal. He, however, has his own agenda and is surrounded by Yehudite interests. Next to his loyalty towards the Persian king stands his loyalty towards his people and their religious and moral code. It is hardly conceivable that Artaxerxes would have been interested in the question of exogamous or endogamous marriages among the inhabitants of the province of Yehud. Ann Fitzpatrick-McKinley (2015) has shown clearly that the Persians were not very much interested in local affairs as long as the provinces contributed to the imperial coffers. Hence, while performing the task given by Artaxerxes, Ezra had the freedom to execute his own agenda: purifying the community from strange elements. In everything he does, he is "between fires." He is in the unenviable position between "above" and "beneath," between Persian power and Yehud's desire for autonomy and the continuation of its own religion.

I come to a conclusion. Ezra – and especially Ezra B – is best be seen as a middleman who was able to remain loyal to two sides: the Persian government and the Yahwistic religion (as he saw it). He was simultaneously a Persian and a Yehudite leader.

5 Pre- and Postexilic Leadership

I would like to round off with a remark on one of the focal questions of the present volume by asking to what degree postexilic leadership differed from preexilic leadership. My short answer based on the study of the book of Ezra within its historical context is as follows. After the exile, the need for a double loyalty arose out of the loss of Judean independence and being incorporated into a vast empire. This situation caused an act of compromising and balancing between the two poles of power. Apparently, Ezra A as well as Ezra B found ways to manoeuvre between the two, which also explains why neither can be classified fully as charismatic leaders. Both were restricted in their roles either of seconding Nehemiah or as an intermediary middleman.

Bibliography

Andersson, Greger. 2019. "Narrating Selves and the Literary in the Bible." *Partial Answers: Journal of Literature and the History of Ideas* 17:87–105.
Basak, Rishi. 2017. "Agency Theory and International Climate Change Financing Accountability Regimes." *World Bank Research Observer* 19:41–60.
Becker, Joachim. 1990. *Esra, Nehemia*. NEB 25. Würzburg: Echter Verlag.
Becking, Bob. 2009. "On the Identity of the 'Foreign' Women in Ezra 9–10." In *Exile and Restoration Revisited: Essays on the Babylonian and Persian Periods in Memory of Peter R. Ackroyd*, edited by Lester L. Grabbe and Gary N. Knoppers, 31–41. Library of Second Temple Studies 73. London and New York: Bloomsbury T&T Clark.
Becking, Bob. 2018. *Ezra and Nehemiah*. HCOT. Leuven: Peeters.
Blenkinsopp, Joseph. 1989. *Ezra-Nehemiah: A Commentary*. OTL. London: SCM Press.
Blenkinsopp, Joseph. 2009. *Judaism, the First Phase: The Place of Ezra and Nehemiah in the Origins of Judaism*. Grand Rapids: Eerdmans.
Briant, Pierre, 1996. *Histoire de l'Empire Perse: De Cyrus à Alexandre*. Paris: Fayard.
Clines, David J. A. 1984. *Ezra, Nehemiah, Esther*. NCBC. Grand Rapids: Eerdmans.
Coggins, Eric. 2012. "Contrasting Leadership Styles in Postexilic Judaism: A Comparative Analysis of Ezra 9:1–5 and Nehemiah 13:23–27." *Journal of Biblical Perspectives in Leadership* 41:33–52.
Davies, Philip R. 2018. "Cultural Memory in Practice: Ezra and Nehemiah." In *Even God Cannot Change the Past: Reflections on Seventeen Years of the European Seminar on Historical Methodology*, edited by Lester L. Grabbe, 114–124. LHBOTS 663. London and New York: Bloomsbury T&T Clark.
Eskenazi, Tamara C. 1988. *In an Age of Prose: A Literary Approach to Ezra-Nehemiah*. SBL.MS 36. Atlanta: Scholars Press.
Fantalkin, Alexander, and Oren Tal. 2006. "Redating Lachish Level 1: Identifying Achaemenid Imperial Policy at the Southern Frontier of the Fifth Satrapy." In *Judah and the Judaeans in the Persian Period*, edited by Oded Lipschits and Manfred Oeming, 167–197. Winona Lake: Eisenbrauns.

Faust, Avraham. 2018. "Forts or Agricultural Estates? Persian Period Settlement in the Territories of the Former Kingdom of Judah." *PEQ* 150:34–59.

Fensham, F. Charles. 1982. *The Books of Ezra and Nehemiah*. NICOT. Grand Rapids: Eerdmans.

Fitzpatrick-McKinley, Ann. 2015. *Empire, Power, and Indigenous Elites: A Case Study of the Nehemiah Memoir*. JSJ.S 169. Leiden: Brill.

Frevel, Christian. 2014. "Transformationen des Charismas: Überlegungen zum Buch Numeri vor dem Hintergrund von Max Webers Veralltäglichungstheorem." In *Glaube in Gemeinschaft: Autorität und Rezeption in der Kirche*, edited by Markus Knapp and Thomas Söding, 261–287. Freiburg i. Br.: Herder.

Frevel, Christian. 2018. "Leadership and Conflict: Modelling the Charisma of Numbers." In *Debating Authority: Concepts of Leadership in the Pentateuch and the Former Prophets*, edited by Katharina Pyschny and Sarah Schulz, 89–114. BZAW 507. Berlin and Boston: de Gruyter.

Fried, Lisbeth S. 2014. *Ezra and the Law in History and Tradition*. Columbia: University of South Carolina Press.

Fried, Lisbeth S. 2015. *Ezra: A Commentary*. Sheffield: Phoenix Press.

Gnuse, Robert K. 2015. *Trajectories of Justice: What the Bible Says About Slaves, Women, and Homosexuality*. Eugene: Wipf and Stock Publishers.

Grabbe, Lester L. 1980. *Ezra-Nehemiah*. Old Testament Readings. London and New York: Routledge.

Grabbe, Lester L. 2004. *A History of the Jews and Judaism in the Second Temple Period. Vol. 1: Yehud: A History of the Persian Province of Judah*. LSTS 47. London et al.: Bloomsbury T&T Clark.

Grabbe, Lester L. 2015. "Penetrating the Legend: In Quest for the Historical Ezra." In *Open-Mindedness in the Bible and Beyond: A Volume of Studies in Honour of Bob Becking*, edited by Lester L. Grabbe and Marjo C. A. Korpel, 97–111. LHBOTS 616. London et al.: Bloomsbury T&T Clark.

Grätz, Sebastian. 2004. *Das Edikt des Artaxerxes: Eine Untersuchung zum religionspolitischen und historischen Umfeld von Esra 7,12–26*. BZAW 337. Berlin and New York: de Gruyter.

Guesnerie, Roger, and Jean-Jaques Laffont. 1984. "A Complete Solution to a Class of Principal-Agent Problems with an Application to the Control of a Self-Managed Firm." *Journal of Public Economics* 25:329–369.

Heltzer, Michael, and Yitsḥak Avishur. 2002. "The Term sōfēr māhīr as Designating a Courtier in the Old Testament and the Ahiqar Story." *UF* 34:217–222.

Hogewood, Jay C. 2006. "The Speech Act of Confession: Priestly Performative Utterance in Leviticus 16 and Ezra 9–10." In *Seeking the Favor of God. Vol. 1: The Origins of Penitential Prayer in Second Temple Judaism*, edited by Mark J. Boda, Daniel K. Falk, and Rodney A. Werline, 69–82. EJIL 21. Atlanta: SBL Press.

Hoglund, Kenneth G. 1992. *Achaemenid Imperial Administration in Syria-Palestine and the Missions of Ezra and Nehemiah*. SBLDS 125. Atlanta: Scholars Press.

Holstein, Jay A. 1975. "Max Weber and Biblical Scholarship." *HUCA* 46:159–179.

Janzen, David. 2002. *Witch-Hunts, Purity and Social Boundaries: The Expulsion of the Foreign Women in Ezra 9–10*. JSOTSup 350. Sheffield: Sheffield Academic Press.

Karrer, Christiane. 2001. *Ringen um die Verfassung Judas: Eine Studie zu den theologisch-politischen Vorstellungen im Esra-Nehemia-Buch*. BZAW 308. Berlin and New York: de Gruyter.

Lepsius, M. Rainer. 1993. "Das Modell der charismatischen Herrschaft und die Anwendbarkeit auf den 'Führerstaat' Adolf Hitlers." In *Demokratie in Deutschland: Soziologisch-historische Konstellationsanalysen*, edited by M. Rainer Lepsius, 95–118. KSG 100. Göttingen: Vandenhoeck & Ruprecht.

Löwisch, Ingeborg S. 2015. *Trauma Begets Genealogy: Gender and Memory in Chronicles*. Sheffield: Sheffield Phoenix Press.

Maciariello, Joseph. 2003. "Lessons in Leadership and Management from Nehemiah." *ThTo* 60:397–407.

McKenna, David L. 2005. *Becoming Nehemiah: Leading with Significance*. Kansas City: Lillenas Publishing.

Moffat, Donald P. 2013. *Ezra's Social Drama: Identity Formation, Marriage and Social Conflict in Ezra 9 and 10*. LHBOTS 579. London and New York: Bloomsbury T&T Clark.

Myers, Jacob M. 1965. *Ezra Nehemiah: A New Translation with Introduction and Commentary*. AB 14. New York: Doubleday.

Otto, Eckart. 1994. *Theologische Ethik des Alten Testaments*. ThW 3.2. Stuttgart, Berlin, and Cologne: Kohlhammer.

Pakkala, Juha. 2006. "The Original Independence of the Ezra Story in Ezra 7–10 and Neh 8." *BN* 129:17–24.

Patton, Cheryl. 2007. "What Made Nehemiah an Effective Leader?" *The Journal of Applied Christian Leadership* 11:8–14.

Rees, Ray. 1985a. "The Theory of Principal and Agent: Part I." *Bulletin of Economic Research* 37:3–26.

Rees, Ray. 1985b. "The Theory of Principal and Agent: Part II." *Bulletin of Economic Research* 37:75–97.

Roach, Charlene M. L. 2016. "An Application of Principal Agent Theory to Contractual Hiring Arrangements within Public Sector Organizations." *Theoretical Economics Letters* 6:28–35.

Rodd, Cyril S. 1981. "On Applying a Sociological Theory to Biblical Studies." *JSOT* 19:95–106.

Rom-Shiloni, Dalit. 2013. *Exclusive Inclusivity: Identity Conflicts Between the Exiles and the People Who Remained (6th–5th Centuries BCE)*. LHBOTS 543. London and New York: Bloomsbury T&T Clark.

Schulze, William S., Michael H. Lubatkin and Richard N. Dino. 2003. "Toward a Theory of Agency and Altruism in Family Firms." *Journal of Business Venturing* 18:473–490.

Shepherd, David and Christopher J. H. Wright. 2018. *Ezra and Nehemiah*. The Two Horizons Old Testament Commentary. Grand Rapids: Eerdmans.

Southwood, Katherine E. 2011. "An Ethnic Affair? Ezra's Intermarriage Crisis Against a Context of 'Self-Ascription' and 'Ascription of Others'." In *Mixed Marriages: Intermarriage and Group Identity in the Second Temple Period*, edited by Christian Frevel, 46–59. LHBOTS 547. London and New York: Bloomsbury T&T Clark.

Southwood, Katherine E. 2012. *Ethnicity and the Mixed Marriage Crisis in Ezra 9–10: An Anthropological Approach*. Oxford: Oxford University Press.

Throntveit, Mark A. 1992. *Ezra-Nehemiah*. Interpretation. Louisville: John Knox Press.

Unterman, Jeremiah. 2017. *Justice for All: How the Jewish Bible Revolutionized Ethics*. Philadelphia: University of Nebraska Press.

VanderKam, James C. 2004. *From Joshua to Caiaphas: High Priests After the Exile*. Minneapolis: Fortress Press.

Weber, Max. 1980. *Wirtschaft und Gesellschaft*. Tübingen: Mohr Siebeck.

Weisman, Ze'ev. 1977. "Charismatic Leaders in the Era of the Judges." *ZAW* 89:399–411.

White, John. 1986. *Excellence in Leadership: The Pattern of Nehemiah*. Westminster: IVP.
Wiesehöfer, Josef. 1994. *Das antike Persien von 550 v. Chr. bis 650 n. Chr.* Munich and Zurich: Artemis & Winkler.
Willi, Thomas. 2012. *Esra: Der Lehrer Israels*. Biblische Gestalten 26. Leipzig: Evangelische Verlagsanstalt.
Williamson, Hugh G. M. 1983. "The Composition of Ezra I–VI." *JThS Studies* 34:1–30.
Williamson, Hugh G. M. 1985. *Ezra, Nehemiah*. WBC 16. Waco: Word Books.
Wilson, Robert. 1977. *Genealogy and History in the Biblical World*. New Haven: Yale University Press.
Wright, Jacob L. 2004. *Rebuilding Identity: The Nehemiah Memoir and Its Earliest Readers*. BZAW 348. Berlin and New York: de Gruyter.
Yoder, John C. 2015. *Power and Politics in the Book of Judges: Men and Women of Valor*. Minneapolis: Fortress Press.

Ehud Ben Zvi
Leadership in the World of Memories Evoked by Chronicles in the Context of the Late Persian/Early Hellenistic Period

1 Establishing a Starting Point: An Array of Opening Considerations

The memories of past Israel evoked by reading Chronicles among the literati of the period could not but raise, in one way or another, issues of leadership, especially (but not necessarily limited to) the central leadership of Israel. Although Chronicles was, in the main, about Israel and YHWH, it was still generally structured around human kings and their deeds, and thus directly and indirectly addressed matters of leadership.[1]

Conversely, much of the exploration of matters of central leadership among the readers of Chronicles in the late Persian/early Hellenistic period was carried out through narratives about the past and the memories evoked by them (cf. Edelman and Ben Zvi 2016). The literati reading Chronicles were by no means unique in this regard.

Obviously, the access to these narratives and the world of memories they construed required a primary group, namely the literati who read and reread the book. This simple and self-evident fact raises three crucial sets of considerations, which will serve as guideposts in the present study.

1.1 Memories and meanings evoked by comprehensive narratives informed, balanced, and complemented those evoked by "narrower" narratives and *vice versa*

The literati who read Chronicles read and remembered particular stories about this or that king or event (e.g., the stories about the main villain Ahaz, or about Manasseh whose life partially embodies the story of Israel; see Ben Zvi 2019), but they also read, construed and remembered large scale narratives shaping

---

[1] As is the case of the books of Kings and most ancient Near Eastern works that may be considered historiographic. I have purposefully kept some of the oral tone of the original paper read at the relevant session at the 2018 EABS meeting.

their general understanding of Israel's past (and hinting at its present and future), such as the narrative trajectory from Adam to David/Solomon, or from the creation of the human world to the creation of the temple in Jerusalem; or the array of multiple mutually informing, complementary trajectories that begin with either Saul or David on the one hand and end with Cyrus or sinful Judah about to be exiled on the other, and which reflect on a plethora of issues involving a second instantiation of "the temple" – which in itself assumes an abstract concept of "the temple," "proper" configurations and roles of local elites in a subaltern polity, Davidic and non-Davidic monarchy/ies and their multiple potential instantiations, and so on.

The memories evoked by the larger, summarizing, comprehensive narratives informed, balanced, and complemented those of the narrower narratives, but also *vice versa*. This dynamic process of complementarity must be taken into serious consideration when we attempt to construct a historical reconstruction of the ways the literati explored and construed matters of central leadership, whether in ways "visible" or – more importantly – "invisible" to them, for that which is "transparent" and "unseen" for a group is usually the most important evidence for reconstructing its social mindscape.

1.2 Reading Chronicles and remembering its world did not take place in a social, cultural vacuum and every new book changes the mental "library" of the literati and vice versa

The readers of Chronicles could not have read the book outside of their world of knowledge and without recourse to their general social mindscape, which in turn was intertwined with their world of knowledge.[2] Particularly relevant for the present purposes is that they read several other books that also constructed each a past and as such served also as a safe playground for social exploration on matters of leadership. This simple fact raises two important – and not so self-evident – considerations.

First, in order to understand what reading Chronicles *uniquely and substantially* contributed to a socially shared web of explorations on issues of leadership among the literati, one has to think in terms of the ways in which *the web*

---

[2] Cf. Umberto Eco's concepts of the "encyclopedia" and "encyclopedic knowledge." Moreover, like Eco, I would argue that each new book that is added to the library reshapes, to a certain extent, the meaning of the other books in the library and *vice versa*. See below.

of explorations about leadership in the group would have been different, had Chronicles not existed among these literati. As Eco and others have long maintained, every new "book" added to the textual repertoire or "library" of a group impacts the accepted meanings communicated by the other books in the said repertoire, because it informs and is informed by the others.

Second, the general narrative in Chronicles must differ from the general narrative in the Primary Historical Collection (Gen–2 Kgs; hereafter PHC) and that of Deuteronomistic Historical Collection (Deut–2 Kgs; hereafter DHC) to be able to emerge within the community. Even so, Chronicles came into being among them, and above all was read among literati who not only read the other collections, but also shared a comprehensive social mindscape. Reading Chronicles within this context went together with addressing, even if often implicitly, core matters within this mindscape. Obviously the same held true for their reading the other stories/works/collections. Thus, the unavoidable outcome of this situation is that the literati's Chronicles entered into a conversation and at times complementary tension with conceptual frames on matters of leadership conveyed or evoked by the literati's DHC and PHC.

1.3 Prioritizing the "pragmatic" meaning of reading and remembering

I would argue that the key to reconstruct the way in which reading Chronicles – or indeed any other pastshaping book served to explore issues of leadership is often not found at the level of the basic narrative "content" of specific stories about the past, even if this level is the most obvious to all of us, but at that of the "pragmatic" meaning of reading and remembering these texts within a certain social location and historical setting.

For the present purposes, the most profitable way to demonstrate the usefulness of this approach is not to develop a lengthy, abstract, theoretical discussion, but to bring to bear some examples that clearly demonstrate the point. The examples I have in mind come from broadly the same time period and from a group of literati that shares some "systemic" features with the Yehudite literati, namely the priestly literati in places such as Babylonia or Uruk in the late Persian and Seleucid periods, and their world of thought as it has emerged in some recent studies (see, e.g., Waerzeggers 2015; De Breucker 2015; Jursa and Debourse 2017).

According to De Breucker (2015, 83–84), for instance, three main motifs are particularly important in "late" historical-literary texts which deal with Babylonian kings: (a) the "heroic liberator" who fought against foreign domination;

(b) the king "who revered Bel-Marduk, his temple Esagil and his city Babylon gained divine protection and were successful rulers" along with his negative counterpart, the king who did not and was "severely punished," and (c) the sinful king who confesses, repents and becomes successful.

The first and second motifs are rooted in literature earlier than the Persian or Hellenistic periods, but the third seems to have emerged at that time. Another feature of this literature that is directly relevant to our discussion here is the "pervasive interest in the interaction between the king and the priest, in cultic correctness and in the consequences of royal impropriety" that characterizes "all the priestly literature of the Late Period in the form we know it today," "notwithstanding possible roots in earlier periods" (Jursa and Debourse 2017, 87).

To be sure, as the Babylonian priests shaped and remembered their past, they involved themselves, to an extent, in nostalgia, but above all they engaged in their memory project because it addressed and supported their own sense of identity, the importance of the temple and its personnel and the role of the priests in the new political framework. The latter included their role *vis à vis* the foreign kings, both as their potential educators, but also, when necessary, as their challengers to the point of martyrdom (Jursa and Debourse 2017).[3] It is worth stressing that at times these features were conveyed *not* by the main narrative, but by seemingly "secondary" details and characters in it, as the case of the Nabonaid Chronicle clearly shows (see, e.g., ii.6–8, 10–12, 24–25; for another reference to the *šešgallû*-priest and his role, see the so-called Religious Chronicle, ii.5).[4]

Of course, Persian or early Hellenistic Jerusalem was very different from Babylon or Uruk or any other large Mesopotamian city. Nevertheless, all of the motifs mentioned above are also central to Chronicles, with one possible exception, the heroic liberator, to which I will come back below. This convergence is *not* the result of borrowing.[5] Instead, it is based on the pragmatic meaning of producing and reading past-shaping texts by temple-centered literati living in a subordinate, local polity within an empire whose hegemonic center was elsewhere. It is in this context that, in both cases, the focus on seemingly secondary characters is heuristically so important to understand the pragmatic role of reading and shaping a monarchic past in a non-monarchic setting.

---

3 Challenging the king, when necessary, may be seen also as an educational act, even if, or perhaps even more so, when it involves martyrdom.
4 On potential connections between these texts, see Waerzeggers 2017, especially 113–114.
5 A point that emerges even out of the most cursory comparison of the texts.

Further, subordinate groups tend to remember the past differently than hegemonic centers and to construe the political field and matters of leadership differently as well. For instance, subordinate groups are more likely to focus on local cultural institutions and traditions, but less on the power of the empire and the tools and institutions that it needs to exercise control over subaltern groups and imperial peripheral areas (e.g., the army, taxation, etc.). This is not surprising, since remembering the past serves directly or indirectly as a way to advance claims for community leadership in the present, either in the "real" world or in the "imaginary" worlds experienced by the literati in which they serve as leaders (cf. the role of the rabbis in early rabbinic literature).

At times, even an implied acknowledgement of the gap between their "ideal" role and the current role served to configure the lenses with which the past and its leaders were construed. For instance, as Stemberger has noted in relation to the Moses of the rabbis, "[t]he image of the leadership of Moses is not only based on the biblical image, but also on the presuppositions of the rabbis about how an ideal leader of the Jewish community should act [...]. Because [...] [they] were themselves usually not yet in a leadership position, they were interested in a conciliatory, service-minded community leader, who does not become angry, who does not follow his own interests, who is not authoritarian [...]. All this may have played on the background of the passive image that Moses has in rabbinic literature."[6] In other words, not only the subordinate position of the ethnie plays a role, but also the subordinate position of the literati within the ethnie contributes to their construction of the past and their explorations on ethnie leadership.

Having set this array of considerations as a starting point for exploring the issue of "Leadership in the World of Memories Evoked by Chronicles," in what follows, the focus of this contribution shifts, within the limits of space, to a discussion of a set of diverse examples that each contributes to our understanding of leadership in the world of memory evoked by Chronicles, while at the same time, all together demonstrate the heuristic potential of the mentioned considerations, and as such, may stimulate further research. Given the limitations of space, I will begin with two case studies and will then move to sets of broader observations, each based on clear examples.

---

6 Stemberger 2016, 184–185. The English translation of the cited text offered above follows that of Lieve Teugels see https://parabelproject.nl/parable-of-the-month-make-someone-else-your-agent-an-ambivalent-picture-of-moses/.

2 Case Studies

2.1 The Case of Azariah, the Heroic Priest

The most obvious memory about a heroic priest evoked in Chronicles is that of Azariah, the priest who, with support of eighty other priests, stopped king Uzziah from burning incense on the altar of incense (2 Chr 26:16–21). Not only is the action of the priests described as heroic, but also a narrative of martyrdom interrupted by divine actions plays a substantial role in this story and the memories it evokes. Unlike the Babylonian case, however, "evil" is not caused by a "foreigner," but is of local origin. The danger to the temple is from the inside.

From the perspective of the memory landscape of the literati, the characterization of Uzziah in Chronicles informs and is informed by that of the same king, but recalled by the name Azariah, in the corresponding regnal account in Kings.[7] The exchange of names is significant. When these literati read (and re-read) Chronicles, they noticed and remembered that the name Azariah shifts from being the one carried by a king who imperils the temple to that of the priest who saves the temple. Moreover, Chronicles underscores the exchange by upending expectations.[8] The readers learned how YHWH helped the king against his enemies at some point (ויעזרהו in 2 Chr 26:7; cf. כי־הפליא להעזר in 2 Chr 26:15), but contrary to all expectations shaped by these texts, the one who gets to carry the name "YHWH has helped" is the priest who was helped by YHWH to save the temple. Further, the eighty priests led by him are explicitly characterized as בני חיל (2 Chr 26:17), an expression that evokes a warrior image

---

[7] Azariah/u occurs in 2 Kgs 14:21; 15:1, 6, 7, 8, 17, 23, 27; Uzziah/u only in 2 Kgs 15:13, 30, 32, 34, all of which stand outside the boundaries of Kings' royal account of Azariah. The name Uzziah/u appears throughout the royal account of the king in 2 Chr 26 (see vv. 3, 8, 9, 11, 14, 18, 19, 21, 22, 23), see also 2 Chr 27:2. The only place in which the king is referred to as Azariah in Chronicles occurs in the genealogies, well outside the regnal account in the main historical narrative (see 1 Chr 3:12). Uzziah/u is, of course, the only name associated with this king in prophetic literature (see Isa 1:1; 6:1; 7:1; Hos 1:1; Amos 1:1; Zech 14:5). The point advanced here has to do only with the effects of the use of one or the other name for the construction of the character as a site of social memory.

[8] Chronicles shows a tendency to associate royal names with stories told about them in midrashic fashion. The most obvious cases are Asa and Jehoshaphat, but see also some of the other examples discussed in Jarick 2012. All in all, the very fact that it is not the king who bears the name Azariah likely served as an attention-getter, first to itself and second to the significance of the exchange of names for the narrative and the memory of the relevant individuals and those with whom they engaged.

(cf. Deut 3:18; 1 Sam 14:52; 18:17; 1 Chr 5:18; 11:22). Azariah the priest thus becomes the leader of a small "militia," and this is the only "force" that counts when it comes to defending the proper order of the temple and – within the world of Chronicles and the literati – Israel.

On one level, there is little doubt about the pragmatic meaning of the text for Jerusalem-centered literati, and especially the priests among them, in terms of both the temple as an institution and its priests, without whom and without whose work the temple cannot properly function. A proper temple is protected by proper priests under proper leadership. Moreover, the construction of danger from the inside, from those who were supposed to know better, is also particularly interesting in this context. Contextually, it fits well with a construction of the period of Persian hegemony over Yehud, in which the temple in Jerusalem was not in danger from foreign Persian kings, governors or commanders.[9]

That said, it seems that closer attention to the story as construed and remembered by these literati raises questions about the social and ideological centrality of the priests as such. The literati's memory of Uzziah evoked through reading and rereading Chronicles was strongly informed by the key interpretative statement that (a) he was successful as long as he "sought" YHWH (2 Chr 26:5b), and (b) he did so during the days of Zechariah, a person who is characterized as one who understands the visions (or according to some textual variants, "the fear") of YHWH or teaches them (presumably to Uzziah, but perhaps to godly characters, or to the priests, or to the people in general, or some combination of the above, see 2 Chr 26:5a).[10]

This Zechariah served as a prophetic voice guarding the king, and through the king, the people. His very name evokes the memory of the martyred priest Zechariah (2 Chr 24:20–22) whose prophetic (in the sense of Chronicles) guardianship,[11] along with the guardianship of other unnamed, secondary prophetic

---

9 The contrast with the case in late Seleucid or Roman times is sharp and self-evident.

10 The MT reads: המבין בראת האלהים. The seemingly unusual choice of an inf. cs. of the root ראה instead of יראת may be a function of the desire to create a textually inscribed attention-getter and a clear signpost linking this verse and the story of Uzziah with that of Zechariah the priest and other prophetic voices who confronted Joash in 2 Chr 24:17–22. For the textual traditions that reflect the more common expression "the fear of God" (cf. Gen 20:11; 2 Sam 23:3; Neh 5:9, 15) see LXX, Peshitta, Targum, some MT mss. and some rabbinic (y. Soṭah 45b [9.13]) and mediaeval Jewish commentators (e.g., Rashi and Ralbag on 2 Chr 26:5). It is worth noting, however, that there is no attestation of the precise expression ביראת האלהים in the Masoretic text of the Bible; even יראת אלהים is rare and occurs only in Gen 20:11; 2 Sam 23:3; Neh 5:9, 15.

11 I have written about the centrality of the concept of "guardianship" within the political thought of the literati of the late Persian/early Hellenistic period in Ben Zvi 2016. This contribution continues this path and expands on a number of substantial matters.

characters (v. 19) that the king (here, Joash) and his officers (שׂרים) rejected. Moreover, textually-inscribed key terms used in 2 Chr 26:5 recalled and complemented the system of signposts interweaving the relevant narratives about Zechariah and Azariah. In other words, markers of mutual recalling between the two narratives went beyond the thematic level of complementary stories of confrontation of a godly group led by a godly, prophetic individual, who may or may not be a priest, with a king and which may lead to actual or potential martyrdom.[12]

In addition, the readers of this didactic story about the heroic priest Azariah understood that the narrative and the memory of the event was meant to socialize Israel, and thus guard it. But they were asked also to remember that they were able to know about it, because of the deed of another prophetic voice, this time, not an *ad hoc* one, but a major prophet of memory, namely Isaiah, the son of Amoz (2 Chr 26:22).

Significantly, King Uzziah vanishes from the story after being punished by YHWH for his deed, but so do Azariah the priest and his fellow priests after their heroic stand. The priest may have been heroic, but nothing is worth remembering about him except that he stood firm to stop a desecration that would never have happened if the prophetic voice had been heeded. Moreover, without another prophetic voice, the event would not have been remembered and thus become relevant for Israel's education and its well-being many generations after the event.[13]

In other words, although the leadership of the priests as such may be temporarily crucial, when others fail, that of prophetic guardianship is far more essential for the well-being of Israel/Judah/Yehud. Reading the story from a pragmatic perspective indicates a significant emphasis on guardianship and a shift away from royal leadership, while at the same time constraining the potential roles of the priests as such (compare and contrast with the Mesopotamian tendencies mentioned above).

---

12 For textually marked signposts, see ובימי דרשו את־יהוה הצליחו האלהים (2 Chr 26:5b), לא תצליחו (2 Chr 24:20), and ירא יהוה וידרש (2 Chr 24:22b; the final words of the martyred Zechariah); see also ירא יהוה and בראת האלהים (see the preceding note). Since the latter expression is "unexpected," it is far more helpful as an attention-getter, drawing attention first to itself and then to this system of mutually informing signposts.

13 Of course, there is another prophetic, guarding voice at work here: that of the Chronicler, the constructed author of the book of Chronicles as imagined by its readers (i.e., the literati). Needless to say, as they read the book, these literati bring this author to life and thus also assume to a certain extent the role of bearers of a prophetic voice guarding Israel. See below.

2.2 The Case of the Priest Jehoiada

Several additional stories show a similar pragmatic emphasis. The most obvious of these is the one about Jehoiada, a priest depicted in quasi-royal terms (see, e.g., 2 Chr 23:1, 16; 24:3, 15–16) and remembered as having his son, Zechariah, succeeding him in his leadership role (2 Chr 24:20–22).

Jehoiada was remembered as a priest who commanded a temple militia of Levites who saved Israel/Judah and its/YHWH's temple, again not from an imperial foreign power, but from an otherized local queen and her supporters. Within the world of Chronicles, the actions in the temple at the time of the rebellion demanded the leadership of a priest. When the narrative moves towards the restoration of the temple, a royal order was anticipated within that world, but the narrative construes a king and a priest who closely work as a team in a way reminiscent of that of the Zerubbabel and Joshua of memory (see especially 2 Chr 24:11–14). Moreover, the conclusion of the story, in addition to shaping the continuation of the historical narrative in Chronicles (2 Chr 24:15–22), construed and instilled among the readers a memory in which the very presence of Jehoiada, the proper priest, rather than that of the king, served as the necessary condition for the continuation of proper offerings (2 Chr 24:14b) and the blessings and cosmic order that they provided. Significantly, his previous partner, the king, who is usually construed in the ancient Near East as responsible for the maintenance of the proper cult, becomes the very embodiment of the "inner danger" threatening it in this memory of the past.

The most crucial roles associated with the Jehoiada of memory (and his son Zechariah) are those of prophetic guardianship (see, e.g., 2 Chr 24:2 [cf. 2 Chr 26:5]; 2 Chr 24:17–19; and notice the exact language of 2 Chr 24:19; cf. 2 Chr 24:27, on the latter see also below).[14] Moreover, this Jehoiada of memory, although no Moses, goes in some respects even beyond that of the common image of the archetypal prophetic figure of Moses. This Jehoiada, as the godly leader of the community, sealed a covenant *between himself*, the people, and the king to be,

---

14 Significantly, this role is not a necessary condition of the narrative plot, i.e. the type of a crime that must take place in a crime novel or a temple in need of restoration in a narrative about restoring a temple, etc. Any narrative about the restoration of order requires a depiction of a prior chaotic situation. The most significant ideological messages in all these stories – besides the reaffirmation that order is eventually restored – are not to be found in these necessary conditions, but in those that are not essential to the plot, e.g., the identity and character of the crime investigator who solves the crime and thus restores order (and those of the "agents of chaos" in the narrative), the identity and character of those who, against all odds, succeed in restoring the proper cult or "religion" (and those responsible for the prevalence of chaos before) and the like.

i.e., to behave again as YHWH's people. The order in which these three are mentioned in the text is particularly significant and was hardly missed by the readers as they involved themselves in an act of reconfiguring their memories of the events, by reading 2 Chr 23:16 and thus balancing the image with the one they gathered from 2 Kgs 11:17, and *vice versa*, shaping a mutually informing link between the two texts, in which the matters mentioned above play a central role.

In addition, in Chronicles, Jehoiada serves not only as the prophetic covenant mediator but, in his role as prophetic representative of YHWH, also symbolically takes YHWH's position among the covenant partners.[15]

Finally, also here the readers of the book were asked to keep in mind that they are able to know about this past because of prophetic (in the sense of Chronicles) activity in the past, as the Chronicler explicitly brings to their memory a written source referred to as "the Study on the Book of Kings" מדרש ספר המלכים (2 Chr 24:27).[16]

3 Six Observations Regarding Memories of Kings Evoked by Chronicles

Chronicles is by necessity a book about kings. Ancient Israelite historiography was organized around kings and their regnal periods (see the book of Kings). That said, there are a few seemingly "odd" ways of constructing the kings of old that shed light on the milieu of the remembering group, (that is, the literati), that are particularly relevant to the present discussion.[17]

---

[15] It is worth noting that Jehoiada dies at the age of 130 in Chronicles (2 Chr 24:15; cf. with Moses' 120 years in Deut 34:7; see also Gen 6:3). In Chronicles, a long life is usually understood as a divine blessing.

[16] מדרש appears only twice in the Hebrew Bible, both times in Chronicles. The only other occasion is explicitly related to prophetic activities; see מדרש הנביא עדו (2 Chr 13:22). Significantly, the reference in 2 Chr 13:22 is to the stories about Abijah, a king who himself served the role of a godly speaker, a guardian voice in his own time. I have translated the Hebrew מדרש as "study" instead of "midrash" to avoid confusing the text portrayed in the world of Chronicles with the much later genre, or better set of genres, associated with the term "midrash."

[17] Obviously, these five observations are not meant to cover the entire conceptualization of kingship in Chronicles. They are simply meant to shed light on some particular aspects of it. Moreover, they serve as good examples of the way in which some seemingly minor choices in the construction of the past and some seemingly "odd" features of texts and personages of old may provide extremely helpful information about the general social mindscape of the group

First, the warrior-like heroic aspect of the king is generally downplayed in Chronicles (see, e.g., the portrayals of Abijah, Hezekiah, etc.), as is the case in the construction and reproduction of memories about Moses, Abraham, Joshua among the literati of the late Persian/early Hellenistic periods.[18] Chronicles includes multiple manifestations of a generative grammar that – like all generative grammars governing the social production and reproduction of memories – are not and cannot be restricted within the limits of individual books, collections, or literary genres, because they "belong" to the remembering community as a social group and directly relate to its social mindscape, rather than being an attribute of a particular text, collection, or literary genre.

Second, Chronicles shaped a world in which tribes or groups within a tribe may take an independent role in local warfare aimed at expanding territory or fulfilling ideological goals (see 1 Chr 4:38–43; 5:7–10, 18–22). The concept of a centralized kingdom, necessary for a historical narrative structured around kings, is thus balanced by other memories encoded and communicated by Chronicles, and so are matters of royal leadership. Locals do have power, even when the king is pious and follows pious policies.[19]

Third, Chronicles construes, as expected, kings as historical agents, but stress that they cooperate with others, e.g., officers and "the people" (cf., e.g., Japhet 1997, 416–428), and the former are often described as having much influence on the decisions of the king. Again, the idea of an autocratic king is strongly balanced. From a pragmatic perspective, this non-autocratic tendency is relevant and reminds us of the Moses of the rabbis. Both exemplify how memory about leaders of the past is influenced by the lack of an autocratic system within the remembering community.

Fourth, Israel is certainly able to behave piously without a king ruling over it (see 2 Chr 28:9–15). Moreover, even a Davidide king may "disappear" from a

---

on matters of leadership. A full study of kingship in Chronicles requires, of course, a separate monograph. For recent monographs on the concept of kingship in postmonarchic Israel, see, e.g., Wilson 2017; Janzen 2013.

18 I discussed these matters at some length elsewhere. See, e.g., Ben Zvi, "Squaring Circles and The Social Benefits of Squaring Them: Joshua as a Case Study for Constraints, Preferences, Balances and Flexibility within the Complex Memory System of the Literati of the late Persian/ early Hellenistic Period" in Ben Zvi 2019 and bibliography.

19 Within the memory world informed by Chronicles, the Simeonites are those imagined having destroyed the remnant of Amalek, something that previous kings seem not to have been able to achieve. Significantly, their victories took place during the time of Hezekiah, the great king of the post-David/Solomon period, but without his intervention. As a reward for their actions, the Simeonites were exempted from exile. On these matters, see my "Contributions of the Genealogies in Chronicles to the Shaping of the Memory of the Monarchic Period: The Case of Some Simeonites's Vignettes," in Ben Zvi 2019.

key narrative within the memoryscape of the literati, as is clear from the fact that Zedekiah is not mentioned after 2 Chr 36:14. Significantly, his fate was presented as not worth remembering, and thus not worth mentioning in Chronicles, whereas the fate of the temple and the people were surely considered worth remembering. That said, when it comes to rebuilding the temple, in the very same world of Chronicles, YHWH has to contact a king and turn him into his "prophetic voice" to rebuild the temple, even if the king is a foreigner. One may compare with the need for a David – and Solomon – for the establishment of the temple in the world of memory evoked by Chronicles, but also notice the difference. In the case of a Davidic king in the land, even if the king bears, to an extent, a prophetic voice and message, the remembered narrative includes a separate figure of a prophet as an intermediary. In the case of a foreign king who also bears a prophetic voice and message from YHWH, no other separate figure is recalled as an intermediary (see also the case of Necho, 2 Chr 35:20–22).

Fifth, the literati reading Chronicles remembered that monarchic Judah stands for the kingdom of YHWH by the hands of the sons of David (ממלכת יהוה ביד בני דויד; 2 Chr 13:8), but they also knew all too well that, unlike the situation during the days of Abijah, Judah was defeated and there was no Davidide reigning among them. They remembered that a main reason for their situation was that their ancestors rejected YHWH and his ways. If the role of the king is to "guard" and protect the people, to be a shepherd, then his main role had to be imagined as a "prophetic" voice embodying the role of the guardian, and some kings served that function in Chronicles.

But most significantly, and particularly relevant from a pragmatic perspective within the remembering community, Davidic kings were not alone serving as guardians of Israel. Prophets, priests, and even foreign kings could and did serve as guardians. Moreover, the imagined author of Chronicles was also a sort of guardian, as were – indirectly – the literati who vicariously experienced the past shaped in Chronicles and who communicated it to others in Yehud and thus socialized them.

In this regard, the literati themselves become a new instantiation of the prophetic voices of old. Since, obviously, none of the literati was king over Yehud and not all the literati were priests,[20] it is not surprising that neither kings nor priests of old were imagined as having a monopoly on the key role of being a guardian of a prophetic voice for Israel. Moreover, the crucial leadership as

---

20 It is most likely that the literati depended directly or indirectly on support from the temple and *vice versa* and that some of them were priests, but there is no reason to assume, nor any text that suggests that all or even most of the literati had to be priests.

imagined by the literati reading Chronicles was not even a hereditary affair.[21] One may easily compare and contrast their case with that of the priestly literati of Babylonia mentioned above.

Sixth, time and again, Chronicles conveyed to the literati a sense that the king is neither a sufficient nor a necessary safeguard against chaos. The only matter that required an explicit command from YHWH to a king – and thus required a king – in a post-Moses and post-David/Solomon period such as the one in which the literati lived was the (re)building of the temple of YHWH in Jerusalem according to the rules set up by Moses and David.[22]

Thus, the most common, positive argument for the *need* for a (local, human) king in terms of political thought[23] seems to have been downplayed in Chronicles and for its readers in the late Persian/early Hellenistic period. To be sure, the very same literati also read and remembered the heightened end of the book of Judges (i.e., Judg 17:1–21:25) that communicated to the readers quite explicitly that kingship was a very necessary institution, even when there is no external, military pressure,[24] because according to these texts and memories, a society without a king devolves into chaos. But the very same literati vicariously experienced through their reading of 2 Chr 28 (esp. 2 Chr 28:8–15) that when the king of (northern) Israel disappeared from the scene, society actually behaved in pious ways and listened to the prophetic voice, unlike its contemporary monarchic, Davidic-led Judah. Chronicles is not alone in engaging with and balancing this voice at the end of Judges. See, for instance, the portrayal of the period of Judges in Ruth. When reading Ruth, the literati are asked to consider that the reason for a king is not that chaos necessarily engulfs society without one, but that there was a divine choice of David, which in itself does not require explanation in human terms.

Although the very choice of David – like all important divine selections in Chronicles (e.g., Israel, Jerusalem, the priests) – is presented as not explainable

---

21 To be sure, none of this means that there were no limitations. For instance, prophetic voices may be instantiated through kings, even foreign kings, very often through "professional" prophets and priests, but rarely through a woman and never through a slave. The social composition of the literati group in the late Persian/early Hellenistic period seems to have played an important role here.
22 It was widely held in the ancient Near East that temple-building was a royal task.
23 Any student of Political Science would immediately suggest a reference to Hobbes, but see already the stories at the end of the book of Judges (Judg 17:1–21:25).
24 The argument in 1 Samuel is more complex and includes several threads, but military challenges from non-Israelites are not necessarily the main reason for the people's desire for a king (see 1 Sam 8:5–8). Both Samuel and Judges contain a number of memorable episodes hammering the point that military challenges do not have to resolved by appointing a king.

in human terms, it is clear that the main and the only role for which a David is *necessary* in Chronicles is to establish the temple and its regulations; even his wars were meant to allow for the conditions necessary for the establishment of the temple. But given what was mentioned at the beginning of this section, what about the situation in Yehud in the late Persian/early Hellenistic period? In terms of political thought, the Chronicler seems to have indirectly raised and addressed the question of whether the community in Yehud could prosper with an "outsourced" human king, in an empire run by foreigners and foreign kings.[25] But if so, then the crucial question for the literati became: What can they and their larger Yehudite community – with which they identify and which they also socially construe – not outsource?[26] The answer to this question would have seemed clear to the literati reading Chronicles within the context of their own world of knowledge, ideological horizons and social mindscape: The literati themselves and their "prophetic" leadership, and, of course, books such as Chronicles, that are the outcome and expression of earlier cases of prophetic leadership, and which require them as readers – and thus, from our historical perspective, as "producers of their meanings." Significantly, similar responses seem to characterize comparable subaltern groups in large imperial polities, e.g., the priests in Babylonia, or in much later times, the rabbinical leaders in the late Roman period. In all these cases, the main and most substantive role for in-group leadership, in its own mind at least, was to "guard" the people and the past and future worlds of memory (embodied and evoked by texts) that the guardians consider necessary for the social reproduction of the group, and thus for their "guardianship" roles.

4 Some Concluding Thoughts

To be sure, the methodological considerations advanced in the introduction may have led to different observations depending on the case studies selected

---

[25] The saliently lengthy genealogy of the Saulides who lived for many generations – implicitly under the rule of the Davidides (see 1 Chr 8:33–40; 9:39–44) – serves as a kind of indirect exploration of living within a polity ruled by the "Other," especially given the roles of the figure of Saul in Chronicles. See Ben Zvi 2020.

[26] It is worth stressing that none of these questions was anchored on utopian constructions or socially shared memories of ideal futures. Although the latter did exist and played an important role in the lives of the literati and provided much hope, these questions directly related to the here and now experienced by the literati, even if necessarily through their own ideological lenses, social mindscape, and memoryscape.

for examination. But looking back, the emphasis on guardianship as the most essential form of leadership is not surprising and most likely would have appeared in one way or another no matter which set of "representative" cases were selected.

For one, this emphasis on guardianship fits well with literati whose identity was directly related to writing, composing, redacting, reading and rereading, and performative acts of reading and rereading to others (cf. 2 Chr 17:7–9) the relevant texts. It fits well their key concept of an Israel-centered Torah, which by necessity requires guardianship for Israel. Moreover, when Torah is central and following or forsaking it is what really counts, then when the ultimate king of Israel, YHWH, is imagined as fulfilling the primary function of a king as protector of his people, YHWH, as king, was not to be imagined, in the main, as raising armies, but as instructing Israel to follow Torah, or at least, attempting to do so. Within the world of this literati, YHWH requires human voices whose role is to convey godly messages to fulfill this crucial job; in other words, prophetic voices, in all their variations and types (see Chronicles). Finally, this emphasis on guardianship fits well the historical fact that Moses (the main prophetic voice/guardian) served as the most prominent site of memory for the group, not Aaron the priest or, for that matter, David the king, or Israel/Jacob by whose name the ethno-cultural group identified itself. Of course, this emphasis on guardianship is very much historically and socially contingent. The very realia of the world of the literati played important roles in shaping it. In all these aspects, Chronicles was not an "odd" book, but one that embodied larger tendencies among the literati and their readings of their core repertoire.

In sum, Chronicles provides a very good example of how multiple approaches, concepts, ideas, and memories related to leadership that existed within the general world of knowledge and social mindscape of the literati came to interact and inform each other via this book. By doing so, this book helped the literati reading it to explore what leadership is about, while construing and remembering their (didactic, socializing) past, and as it did so it taught them why it was so important to remember that past also in the way their Chronicler did.

Bibliography

Ben Zvi, Ehud. 2016. "Memory and Political Thought in the Late Persian/Early Hellenistic Yehud/Judah: Some Observations." In *Leadership, Social Memory and Judean Discourse in the 5th–2nd Centuries BCE*, edited by Diana V. Edelman and Ehud Ben Zvi, 9–26. Worlds of the Ancient Near East and Mediterranean. London: Equinox.

Ben Zvi, Ehud. 2019. *Social Memory among the Literati of Yehud*. BZAW 509. Berlin and Boston: de Gruyter.

Ben Zvi, Ehud. 2020. "Reading Chronicles and Remembering Saul in the Late Persian/Early Hellenistic Period." In *Fortgeschriebenes Gotteswort: Studien zu Geschichte, Theologie und Auslegung des Alten Testaments*. FS Christoph Levin, edited by Reinhard Müller, Urmas Nõmmik and Juha Pakkala, 369–380. Tübingen: Mohr Siebeck.

De Breucker, Geert. 2015. "Heroes and Sinners: Babylonian Kings in Cuneiform Historiography of the Persian and Hellenistic Periods." In *Political Memory in and after the Persian Empire*, edited by Jason M. Silverman and Caroline Waerzeggers, 75–94. Ancient Near East Monographs 13. Atlanta: SBL Press.

Edelman, Diana V., and Ehud Ben Zvi, eds. 2016. *Leadership, Social Memory and Judean Discourse in the 5th–2nd Centuries BCE*. Worlds of the Ancient Near East and Mediterranean. London: Equinox.

Janzen, David. 2013. *The Necessary King: A Postcolonial Reading of the Deuteronomistic Portrait of the Monarchy*. HBM 57. Sheffield: Sheffield Phoenix Press.

Japhet, Sara. 1997. *The Ideology of the Book of Chronicles and Its Place in Biblical Thought*. 2nd rev. edition. BEATAJ 9. Bern: Peter Lang.

Jarick, John. 2012. "The Sting in the Tales of the Kings of Judah." In *Far From Minimal: Celebrating the Work and Influence of Philip R. Davies*, edited by Duncan Burns and John W. Rogerson, 226–236. LHBOTS 484. London: Bloomsbury T&T Clark.

Jursa, Michael, and Céline Debourse. 2017. "A Babylonian Priestly Martyr, a King-like Priest, and the Nature of Late Babylonian Priestly Literature." *WZKM* 107:77–98.

Waerzeggers, Caroline. 2015. "Facts, Propaganda or History? Shaping Political Memory in the Nabonidus Chronicle." In *Political Memory in and after the Persian Empire*, edited by Jason M. Silverman and Caroline Waerzeggers, 95–124. Ancient Near East Monographs 13. Atlanta: SBL Press.

Stemberger, Günter. 2016. *Mose in der rabbinischen Tradition*. Freiburg i. Br.: Herder.

Wilson, Ian D. 2017. *Kingship and Memory in Ancient Judah*. New York: Oxford University Press.

Louis C. Jonker
Reflections on Leadership in Achaemenid Yehud: Case Studies from the Chronicler's Imperial, Provincial, Tribal, and Cultic Rhetoric

1 Introduction: A Multilayered Socio-Historical Existence in Achaemenid Yehud

There is often the misconception among biblical scholars that the book of Chronicles communicated only on one socio-historical level. It is almost generally accepted today that Chronicles originated toward the end of the Achaemenid period (or early in the Hellenistic period) in Jerusalem and was most probably written by cultic *literati* (hereafter the Chronicler, used in a collective sense).[1] We are aware of the fact that Yehud was proclaimed a separate province of the Persian Empire probably in the second half of the fifth century BCE. Past research has shown that the conditions in the later Achaemenid period were different from the earlier period, when Jerusalem had not yet been established as the capital of a separate Persian province.[2]

Few scholars, however, differentiate between the different levels of socio-historical existence that prevailed during the later Achaemenid period. I have argued elsewhere (in more detail) that at least the following spheres or levels should be distinguished (see particularly Jonker 2016, ch. 3):

1.1 The Imperial Sphere

The time during which Chronicles originated was the period of turmoil which Persia experienced more or less from the time of Artaxerxes I (465–405 BCE) to the rule of Darius III (336–330 BCE), the last Persian king before the invasion by Alexander the Great of Macedonia. During this period, the Levant was heavi-

---

[1] For a broader discussion of the dating and authorship of Chronicles, see Jonker 2016, 66–71.
[2] For the distinction between Persian 1 and Persian 2 periods, see Ben Zvi 1997; Carter 1999, 172–248.

ly affected by the difficult relationship between Egypt and Persia.³ A revolt broke out against the Persian rule in Egypt during the reign of Artaxerxes I, but the latter emerged victorious by suppressing the Egyptian revolt and by securing the Levantine coast and Palestine for the Persians.⁴ After the death of Artaxerxes I, further turbulence followed. During the troublesome succession history from Xerxes II through Darius II to Artaxerxes II, the Persian grip on Egypt was lost and was regained only much later during the reign of Artaxerxes III in 343 BCE. For approximately sixty years, Yehud and Idumea served as the Persian frontier with Egypt. During this period, the Levant was of particular strategic importance for Persia, as Wiesehöfer indicates:

> Although Judah's importance for the development of a Jewish consciousness and community in the early Second Temple period may seduce biblical scholars into overestimating the region's relevance for Persian imperial policy, one should not forget that Palestine was a major land-bridge and that its route network must have been highly responsible for the demographic expansion and economic growth of Persian-period Palestine. Besides, Persian fortified places in Yehud and Idumea must have served to police communications with Egypt (Wiesehöfer 2011, 182).

The proclamation of Yehud as a separate province (formerly probably under Samarian control) was likely a direct result of this development. Two issues that dominated this period were the political or royal ideology as well as the economic changes in Yehud. Regarding the first issue, the notion of peace had always been an important issue in Achaemenid ideology. The so-called *pax Achaemenidica* was given expression in various ways, through inscriptions, but also through iconography in the great Persian cities like Persepolis and Susa, from the period of Cyrus II the Great and following.⁵ However, the notion of peace became particularly important during the tumultuous period mentioned above. Particularly during the reign of Artaxerxes II it seems that peace treaties played an important role. Josef Wiesehöfer describes this period as follows:

> Although the succession to the throne from Darius to his eldest son Arses (throne name: Artaxerxes II) proceeded smoothly, the new king soon had to tackle a two-front crisis. Egypt was lost between 401 and 399 BCE; and at exactly that time, the younger brother Cyrus made a futile attempt to replace his brother on the throne with the help of Spartan and Greek mercenaries. As in the battle for the throne, Artaxerxes II was similarly successful in securing Syria and Palestine and in fending off Spartan interventions in Asia Minor.

---

3 For good discussions on this history, see Briant 2002, 515–692; Brosius 2006, 15–32; Waters 2014, chs. 9–11.
4 See Wiesehöfer 2013, 202.
5 For further background, see Jonker 2008.

The king not only became the negotiator and guarantor of the Greek general peace of 387/6 BCE ("The King's Peace"), which confirmed his right of rule over the cities of Asia Minor and Cyprus; he was also able to thwart the plans of the Salaminian king Euagoras to make himself lord of Cyprus, and he succeeded in putting an end to the so-called Great Satraps Revolt in the 360s (Wiesehöfer 2013, 202).[6]

It is thus clear that the Persian ideology of peace was very much under pressure during these days of revolt and uprisings. However, the military actions against these revolts – surely also those conducted from the fortresses in Idumea and Yehud – were portrayed as actions that would restore peace to the Persian Empire.[7]

Another significant issue of the time, which is closely related to the military aspects mentioned above, is that the temple in Jerusalem apparently became the economic center through which the Persian taxes and tributes were channeled.[8] We know from archaeology that Jerusalem was not a large city at the time, consisting mainly of groups of clergy and literati associated with the temple.[9] However, these clergy were influential in the provincial area under their control, and they probably had to occupy a middle position of some sort between the Persian imperial demands and the rural supply of crops, livestock, etc.[10] The Persian military bases on the southern border with Egypt had to be sustained, and imperial taxes had to be paid by nearby Yehud. By situating this function in the temple in Jerusalem, the local Yahweh cult was utilized to motivate the extraction of produce from the rural areas to the sanctuary. This situa-

---

6 See also the following background information in Jonker (2016, 81) "[T]he so-called King's Peace (or, Peace of Antalcidas) of 386 B.C.E. [was concluded] after a period of disagreement among the Greek city states about whether Persia's claim on the Asiatic Greeks should be accepted. Antalcidas of Sparta made an alliance with Tiribazus (who was reinstated as Persian satrap in Sardis), and together they defeated the Athenians and recovered control of the Hellespont. After these successes Antalcidas felt he could depend on the support of the other Greek city states and accordingly negotiated a peace treaty with the Persian satrap, Tiribazus, which was proclaimed in 386 B.C.E. [...] [T]hese circumstances probably contributed to the Peace of Callias becoming so important [...] [A]lthough one cannot state for certain that the last-mentioned peace treaty between Athens and Persia was concluded in 449 B.C.E., one can be confident in stating that the idea of such a treaty, as a projection into the past, was a reality in the first half of the 4th century B.C.E. (which is also the most likely time when the Chronicler constructed his history)."
7 See Wright's study on how war and battles are portrayed in the narrative literature of Chronicles (Wright 1997).
8 For more information, consult Bedford 2007; West 2011.
9 See the discussions in Lipschits 2005, ch. 3, 2006; Ussishkin 2006; Finkelstein 2010a, 2010b.
10 For supporting arguments, see Jonker 2015.

tion probably prevailed until Egypt was regained shortly before the end of the Achaemenid period.

The Chronicler's portrayal of King Solomon will be read against this background in a section below, which will also consider how the imperial level of socio-historical existence influenced the Chronicler's rhetoric.

1.2 The Provincial Sphere

The province of Yehud existed among other provinces, such as Samaria to the north, Philistia or Ashdod to the west, Ammon and Moab to the east, and Idumea and Arabia to the south. These provinces had more or less the same status within the Persian Empire, although the circumstances in each province differed significantly. Samaria, in particular, was much more developed and affluent than its southern neighbor, Yehud, and the effects of the exile were not so visible in the north.[11] Provinces such as Philistia, Idumea, the Transjordanian provinces, and Arabia also profited much more than Yehud from trade during the time.

Some of the surrounding areas (such as Idumea, as reflected in some ostracon-texts that were found at Maresha and Khirbet el-Qom) also seem to have served Yahweh as their god, and it might even be that there was a local sanctuary to Yahweh at Khirbet el-Qom (see the arguments in Lemaire 2006). The diversity of Yahwisms during the time is further illustrated in Yehud's relationship with Samaria to the north. The rivalry between the kingdom of Judah and the kingdom of Israel of earlier times was mainly focused on religious differences. Although both of these kingdoms practiced a monotheistic form of Yahwism, the southern kingdom of Judah believed that its version of Yahwism, with the temple in Jerusalem as the central sanctuary, was the 'correct' version, and they despised the aberrations practiced in the north. There is thus a shared past which influenced the inter-provincial relationship between Yehud and Samaria (see Knoppers 2006, 279). Some scholars are sure that there was also a Yahweh sanctuary on Mount Gerizim in the province of Samaria during the Persian period, which would have extrapolated the earlier religious rivalry into the postexilic era (see Magen 2017; Knoppers 2013, chs. 3, 5).

Apart from the above-mentioned economic and religious differences, there were also some political factors involved in the interaction among provinces, particularly in the interaction between Yehud and Samaria. The provinces of

---

11 See, e.g., the discussions in Knoppers 2006, 272–273; Cornelius 2011.

Yehud and Samaria comprised more or less the same territories as the former divided kingdoms of Judah and Israel. Some scholars hypothesize that during the early postexilic period, Yehud was placed under the authority of the provincial governor in Samaria. Yehud was therefore proclaimed as a province only much later than Samaria and was subjugated to its northern rival for the initial years of Persian imperial domination (Willi 1995, ch. 2). This factor also played a decisive role in the later relationship between Yehud and Samaria. We will see in the analysis of an example text below that the Chronicler's portrayal of Samaria is often ambiguous; sometimes Samaria (or the northern kingdom) is portrayed as part of the "All-Israel" family, while in other cases it is portrayed as the instrument in Yahweh's hand to act against the southern kingdom. Various royal narratives in Chronicles will serve to illustrate this observation.

1.3 The Tribal Sphere

The province of Yehud was mainly situated in what used to be Judahite and Benjaminite territory in former times. It is very difficult to determine the borders of Yehud as well as the earlier border between Judah and Benjamin. It seems that this was not a fixed line, but that the situation remained fluid in different time periods, and that Benjamin might even have switched allegiance between north and south at certain time periods. However, the identities associated with these former tribal areas persisted into the postexilic period in various ways.

It is clear that polemics against Benjamin continued into the Persian period.[12] This can be deduced, *inter alia*, from how some biblical materials portray King Saul. Although he is revered as the first king of the united monarchy of Israel in the so-called Deuteronomistic History, the Chronicler narrates only Saul's death. It seems as if Chronicles wanted to emphasize David and Solomon as founder kings, and not Saul.

The political and religious tensions between Judah and Benjamin might also have been the result of the exilic period. We know from archaeology that during the Neo-Babylonian period, the capital of the region was situated at Mizpah in Benjaminite territory, and some other Benjaminite sites like Gibeon, Bethel, and Gibeah had religious influence during the time. Archaeological excavations confirm that these places, and Benjaminite territory in general, lost influence again at the end of the fifth and beginning of the fourth centuries

---

12 For further discussion, see Davies 2007; Giffone 2016.

BCE. This coincided with the proclamation of Yehud as a separate province and with Jerusalem gaining influence again as capital.[13]

It seems that these shifts in political power between the two regions also played out in some of the texts from the late Persian period. We will particularly look at the Chronicler's portrayal of Saul as a case study in section 4.

1.4 The Cultic Sphere

Although Jerusalem was not a large city in the late Persian period (as indicated above), it was a complex society. The population at the time consisted mainly of cultic elites, but different fault lines ran through the community. Richard Horsley (2007, 22) described the situation in Yehud as follows:

> Despite, or perhaps rather because of, the arrangements imposed by the imperial regime, it is difficult to imagine that Yehud ever became a unified society under the Persians. Our sources for the period indicate several interrelated conflicts. The most fundamental, because rooted in the very structure of imperial Yehud, were two conflicts that persisted throughout second-temple history: (1) the division between those who had remained on the land after the Babylonian conquest, and the restored elite who controlled the temple-state, initially as a virtual colony of immigrants in and around Jerusalem; and (2) the division between the peasants living in village communities and the Jerusalem aristocracy centered in the high priesthood. Compounding those overlapping structural conflicts were (3) divisions between various priestly factions, which overlapped the conflict between immigrants and indigenous, and (4) struggles and maneuvering for power both between local magnates and between local magnates and the Persian governors.

Although Horsley has been criticized for an overly creative description of the situation in Jerusalem (see Brooke 2008), the point that he is making remains valuable and valid, namely that various lines of division and tension ran through the community. Particularly the third point mentioned above, divisions between various priestly factions, seems to be significant for the interpretation of the book of Chronicles. It seems that the tensions between the dominant (Aaronide, or Zadokite) priesthood and the Levites drive the rhetoric of the book in order to create a profile of the Levites which is – with one exception, namely, officiating at sin offerings – on a par with that of the priests. The notion of priestly leadership was thus a contentious matter at this time. Section 5 will discuss the portrayal of the Levites more fully, in order to serve as case study for this socio-historical level.

---

[13] For more elaborate discussions, see Lipschits 2003, 2006.

These four socio-historical levels are particularly important when it comes to the interpretation of literature from this time period. The distinction between different levels is not meant to suggest consecutive phases of growth in the book, different authorship, or different places of origin. These four spheres were overlapping dimensions of a multilayered society in Achaemenid Yehud (see Jonker 2011). One may perhaps see some hierarchical power structure here, with the imperial level right at the top and the other levels dependent on and determined by the imperial level. This power dynamics should be taken into consideration in our interpretation of literature from this period. Literature, including biblical literature, does not communicate in a vacuum; rather, it communicates in such a way that its rhetorical effect will be appropriate for its specific context. One may expect that the Chronicler engaged with all four of the aforementioned socio-historical spheres and was responsive to the power structures on all levels.

When concepts of leadership are investigated in the book of Chronicles, it will benefit the task when these different levels are taken into consideration. There is not one portrayal of leadership in Chronicles; rather, the discourses on leadership differ according to the socio-historical sphere that is addressed. In what follows, selected texts from Chronicles will serve as case studies of conceptions of leadership in operation on each of the four levels. By considering these differing conceptions in Chronicles, biblical scholars may potentially gain a richer understanding of how leadership is reflected in this book.

2 Discourse on Imperial Leadership: Solomon in Chronicles (1 Chr 22:6–10)

Although the narrative about Solomon's reign is actually narrated in 2 Chr 1–9, we already encounter the preparation of and commissioning of Solomon for the building of the temple as part of the David narrative in the last part of 1 Chr (22:6–19; 28:9–21). These sections form part of the Chronicler's own material. The following verses in 1 Chr 22 are of particular importance for our discussion:

> [6] Then he called for Solomon his son and charged him to build a house for the Lord, the God of Israel. [7] David said to Solomon, "My son, I had it in my heart to build a house to the name of the Lord my God. [8] But the word of the Lord came to me, saying, 'You have shed much blood and have waged great wars. You shall not build a house to my name, because you have shed so much blood before me on the earth. [9] Behold, a son shall be born to you who shall be a man of rest [איש מנוחה]. I will give him rest [והנחותי לו] from

all his surrounding enemies. For his name shall be Solomon [שְׁלֹמֹה], and I will give peace [שָׁלוֹם] and quiet [שֶׁקֶט] to Israel in his days. ¹⁰ He shall build a house for my name. He shall be my son, and I will be his father, and I will establish his royal throne in Israel forever'. (ESV, with addition of Hebrew lemmas by the author)

It is clear that these verses want to draw a contrast between David, who has shed much blood and has waged great wars, and Solomon, who is a man of peace and rest. The close association of Solomon with the temple in Jerusalem is emphasized when the temple is also called a "house of rest" [בית מנוחה] in 1 Chr 28:2. The collocations איש מנוחה and בית מנוחה occur only here in the Hebrew Bible, in the Chronicler's *Sondergut*. This is also the only place in the Hebrew Bible where the name of Solomon [שְׁלֹמֹה] is etymologized and related to the theme of peace [שָׁלוֹם].[14]

The theme of peace and rest seems to become a structuring feature in the rest of the book of Chronicles. In further royal narratives (and always as *Sondergut* additions to the deuteronomistic *Vorlage*) these themes are associated with those kings who relied on and sought Yahweh. Peace, rest and quietness are often the outcome of a royal figure putting his full trust in Yahweh, and not in human agents (e.g., Kings Asa, Jehoshaphat, Joash, and Josiah). The Chronicler thus constructs an interesting relationship between Solomon, the temple, dedication to Yahweh, and the theme of peace and rest.

Why these deviations from the Solomon narrative as recounted in the book of Kings? Elsewhere, I have argued that the portrayal of Solomon as the "man of rest" and the temple as "the house of rest," closely linked with the theme of peace and rest, represents a subtle polemic by the Chronicler against the Persian imperial leadership. We are aware of the fact that the Persian government often employed local citizens as governors of provinces, and we may therefore expect these local governors (such as those who were apparently situated at nearby Ramat Rahel) to have overheard the discourses expressed in Chronicles.

During the same period when Chronicles was written, the so-called *pax Achaemenidica* was a prominent part of the Persian royal ideology, as we have seen above. We find in some Persian inscriptions of the time (e.g., the Bisitun inscription of Darius I and the inscriptions on his tomb at Naqš i-Rustam) deliberate portrayals of the Persian emperor as a seeker of peace and rest in his empire. Even the architecture at cities like Persepolis (which was built more or less at the same time as the Second Temple in Jerusalem) symbolized a realm of peace. The reliefs on the Apadana staircase at Persepolis are well-known in this regard. All known nations are portrayed as coming peacefully with their

---

[14] See a broader discussion in Jonker 2008.

gifts to pay tribute and to honor the Persian king, who is sitting on his throne in the audience hall. The parlance around the so-called Kings' peace of 386 BCE, and the memory of a Peace of Callias (see note 6 above) were, of course, also in the background. The specific understanding of and propaganda around peace were influenced by political factors and should therefore not be interpreted as some sort of pacifist inclination on the part of the Persians.

An interesting feature of Persian society of this period is, however, that they did not build and maintain temple complexes. It seems as if the royal palace, and particularly the audience hall, served the function that temples in other ancient Near Eastern contexts had.[15]

The portrayal of Solomon as the "man of rest and peace" and of other Judean kings of the past as kings who brought rest and peace by relying on and seeking Yahweh might therefore have been the Chronicler's way to show that the real king of peace is Yahweh, the God of Israel (and not the Persian king). The temple in Jerusalem being portrayed as the "house of rest" was the Chronicler's way of indicating that the sanctuary in Jerusalem is actually the place where peace is to be found (and not in the audience halls of the Persian Empire). Although the Chronicler highlights the reign of Solomon, it seems that the idea was nowhere to portray this early king of Israel in contrast to the Persian king. It is rather that Solomon, like all further Judahite kings that are associated with peace and rest by the Chronicler, are portrayed as those who benefit from the peace of Yahweh when relying on and seeking him. The real contrast is therefore between Yahweh and the Persian king, and between the Jerusalem temple and the audience hall of the Persian king.

The Chronicler's communication on the imperial level therefore functioned as a subtle polemic to indicate what the real qualities of the founder king of Israel, Solomon, were. He was somebody who built the temple in Jerusalem and began the tradition of relying on and seeking Yahweh, the real king of peace. This is a qualitatively different portrayal of kingship compared to the Persian understanding of kingship. In the Persian context, the king is not only the embodiment of peace by the grace of the deity Ahuaramazda, but peace can also be obtained by bringing tribute to the Persian emperor on his throne in the audience hall. According to the Chronicler's understanding, peace and rest can only be obtained by relying on Yahweh, the God of Israel, and by serving him in the sanctuary, which is seen as "the house of rest."

---

15 For supporting arguments, see Cool Root 2010; Lynch 2014.

3 Discourse on Provincial Leadership: Various Kings in Chronicles

It is well-known that the Chronicler omits from his own account the bulk of the history of the northern kingdom as narrated in the book of Kings. The existence of Israel is acknowledged, and where the northern kingdom's history impinged on that of Judah, it is indeed referenced. Much more than in Kings, the focus in Chronicles is on the southern kingdom, Judah. However, the relationship between the kingdoms of Judah and Israel is sketched in a very complex way. Sometimes, Judah and Israel are portrayed as opponents of one another. On occasion, Israel is seen as Yahweh's instrument to punish Judah for transgressing against him. In other instances, however, Judah and Israel are assimilated, or the boundaries between the southern and northern royal houses are blurred. The following examples provide a brief overview of this variety of portrayals in the Chronicler's narratives about some of Judah's kings.

3.1 Judah and Israel in Opposition

Particularly the Chronicler's narratives about Abijah and Ahaz, both kings of Judah, show Judah and Israel in opposition to one another. In 2 Chr 13:1–14:1a Abijah's campaign against Jeroboam of Israel is mentioned. The Chronicler significantly expanded on the *Vorlage* in 1 Kgs 15:1–8a, and thereby altered the portrayal of Abijah from a king who was not fully devoted to Yahweh (according to 1 Kgs 15:3) to a pious leader who leads his people to victory against the northern kingdom, Israel.[16]

Second Chronicles 13:3 mentions that Abijah started a war against Jeroboam of Israel. Jeroboam had twice the number of soldiers than Abijah of Judah. A victory for Judah over Israel was therefore almost impossible. Before the battle, however, Abijah addresses his men. He emphasizes the eternal kingship that Yahweh promised to David: "Ought you not to know that the Lord God of Israel gave the kingship over Israel forever to David?" (13:5 ESV). Then follows an accusation: "Yet Jeroboam the son of Nebat, a servant of Solomon the son of David, rose up and rebelled against his lord" (13:6 ESV). The Chronicler indicates that Jeroboam's rebellion directly opposes the eternal covenant that Yahweh made with the house of David. Jeroboam is characterized as "a servant of Solomon the son of David," but not as monarch over Israel, thereby emphasiz-

---

[16] For a broader discussion, see Jonker 2007, 2013, 216–220.

ing Jeroboam's apostasy. In 13:8–9 Abijah refers to the unfaithfulness of Israel. Not only does he mention Jeroboam's golden calves, but also the fact that Jeroboam ill-treated the sons of Aaron and the Levites. The piety of the Judahites is emphasized in 13:10–11, in sharp contrast to the apostasy of the northerners. Aaronide priests, assisted by Levites, were observing the requirements of Yahweh by attending to all the aspects of the temple cult. The Judahites did not forsake (לֹא עָזַב) Yahweh (13:10), while the Israelites did (עָזַב) (13:11). Therefore, in 13:12 it is claimed that God is with them as their leader. Israel should be warned that Yahweh is fighting a holy war for Judah. Therefore, the "sons of Israel" are warned not to oppose Yahweh, for they will lose the battle. Subsequently, God destroys Jeroboam of Israel before Abijah of Judah. It is indicated that the men of Judah were victorious because they relied (שָׁעַן) on Yahweh, the God of their fathers (13:18). Jeroboam was totally destroyed (13:20), while Abijah could extend his territory into the border regions between Judah and Israel (13:19).

The Chronicler's version of Abijah's history seems to have had the aim of making good on the blemishes caused by the division of the kingdom under Rehoboam. Whereas the idealized image of the Davidic kingdom and Solomonic cult became tainted during Rehoboam's reign, the Chronicler's version of Abijah restores the splendor and dedication of that reputation. Abijah now serves as a model of proper kingship and fullhearted dedication to Yahweh, standing in stark contrast to the northern king who did not rely on Yahweh.

Another example of opposition between Judah and Israel occurs in 2 Chr 28:5b–15, the history of Ahaz, although the tables are turned in this narrative compared to Abijah's. The Chronicler changed the information of the *Vorlage* (2 Kgs 16) to a fully negative portrait of King Ahaz of Judah, who serves as a warning against unrestrained apostasy. The Chronicler added a section (28:6–15) about another encounter with Israel. This is the final occurrence of an Israelite king in Chronicles. The Chronicler explains Judah's heavy losses against Israel in theological terms, namely that Judah had forsaken (עָזַב) Yahweh, the God of their fathers (28:6). The section in 29:5b–15 contains a number of ironic twists. Israel, which is normally portrayed very negatively, now becomes Yahweh's instrument for punishing the apostasy of Ahaz and Judah. Furthermore, Yahweh's prophet Oded warns these Israelite soldiers not to take the Judahites to Samaria (28:8–9), so that Yahweh's anger (28:13) will not come upon Israel. The Israelite army does not have the right to slaughter the Judahites in a rage that reaches to heaven (28:9). They themselves are also guilty of sins against Yahweh (28:10). Some Ephraimite leaders then convince the warriors to release the captives. After clothing them and providing sandals, food and drink, they anointed the captives and let them go back to Jericho (28:14–15).

The second example therefore also portrays an oppositional relationship between Judah and Israel, but the roles are reversed. By juxtaposing these two narratives, it becomes clear that the Chronicler had a multi-faceted view of Judah and Israel and of their kings. Both could be in the wrong, and both could rely on Yahweh's assistance.

3.2 Assimilation of Judah and Israel

The Chronicler's version of the narrative about Asa's reign (2 Chr 13:23b–16:14) differs significantly from its *Vorlage* (1 Kgs 15:9–24).[17] The Chronicler reworked this narrative creatively to fit into a coherent theological framework. The section in 2 Chr 15:1–19 stems almost entirely from the Chronicler's own hand. The first seven verses narrate how the prophet Azariah, the son of Oded, was stirred by the spirit of God and how he delivered a message to king Asa of Judah. The core of the message is that, provided that Judah and Benjamin "seek" (דרשׁ) Yahweh, Judah will have peace and rest. The next pericope, vv. 8–15, reports on Asa's cultic reforms in Judah and Benjamin. Verses 8–9 also refer to the northern territories. It is stated that Asa's reforms were also undertaken in some Ephraimite cities (which were traditionally associated with the northern kingdom of Israel). Furthermore, Asa gathered all Judah and Benjamin and all from Ephraim, Manasseh, and Simeon to Jerusalem to take an oath to Yahweh and to participate in celebrating a festival there. It is specifically mentioned that many members from these tribes joined the south when they heard that Yahweh was with Judah.

It is significant that Ephraim and Manasseh are included as supporters of Asa's reform. The designation "Ephraim and Manasseh" often refers to the northern kingdom, Israel. The Chronicler's suggestion is that the cooperation between south and north contributed to the peaceful period of Asa's reign. Judah and Israel are not in opposition, but are both part of Yahweh's people, seeking (דרשׁ) him and relying (שׁען) on him.

3.3 Blurred Lines between Judah and Israel

The narrative about Jehoram is found in 2 Chr 21:2–22:1. Although the previous three kings, Abijah, Asa, and Jehoshaphat, are portrayed positively in Chroni-

---

17 For more in-depth discussions of these texts, see Jonker 2006, 2013, 221–226.

cles, like in Kings, the same does not apply to Jehoram. The Chronicler portrays him very negatively, stating early on that Jehoram "walked in the ways of the kings of Israel" (21:6).

The first three verses (21:2–4) come from the Chronicler's own hand, describing Jehoram's initial attempts to establish his kingship. These verses provide new information that is not included in the *Vorlage* in 2 Kgs 8, and it is not completely clear whether the events took place in Israel or in Judah. Verse 2 suggests that the brothers of Jehoram were all sons of Jehoshaphat king of Israel, although Jehoshaphat was actually the king of Judah. Verse 3 mentions, however, that fortified cities in Judah were given to these brothers and that the kingship was given to Jehoram, who was his firstborn son. After establishing his power, Jehoram killed all his brothers along with some of the princes of Israel (21:4). This statement is again confusing Judah and Israel.

What function would this confusion about Judah and Israel serve? One should remember that this literature stood in the service of the Second Temple Jerusalemite community in the process of negotiating a new identity in Achaemenid Yehud. It seems that the community was trying to come to terms with the new postexilic reality, in which the boundaries between the south and the north were no longer defined in terms of two separate monarchies. The monarchic political realities of the past were forever gone, and those realities were now substituted by a common political fate as provinces under Persian imperial rule. This common fate motivated those in the south to remember their continuity with their northern neighbor, knowing well that Samaria was a "larger, better-established, and considerably more populous" province than Yehud (Knoppers 2006, 272–273).

However, this narrative also witnesses to discontinuities between south and north. Although the lines between Judah and Israel, between Yehud and Samaria, were deliberately blurred by the Chronicler, it is also made clear that the Jerusalemite community was steadfast in its trust that the continuation of the Davidic line (not as a political reality but as a religious-theological one) was their assurance for the future. Yahweh's covenant with David sheltered them against destruction in the exile. The "ways of their father David" therefore stand in sharp contrast to the "ways of the Ahabites" of the north. There was no doubt that the people of Jerusalem had to differentiate themselves from the northern religious ways. This would have been a powerful message at a time when a Yahweh sanctuary likely already existed in Samaria on Mount Gerizim (see again Magen 2007).

3.4 Synthesis

We have seen in the royal narratives discussed above that the portrayal of the kings' leadership stood in the service of the Chronicler's engagement with the reality of separate Persian provinces in north and south. Due to the fact that these provinces approximately coincided with the respective geographical areas and populations of the former kingdoms of Judah and Israel, the Chronicler was eager to explain the similarities between these provinces, but also the differences. Through narratives of assimilation and differentiation, the Chronicler succeeded in expressing the continuities and discontinuities between Samaria and Yehud, clearly in the service of a process of identity negotiation.

4 Discourse on Tribal Leadership: Saul in Chronicles (1 Chr 10:1–14)

The tribe of Benjamin features prominently in the Chronicler's genealogical construction. In 1 Chr 8:1–40 we find the Benjaminite (and Gibeonite) genealogies as the counterpart of the tribe of Judah in the second part of the ring macrostructure (1 Chr 2.3–4:23). This macrostructure in the "genealogical vestibule" emphasizes that Judah and Benjamin form the two pillars upon which "All-Israel" is founded. After the last part of the ring construction in which the inhabitants of Jerusalem are listed (1 Chr 9:1–34) follows another genealogy that focuses on the Benjaminites, including a passing remark about Saul (1 Chr 9:35–44). Some scholars see this addition at the end of the "genealogical vestibule" as a transition to the narrative about Saul which follows in 1 Chr 10:1–14. Although Benjamin is portrayed as one of the pillars of "All-Israel," not much emphasis is placed on Saul, who was the first king of Israel according to the book of Samuel. This ambiguity increases when the reader reaches 1 Chr 10.

The narrative in 1 Chr 10 deviates significantly from the deuteronomistic version in 1 Sam 31. Although we find an elaborate narrative about Saul in Samuel, the Chronicler focuses only on the death of this king. In the first two sections of the pericope in 1 Chr 10 (vv. 1–7 focus on Saul's death, and vv. 8–12 focus on the benevolence of the people of Jabesh-Gilead) the writer strictly follows his *Vorlage* in 1 Sam 31, but in vv. 13–14 the Chronicler's own hand can be observed. These two verses state:

> [13] So Saul died for his breach of faith [מעל]. He broke faith with the Lord in that he did not keep [לא שמר] the command of the Lord, and also consulted a medium, seeking

[דרש] guidance. ¹⁴ He did not seek [לֹא דרשׁ] guidance from the Lord. Therefore the Lord [literally: "he" – LCJ] put him to death and turned the kingdom over to David the son of Jesse. (ESV, with addition of Hebrew lemmas by the author)

This passage is full of programmatic concepts which also appear prominently in other parts of the Chronicler's *Sondergut*. It seems as if the Chronicler wanted to heap up the accusations against Saul. Although the subject of the verb "kill" (מות *hiphil*) in v. 14 is unspecified, there is no doubt from the context that it is Yahweh who killed him in order to give the kingdom to David. This very fierce turn of events emphasizes not only that David's reign began on account of a deliberate intervention by Yahweh (thus providing a theological backing for David's reign) but also that Saul surely did not live up to Yahweh's expectations.

This evaluation of Saul's leadership in Chronicles fits into the ambiguous portrayal of Benjamin in the book. On the one hand, Benjamin is seen as a foundational part of "All-Israel." In fact, in 1 Chr 21 it seems that the Chronicler deliberately tailored the narrative in order to show that the threshing floor of Arauna (which was most probably in the border region between the tribal areas of Benjamin and Judah) was chosen as the future site of the temple. This indicates that the writer definitely wanted to incorporate Benjamin in the formation of a new identity for "All-Israel." However, the mainly negative portrayal of Saul, as well as the indication that the religious center shifted from Gibeon to Jerusalem, most probably signaled to the Benjaminites that their political and religious aspirations would not be tolerated in the new postexilic dispensation.

The portrayal of Saul's leadership (in fact, the absence of any narrative about his leadership) is therefore no evaluation of the individual, but rather fits into the overall rhetoric *vis-à-vis* Benjamin. The Chronicler constructs an identity for "All-Israel" in late Persian period Yehud which builds upon the two foundational tribal pillars of Judah and Benjamin. But the focus is rather on the central element of the initial genealogies, namely the Levites. The next section therefore moves over to a discussion of discourse on leadership in the cultic context of Jerusalem.

5 Discourse on Cultic Leadership: The Levites in Chronicles (2 Chr 29–32)

The concept of "holiness" occurs frequently in Chronicles – 32 times as a verb (mostly *hiphil* or *hithpael*), 47 times as a noun, and once as an adjective. It seems, however, that there is a development in Chronicles in the associations made with the issue of consecration and holiness. In the earlier parts of the book, 1 Chr 23:13 is programmatic: "The sons of Amram: Aaron and Moses. Aaron was set apart to dedicate (קדשׁ) the most holy things, that he and his sons forever should make offerings before the Lord and minister to him and pronounce blessings in his name forever" (ESV).

The view that Aaron and his descendants are set apart to deal with the holy things continues into the narrative of Solomon's dedication of the temple in Jerusalem. Although 2 Chr 5:5, 7 indicate that the Levites carried the ark, the tent of meeting, and the consecrated utensils into the temple (and even into the holy of holies), 2 Chr 5:11 clearly states that the priests consecrated themselves and that the Levites stood nearby lending support.

The first indication of the Levites being consecrated comes in 2 Chr 23:6, which states that only those priests and Levites who were on duty could enter the temple because they were holy. From 2 Chr 29, in the narrative about king Hezekiah's reign, the tide turns, however. From now on, the term קדשׁ (as a verb and a noun) is used frequently – 26 times in the Hezekiah narrative (2 Chr 29–32) and four times in the Josiah narrative (2 Chr 34–35).

In 2 Chr 29:5–11 the king commands the Levites to consecrate themselves to perform the purification of the temple. The same happens (in 2 Chr 35:6) when Josiah instructs the Levites to consecrate themselves and to slaughter the lambs for the Passover offering. Second Chronicles 29:34 even sets up a contrast between the priests and Levites by indicating that the latter were more conscientious in consecrating themselves than the priests. The contrast continues into the narrative of the celebration of Passover in Hezekiah's days. The Passover had to be postponed until the second month, since there were not enough consecrated priests to perform the offerings (2 Chr 30:3). Another interesting turn of events occurs when a very large crowd of people begins slaughtering the Passover lamb (2 Chr 30:13–15). The priests and the Levites were put to shame by this, and they therefore consecrated themselves and brought burnt offerings. For those in the crowd who were not consecrated, the Levites performed the slaughtering of the Passover lambs (2 Chr 30:17). After the whole assembly insisted on continuing the feast for another seven days, a great number of priests consecrated themselves (2 Chr 30:24). After an abundance of freewill offerings were brought to the temple, the distribution started taking place according to those enrolled in the family lists. Interestingly enough, 2 Chr 31:18 states: "They [male Levites and priests] were enrolled with all their little children, their wives, their sons, and their daughters, the whole assembly, for they were faithful in keeping themselves holy (כי באמונתם יתקדשׁו־קדשׁ)" (ESV).

This is unique in Chronicles, because Levites are never called "holy" in the priestly literature and in Ezekiel (see Knoppers 1999, 71). The development is thus clear: Whereas the book of Chronicles reflects in its earlier parts the ideological position that the priests were the consecrated ones and that the Levites played a supporting role, the position changes particularly beginning with the Hezekiah narrative, where the Levites become the primary consecrated ones who assist in the slaughtering and offering of the Passover lambs. There are even glimpses (in 2 Chr 30:15 and 31:18) of community members being viewed as holy.

It therefore seems that the relationship between the Aaronide priests and the Levites grows from a position of subordination to a coordinate relationship. Toward the end of the book, particularly as seen in the Passover narratives in 2 Chr 30 and 35, the Levites occupy at least an equal position with the Aaronide priests, and in some cases are even seen as more obedient in terms of their consecration.

It is clear that this portrayal of the relationship between the Aaronide priests and the Levites in Chronicles engaged with the issue of cultic leadership in Persian-period Jerusalem against the background of inner-cultic tensions and fault lines (see above).

6 Conclusion: A Multilayered Reflection on Leadership in Achaemenid Yehud

Where do these different perspectives on and uses of the theme of kingship leave us in our endeavor to study leadership in the late postexilic literature of the Hebrew Bible? First of all, one has to acknowledge that the portrayal of kingship, or of other types of leadership (e.g., of tribal areas, of cultic groups, etc.) in Chronicles is fully determined by the socio-historical level involved in the rhetorical situation. I have indicated above that these levels were overlapping and coinciding, and they exerted mutual influence on one another. However, each of these levels constituted a unique rhetorical situation, which determined how the notion of leadership functioned in literature that aimed at addressing the specific rhetorical situations.

It should further be acknowledged that all narratives about kings or other types of leadership did not necessarily have the intention to provide a model or models of leadership, but rather contributed with these narratives to processes of identity negotiation, and the negotiation of power relations in the late Achaemenid period. The reflections of leadership that we see in Chronicles are not primarily models of the monarchic past that are presented in order to be followed in a new dispensation. It is rather a matter of a specific way of remembering models of leadership in the past in order to contribute to ideological discourses in the present of the Achaemenid period.

If my assessment is correct in the above two observations, the following insights could be gathered from the present study:

- Although it seems that the Chronicler reflects a time period in postexilic Yehud when the emerging Jewish community in Jerusalem and its surroundings was encouraged to assimilate into the new imperial dispensation, the book also reflects a subtle polemic against the imperial center. This polemic particularly plays out in the relationship that the Chronicler constructs between the ideological notion of "peace" and the triad of king – deity – sanctuary. It seems that the Chronicler is latching onto the Achaemenid royal ideology as expressed in certain royal inscriptions and Persian architectural features. However, he brings the memories of a distant monarchic past into discourse with the Achaemenid royal ideology by pointing out that Solomon, their model king who was "a man of rest," built the temple in Jerusalem which was "a house of rest." Rest and peace could be obtained when the people, including their kings, relied on Yahweh, the deity of the temple, and when they sought him in all their doings. The idealized leadership model of a past king like Solomon is therefore used as a polemical counter-image to kingship in the Persian Empire. The suggestion was that, if they wanted real peace, the Persians should not be looking for it in the deeds of their kings or in their audience halls, but rather in the temple in Jerusalem where the deity Yahweh lived to make it "a house of rest."
- While the aforementioned leadership model forms the overarching framework in the Persian Empire, the Chronicler also engaged in the question of who could claim leadership of All-Israel on a provincial level. On the one hand, those areas included in Yehud's northern provincial neighbor, Samaria, could not be estranged within the imperial context. Strife between these provinces would definitely not go unpunished under the Persian authorities. The Chronicler is therefore careful to point out that the northerners (read: those living in Samaria) were blood brothers and sisters of those living in the south (in Yehud). However, the inner-provincial polemic on whose version of Yahwism was really the true version continued simultaneously. We therefore see that the kings of the former northern kingdom, Israel, are omitted from the Chronicler's narrative line, but also that those mentioned in his narrative are accused of having allowed foreign elements into their religion. We therefore find a very ambiguous picture of Samaria, and of leadership in Samaria in the book of Chronicles. What stands out, however, is that the kings of the southern kingdom are evaluated according to the same criterion, namely whether they sought Yahweh wholeheartedly. Only a few of the southern kings fall into that category. The Chronicler's portrayal of these kings focuses more on how their individual conduct de-

termined their relationship with Yahweh. Whereas the notion of kingship is more at stake in the deuteronomistic *Vorlage*, the Chronicler turns the narratives into models of individual royal dedication to Yahweh (or of its absence).

- It is clear from the Saul narrative in Chronicles that there were still some leadership tensions between Benjamin and Judah – both on political and religious levels – prevailing during the late Persian period. The remembrance of Saul (a Benjaminite) as someone who was killed by Yahweh so that the kingship could go over to David (a Judahite) is telling. It reflects that the political and religious leadership in Achaemenid Yehud probably wanted to make clear that the influence of the Judahite line should not be questioned or underestimated in the restoration society. The leadership aspirations of Judahites in the Persian province of Yehud become clear from this portrayal.
- Leadership in the Jerusalemite cult was a sensitive topic in late Persian-period Yehud. We have seen above that the fault lines ran deep in the restoration community due to the overlapping aspirations of Aaronide priests and Levites, and of remainees and returnees. A unique element in the Chronicler's portrayal, however, is the association of cultic leadership with the notion of holiness. We have seen that the Chronicler develops the profile of the Levites gradually throughout the book in terms of the understanding of holiness as a quality that can be obtained by all parts of society, including the so-called "minor cultic personnel" (probably related to the understanding of holiness propagated in the Holiness Legislation in Leviticus). The Chronicler therefore portrays the Levites and Aaronide priests as on a par in terms of cultic leadership. The only difference that remains is the bringing of the sin offerings, which remains the privilege of the Aaronides. However, the profile developed in Chronicles is far removed from the "singers and temple guardians" profile that we find elsewhere in the Hebrew Bible.

When observing Chronicles against the background of the four socio-historical levels discussed above, the interpreter of this book notices a multilayered and multifaceted understanding of leadership in this late Persian-period literature. It would thus do scholars well to incorporate this more complex portrayal of leadership in Chronicles into the ongoing interpretation of the book.

Bibliography

Bedford, Peter. 2007. "The Economic Role of the Jerusalem Temple in Achaemenid Judah: Comparative Perspectives." In *Shai le-Sara Japhet: Studies in the Bible, Its Exegesis and Its Language*, edited by Moshe Bar-Asher et al., 3–20. Jerusalem: The Bialik Institute.

Ben Zvi, Ehud. 1997. "The Urban Center of Jerusalem and the Development of the Literature of the Hebrew Bible." In *Urbanism in Antiquity: From Mesopotamia to Crete*, edited by Walter Aufrecht et al., 194–209. Sheffield: Sheffield Academic Press.

Briant, Pierre. 2002. *From Cyrus to Alexander: A History of the Persian Empire*, translated by P. T. Daniels. Winona Lake: Eisenbrauns.

Brooke, George. 2008. "Review of Richard Horsley's Scribes, Visionaries, and the Politics of Second Temple Judea." *JSS* 53:380–381.

Brosius, Maria. 2006. *The Persians: An Introduction*. London: Routledge.

Carter, Charles. 1999. *The Emergence of Yehud in the Persian Period: A Social and Demographic Study*. Sheffield: Sheffield University Press.

Cool Root, Margaret. 2010. "Palace to Temple – King to Cosmos: Achaemenid Foundation Texts in Iran." In *From the Foundations to the Crenellations: Essays on Temple Building in the Ancient Near East and Hebrew Bible*, edited by Mark Boda and Jamie Novotny, 165–210. Münster: Ugarit-Verlag.

Cornelius, Izak. 2011. "'A Tale of Two Cities': The Visual Imagery of Yehud and Samaria, and Identity/Self-Understanding in Persian-Period Palestine." In *Texts, Contexts and Readings in Postexilic Literature: Explorations into Historiography and Identity Negotiation in Hebrew Bible and Related Texts*, edited by Louis Jonker, 213–237. FAT II/53. Tübingen: Mohr Siebeck.

Davies, Philip R. 2007. "The Trouble with Benjamin." In *Reflection and Refraction: Studies in Biblical Historiography in Honour of A. Graeme Auld*, edited by Robert Rezetko, Timothy Lim, and Brian Aucker, 93–112. Leiden: Brill.

Finkelstein, Israel. 2010a. "The Territorial Extent and Demography of Yehud/Judea in the Persian and Early Hellenistic Periods." *RB* 117:39–54.

Finkelstein, Israel. 2010b. "Persian Period Jerusalem and Yehud: A Rejoinder." *JHS* 9: Article 24.

Giffone, Benjamin D. 2016. *"Sit at my Right Hand": The Chronicler's Portrait of the Tribe of Benjamin in the Social Context of Yehud*. LHBOTS 628. London: Bloomsbury T&T Clark.

Horsley, Richard. 2007. *Scribes, Visionaries, and the Politics of Second Temple Judea*. Louisville: Westminster John Knox Press.

Jonker, Louis. 2006. "The Cushites in the Chronicler's Version of Asa's Reign: A Secondary Audience in Chronicles?" *OTE* 19:863–881.

Jonker, Louis. 2007. "Refocusing the Battle Accounts of the Kings: Identity Formation in the Books of Chronicles." In *Behutsames Lesen: Alttestamentliche Exegese im inderdisziplinären Methodendiskurs*, edited by Louis Jonker et al., 245–274. Leipzig: Evangelische Verlagsanstalt.

Jonker, Louis. 2008. "The Chronicler's Portrayal of Solomon as the King of Peace Within the Context of the International Peace Discourses of the Persian Era." *OTE* 21:653–669.

Jonker, Louis. 2011. "Engaging with Different Contexts: A Survey of the Various Levels of Identity Negotiation in Chronicles." In *Texts, Contexts and Readings in Postexilic Literature: Explorations into Historiography and Identity Negotiation in Hebrew Bible and Related Texts*, edited by Louis Jonker, 63–93. FAT II/53. Tübingen: Mohr Siebeck.

Jonker, Louis. 2013. *1 & 2 Chronicles*. Grand Rapids: Baker Books.
Jonker, Louis. 2015. "Agrarian Economy Through City Elite Eyes: Reflections of Late Persian Period Yehud Economy in the Genealogies of Chronicles." In *The Economy of Ancient Judah in Its Historical Context*, edited by Marvin Miller, Ehud Ben Zvi, and Gary Knoppers, 77–101. Winona Lake: Eisenbrauns.
Jonker, Louis. 2016. *Defining All-Israel in Chronicles: Multi-Levelled Identity Negotiation in Late Persian Period Yehud*. FAT 106. Tübingen: Mohr Siebeck.
Knoppers, Gary. 1999. "Hierodules, Priests, or Janitors? The Levites in Chronicles and the History of the Israelite Priesthood." *JBL* 118:49–72.
Knoppers, Gary. 2006. "Revisiting the Samarian Question in the Persian Period." In *Judah and the Judeans in the Persian Period*, edited by Oded Lipschits and Manfred Oeming, 265–290. Winona Lake: Eisenbrauns.
Knoppers, Gary. 2013. *Jews and Samaritans: The Origins and History of Their Early Relations*. Oxford: Oxford University Press.
Lemaire, Andre. 2006. "New Aramaic Ostraca from Idumea and Their Historical Interpretation." In *Judah and the Judeans in the Persian Period*, edited by Oded Lipschits and Manfred Oeming, 413–456. Winona Lake: Eisenbrauns.
Lipschits, Oded. 2003. "Demographic Changes in Judah Between the Seventh and the Fifth Centuries B.C.E." In *Judah and the Judeans in the Persian Period*, edited by Oded Lipschits and Manfred Oeming, 323–376. Winona Lake: Eisenbrauns.
Lipschits, Oded. 2005. *The Fall and Rise of Jerusalem: Judah under Babylonian Rule*. Winona Lake: Eisenbrauns.
Lipschits, Oded. 2006. "Achaemenid Imperial Policy, Settlement Processes in Palestine, and the Status of Jerusalem in the Middle of the Fifth century BCE." In *Judah and the Judeans in the Persian Period*, edited by Oded Lipschits and Manfred Oeming, 19–52. Winona Lake: Eisenbrauns.
Lynch, Matthew. 2014. *Monotheism and Institutions in the Book of Chronicles: Temple, Priesthood, and Kingship in Post-exilic Perspective*. FAT II/64. Tübingen: Mohr Siebeck.
Magen, Yigal. 2007. "The Dating of the First Phase of the Samaritan Temple on Mount Gerizim in Light of the Archaeological Evidence." In *Judah and the Judeans in the Fourth Century B.C.E.*, edited by Oded Lipschits, Gary Knoppers, and Rainer Albertz, 157–211. Winona Lake: Eisenbrauns.
Ussishkin, David. 2006. "The Borders and De Facto Size of Jerusalem in the Persian Period." In *Judah and the Judeans in the Persian Period*, edited by Oded Lipschits and Manfred Oeming, 147–166. Winona Lake: Eisenbrauns.
Waters, Matthew. 2014. *Ancient Persia: A Concise History of the Achaemenid Empire, 550–330 BCE*. Cambridge: Cambridge University Press.
West, Gerald. 2011. "Tracking an Ancient Near Eastern Economic System: The Tributary Mode of Production and the Temple-State." *OTE* 24:511–532.
Wiesehöfer, Josef. 2011. "Achaemenid Rule and Its Impact on Yehud." In *Texts, Contexts and Readings in Postexilic Literature: Explorations into Historiography and Identity Negotiation in Hebrew Bible and Related Texts*, edited by Louis Jonker, 171–185. FAT II/53. Tübingen: Mohr Siebeck.
Wiesehöfer, Josef. 2013. "Iranian Empires." In *The Oxford Handbook of the State in the Ancient Near East and Mediterranean*, edited by Peter Bang and Walter Scheidel, 199–231. Oxford: Oxford University Press.

Willi, Thomas. 1995. *Juda, Jehud, Israel: Studien zum Selbstverständnis des Judentums in persischer Zeit*. FAT 12. Tübingen: Mohr Siebeck.

Wright, John. 1997. "The Fight for Peace: Narrative and History in the Battle Accounts in Chronicles." In *The Chronicler as Historian*, edited by Matt Graham, Kenneth Hoglund, and Steven L. McKenzie, 150–177. Sheffield: Sheffield Academic Press.

Yigal Levin
Judges, Elders, and Officers in Chronicles

The book of Chronicles is, to a large extent, a book about kings: the kings of the House of David. The entire narrative part of the book is built around these kings, and they also feature prominently in the genealogies.[1] Besides kings, Chronicles is also full of priests and Levites (on which see Levin 2019) and also mentions dozens of prophets in various roles (see, e.g., Knoppers 2010; Person 2013). It is obvious that when the Chronicler looked back at preexilic Israel, he imagined it as being a society led by kings, priests, Levites, and prophets; it is thus not surprising that these also stand at the center of most modern scholars' conception of Chronicles (see, e.g., Ben Zvi 2016; Bos 2016).

But the society of ancient Israel was led not only by kings, priests, Levites, and prophets. Within the Bible, we find many additional forms of leadership – the entire book of Judges is all about different kinds of leadership (see Brettler 1989; Levine 2009; Niditch 2009). And even in the rest of the Bible, we find teachers, generals, officers, elders, judges, nobles, and villains – each with their own leadership qualities and capabilities (see the essays in Pyschny and Schulz 2018). In this paper, I wish to examine three specific types of leaders that appear in various biblical texts, and to see how they are represented in Chronicles. I intend to compare their appearance in Chronicles to the way they are used in the Chronicler's "preexilic sources" (the Pentateuchal sources and the Deuteronomistic History) and to examine the way in which these office-holders are envisioned in Chronicles: their relationship to the monarchy, to the priesthood, to the temple, and to the tribal institutions. Is the Chronicler's vision of these office-holders fundamentally different from that of the earlier sources? If so, does this different vision reflect the reality of Persian-period Yehud, or is it a utopian vision, more reflective of the Chronicler's ideology than of any historical reality?[2] The three types of leaders that this paper will examine are the $šōp^eṭîm$ ("judges"), the $šōṭ^erîm$ ("officers"), and the $z^eqenîm$ ("elders"). What does Chronicles have to say about these types of leaders?

---

[1] On the ideology of kingship in Chronicles, see Japhet 1997, 395–491.
[2] For the widely accepted view that Chronicles was composed in the province of Yehud/Judah during the late fourth century BCE, either just before or just after the Macedonian conquest, see Knoppers 2003, 101–117; Klein 2006, 13–16, and many others. On the idea of Chronicles as utopian literature, see the essays in Schweitzer and Uhlenbruch 2016.

1 Judges (šōpᵉṭîm)

The noun שפט, in its various forms, appears about 60 times in the Bible. Technically, the noun is derived from the verbal root שפט, which can mean "to judge," "to lead," or "to rule" (Easterly 1997). But when an individual is said to be a šōpēṭ, the line between the verb "he judges" or "he rules" and the noun "judge" or "ruler" can be blurred. For example, when 2 Chr 26:21, copied almost verbatim from 2 Kgs 15:5, tells us that Jotham son of Uzziah שופט את עם הארץ, does this mean that he was "ruling" or "judging" the people, or that he was "ruler" or "judge" of the people? The same can be asked of Deborah, who is described in Judg 4:4 as šōpᵉṭâh yiśrā'el, which NRSV translates "was judging Israel" while NJPS has "she led Israel."[3]

In Deuteronomy, the context makes it clear that most šōpᵉṭîm are, indeed, "judges." According to such passages as Deut 1:16–17 and 16:18–20, these šōpᵉṭîm were situated in the city gates and were supposed to hear cases with fairness and impartiality. As pointed out by Fox (2000, 165–166), they were supposed to deal with certain types of cases, while others, such as those of rebellious sons (Deut 21:19), brides accused of not being virgins (22:15–19) and so on are to be adjudicated by the town zᵉqenîm, the "elders" (see below).

What Fox does not emphasize is the non-mention of šōpᵉṭîm, or even of the verb špṭ with reference to human judgment, in the rest of the legal sections of the Pentateuch outside of Deuteronomy, especially the priestly corpus.[4] The main exception to this is of course Exod 18, in which Jethro is said to guide Moses in the appointment of judges, although the assignment of this passage to the "Pentateuchal legal corpus" and its relationship to the various Pentateuchal sources is debated (cf. Schwartz 2009; Baden 2011, 328–336; Jeon 2017). But even within this chapter, it is only the verb špṭ that appears, never the noun šōpēṭ. The officers of thousands and hundreds and fifties and tens that are supposed to judge the people are never actually called "judges."

---

[3] The comparison made by Avishur (1999) between the language and imagery of the depiction of Deborah and those used in to describe Dan'il in the Ugaritic story of Aqhat, however, supports understanding her role as that of a judge as well as a leader.

[4] The emphases on human judgment and the legal corpus are meant to exclude references to divine judgement such as in Gen 18:25 ("Shall not the judge of all the earth do what is just?"), and anecdotal references to someone being, or not being, in a position to judge, such as Gen 19:9 (האחד בא־לגור וישפט שפוט), which NRSV translates "This fellow came here as an alien, and he would play the judge!", while NJPS renders "The fellow [...] came here as an alien, and already he acts the ruler!") or Exod 2:14 (שר ושפט), which NRSV gives as "ruler and judge" and NJPS "chief and ruler").

Besides this, "judging" by humans is mentioned in just three legal passages. The first of these is Lev 19:15, which admonishes, "You shall not render an unjust judgment; you shall not be partial to the poor or defer to the great: with justice you shall judge your neighbor."[5] This chapter is usually considered to be part of the "Holiness Code" (commonly delimited as Lev 17–26), the relationship of which to the priestly and deuteronomic legislation is debated (for which see, for example, Stewart 2015; Meyer 2017). But there, too, it is "all the assembly of the sons of Israel" (v. 2) who are addressed, with no mention of "judges."

Next comes Num 25:5, in which Moses orders "the judges of Israel" (*šōpᵉṭê yiśrā'el*) to kill those who had worshiped Baal-peor. However, many scholars relate vv. 1–5 of this chapter to the Yahwistic or the "JE" tradition, distancing it from the priestly legislation (for discussion see Kislev 2011). Both Budd (1984, 275) and Ashley (1993, 519) specifically connect the "judges" mentioned here with those of Exod 18 (which, as mentioned above, are not actually called *šōpᵉṭîm*). Levine (2000, 285) makes the same connection, but confuses the issue by translating *šōpᵉṭê yiśrā'el* as "the Israelite commanders" rather than "judges."

Finally, in Num 35:24, "the assembly" (העדה) is supposed to judge between an accidental killer and the dead person's relatives, sending the accidental killer to a city of refuge. Mattison (2018) ascribes this passage to a corpus of "Holiness Legislation" that goes beyond the "Holiness Code" of Lev 17–26, and in any case, here too, it is "the assembly" that does the judging, not professional judges.

In other words, while Deuteronomy assumes that *šōpᵉṭîm* are professional appointed judges, such judges are lacking in the priestly legislation, while in passages often assigned to JE or to H, the people who do judge are not actually called *šōpᵉṭîm*.

Within the Deuteronomistic History we find a similar pattern. In Joshua, the root *špṭ* appears six times. In Josh 6:15, כמשפט הזה, means "in this manner," which has nothing to do with "judging." In Josh 8:33, "all Israel, and their *zᵉqenîm* and their *šōṭᵉrîm* and their *šōpᵉṭîm*" are pictured as standing with the Levitical priests by the ark. In Josh 20:6, the unintentional killer must remain in the city of refuge "until he has stood before the assembly for judgment," following Num 35:24. In Josh 23:2 and 24:1, Joshua assembles "all Israel, their *zᵉqenîm* and heads, their *šōpᵉṭîm* and *šōṭᵉrîm*." And finally, in Josh 24:25, Joshua lays down חק ומשפט, "statutes and ordinances" (NRSV) for the people.

---

5 The dictum לא־תעשו עול במשפט is repeated verbatim in v. 35. Many modern translations such as NRSV and NJPS obfuscate this by combining this first part of the verse with its second part, such as "You shall not cheat in measuring length, weight, or quantity" (NRSV). Compare KJV, in which "Ye shall do no unrighteousness in judgement" is spelled out in both verses.

Thus, in three of the six texts, šōpᵉṭîm, together with zᵉqenîm, šōṭᵉrîm, "heads," and priests, are listed as office-holders of some sort, without any description of their specific duties. When there is "judging" to be done it is done by the "assembly" rather than by "judges," and twice the word mišpaṭ is used for "rule" or "ordinance," not for "judgement."

In Judges the root špṭ appears 24 times. The first six of these are in Judg 2:16–19, in which the author introduces "the judges" for whom the book is named. In light of the narrative context, however, it is clear that "The Judges in Judges Don't Judge" (Easterly 1997, 44); the term šōpeṭ here means "leader" or "ruler," not "judge." So when the spirit of the Lord came upon Othniel, "*wayyišpōṭ* Israel and he went out to war" (Judg 3:10), he obviously "led" Israel rather than "judged" them. The same is true for the eleven additional times in which this leader or that is said to have šapaṭ/wayyišpōṭ Israel: all of these men were "leaders," not "judges." The only ambiguity is with the role of Deborah, whom we have already discussed, and the only character who is actually called upon to "judge" is God, in Judg 11:27: "the Lord, the judge, judge this day (ישפט יהוה השפט) between the people of Israel and the people of Ammon." Besides this, mišpaṭ is used for "rule" or "custom" in Judg 3:12 and 18:7.

In Samuel and in Kings we find a similar pattern, but there is a shift. mišpaṭ still usually means "rule" or "custom" (such as in 1 Sam 2:13; 8:9, 11; 30:25), and when Samuel is said to *wayyišpōṭ* Israel (7:6, 15), it still obviously means that he "led" or "ruled" them, but when he šapaṭ Israel at Ramah and appointed his sons as šōpᵉṭîm in Beer-sheba (7:17; 8:1–2), the fact that they "did not walk in his ways, but turned after gain; they took bribes and perverted justice (mišpaṭ)" (8:3) shows that their role, at least in part, was in fact "to judge." So when the elders of Israel subsequently ask for a king lᵉšōpṭēnû (8:5–6), the term seems to have a double meaning of both "to lead us" and "to judge us."[6] And when David is said to have "administered justice (mišpaṭ) and equity (ṣᵉdaqâh) to all his people" (2 Sam 8:15), this specifically refers to the king's role as judge. This role is also emphasized in 2 Sam 15:2–6. The role of God as judge also appears several times (1 Sam 12:7; 24:12, 15; 2 Sam 18:19, 31). Also in Kings, God judges (1 Kgs 8:32) and kings judge (1 Kgs 3:9, 17–28; 7:7; 10:9; 20:40; 2 Kgs 15:5).[7] What we do not find at all, beyond 1 Sam 8, is anyone else judging. There seems to be no evidence in the deuteronomistic version of the history of the kingdoms of

---

[6] Nihan (2013, 229–236) emphasizes the connection between 1 Sam 7–8 and the "law of the king" in Deut 17:14–20, although he does not mention that in Deuteronomy, "judging" is not one of the duties of the king.

[7] Although in the case of 2 Kgs 15:5, NRSV and NJPS are probably justified in translating šōpeṭ as "governing."

Israel and Judah of professional judges, sitting in courts of law.[8] The only mentions of šōp^eṭîm are in 1 Sam 7:11, "from the time that I appointed šōp^eṭîm over my people Israel," and then again in 2 Kgs 23:22, "since the days of the šōp^eṭîm who šāp^eṭû Israel," both referring to the "šōp^eṭîm" of the book of Judges, but as we have already noted, those šōp^eṭîm were not really "judges" in the sense that we are discussing here.

What about Chronicles? What are the contexts in which šōp^eṭîm appear in Chronicles, can the choice of words be attributed to the Chronicler himself, and what does the term itself seem to mean?

The first two references to šōp^eṭîm in Chronicles are in the so-called dynastic oracle in 1 Chr 17 (// 2 Sam 7). There, in v. 6, in God's response to David's wish to build a temple, delivered through the prophet Nathan, God asks, "Wherever I have moved about among all Israel, did I ever speak a word with any of šōp^eṭê yiśra'el (the judges of Israel), whom I commanded to shepherd my people, saying, Why have you not built me a house of cedar?" Here šōp^eṭê yiśra'el quite definitely refers to the previous leaders of Israel, the so-called judges of the book of Judges. Verse 10 of the same chapter, "from the time that I appointed šōp^eṭîm over my people Israel," refers to the same "judges." In any case, since this whole chapter in Chronicles is taken with minimal changes from Samuel, the use of šōp^eṭîm here first of all reflects the deuteronomistic use of the term, and only secondarily the fact that the Chronicler preserved this use in his retelling of the story.[9]

The remaining five appearances of šōp^eṭîm in Chronicles are in passages that are uniquely the Chronicler's. The first two of these are within the long lists of Levitical officials that the Chronicler attributes to the time of David. In 1 Chr 23:2–5, as David is passing his reign to Solomon:

> He assembled all the leaders of Israel and the priests and the Levites. And they counted the Levites, thirty years old and upward, and their number, the men, was thirty thousand and eight hundred heads. Twenty-four thousand of these, to take charge of the work in the house of the Lord, and šōṭ^erîm and šōp^eṭîm ("officers and judges") six thousand. Four thousand gatekeepers, and four thousand shall offer praises to the Lord with the instruments that I have made for praise.

---

[8] This is also true in the story of the false trial of Naboth in 1 Kgs 21:8–13. There, the trial was conducted by the z^eqenîm and the ḥōrîm, "the elders and the nobles," who seem to have been assembled ad hoc. They are never called šōp^eṭîm, and the story makes no use of the term špṭ in any way.

[9] In the Samuel version, 2 Sam 7:7 reads šibṭê yiśra'el, "the tribes of Israel" where Chronicles reads šōp^eṭê yiśra'el. McCarter (1984, 192) prefers the Samuel version as a *lectio facilior*, reading it as šōb^eṭê yiśra'el, which he translates "the staff bearers of Israel." See also Caquot and de Robert 1994, 427–428 and the references there.

Mention is made to *šōpᵉṭîm* again in 1 Chr 26:29, where some of the Levites are appointed for "outside duties for Israel [meaning outside of the temple], as *šōṭᵉrîm* and *šōpᵉṭîm*." So in both of these related passages, attributed by the Chronicler to David, *šōpᵉṭîm* come together with *šōṭᵉrîm*, and they both seem to come from the tribe of Levi. Their actual functions, however, are not spelled out – presumably the reader was supposed to know what a *šōpeṭ* does.

In 2 Chr 1:2, as Solomon is taking control of Israel after the death of David, "Solomon summoned all Israel, the commanders of the thousands and of the hundreds, the *šōpᵉṭîm*, and every *naśi* ('leader') of all Israel, the heads of families." This passage, which is part of the Chronicler's expansion of Kings' description of Solomon's pilgrimage to Gibeon, includes the *šōpᵉṭîm* in what seems to be a list of military leaders, based roughly on Deut 1:15–16: "So I took the leaders of your tribes, wise and reputable individuals, and installed them as leaders over you, commanders of thousands, commanders of hundreds, commanders of fifties, commanders of tens, and officials (*šōṭᵉrîm*), throughout your tribes. And I charged your judges (*šōpᵉṭîm*) at that time: Give the members of your community a fair hearing, and judge rightly between one person and another, whether citizen or resident alien." Officers of thousands and of hundreds are also mentioned in Num 31, together with *kol nᵉśi'ê ha'edâh* (v. 13, NRSV "all the leaders of the congregation"; NJPS "all the chieftains of the community"). Finally, in Jethro's advice to Moses (Exod 18:21–26), officers of thousands and of hundreds (and of fifties and of tens) are actually part of the judicial system, with Moses himself as the supreme judge. So when the Chronicler lists *šōpᵉṭîm* together with *nᵉśi'îm* and with officers of thousands and hundreds, he is taking his cue from Exodus, Numbers, and Deuteronomy. In fact, since, as mentioned above, Exodus does not actually call these "judges" *šōpᵉṭîm*, while *nᵉśi'îm* never appear in Deuteronomy, the Chronicler can be described as combining the various terms that he found in his Pentateuchal sources in order to form what he considered to be a comprehensive description.

Finally, *šōpᵉṭîm* are mentioned twice in the famous "judicial reform" of Jehoshaphat in 2 Chr 19. This might be expected, but there is a twist. As many have pointed out, this passage envisions a "two-tiered" judicial system. Verses 5–7 tell of Jehoshaphat's positioning *šōpᵉṭîm* in every town in Judah, and admonishing them to judge by fear of God:

> He appointed judges (*šōpᵉṭîm*) in the land in all the fortified cities of Judah, city by city, and said to the judges, Consider what you are doing, for you judge not on behalf of human beings but on the Lord's behalf; he is with you in giving judgment. Now, let the fear of the Lord be upon you; take care what you do, for there is no perversion of justice with the Lord our God, or partiality, or taking of bribes.

When this passage is compared to Deut 16:18–20, the dependence is clear, even to the extent of Chronicles' "in the land in all the fortified cities of Judah, city by city" reflecting Deuteronomy's "throughout your tribes, in all your towns":

> You shall appoint judges and officials throughout your tribes, in all your towns that the Lord your God is giving you, and they shall render just decisions for the people. You must not distort justice; you must not show partiality; and you must not accept bribes, for a bribe blinds the eyes of the wise and subverts the cause of those who are in the right. Justice, and only justice, you shall pursue, so that you may live and occupy the land that the Lord your God is giving you.

Verses 8–11 then discuss a different court in Jerusalem, which is specifically staffed with priests, Levites, and the heads of the fathers' houses, together with šōṭ^{e}rîm. And while a real analysis of Jehoshaphat's judicial system is far beyond the limits of this paper,[10] I do wish to emphasize one thing: šōp^{e}ṭîm – that is, people whose main task is to judge, what we might call "professional judges" – are only mentioned in the "lower" courts, and they are not said to be priests or Levites. In the "upper" court in Jerusalem, the people who are appointed to judge (העמיד למשפט) are priests, Levites and heads of the fathers' houses, but they are never actually called šōp^{e}ṭîm.

What kind of picture do we have so far? Of the five contexts in which šōp^{e}ṭîm are mentioned, in 1 Chr 17 the term refers to the premonarchic leaders of Israel, as in the deuteronomistic source for this pericope. In 1 Chr 23 and 26, the šōp^{e}ṭîm, together with the šōṭ^{e}rîm, are Levites who are appointed by David for various administrative tasks outside the sanctuary, although just what those tasks are is not specified. In 2 Chr 1:2 the šōp^{e}ṭîm appear, together with other leaders such as the n^{e}śî'îm, the commanders of the thousands and of the hundreds, and the heads of families, as part of Solomon's entourage, but again, their specific tasks are not mentioned. And finally, in 2 Chr 19, the šōp^{e}ṭîm are said to be appointed judges in the "usual" sense of the word, but here they seem not to be Levites or priests, while the Levites and priests who do the mišpaṭ in the Jerusalem court are never called šōp^{e}ṭîm. And in at least two of these contexts, the šōp^{e}ṭîm are accompanied by šōṭ^{e}rîm.

2 Officers (šōṭ^{e}rîm)

The noun šōṭēr is usually assumed to be connected to the Akkadian verb šaṭāru, "write, copy, register" and the noun šaṭāru(m), "document, copy," and to the

---

10 For such a discussion see Levin 2017, 121–136 and references there.

later Aramaic שטר, "document" as well, leading to the Greek and Syriac translations of the term as "scribe." Moshe Weinfeld (1977, 83) claimed that the *šōṭēr* "fulfilled secretarial functions [...] סופר and שוטר are very close in meaning".[11] Alexander Rofé (2001, 98–99) went even further, claiming that *sōpēr* and *šōṭēr* actually are synonymous, the former being preferred in most of biblical historiography, the latter, derived in his opinion from the Aramaic, used in the Pentateuch and Joshua for its "archaic quality." Only in Chronicles do the two appear together, perhaps because the much later writer of Chronicles thought that they represented two different functions. However, as noted by Fox, Akkadian does not have a noun *šaṭāru(m)* that means "scribe," and Biblical Hebrew has neither a verb from this root which means "to write," nor are *šōṭerîm* ever explicitly described as writing (Fox 2000, 192–196). While the terms may be related etymologically, the only actual information we have about the biblical *šōṭēr* is from the Bible itself.[12] Within the Bible, most *šōṭerîm* seem to be government officials, but their specific function is not clear. In Exod 5, they are part of the Egyptian slave-drivers, but designated "the *šōṭerîm* of the children of Israel," perhaps indicating they were chosen from among the Israelites. Numbers 11:16, usually assigned to the "JE" narrative (Levine 1993, 311), speaks of "the elders of Israel, whom you know to be the elders of the people and their officers (*šōṭerāw*)." This is the only mention of *šōṭerîm* in the Pentateuch outside of Deuteronomy; they are totally absent from P and H. In Deut 1:15; 20:5–8; and Josh 1:10; 3:2 they seem to have a military function, perhaps as orderlies or sergeants-major. In Deut 29:9 and 31:28 they are listed together with the elders, the *zeqenîm*. In Josh 8:33 it is "their elders and their *šōṭerîm* and their judges." Joshua 23:2 and 24:1 are similar: "their elders and heads, their *šōpeṭîm* and *šōṭerîm*." And finally, Prov 6:7 speaks allegorically of the energetic ant, who does not have "any officer (*qaṣîn*) or *šōṭēr* or ruler (*mōšēl*)." But besides this verse in Proverbs, *šōṭerîm* are not mentioned in the Bible beyond Joshua, as if the position itself existed only in the days of the Exodus, the wilderness wanderings, and the conquest. Once Israel had settled in the land, they no longer needed *šōṭerîm*. They are never mentioned in the "later" stories of Judges, Samuel or Kings – until they are "revived" by the Chronicler.

Within Chronicles, *šōṭerîm* appear six times, three of which we have already mentioned. In 1 Chr 23:4, six thousand "*šōṭerîm* and *šōpeṭîm*" are appointed by

---

11 See also Mark Leuchter's essay (2014) on this subject, http://thetorah.com/judges-who-are-magistrates, and more recently Elitzur 2018a, 135–137.
12 To quote Tigay (1996, 345 n. 59): "Since offices often evolve into something considerably different form the functions from which they derived their names, etymology is a poor guide to their functions. 'Secretary' originally meant 'one entrusted with secrets,' 'clerk' meant 'clergyman,' and 'constable' meant 'count of the stable.'"

David from among the Levites. In 1 Chr 26:29, Chenaniah and his sons, of the Izharite Levites, were appointed "for outside duties for Israel" (i.e. outside the Temple), "as šōṭ^{e}rîm and šōp^{e}ṭîm." In both of these cases, the šōṭ^{e}rîm are Levites, and they are somehow connected to the šōp^{e}ṭîm.

In 1 Chr 27:1, the šōṭ^{e}rîm are listed in a non-Levitical context, one that seems more military or administrative: "This is the list of the people of Israel, the heads of families, the commanders of the thousands and the hundreds, and their šōṭ^{e}rîm who served the king in all matters concerning the divisions that came and went, month after month." This is very similar to Deut 1:15: "So I took the leaders of your tribes, wise and reputable men, and installed them as leaders over you, commanders of thousands, commanders of hundreds, commanders of fifties, commanders of tens, and šōṭ^{e}rîm for your tribes" – only there they are responsible to Moses rather than to David. Also, the next verse in Deuteronomy is about šōp^{e}ṭîm, who are not mentioned in this context in Chronicles.

A summary of the functions of Jehoshaphat's Jerusalem court, mentioned above, appears in 2 Chr 19:11: "And behold, Amariah the chief priest is over you in all matters of the Lord; and Zebadiah the son of Ishmael, the governor of the house of Judah, in all the king's matters; and the šōṭ^{e}rîm-Levites (ושטרים הלוים) are before you." So here, the šōṭ^{e}rîm, who are Levites, have some sort of function within that court, which is not staffed with "professional šōp^{e}ṭîm."

In 2 Chr 26:11 the šōṭ^{e}rîm again seem to have a military-administrative function: "Uzziah had an army [...] according to the muster made by Jeiel the scribe (sōpēr) and Maaseiah the šōṭēr, under the direction of Hananiah, of the king's officers." And finally, in a chronistic addition to the story of Josiah's renovation of the temple in 2 Kgs 22, 2 Chr 34:13 tells us that other Levites were "over the burden bearers and directing all who did work in every kind of service; and some of the Levites were scribes, and šōṭ^{e}rîm, and gatekeepers." Based on the mention of both scribes and šōṭ^{e}rîm in 2 Chr 34:13, de Vaux (1961, 155) concluded that the šōṭ^{e}rîm "were not mere scribes [...]. They seem to have been clerks of the court, and more generally, clerks attached to the judges [...]. 'Clerk' would also be a good translation of the other uses of the word, which denotes the officials in charge of forced labour (Ex 5:6 f.; perhaps 2 Ch 34:13), and also administrative officers of the army (Dt 20:5 f.)."

Thus, of the six times šōṭ^{e}rîm appear in Chronicles, in four they are specifically said to have been Levites. In three of these, they are connected to the judiciary. In the other three, they seem to have administrative functions in the king's court or military. And in none of these did the Chronicler get his specific information from earlier biblical books, since, as we saw, šōṭ^{e}rîm are totally absent from the earlier accounts of the monarchy. Analyses of their functions such as those of de Vaux, Weinfeld, and Fox, which combine the information gleaned from both Chronicles and Exodus–Joshua, tend to ignore both the chronological gap between the narrative settings and the chronological gap between the presumed dates of composition of the different books. A more diachronic approach was taken by Tigay (1996, 345 n. 61): "Since none of the earlier works dealing with that period uses the term, however, the use in Chronicles may be the revival of an old, pre-monarchic term, based on an interpretation of the usage in Deuteronomy, and not a reflex of the original meaning." I tend to agree, but would add that the Chronicler was probably influenced by the use of the term in Numbers and in Joshua as well.

3 Elders ($z^eqenîm$)

$Z^eqenîm$, "elders," in the plural, including plural constructs, appear well over 130 times in the Bible, in many different contexts, and much has been written about the status of the "elders" in biblical society, law, ideology, and wisdom literature (for example, see Reviv 1989; Fox 2000, 63–72). In general, we find elders in the community of Israel, Moses' seventy elders in the wilderness, village or town elders, who at least in Deuteronomy have local-judicial authority as well (de Vaux 1961, 138; Reviv 1989, 57–75; contra Tigay 2011),[13] elders as advisors to kings, and elders as epitomizing wisdom and experience (Walzer 2008). Elders appear in similar roles throughout the ancient Near East (see, e.g., Malamat 1963; Fox 2000, 63–72; Wells 2010). They appear in almost every book of the Bible, in all types of biblical literature, although Reviv (1989, 7) emphasizes that they are much more common in the historiographical books than in the Prophets or the Writings. Since the term $z^eqenîm$ is what Fox (2000, 63) calls "multivocal," it is not always clear from the context when $z^eqenîm$ are simply "old people" and when they are "elders." For example, in Lam 5:12 ("Princes are hung up by their hands; no respect is shown to $z^eqenîm$"), both NRSV and NJPS translate $z^eqenîm$ as "elders," but in v. 14 of the same chapter ("$z^eqenîm$ have left the city gate, young men their music"), both translate the same word as "old men."

The first $z^eqenîm$ that we meet in Chronicles are in 1 Chr 11:3, when "all the elders of Israel" come to Hebron in order to make David king over Israel. This pericope is taken directly from 2 Sam 5, and while the differences between the

---

[13] Tigay has argued that the elders who deal with cases such as those of rebellious sons (Deut 21:19) or brides accused of not being virgins (22:15–19) are not required to "judge," but rather to serve as "public witnesses" in order to ensure that the procedures are carried out properly.

two versions are interesting, the use of $z^eqenîm$ here is unchanged from that in Samuel and thus does not reflect any special use by the Chronicler.[14]

The next chapter in Samuel, 2 Sam 6, tells of David's bringing the ark from Kiriath-jearim to Jerusalem. In Chronicles, this story is expanded into three chapters, 1 Chr 13 and 15–16. Most of the expansion, especially in ch. 15, describes the role of the priests and the Levites in the transportation of the ark, but when the actual deed is done, v. 25 reads, "So David and the elders of Israel (זקני ישראל), and the commanders of the thousands, went to bring up the ark of the covenant of the Lord from the house of Obed-edom with rejoicing." This particular verse is an expansion of v. 12b in the Samuel version, which reads: "So David went and brought up the ark of God from the house of Obed-edom to the City of David with rejoicing." And while we can assume that the author of Samuel did not intend us to understand that David really went to Kiriath-jearim on his own, he does not mention any priests, Levites, commanders of thousands, or, of course, elders of Israel as going with him. The addition of priests and especially Levites to the story is typical of the Chronicler, and has been dealt with many times (see, e.g., Hanson 1992; Levin 2019). Many commentators see the addition of "the elders of Israel and the commanders of the thousands" as the Chronicler's way to emphasize that the bringing up of the ark was a collective national effort, rather than a personal whim of David's. Knoppers (2004, 625) suggests that "the commanders of the thousands" refers to the same "commanders of the thousands and of the hundreds" with whom David took council before his first attempt to bring up the ark in 1 Chr 13:1. The reference to the elders, according to Knoppers, "recalls the involvement of 'all the elders of Israel' in David's anointing" in 1 Chr 11:3. Klein (2006, 355) actually refers to Solomon's bringing the ark up from the City of David in 2 Chr 5:2, 4, in which "the elders of Israel" are also mentioned. Both Knoppers and Klein assume that the addition of "the elders of Israel" here is intended to bring this story in line with another pericope, one in which "the elders of Israel" in Chronicles is based on Samuel–Kings, and is not original to Chronicles. In fact, Klein points out that "the elders of Israel" are "relatively rare in the Chronicler," citing 1 Chr 11:3; 21:16; and 2 Chr 5:2, 4 as the "only" examples, presumably in addition to 1 Chr 15:25. However, 1 Chr 21:16 is different from the other examples that he cites.

First Chronicles 21 is of course the dramatic story of Joab's census and its aftermath. The Chronicles version is based on 2 Sam 24, with many significant differences, upon which we will not expound here (see, e.g., Rofé 2014). But

---

14 On the role of the $z^eqenîm$ in this story, albeit with no special reflection on Chronicles, see Reviv 1989, 83–84.

where 2 Sam 24:17 says, "When David saw the angel who was destroying the people, he said to the Lord, I alone have sinned, and I alone have done wickedly; but these sheep, what have they done? Let your hand, I pray, be against me and against my father's house," 1 Chr 21:16–17 have:

> David looked up and saw the angel of the Lord standing between earth and heaven, and in his hand a drawn sword stretched out over Jerusalem. Then David and the elders, clothed in sackcloth, fell on their faces. And David said to God, Was it not I who gave the command to count the people? It is I who have sinned and done very wickedly. But these sheep, what have they done? Let your hand, I pray, O Lord my God, be against me and against my father's house; but do not let your people be plagued!

So, besides everything else, we suddenly learn that David, who up until that point seemed to be alone with Gad and with the destroying angel, was also accompanied by "the elders, clothed in sackcloth." Now it is true that v. 16, much of which is missing in the MT of Samuel, does seem to be in the Qumran version of Samuel, but we should note that the reference to the elders is only reconstructed there (see Auld 2010; Himbaza 2010). As argued by Dirksen (2005, 260–261), since the MT of 2 Sam 24:17 does not seem to have been corrupted in any way, what the Qumran version shows, is that there were two versions of the Samuel text, and that the Chronicler's *Vorlage* differed from the MT text of Samuel. Thus, the elders here are not original to Chronicles either. In any case, there is no explanation of just where these elders, sackcloth and all, came from in the first place and what their function is within the text.[15]

The next time that "elders" appear in Chronicles is in the story of Solomon's transferring the ark from the City of David to the newly-built temple in 2 Chr 5. There, "the elders of Israel" are mentioned twice, in vv. 2 and 4, and in both cases the text seems to have been taken almost verbatim from 1 Kgs 8. The same is true for 2 Chr 10, in which "the elders" – this time Solomon's counselors to whom Rehoboam did not listen – appear in vv. 6, 8 and 13, taken from 1 Kgs 12.[16] And the final appearance of $z^e qen\hat{\imath}m$ in Chronicles is in 2 Chr 34:29, in which Josiah gathers "all of the elders of Judah and Jerusalem," taken word-for-word from 2 Kgs 24:1.

---

15 This despite the very compelling argument made by Amit (2011, 138) that the elders in sackcloth were meant to recall the behavior of Hezekiah and his officials during the siege of Jerusalem by Sennacherib (2 Kgs 19:1–2), which, like David's act here, resulted in the saving of Jerusalem. There, among the supplicants were *ziqnê hakkōhanîm*, which NRSV and NJPS translate as "the senior priests."

16 See Reviv 1989, 99–101. Fox (2000, 64–66) discusses the question of whether these and other $z^e qen\hat{\imath}m$ who appear as a group of advisors to kings constitute a permanent gathering of tribal elders or a group of "senior courtiers" and concludes in favor of the latter.

So, of the six contexts in which the $z^eqenîm$ appear in Chronicles, four are taken directly from the text of Samuel–Kings, 1 Chr 21:16 seems to be based on an alternative version of Samuel, while their mention in 1 Chr 15:25 – which is not taken directly from the Samuel "source" – can easily be understood as an attempt to tie in this story with similar stories in which the $z^eqenîm$ are taken from Samuel–Kings. We have absolutely no independent treatment of "elders" that could reveal the Chronicler's own view of them.

4 Šōp^{e}ṭîm, šōṭ^{e}rîm, and z^{e}qenîm in Postexilic Biblical Literature

Was the Chronicler's view of $šōp^eṭîm$, $šōṭ^erîm$ and $z^eqenîm$ influenced in any way by the reality of his own day, in Persian period Yehud? Our sources are limited, but we can say the following:

1. $Šōṭ^erîm$ do not appear in any literature of the period, except perhaps in the reference to the ant in Proverbs.[17]
2. $Šōp^eṭîm$ and $z^eqenîm$ actually do appear in Ezra, in the postexilic prophets,[18] and in the wisdom literature in many different contexts and with

---

[17] There is a wide range of opinions as to the composition-history of Proverbs and the date of its various component parts. See, for example, Waltke 2004, 31–37, who sees no reason to question the Solomonic origin of the earliest parts of the book, and Loader 2014, 9, who considers chapters 1–9 to be the latest part of the book dating to "the end of the Persian and beginning of the Hellenistic period." If so, the use of $šōṭēr$ in Prov 6:7 is probably an anachronism or what Joosten would call a "pseudo-classicism" (Joosten 2016b, although he does not mention this particular case).

[18] The issue of the dating of the various biblical corpora is one that is highly contested in contemporary scholarship, with linguistics being one of the methodologies that are used. In general, we accept the "classical" diachronic distinction between "Classical (or Standard) Biblical Hebrew" as relating to the preexilic period, and "Late Biblical Hebrew" as reflecting the postexilic period, obviously with a transitional period in between. From this point of view, the Pentateuchal sources, the Deuteronomistic History and the "preexilic" prophets are written in SBH, while Chronicles and Ezra-Nehemiah are written in LBH, with Haggai, Zech 1–8, and Malachi probably representing the transitional phase (for which see Hendel and Joosten 2018, 73–74). We do, however, recognize that there are also "grey areas" in which the date of texts is impossible to ascertain, and there is always, of course, the possibility of later redactional work influencing the final form of a text. For a recent overview of some of the issues, see Gesundheit 2016. See also Joosten 2016a; Elitzur 2018a, 2018b; and most recently Hendel and Joosten 2018. For the purposes of this paper, we will consider Chronicles, Ezra-Nehemiah, Haggai, Zech 1–8, and Malachi as representing the "postexilic period" from a linguistic point of view.

various meanings, but it is difficult to see any specific connections between these and the way these posts are used in Chronicles. The closest we can get is in Ezra 10:14, זקני־עיר ועיר ושפטיה, "the elders of each town and its judges," but we should remember that Chronicles never mentions "town elders" and also never mentions šōpᵉṭîm and zᵉqenîm together, so we should be careful before drawing any conclusions.

3. Besides šōpᵉṭîm and zᵉqenîm, Ezra-Nehemiah also mentions other forms of local political leadership: the peḥâh ("governor"), ḥorîm and sᵉganîm (often translated "nobles and prefects"), and śar pelek (either district governor or corvée chief).[19] None of these appear in Chronicles.

4. A similar pattern can be seen in Haggai, Zechariah, and Malachi, widely seen as reflecting the same period: Haggai mentions the peḥâh of Judah four times, but never mentions šōpᵉṭîm or zᵉqenîm. Zechariah 8:4 mentions zᵉqenîm and zᵉqenôt as "old men and old women," not as "elders," and when Zech 7:9 and 8:16 enjoin to "judge true judgments" and to "judge judgments of peace in your gates," the words are aimed at "Judah" in general, with no mention of "judges."[20] Malachi 1:8 mentions the peḥâh, and 2:17 asks "where is the God of justice?" but no šōpᵉṭîm, šōṭᵉrîm, or zᵉqenîm are mentioned.

5 Conclusions

In other words, there seems to be no relationship at all between the Chronicler's use of šōpᵉṭîm, šōṭᵉrîm, and zᵉqenîm and the other literature of the postexilic period. Šōṭᵉrîm are never mentioned in postexilic literature (except the ant!), and while šōpᵉṭîm and zᵉqenîm are mentioned, there seems to be no relationship between their tasks in that literature and the way in which they appear in Chronicles. And since the other terms of "civil" leadership that do appear in postexilic literature, such as peḥâh, ḥorîm, sᵉganîm, and śar pelek, never appear in Chronicles, it seems safe to say that the Chronicler's picture of the "civil" leadership of preexilic Israel is not based on what he knew in his own day.

So where did the Chronicler get his conception of the šōpᵉṭîm, šōṭᵉrîm, and zᵉqenîm in preexilic Israel? In all three cases, the Chronicler's use of these terms

---

[19] For a study of these terms of local political leadership in the Nehemiah Memoir, see Fitzpatrick-McKinley 2016. For the understanding of śar pelek as "corvée chief," see Demsky 1983.
[20] Since all of these references are in Zech 1–8, the question of the date of Zech 9–14 and their relationship to chapters 1–8 is irrelevant for our discussion.

seems to rely heavily on his sources. In some cases, this reliance is direct: The Chronicler simply retains the terms as he found them in his earlier source. In other cases, however, especially in his use of šōp^{e}ṭîm and šōṭ^{e}rîm, the Chronicler seems to have taken his understanding of their functions from the various parts of the Pentateuch and the Deuteronomistic History, and written them into his own narratives. Examples of this can be found in the lists of David's officials or in the story of Jehoshaphat's judiciary, the basic historicity of which is beyond the scope of this paper. In any case, the Chronicler does not seem to have any special vision of any of these three terms.

What can this teach us about the Chronicler's use of sources in general? This, of course, is an issue which is way beyond our discussion here. However, I would like to emphasize two of the main points on which there is broad agreement:

1. The Chronicler's account of the time of the monarchy, from Saul to the destruction of Jerusalem, is based on that of the Deuteronomistic History (see Glatt-Gilad 2011, 68).
2. In many (but not all) of the places in which Chronicles adds material to the account that he derived from the DH, this material is informed by references to "the Torah of Moses." One can argue about the extent to which this "Torah of Moses" corresponds to what we know as the Pentateuch, but he is undoubtedly familiar with much of the material that is conventionally attributed to the all of the assumed Pentateuchal sources, including JE, P, H, and D (see, e.g., Shaver 1989, 127–128). As stated by Glatt-Gilad (2011, 68), "The Chronicler not only refers to Moses' Torah as a source of authority but also looks to it as a recent model to emulate in his own quest for achieving authoritative status."

In our attempt to understand the Chronicler's picture of the šōp^{e}ṭîm, šōṭ^{e}rîm, and z^{e}qenîm as leaders in Israel's preexilic past, we have seen that the Chronicler does not seem to have his own preconceptions of these people and their roles. He is also not influenced by the roles played (or not played) by such people in the present. Instead, he uses the "raw material" found in his various sources in order to create what to him is a more complete picture of Israel's past.[21]

Bibliography

Amit, Yairah. 2011. "Arunah's Threshing Floor: A Lesson in Shaping Historical Memory." In *What Was Authoritative for Chronicles?*, edited by Ehud Ben Zvi and Diana V. Edelman, 133–144. Winona Lake: Eisenbrauns.

---

[21] For more on the way in which the Chronicler re-wrote the history of Israel, see Levin 2020.

Ashley, Timothy R. 1993. *The Book of Numbers*. NICOT. Grand Rapids: Eerdmans.

Auld, Graeme. 2010. "Imag[in]ing Editions of Samuel: The Chronicler's Contribution." In *Archaeology of the Books of Samuel: The Entangling of the Textual and Literary History*, edited by Phillipe Hugo and Adrian Schenker, 119–131. VTSup 132. Leiden and Boston: Brill.

Avishur, Yitzhak. 1999. "A Common Formula for Describing a Judge Fulfilling his Duty: Daniel the Canaanite and Deborah the Israelite." In *Studies in Biblical Narrative: Style, Structure, and the Ancient Near Eastern Literary Background*, edited by Yitzhak Avishur, 239–249. Tel Aviv-Yafo: Archaeological Center Publication.

Baden, Joel S. 2011. "The Deuteronomic Evidence for the Documentary Theory." In *The Pentateuch: International Perspectives on Current Research*, edited by Thomas B. Dozeman, Konrad Schmid, and Baruch J. Schwartz, 327–345. FAT 78. Tübingen: Mohr Siebeck.

Ben Zvi, Ehud. 2016. "Memory and Political Thought in the Late Persian/Early Hellenistic Yehud/Judah: Some Observations." In *Leadership, Social Memory, and Judean Discourse in the 5th–2nd Centuries BCE*, edited by Diana V. Edelman and Ehud Ben Zvi, 9–26. Sheffield: Equinox.

Bos, James M. 2016. "Memories of Judah's Past Leaders Utilized as Propaganda in Yehud." In *Leadership, Social Memory, and Judean Discourse in the 5th–2nd Centuries BCE*, edited by Diana V. Edelman and Ehud Ben Zvi, 27–40. Sheffield: Equinox.

Brettler, Marc Zvi. 1989. "The Book of Judges: Literature as Politics." *JBL* 108:395–418.

Budd, Philip J. 1984. *Numbers*. WBC. Waco: Word Books.

Caquot, André, and Philippe de Robert. 1994. *Les livres de Samuel*. Geneva: Labor et Fides.

Demsky, Aaron. 1983. "'Pelekh' in Nehemiah 3." *IEJ* 33:242–244.

Dirksen, Peter B. 2005. *1 Chronicles*. HCOT. Leuven: Peeters.

Easterly, Ellis. 1997. "A Case of Mistaken Identity: The Judges in Judges Don't Judge." *BiRe* 13:41–43, 47.

Elitzur, Yoel. 2018a. "The Interface Between Language and Realia in the Preexilic Books of the Bible." *HebStud* 59:129–147.

Elitzur, Yoel. 2018b. "Diachrony in Standard Biblical Hebrew: The Pentateuch vis-à-vis the Prophets/Writings." *JNSL* 44:81–101.

Fitzpatrick-McKinley, Anne. 2016. "Models of Local Political Leadership in the Nehemiah Memoir." In *Leadership, Social Memory, and Judean Discourse in the 5th–2nd Centuries BCE*, edited by Diana V. Edelman and Ehud Ben Zvi, 67–75. Sheffield: Equinox.

Fox, Nili Sacher. 2000. *In the Service of the King: Officialdom in Ancient Israel and Judah*. Cincinnati: Hebrew Union College Press.

Gesundheit, Shimon. 2016. "Introduction: The Strengths and Weaknesses of Linguistic Dating." In *The Formation of the Pentateuch: Bridging the Academic Cultures of Europe, Israel, and North America*, edited by Jan C. Gertz, Bernard M. Levinson, Dalit Rom-Shiloni, and Konrad Schmid, 295–302. FAT 111. Tübingen: Mohr Siebeck.

Glatt-Gilad, David. 2011. "Chronicles as Consensus Literature." In *What Was Authoritative for Chronicles?*, edited by Ehud Ben Zvi and Diana V. Edelman, 133–144. Winona Lake: Eisenbrauns.

Hanson, Paul D. 1992. "1 Chronicles 15–16 and the Chronicler's Views on the Levites." In *"Shaarei Talmon": Studies in the Bible, Qumran, and the Ancient Near East Presented to Shemaryahu Talmon*, edited by Michael Fishbane and Emanuel Tov, 69–77. Winona Lake: Eisenbrauns.

Hendel, Ronald, and Jan Joosten. 2018. *How Old Is the Hebrew Bible? A Linguistic, Textual, and Historical Study*. New Haven and London: Yale University Press.

Himbaza, Innocent. 2010. "4QSam^a (2 Sam 24:16–22): Its Reading, Where It Stands in the History of the Text and Its Use in Bible Translations." In *Archaeology of the Books of Samuel: The Entangling of the Textual and Literary History*, edited by Phillipe Hugo and Adrian Schenker, 39–52. VTSup 132. Leiden and Boston: Brill.

Japhet, Sara. 1997. *The Ideology of the Book of Chronicles and Its Place in Biblical Thought*, translated by Anna Barber. BEAT 9. Frankfurt am Main: Peter Lang.

Jeon, Jaeyoung. 2017. "The Visit of Jethro (Exodus 18): Its Composition and Levitical Reworking." *JBL* 136:289–306.

Joosten, Jan. 2016a. "Diachronic Linguistics and the Date of the Pentateuch." In *The Formation of the Pentateuch: Bridging the Academic Cultures of Europe, Israel, and North America*, edited by Jan C. Gertz, Bernard M. Levinson, Dalit Rom-Shiloni, and Konrad Schmid, 327–344. FAT 11. Tübingen: Mohr Siebeck.

Joosten, Jan. 2016b. "Pseudo-Classicisms in Late Biblical Hebrew." *ZAW* 128:16–29.

Kislev, Itamar. 2011. "P, Source or Redaction: The Evidence of Numbers 25." In *The Pentateuch: International Perspectives on Current Research*, edited by Thomas B. Dozeman, Konrad Schmid, and Baruch J. Schwartz, 387–399. FAT 78. Tübingen: Mohr Siebeck.

Klein, Ralph W. 2006. *1 Chronicles: A Commentary*. Hermeneia. Minneapolis: Fortress Press.

Knoppers, Gary N. 2003. *I Chronicles 1–9: A New Translation with Introduction and Commentary*. AB 12. New York: Doubleday.

Knoppers, Gary N. 2004. *I Chronicles 10–29: A New Translation with Introduction and Commentary*. AB 12A. New York: Doubleday.

Knoppers, Gary N. 2010. "Democratizing Revelation? Prophets, Seers and Visionaries in Chronicles." In *Prophecy and Prophets in Ancient Israel: Proceedings of the Oxford Old Testament Seminar*, edited by John Day, 391–409. New York and London: Bloomsbury T&T Clark.

Leuchter, Mark. 2014. "Judges Who Are Magistrates: Who Were the Shoftim?" Essay on *TABS* website, http://thetorah.com/judges-who-are-magistrates (accessed 31. 10. 2018).

Levin, Yigal. 2017. *The Chronicles of the Kings of Judah: 2 Chronicles 10–36: A New Translation and Commentary*. London: Bloomsbury T&T Clark.

Levin, Yigal. 2019. "The Role of the Levites in Chronicles: Past, Present, or Utopia?" In *Ben Porat Yosef: Studies in the Bible and its World – Essays in Honor of Joseph Fleishman*, edited by Michael Avioz, Omer Minka, and Yael Shemesh, 133–146. Münster: Ugarit-Verlag.

Levin, Yigal. 2020. "The Chronicler's Rewriting of the History of Israel: Why and How?" In *Writing and Rewriting History in Ancient Israel and Near Eastern Cultures*, edited by Isaac Kalimi, 173–188. Wiesbaden: Harrassowitz.

Levine, Baruch A. 1993. *Numbers 1–20: A New Translation with Introduction and Commentary*. AB 4. New York: Doubleday.

Levine, Baruch A. 2000. *Numbers 21–36: A New Translation with Introduction and Commentary*. AB 4A. New York: Doubleday.

Levine, Baruch A. 2009. "Religion in the Heroic Spirit: Themes in the Book of Judges." In *Thus Says the Lord: Essays on the Former and Latter Prophets in Honor of Robert R. Wilson*, edited by John J. Ahn and Stephen L. Cook, 27–42. New York and London: Bloomsbury T&T Clark.

Loader, James A. 2014. *Proverbs 1–9*. HCOT. Leuven: Peeters.

Malamat, Abraham. 1963. "Kingship and Council in Israel and Sumer: A Parallel." *JNES* 22:247–253.

Mattison, Kevin. 2018. "Contrasting Conceptions of Asylum in Deuteronomy 19 and Numbers 35." *VT* 68:232–251.

McCarter, P. Kyle Jr. 1984. *II Samuel: A New Translation with Introduction, Notes and Commentary.* AB 9. New York: Doubleday.

Meyer, Esias E. 2017. "When Synchrony Overtakes Diachrony: Perspectives on the Relationship Between the Deuteronomic Code and the Holiness Code." *OTE* 30:749–769.

Niditch, Susan. 2009. "Judges, Kingship, and Political Ethics: A Challenge to the Conventional Wisdom." In *Thus Says the Lord: Essays on the Former and Latter Prophets in Honor of Robert R. Wilson*, edited by John J. Ahn and Stephen L. Cook, 59–70. New York and London: Bloomsbury T&T Clark.

Nihan, Christophe. 2013. "1 Samuel 8 and 12 and the Deuteronomistic Edition of Samuel." In *Is Samuel Among the Deuteronomists? Current Views on the Place of Samuel in a Deuteronomistic History*, edited by Cynthia Edenburg and Juha Pakkala, 225–273. Ancient Israel and its Literature 16. Atlanta: SBL Press.

Person, Raymond F. Jr. 2013. "Prophets in the Deuteronomistic Literature and the Book of Chronicles: A Reassessment." In *Israelite Prophecy and the Deuteronomistic History: Portrait, Reality, and the Formation of a History*, edited by Mignon R. Jacobs and Raymond F. Person Jr. 187–199. Atlanta: SBL Press.

Pyschny, Katharina, and Sarah Schulz, eds. 2018. *Debating Authority: Concepts of Leadership in the Pentateuch and the Former Prophets.* BZAW 507. Berlin and Boston: de Gruyter.

Reviv, Hanoch. 1989. *The Elders in Ancient Israel: A Study of a Biblical Institution*, translated by Lucy Plitmann. Jerusalem: Magnes.

Rofé, Alexander. 2001. "The Organization of the Judiciary in Deuteronomy (Deut. 16.18–20; 17.8–13; 19.15; 21.22–23; 24.16; 25.1–3)." In *The World of the Aramaeans*. Vol. 1, edited by P. M. Michèle Daviau, John W. Wevers, and Michael Weigl, 92–112. JSOTSup 324. Sheffield: Sheffield Academic Press.

Rofé, Alexander. 2014. "Writing, Interpolating and Editing: 2 Samuel 24 and 1 Chronicles 21 as a Case Study." *Hebrew Bible and Ancient Israel* 3:317–326.

Schwartz, Baruch J. 2009. "The Visit of Jethro – A Case of Chronological Displacement? The Source-Critical Solution." In *Mishneh Todah: Studies in Deuteronomy and Its Cultural Environment in Honor of Jeffrey H. Tigay*, edited by Nili Sacher Fox, David A. Glatt-Gilad, and Michael J. Williams, 29–48. Winona Lake: Eisenbrauns.

Schweitzer, Steven J., and Frauke Uhlenbruch, eds. 2016. *Worlds That Could Not Be: Utopia in Chronicles, Ezra, and Nehemiah.* London: Bloomsbury T&T Clark.

Shaver, Judson R. 1989. *Torah and the Chronicler's History Work.* Atlanta: Scholars Press.

Stewart, David Tabb. 2015. "Leviticus 19 as Mini-Torah." In *Current Issues in Priestly and Related Literature: The Legacy of Jacob Milgrom and Beyond*, edited by Roy E. Gane and Ada Taggar-Cohen, 299–323. Atlanta: SBL Press.

Tigay, Jeffrey H. 1996. *Deuteronomy.* JPSTC. Philadelphia and Jerusalem: Jewish Publication Society.

Tigay, Jeffrey H. 2011. "The Role of the Elders in the Laws of Deuteronomy." In *A Common Cultural Heritage: Studies on Mesopotamia and the Biblical World in Honor of Barry L. Eichler*, edited by Grant Frame, Erle Leichty, Karen Sonik, Jeffrey Tigay, and Steve Tinney, 89–96. Bethesda: CDL.

de Vaux, Roland. 1961. *Ancient Israel: Its Life and Institutions*, translated by John McHugh. New York: McGraw-Hill.

Waltke, Bruce K. 2004. *The Book of Proverbs Chapters 1–15*. NICOT. Grand Rapids and Cambridge: Eerdmans.

Walzer, Michael. 2008. "Biblical Politics: Where Were the Elders?" *Hebraic Political Studies* 3:225–238.

Weinfeld, Moshe. 1977. "Judge and Officer in Ancient Israel and in the Ancient Near East." *IOS* 7:65–88.

Wells, Bruce. 2010. "Competing or Complementary? Judges and Elders in Biblical and Neo-Babylonian Law." *ZABR* 16:77–104.

Isabel Cranz
Diseased Leadership

This study analyzes the social, historical, and literary contexts that shape the representation of royal illness in the Bible. If modern politics is any indication, the declining health of rulers can lead to political instability, regime change, and even wars.[1] Yet, rather than focusing only on the political ramifications of royal illness, scribes in antiquity used this motif also to reflect on the nature of kingship and its relation to gods, dynasties, and nations. Taking this observation as a starting point, the goal of this study is twofold. First, I will describe and analyze how royal illnesses are represented in the Deuteronomistic History and in the book of Chronicles.[2] Second, I will trace how scribes use depictions of royal illness to craft their views about history, dynastic and religious crises, and the concept of kingship. It is likely that these accounts used the bodily integrity of the king as a starting point for formulating ideas about the expectations concerning Judah's and Israel's leadership and how this leadership had shaped Judah's and Israel's past.[3] Consequently, analyzing royal illness in the Bible provides insight into the articulation of national identity and the memory of kingship in Judah and Israel.

---

[1] This is the case for both dictatorships and parliamentary systems, although the degree to which an ailing ruler can affect the course of politics differs depending on the different forms of leadership. For studies about ill rulers in modern times, see Post and Robins 1993; Owen 2008.
[2] The term "Deuteronomistic History" (*Deuteronomistisches Geschichtswerk*) was first coined by Noth (1943). Noth's understanding of the Deuteronomistic History was based on the assumption that all of Deuteronomy–2 Kings was the exilic creation of one author who sought to explain the destruction of Judah as punishment for cultic aberration. Today, some seven decades after Noth's first publication of *Überlieferungsgeschichtliche Studien*, the Deuteronomistic History is deemed the product of many different authors and redactions. It is also said to display a multifaceted range of theological concerns. Studies about the Deuteronomistic History no longer apply to all of Deuteronomy–2 Kings, but rather focus on distinct themes appearing in shorter sections of this work. Similarly, we are faced with different models pertaining to the date of composition as well as the sources available to the scribes involved in the composition of the Deuteronomistic History. For an overview of past and current trends in research, see Blanco Wißmann 2008, 1–14; Hutton 2009, 81–156. For the present study, the term Deuteronomistic History applies only to Samuel–Kings.
[3] For a full exploration of political thought as it is expressed within the Hebrew Bible, see Ben Zvi 2016.

Note: This essay is based on the monograph *Royal Illness and Kingship Ideology in the Hebrew Bible* (see Cranz 2020).

https://doi.org/10.1515/9783110650358-013

1 Methodology: Illness as Frame, Framing of Illness, and Illness as Social Diagnosis

A variety of different models can be applied to descriptions of illness as they appear in ancient sources.[4] I will draw from existing models used to approach ancient concepts of illness, including the field of disability studies and the history of medicine. For the purpose of this study, these models will be combined with the approach of "framing." In the medical humanities, the metaphor of "frame" was developed by Charles E. Rosenberg, who sought to articulate an alternative approach to social constructivism. Especially relevant are Rosenberg's concepts of "disease as frame" and "framing disease," which I will adapt and apply to the study of royal illness.

According to Rosenberg (1992, xviii), disease functions as a frame when it "serves as structuring factor in social situations, as a social actor and as mediator," particularly when it comes to societal response to disease and its diagnosis. A comparable trend can be observed in biblical historiography. In this case, royal illness is used to introduce prophetic oracles about individual dynasties, the state of the nation, cultic policies, and impending doom. Furthermore, royal illness can be used to structure a narrative by allowing for conclusions about characters that are not ill or introducing new actors onto the scene.[5] The use of illness as a frame is more prevalent in the Deuteronomistic History. Illness can, however, also be framed. The framing of disease is carried out in "attempts to find restored health and an explanation for [...] misfortune" (Rosenberg 1992, xvi). For Rosenberg (1992, xvi–xviii) the framing of disease consists of the physician's quest to find the cause of any given ailment. When applying this approach to the analysis of royal illness, the framing of disease constitutes the detailed description of the king's moral predisposition which has led him to suffer from an illness. This description, in turn, allows for insights into the po-

---

[4] Some scholars have applied a diagnostic model as, for example, Scurlock and Andersen 2005. Other scholars prefer approaching the concept of illness from the perspective of the history of medicine (see, e.g., Geller 2010). Particularly in biblical studies, we have seen different disability models applied also to the concept of illness where it crosses over into disability (Schipper 2006; Raphael 2008; Olyan 2008). On the blurry lines between illness and disability, see Wendell 2001.

[5] In a sense, my observation that an ill king functions as plot device comes close to David T. Mitchell's and Sharon L. Snyder's observation that literary narratives depend upon disability (Mitchell and Snyder 2000, 53). Nonetheless, in the case of royal illness, the king's body rarely stands at the center of the discourse. Rather, the plot is moved along by the fact that the king's ailment leads to the introduction of new characters that later prove essential.

tential drawbacks of kingship as well as the expectations and limits pertaining to the office of kingship and the persona of the king. The framing of disease is encountered more often in the chronistic history.

Beyond the different forms of representation, Rosenberg (1992, xxii) points out that disease can be used as "social diagnosis." That is, illness "frame[s] debates about society and social policy," which includes discussions about "the interrelationship of state policy, medical responsibility and individual culpability." When applying this approach to the Bible, we observe that illness is used to reflect on issues linked to cult, worship, prophecy, and their relation to kingship. Analyzing the way royal illness is integrated into the larger narrative frameworks of the various biblical corpora shows how this motif is used to reflect on Israel's and Judah's monarchic past. Taken together, then, this approach will afford us fresh insights into the multifaceted nature of royal illness, historiography, and the nature of kingship as it is presented in the Bible.

2 Royal Illness in the Deuteronomistic History

When royal illness appears in the Deuteronomistic History, it is mostly used as a frame to address issues related to kingship, individual dynasties, political crises, and cultic policies. The critique of kingship, for example, is an issue in the context of Saul's demise and the physical disintegration of David. For the most part, royal illness in the Deuteronomistic History is used as a frame for prophetic oracles. In the stories about Elijah and Elisha, the oracles speak to cultic policies and anticipate temporary crises. The oracles uttered for the illness of Jeroboam's son and Hezekiah evaluate individual dynasties, while the context surrounding the oracles foreshadows the destruction of Israel and Judah, respectively.

2.1 Royal Illness as a Critique of Kingship: The Disintegration of Saul and David

I begin with the disintegration of Saul and David, which highlights a certain degree of ambivalence toward the institution of kingship. The physical appearance of Israel's kings usually does not receive much attention in the Hebrew Bible. Nonetheless, at two key points in the book of Samuel, the biblical narrator provides detailed descriptions of Saul's and David's physical beauty. In 1 Sam 9:2b, when Saul is first introduced, he is described as young, handsome, and tall (Hertzberg 1964, 80). Later, we see how a similar emphasis is placed on David's beauty. In 1 Sam 16:12, 18, David is described as "ruddy" (אדמוני) with "beautiful eyes" (יפה עינים), "pleasant to look upon" (טוב ראי), and "a man of beauty" (איש תואר).[6] The notion that kings presented an ideal image of male beauty is widespread in the ancient Near East. What is new here is that both Saul's and David's body become subject to physical and mental disintegration. The juxtaposition between physical beauty and physical demise resonates with the frequently voiced suspicion about human kingship over against the kingship of Yahweh (Judg 8:22–23; 1 Sam 8:6–9; 12:12–16).[7]

As a case in point, despite his good looks, Saul succumbs to what can be considered a form of mental illness.[8] He is tormented by an evil spirit which originates from Yahweh (1 Sam 16:14; 18:10; 19:9).[9] It is clear that Saul's mental illness plays an important role in David's rise at the court. The evil spirit leads to the introduction of David as lyre player who would soothe the king during his attacks. In addition, Saul's mental instability disqualifies him as king and lets David appear capable where Saul is lacking (Klein 1983, 167; Olyan 2008, 73). One aspect that has received less attention is the fact that Saul's illness also portrays the inherent dangers of human kingship. Although Saul has been rejected by God and suffers from mental illness, the act of anointing has made him sacrosanct. The inviolability of Saul's body through his status as the "anointed of Yahweh" is emphasized on three separate occasions.[10] Twice David has the opportunity to kill Saul, but refrains from doing so because Saul is "anointed by Yahweh" (1 Sam 24:6, 10; 26:9). Finally, David executes the Amalekite who claims to have killed Saul because he has "slain Yahweh's anointed" (2 Sam 1:16).[11] What these accounts exemplify is that the king takes on a divine status which protects him, no matter how erratic and unqualified he may be. Thus, the juxtaposition between the mental illness of Saul and his sacrosanct

---

[6] That David is not as attractive as Saul is indicated by the rejection of Eliab (Nihan 2013, 251–252).

[7] In recent studies, scholars have been careful to point out that these passages do not denounce kingship in general, but rather criticize the Israelites for placing more trust in their prospective kings than in their deity (McKenzie 2000, 303; Nihan 2013, 242–248).

[8] For the problems associated with defining mental illness in the Bible, see Olyan 2008, 62–63.

[9] For the notion that the evil spirit of Yahweh replaces the spirit that had gripped Saul after his anointment, see McCarter 1999, 319; Tsumura 2007, 287.

[10] It is likely that this status is attained through the ritual process of anointing and coronation (Hamilton 2006, 144–147).

[11] Note that all three instances use the term שחט for the act of killing the anointed of Yahweh. According to McCarter (1980, 407), this verb carries the connotation of "spoliation," "ruination," or "corruption" and as such hint at the elevated status of Saul as Yahweh's anointed.

status as anointed of Yahweh illustrates the potential drawbacks of human leadership and also highlights the tension between divine and human kingship.

Whereas Saul's torment can be viewed as the externalization of divine rejection, we observe a similar physical and perhaps even mental deterioration for David, although he is not divinely rejected. The book of Kings begins with the observation that David had grown old and is suffering from chills (1 Kgs 1:1). Because of the declining health of their master, David's servants decide to find a young virgin who would serve the king by warming him (1 Kgs 1:2). After a nationwide search, the Shunammite Abishag is chosen as David's concubine, but, although she is very beautiful, the account makes it clear that the marriage between her and David is never consummated – the king is impotent (1 Kgs 1:3–4).[12] In its immediate context, David's decrepitude figures as part of Solomon's succession narrative by signaling that the king's death was imminent.[13] In a wider sense, David's decline can be understood as subtle critique of human kingship on two levels.[14] On one level, the chaos and infighting caused at the court by the king's imminent death suggests that the institution of kingship is always open to manipulation and abuse. On an additional level, David's decline can be viewed as an indirect expression of divine disfavor (or at least indifference) toward Israel's king. Contrary to Israel's other prominent leader, Moses, whose eyesight never grew dim and whose strength never abated (Deut 34:7), David retains his status as human and is thus not exempt from the effects of old age.

In sum, accounts about the health problems of Israel's first kings address potential pitfalls of human leadership. Kings can suffer from mental disturbances or may succumb to old age. These incidents have the potential to create social upheaval and suggest that the power of the king should not be limitless. The suffering of Saul and David also illustrates the tension between the divine kingship of God and the earthly kingship of humans. Although Saul is divinely rejected, he retains a quasi-divine status and cannot be assassinated without incurring divine wrath. Likewise, despite being divinely elected, David is not immune to physical and mental decline.

---

12 The servants advertise Abishag's service by stating that "she will lie in your lap" (ושכבה בחיקך). This phrasing suggests that Abishag was expected to become intimate with the king, since the same expression is used in contexts such as Gen 16:5 and 2 Sam 12:8, which clearly presuppose a sexual relationship.
13 By clarifying from the start that David was bedbound, impotent, and in need of constant care, the account vilifies Adonijah and allows Solomon's succession to appear as the result of an artfully executed court intrigue (Kaiser 2000, 106).
14 For similar observations, see Schipper 2007, 111–112.

2.2 Royal Illness in the Prophetic Cycles: Ahaziah and Ben Hadad

The next case of royal illness to be discussed stems from the stories about Elijah and Elisha.[15] It is likely that a large part of these prophetic stories developed independently of the Deuteronomistic History. Although the stories themselves do not necessarily count as deuteronomistic in the strict sense, they are still part of the Deuteronomistic History and therefore will be discussed under this rubric. In the context of the prophetic cycle, Elijah pronounces an oracle concerning the Israelite king Ahaziah who had injured himself during a fall in the palace (2 Kgs 1). Similarly, the Aramean king Ben Hadad consults with Elisha about the outcome of his illness (2 Kgs 8:7–15).[16] Both for Elijah's and Elisha's oracle, royal illness is used to anticipate national turmoil, which is associated with the worship of Baal.

As we learn in 2 Kgs 1, Ahaziah injured himself in a fall and sends messengers to a deity referred to as Baal-Zebub. While the messengers are still on their way, an angel instructs Elijah to intercept them and to communicate the following message: "Is there no god in Israel that you go to inquire of Baal-Zebub, the god of Ekron?! Therefore, thus speaks Yahweh: From the bed you have ascended you will not descend, for you will die!" (המבלי אין־אלהים בישראל אתם הלכים לדרש בבעל זבוב: ולכן כה־אמר יהוה המטה אשר־עלית שם לא־תרד ממנו כי מות תמות, 2 Kgs 1:3b–4). This statement develops into the central theme of the episode and is repeated two more times, once by Ahaziah's servants and a final time by Elijah which directly leads to Ahaziah's death. As it stands, the motif of the ailing monarch allows for the combination of two themes that run through the stories about Elijah and Elisha. These themes include the power of Yahweh over life and death (1 Kgs 17:17–24) and the responsiveness of Yahweh over against other deities (1 Kgs 18:18–46).[17] Against the backdrop of royal illness, the themes of Yahweh's power and responsiveness are combined and transferred to the court allowing for a direct condemnation of the king's cultic policies.

---

15 One of the first scholars to formulate this view is Dietrich (1972). For recent studies based on this approach, see Otto 2011; Lehnart 2003.
16 On the significance of consulting with a prophet in the case of illness, see Avalos 1995, 260–274.
17 Beck (1999, 150–153) argues that the links between 1 Kgs 17:17–24 and 2 Kgs 1:9–14, 15b–16 point to a postexilic supplementary layer which was aimed at emphasizing the importance of Elijah. Although a literary dependence between 1 Kgs 18:21–40 and 2 Kgs 1 cannot be detected, the thematic similarities between the two episodes suggest that they were collected and developed in the same circles (Lehnart 2003, 354–357).

The motif of the sick king reappears in 2 Kgs 8:7–15. This time, the spotlight is not on Elijah, but on his disciple Elisha. Similarly, the king who is in need of a prophetic consultation is neither Israelite nor Judean, but the Aramean king Ben Hadad. When the Aramean king falls ill, he sends his assistant Hazael to Elisha to request an oracle. In the first part of Elisha's answer, the prophet instructs Hazael to tell his master that he will recover (2 Kgs 8:10a). In the second part of his answer, Elisha declares that Ben Hadad will surely die (2 Kgs 8:10b). Following this statement, Elisha's face becomes expressionless and he stares at Hazael for a long time before bursting into tears (2 Kgs 8:11–12). Upon inquiry, Elisha explains that he is weeping because Yahweh has shown him that Hazael will be king of Aram. In this capacity, Hazael will burn down the fortresses of Israel, kill her men and children, and rip open pregnant women (2 Kgs 8:12–13). Elisha's prophecy of doom can be understood as an announcement of punishment against the Israelites, who prefer the worship of Baal over the veneration of Israel's national god Yahweh. This interpretation is not readily apparent from 2 Kgs 8:7–15 but becomes clear once we place this prophetic legend in the context of 1 Kgs 19:15–18 (Würthwein 1984, 321). In these verses, Elijah is commissioned to anoint Hazael, Jehu, and Elisha. We also learn that "the one who will escape the sword of Hazael will be killed by Jehu. The one who escapes the sword of Jehu will be killed by Elisha." According to 1 Kgs 19:18, only the 7000 individuals who have not worshipped Baal will be spared this bloody fate.[18] Reading one passage in light of the other, then, offers a theological interpretation of Elisha's activity concerning Hazael's accession and warfare against Israel, which can now be understood as a punishment for Baal worship. In effect, Ahaziah's illness leads to a prophetic oracle against the cultic conduct of Ahaziah's dynasty, while Ben Hadad's illness leads to an oracle against the Israelite people who are guilty of the same religious aberration. In both instances, it is noteworthy that royal illness is not the punishment for transgressions, but merely presents the opportunity for articulating a punishment.

---

18 To be sure, attempting to view 1 Kgs 19:15–18 as an explanation for the rise of Hazael in 2 Kgs 8:7–15 comes with its own set of problems, the most pressing being that Hazael is not anointed by Elisha, but merely encouraged by Elisha's oracle. Likewise, the prophet in charge is not Elijah, but his disciple Elisha. Nevertheless, it is possible that these verses create a link between the different prophetic story cycles by portraying Elisha as the successor of Elijah, carrying out the unfulfilled deeds of his predecessor. For this interpretation, see Seybold 1973, 14; Hentschel 1977, 56–60; Otto 2011, 190.

2.3 Royal Illness, Royal Dynasties, and the Destruction of Nations

Up to this point, we have seen how royal illness can be used to frame religious crises and crises of human kingship. However, as the oracles concerning the ailing health of Jeroboam's son Abijah (1 Kgs 14:1–18) and Hezekiah (2 Kgs 20) demonstrate, royal illness can also be used to evaluate dynasties and to comment on the fate of cities, nations, and people.[19]

When Jeroboam's son Abijah falls ill, Jeroboam's wife elicits two oracles from the prophet Ahijah. The first oracle reverses God's promise to provide Jeroboam with an enduring dynasty (1 Kgs 11:29–39). After all, Jeroboam did not succeed in keeping to "the statutes and commandments" dictated by Yahweh (1 Kgs 11:38), and consequently, the prophet now has "heavy" news. Surprisingly, this news is only indirectly related to the illness of Jeroboam's son. Instead, we learn that Jeroboam's dynasty will end and that his son's death is a sign announcing the impending disaster (vv. 6–14). The second oracle anticipates the destruction of the newly established kingdom of Israel and the exile of the Israelites (vv. 15–16). In all this, the premature death of Jeroboam's son is to be understood as a blessing, since the rest of Jeroboam's house will be massacred (v. 13). As foretold by the prophet, the son dies the moment the wife enters the city of Tirzah (v. 17).[20] The account ends with the note that Jeroboam's son is buried and lamented by all Israel (v. 18).

Isaiah's oracle for the ailing Hezekiah is somewhat more hopeful than Ahijah's oracle for Jeroboam's son. When Hezekiah falls ill, the prophet Isaiah first predicts his death, but Hezekiah turns his face to the wall to pray and weep (2 Kgs 20:2–3). Isaiah then returns to the king's bedside with the message that God will heal the king and save the city from the Assyrians because he has heard his prayer and seen his tears. In addition, Isaiah's oracle declares that Yahweh

---

19 Fretheim (1999, 205) observes the correlation between the king and his dynasty particularly in 1 Kgs 14:1–18. For scholars who detect a parallel between the survival of Hezekiah and the survival of his city and dynasty, see Hobbs 1985, 292; Long 1991, 238; Sweeney 2007, 420. Cohn (2000, 142) remains one of the few scholars who read the oracles concerning Abijah's and Hezekiah's illness in conjunction with one another.

20 It is unclear why Jeroboam's wife returns to Tirzah in 1 Kgs 14:17. Perhaps this is an indicator that Jeroboam had moved the capital there, as suggested by Cogan (2000, 401). Yet, as has been pointed out by Sweeney (2007, 186), Jeroboam's capitals were Shechem and Mahanaim (1 Kgs 12:25). Other scholars (Geoby 2016, 15) believe that the story of Jeroboam's diseased son was retrospectively associated with Tirzah, possibly because the account was composed during the reign of Baasha, who was the first king explicitly described as reigning from Tirzah (1 Kgs 15:21, 33).

is doing this "for [his] sake and for the sake of David [his] servant" (לְמַעֲנִי וּלְמַעַן דָּוִד עַבְדִּי).²¹ Two interrelated aspects of this passage are of note here, namely, the reference to David and the correlation between the deliverance of the king and deliverance of his city. First, in 2 Kgs 20:6, the king's recovery and the concomitant delivery of the city are justified with the Davidic promise of establishing a perpetual dynasty in Jerusalem (2 Sam 7). In this context, Hezekiah's recovery underscores the importance of prayer and demonstrates God's ongoing commitment to David (Long 1991, 240–241). Second, and relatedly, Yahweh's response indicates that Hezekiah's fate is somehow linked to the fate of Jerusalem and the Davidic dynasty. This correlation between the king and his nation is not unprecedented in the Deuteronomistic History or the ancient Near East for that matter.²² What appears unique is that Hezekiah's righteousness and impeccable behavior protect his city, and consequently his people and dynasty, when in most cases people and dynasties suffer annihilation on account of their flawed leadership. Despite all this praise, the illness of Hezekiah ends on a somber note, as his recovery has attracted the attention of the Babylonians (2 Kgs 20:12). Hezekiah readily shows all of his possessions to the envoys sent by the Babylonian king Merodach-Baladan. For doing so, Isaiah declares that the Babylonians would soon carry away everything they have seen, including Hezekiah's offspring (2 Kgs 20:16–18; Isa 39:5–7). Hence, the ailing health of Jeroboam's son and Hezekiah provides an opportunity to emphasize God's rejection of the north-

---

21 The declaration that Yahweh would save the king for his own glory and in commemoration of his servant David has often been considered to be a gloss from 2 Kgs 19:34, where this statement is associated with the salvation of Jerusalem (Montgomery and Gehman 1960, 507). However, some scholars believe that both 2 Kgs 20:6 and 1 Kgs 19:24 are later additions (Würthwein 1984, 428–429). Supposedly, this verse was meant to stress that the survival of Jerusalem was not the result of Hezekiah's politics, but rather the deed of Yahweh who protects his people for his own glory. In general, it is noteworthy that the notion that Yahweh protects Zion and the Davidic dynasty for his own sake is not limited to Hezekiah's reign. We find similar statements in 1 Kgs 11:12, 13, 36; 2 Kgs 8:19. This suggests that this verse is a deuteronomistic addition (McKenzie 1991, 105). Nonetheless, similar claims of God protecting his people for his own sake are found in later prophetic literature (Isa 43:25 and 48:9, Jer 14:7, 21) and in the Psalms (Pss 23:3; 25:11; 106:8). In addition, we find this attitude during the ten plagues as described in Exod 10:1 and 11:7.

22 Some scholars (Knoppers 1994, 579 n. 58) have argued that Ahab's misconduct results in a drought (1 Kgs 17:1–18:45). Likewise, David's misguided decision to carry out a census caused a plague among his people (2 Sam 24:10–17; cf. 1 Chr 21:1–17). A similar tendency can be observed in 2 Sam 21, where a famine of three years is explained by the guilt of the Saulides, which can only be avenged by executing the seven sons of Saul. This account displays several similarities to the Hittite King Murshili's prayer to the gods in the hope of ameliorating a plague which, as it turns out, was caused by the oath violation of a covenantal agreement set up by Šuppiluliuma (Malamat 1955, 1–12; Klinger 2012, 484–491).

ern dynasties, which stands in contrast to his support of the Davidic dynasty ruling in the south. Nevertheless, both for the north and the south, royal illness serves to prepare for the eventual destruction of the nation.

3 Royal Illness in the Book of Chronicles: The Critique of Individual Kings

So far we have seen how royal illness in Samuel–Kings is used to frame the dangers of human kingship, to assess the conduct of individual dynasties, to announce national crises on grounds of cultic aberration, and to articulate impending destruction. In all this, royal illness is generally not viewed as a punishment for sinful behavior. In fact, it can even be interpreted as a blessing, as was the case for Jeroboam's son. Matters are different in Chronicles. For the Chronicler, royal illness is framed by individual character flaws like arrogance, wickedness, or self-reliance, which lead kings to disrespect Yahweh, the cult, the people, and prophets.[23] Nonetheless, royal illness is also used as a frame, since descriptions of moral transgressions and their consequences contain subtle allusions to the destruction of Jerusalem and Judah.

3.1 The Wickedness of Jehoram of Judah

The first chronistic incident of royal illness to be discussed is the bowel disorder of Jehoram of Judah. This incident deals with the question of how the Davidic dynasty can persist, given that some of the Davidic kings are simply wicked. In the case of Jehoram, the key to survival lies in the covenant between Yahweh and David, which forms the foundation for the Davidic dynasty. As is reiterated in 2 Chr 21:7, God has made a covenant with David and therefore will not destroy

---

[23] Contrary to the Deuteronomistic History, the Chronicler sees no competition between divine and human kingship. This means that kingship is bestowed by Yahweh and the human king is viewed as executing the rule of God on earth. The tendency of depicting human kingship as the universal rule of Yahweh on earth finds particular expression in the book of Chronicles but also appears in other postexilic texts such as the book of Daniel and several Psalms (see Pss 2; 93; 95–98 and Dan 4). In its core, the idea of Yahweh's universal kingship is also present in Jer 27, where we learn that God has appointed Nebuchadnezzar as king over humans and animals. This stands in contrast to texts such as Isa 10:15–19, where God raises foreign rulers to punish the kings of Judah (Koch 1986, 39; further Newsom 2014, 142).

his dynasty.[24] Yet, there will be a price to pay, the nature of which is neatly laid out in a letter sent by the prophet Elijah. This letter summarizes Jehoram's various misdeeds, including his fratricide, his intermarriage, and his cultic aberration. Elijah's letter further announces that Jehoram will be punished through "a great plague" (מגפה גדולה) which will strike his people and his family and that he himself would suffer from a disease that would cause "his bowels to come out" (vv. 14–15).[25] Interestingly, Jehoram's illness is described as "incurable" (לאין מרפא), which calls attention to Judah's eventual annihilation on account of Yahweh's implacable wrath which is also referred to as incurable (לאין מרפא) in 2 Chr 36:16b. In the continuation of Jehoram's reign, Elijah's dire predictions come true. Jehoram's family falls victim to foreign invasion, and the king himself is stricken by an embarrassing illness which leads to a painful and horrible death. Nobody is saddened by this event: Jehoram is not honored by a funerary pyre nor is he buried in the tombs of the kings (2 Chr 21:19–20).[26] In short, although the Davidic dynasty ultimately continues, it appears that the body of Jehoram needs to be tormented, dismembered, and wiped out. Only by carrying out the appropriate punishment can the covenant between Yahweh and the Davidic dynasty continue.

3.2 The Self-Reliance of Asa

Whereas Jehoram is punished for generalized wickedness, Asa's illness is associated with the specific trait of self-reliance which has led him to disrespect

---

24 This reference to the promise to David is taken from the deuteronomistic *Vorlage* of Jehoram's reign in 2 Kgs 8:15. Nevertheless, the Chronicler introduces two modifications: First, it is now stated that Yahweh refrains from destroying the "house of David," not "Judah." Second, the house of David is spared "on account of the covenant that he had made with David," which stands in contrast to the deuteronomistic version where we are informed that Yahweh spares Judah "for the sake of David his servant."
25 Within Chronicles מגפה is usually used for physical ailments, as is also implied in David's census in 1 Chr 21:17, 22 and in the punishment of Jehoram himself in 2 Chr 21:18 (Jarick 2007, 135; Boda 2010, 337). The notion that a ruler's transgression could affect the health of his subjects is widespread. Apart from the plague caused by David's census, the worship of the golden calf in Exod 32:35 led to a plague, as did the rebellion of Korah in Num 17:11–15. Nevertheless, some scholars prefer translating the term מגפה as "blow" (Coggins 1976, 229; McKenzie 2004, 305). For the notion that עמך "your people" refers to Jehoram's family rather than the population of Judah, see Japhet 2003, 272.
26 Several different suggestions exist for translating the phrase וילך בלא חמדה, such as "he died to nobody's regret" (NAS), "He went without being desired" (KJV), or "he departed unpraised" (NJPS). Yet, it has also been speculated that the root חמד refers to the lack of a funerary pyre (Japhet 2003, 275).

prophets and the people. In Chronicles, Asa was considered a relatively successful king whose main achievements consisted of cultic reforms under prophetic guidance and a victorious battle against the Kushites. Only in his later reign did he engage in warfare against the northern kingdom and clashed with the prophets, especially the prophet Hanani, who accused him of relying on Aram when instead he should be relying on Yahweh (2 Chr 16:7–11).[27] Hanani is put into jail, and we are informed that the people also suffered. Then, in his thirty-ninth year, the king becomes ill in his feet, and his illness was "exceedingly great." Yet, "even in his illness he did not turn to Yahweh, but to the physicians" (2 Chr 16:12b).[28]

Several observations can be made concerning Asa's health problems. For one, by specifying that the illness was severe and struck the king in his thirty-ninth year, the text suggests that the king's death was caused by his illness (Fretheim 1999, 90; Klein 2012, 242). Beyond implying the cause of Asa's death, the placement of Asa's illness directly after the incident with Hanani implies that it was a punishment for the king's abuse of people and prophet (Myers 1965, 95; Johnstone 1997, 74; Japhet 2003, 206–207; Jarick 2007, 115; Klein 2012, 242).[29] Finally, the statement that the king did not seek divine help, even when his illness was severe, demonstrates that he lacked trust in God. These factors suggest that Asa's illness serves to underscore the importance of trusting in Yahweh and treating prophets and people with respect. Similar to Jehoram's illness, Asa's health problems also create a link to the events leading up to the destruction of Jerusalem and Judah, since much of the divine wrath is caused by the fact that the prophets were mocked, as we learn in 2 Chr 36:16a, where the people "scorned God's messengers and ridiculed their words" (ויהיו מלעבים במלאכי האלוהים ובוזים דבריו).

3.3 The Arrogance of Uzziah and Hezekiah

After having discussed wickedness and self-reliance as underlying causes of illness, we can now turn to the character trait of arrogance.[30] Arrogance is one of the leading contributors to royal illness in Chronicles. This is most apparent in Uzziah's affliction with צרעת, but may also be observed indirectly for the Chro-

---

27 For an overview of his reign and the way it corresponds to the *Vorlage* in Kings, see Japhet 2003, 201–209; Klein 2012, 236–239; Beentjes 2015, 141–151.
28 On the problems involved in turning to physicians alone, see Cranz 2018, 231–246.
29 Contra Kelly (1996, 97) who believes that the illness was not a punishment.
30 Parts of this section are based on Cranz 2019.

nistic interpretation of Hezekiah's illness. According to 2 Chr 26:16, Uzziah's heart was lifted up and he became inclined to "commit sacrilege" (מעל) by entering the temple and burning incense. After a short confrontation with the priests, Uzziah is stricken by the skin disorder צרעת.[31] Given the debilitating nature of the disorder, the king retires and arranges for his son Jotham to take over the government. We also learn that Uzziah was permanently "cut off from the house of Yahweh" (נגזר מבית יהוה) and that he had to be buried in a field, since his צרעת disqualified him from receiving a normal burial. This interpretation of Uzziah's צרעת is most likely motivated by the Chronicler's interest in restricting the cultic role of kings in the temple cult. Although kings are presented as builders of the temple and benefactors of its cult throughout the Deuteronomistic History and Chronicles, slight differences arise regarding the articulation of royal responsibilities. While the Deuteronomistic History concedes that kings and their offspring could serve in cultic positions, the cultic activities of the king and his offspring are limited in Chronicles.[32] In its most immediate context, therefore, Uzziah's sacrilege and subsequent affliction played a larger part in the chronistic scheme of curtailing the monarchs' privileges in the temple cult.[33] Within the wider context of the chronistic narrative, Uzziah's sacrilege points toward exile, since the time leading up to the destruction of Jerusalem was characterized by the sacrilege (מעל) that priests and people committed at the temple (2 Chr 36:14).

Uzziah is not the only king to become exceedingly arrogant; the same can be observed for Hezekiah as he is portrayed in Chronicles. The chronistic version of Hezekiah's illness is condensed to one verse (2 Chr 32:24): "In those days, Hezekiah fell ill onto death. He prayed to Yahweh. He answered him and gave him a sign" (בימים ההם חלה יחזקיהו עד־למות ויתפלל אל־יהוה יומר לו ומופת נתן לו).[34] Hezekiah's illness poses a theological problem for the Chronicler: Why would a righteous king suffer from an illness? Instead of answering

---

[31] The same occurs 2 Kgs 15:5, although in this case Uzziah has not committed any type of sin.
[32] David's sons are depicted as priests in 2 Sam 8:18, and Solomon may have brought an incense offering in 1 Kgs 9:25. In Chronicles, by contrast, David's sons merely serve alongside their father, and the offering of incense is explicitly limited to the priesthood (1 Chr 6:34; 2 Chr 13:11), see Cranz 2019.
[33] For these observations and additional examples that seem to limit the king's cultic responsibility, see Japhet 2009, 345.
[34] The account of Hezekiah's illness and recovery appears in the broader framework of 2 Chr 32:24–33, which also includes a description of Hezekiah's wealth (vv. 27–29), a note on his building activities relating to water (v. 30), a short reference to the visit of the Babylonian envoys (v. 31) and a concluding note on Hezekiah's reign (vv. 32–33).

this question, the Chronicler reworks the account to place more emphasis on Hezekiah's behavior after he was healed from his ailment. This leads to a direct accusation against the king. In 2 Chr 32:25 we learn that Hezekiah incurs divine wrath "because he did not return the favors that had been done for him, but instead his heart became lifted up" (כי לא־כגמול עליו השיב יחזקיהו כי גבה לבו).[35] Hezekiah manages to mitigate this wrath as is stated in 2 Chr 32:26, where we learn that "Hezekiah humbled himself for his arrogance together with the people of Jerusalem" (ויכנע יחזקיהו בגבה לבו הוא ויושבי ירושלים). This communal act of repentance averts immediate disaster without specifying when or whether the disaster would have occurred (Japhet 2003, 435). It is noteworthy that Hezekiah involves the people in his act of repentance. This makes this episode not only relevant for Hezekiah, but also addresses the Chronicler's contemporaries directly, given that the expressions "Judah and Jerusalem" (יהודה וירושלם) in 2 Chr 32:25 and "the inhabitants of Jerusalem" (יושבי ירושלם) referenced in the following verse are typically employed to address the postexilic community (Ackroyd 1991, 324). As we had observed for Uzziah, Hezekiah's health problems also forge a connection with the eventual destruction of Judah and Jerusalem. In 2 Chr 36:12 we learn that one of the reasons for God's abandonment of the people had to do with the fact that Zedekiah "did evil in the eyes of Yahweh his Lord. He did not humble himself before Jeremiah the prophet [speaking] from the mouth of Yahweh" (ויעש הרע בעיני יהוה אלוהיו לא נכנע מלפני ירמיהו הנביא מפי יהוה). In this sense, then, the health problems of Uzziah and Hezekiah inform us about expectations concerning the office of kingship in its relation to people and priests. Simultaneously, royal illness is indirectly tied in with the greater narrative of sin leading to the annihilation of Judah and Jerusalem.

4 Conclusion

This study shows how biblical historiography uses descriptions of royal illness to make statements about the nature of kingship, cultic conduct, moral expectations and the future of dynasties, cities, nations and people. We encounter these

---

35 It is unclear why Hezekiah became arrogant. Some scholars believe that the arrogance was a holdover from Hezekiah's rescue from Sennacherib and as such also figures as the cause of disease (Klein 2012, 467). Still other scholars believe that Hezekiah's arrogance found expression in his failing to bring the appropriate sacrifice (Kleinig 1993, 128). Yet the most likely explanation is that Hezekiah became arrogant on account of his recovery (Williamson 1982, 386).

themes both in the Deuteronomistic History and in Chronicles, where they are emphasized to different degrees. In the deuteronomistic description of Israel's first kings, Saul and David succumb to mental and physical disorders which stand in contrast to their status as divinely ordained leaders of the nation. In the stories about Elijah and Elisha, royal illness frames the condemnation of Baal worship and anticipates a temporary period of hardship. In the account of the divided kingdoms, royal illness frames prophetic oracles expressing either divine approval or disapproval for the different ruling dynasties of Israel and Judah. Jeroboam's dynasty is bound for destruction while the Davidic dynasty is divinely favored. Yet, even for the Davidic ruler Hezekiah, the oracle of hope is quickly followed up with an oracle of doom. It becomes clear that instances of royal illness are used for casting aspersions on the institution of kingship and to anticipate the future annihilation of dynasties and nations. The same themes can be detected in Chronicles, where the motif of royal illness is taken up and adapted to the chronistic understanding of kingship and outlook on history. The Chronicler frames royal illness by pointing to the moral weaknesses of individual kings. Jehoram is stricken by a disease and loses his intestines because of his evil ways. Asa becomes diseased in his feet because he abused prophets and people. Both Uzziah and Hezekiah struggle with excessive levels of arrogance. Uzziah's arrogance goes unchecked and as a result he is punished for his sacrilege. Hezekiah, by contrast, heeds the divine warning and humbles himself. While the nature of kingship and the correct moral conduct of kings appear to be in the foreground in Chronicles, the destruction of Judah and the end of the Davidic dynasty is never lost from view. The issues raised through royal illness converge in the last chapter of Chronicles when God's incurable wrath is explained by sacrilege, disrespect of the prophets and a general lack of humility. Taken together, then, it can be shown how scribes living in post-monarchic Judah employed the motif of royal illness to draw attention to a broad array of different issues, such as problems relating to kingship, the conduct of individual kings, and the evaluation of dynasties. Despite the wide variety of issues that can be addressed through royal illness, when the motif occurs it typically points toward the eventual destruction of the nation and the end of Israel's and Judah's political independence.

Bibliography

Ackroyd, Peter R. 1991. *The Chronicler in His Age*. JSOTSup 101. Sheffield: JSOT Press.
Avalos, Hector. 1995. *Illness and Health Care in the Ancient Near East: The Role of the Temple in Greece, Mesopotamia, and Israel*. HSM 54. Atlanta: Scholars Press.

Beck, Martin. 1999. *Elia und die Monolatrie: Ein Beitrag zur religionsgeschichtlichen Rückfrage nach dem vorschriftprophetischen Jahweh-Glauben*. BZAW 281. Berlin: de Gruyter.

Beentjes, Pancratius C. 2015. "King Asa and Hanani the Seer: 2 Chronicles 16 as an Example of the Chronicler's View of Prophets and Prophecy." In *Prophecy and Prophets in Stories: Papers Read at the Fifth Meeting of the Edinburgh Prophecy Network, Utrecht, October 2013*, edited by Bob Becking and Hans M. Barstad, 141–151. OTST 65. Leiden: Brill.

Ben Zvi, Ehud. 2016. "Memory and Political Thought in the Late Persian/Early Hellenistic Yehud/Judah: Some Observations." In *Leadership, Social Memory and Judean Discourse in the 5th–2nd Centuries BCE*, edited by Diana V. Edelman and Ehud Ben Zvi, 9–26. Worlds of the Ancient Near East and the Mediterranean. Bristol: Equinox.

Blanco Wißmann, Felipe. 2008. *"Er tat das Rechte ...": Beurteilungskriterien und Deuteronomismus in 1Kön 12–2Kön 25*. ATANT 93. Zurich: TVZ.

Boda, Mark J. 2010. *1–2 Chronicles*. Cornerstone Biblical Commentary. Carol Stream: Tyndale.

Cogan, Mordechai. 2000. *I Kings: A New Translation with Introduction and Commentary*. AB 10. New York: Doubleday.

Coggins, Richard. 1976. *The First and Second Books of Chronicles*. Cambridge: Cambridge University Press.

Cohn, Robert L. 2000. *2 Kings*. Berit Olam. Collegeville: Liturgical Press.

Cranz, Isabel. 2018. "Advice for a Successful Doctor's Visit: King Asa Meets Ben Sira." *CBQ* 80:231–246.

Cranz, Isabel. 2019. "The Motif of Uzziah's צרעת in the Deuteronomistic History, Chronicles and Beyond." *JSOT* 44:233–249.

Cranz, Isabel. 2020. *Royal Illness and Kingship Ideology in the Hebrew Bible*. SOTS Monograph Series. Cambridge: Cambridge University Press.

Dietrich, Walter. 1972. *Prophetie und Geschichte: Eine redaktionsgeschichtliche Untersuchung zum deuteronomistischen Geschichtswerk*. FRLANT 108. Göttingen: Vandenhoeck & Ruprecht.

Fretheim, Terence. 1999. *First and Second Kings*. Louisville: Westminster John Knox Press.

Geller, Markham J. 2010. *Ancient Babylonian Medicine: Theory and Practice*. Chichester: Wiley & Blackwell.

Geoby, Ronald A. 2016. "The Jeroboam Story in the (Re)Formulation of Israelite Identity: Evaluating the Literary-Ideological Purposes of 1 Kings 11–14." *JHS* 16:1–42.

Hamilton, Mark W. 2006. "The Creation of Saul's Royal Body: Reflections on 1 Sam 8–10." In *Saul in Story and Tradition*, edited by Carl S. Ehrlich and Marsha C. White, 139–155. FAT 47. Tübingen: Mohr Siebeck.

Hentschel, Georg. 1977. *Die Elijaerzählungen: Zum Verhältnis von historischem Geschehen und geschichtlicher Erfahrung*. Leipzig: Benno.

Hertzberg, Hans Wilhelm. 1964. *I & II Samuel: A Commentary*, translated by J. S. Bowden. OTL. Philadelphia: Westminster Press.

Hobbs, T. Raymond. 1985. *2 Kings*. WBC 13. Waco: Word Books.

Hutton, Jeremy. 2009. *The Transjordanian Palimpsest: The Overwritten Texts of Personal Exile and Transformation in the Deuteronomistic History*. BZAW 396. Berlin and New York: de Gruyter.

Japhet, Sara. 2003. *2 Chronik*. HThKAT. Freiburg i. Br.: Herder.

Japhet, Sara. 2009. *The Ideology of the Book of Chronicles and Its Place in Biblical Thought*. Winona Lake: Eisenbrauns.

Jarick, John. 2007. *2 Chronicles*. Readings: A New Bible Commentary. Sheffield: Sheffield Phoenix Press.
Johnstone, William. 1997. *1 and 2 Chronicles. Vol. 2: 2 Chronicles 10–36: Guilt and Atonement*. JSOTSup 254. Sheffield: Sheffield Academic Press.
Kaiser, Otto. 2000. "Das Verhältnis der Erzählung vom König David zum sogenannten Deuteronomistischen Geschichtswerk." In *Die sogenannte Thronfolgegeschichte Davids: Neue Ansichten und Anfragen*. OBO 176. Fribourg: Academic Press.
Kelly, Brian M. 1996. *Retribution and Eschatology in Chronicles*. JSOTSup 211. Sheffield: Sheffield Academic Press.
Klein, Ralph W. 1983. *1 Samuel*. WBC 10. Waco: Word Books.
Klein, Ralph W. 2012. *2 Chronicles: A Commentary*. Hermeneia. Minneapolis: Fortress Press.
Kleinig, John W. 1993. *The Lord's Song: The Basis, Function and Significance of Choral Music in Chronicles*. JSOTSup. 156. Sheffield: Sheffield Academic Press.
Klinger, Jörg. 2012. "Krankheit und Krieg im Spannungsfeld zwischen mythischer und realer Katastrophe." In *Disaster and Relief Management = Katastrophen und ihre Bewältigung*, edited by Angelika Berlejung, 471–497. FAT 81. Tübingen: Mohr Siebeck.
Knoppers, Gary N. 1994. "Dissonance and Disaster in the Legend of Kirta." *JAOS* 114:572–582.
Koch, Klaus. 1986. *Daniel*. BK.AT 22. Neukirchen-Vluyn: Neukirchener Verlag.
Lehnart, Bernhard. 2003. *Prophet und König im Nordreich Israel: Studien zur sogenannten vorklassischen Prophetie im Nordreich Israel anhand der Samuel-, Elija und Elischa Überlieferungen*. VTSup 96. Leiden: Brill.
Long, Burke O. 1991. *2 Kings*. Grand Rapids: Eerdmans.
Malamat, Abraham 1955. "Doctrines of Causality in Hittite and Biblical Historiography: A Parallel." *VT* 5:1–12.
McCarter, P. Kyle. 1980. *I Samuel: A New Translation with Introduction, Notes & Commentary*. AB 8. Garden City: Doubleday.
McCarter, P. Kyle. 1999. "Evil Spirit of God רוח אלוהים רעה." *DDD* 319–320.
McKenzie, Steven L. 2000. "The Trouble with Kingship." In *Israel Constructs Its History: Deuteronomistic History in Recent Research*, edited by Albert de Pury, Thomas Römer, and Jean-Daniel Macchi, 286–314. JSOTSup 306. London: Bloomsbury T&T Clark.
McKenzie, Steven L. 2004. *1–2 Chronicles*. AOTC. Nashville: Abingdon Press.
Mitchell, David T., and Sharon L. Snyder. 2000. *Narrative Prosthesis: Disability and the Dependencies of Discourse*. Ann Arbor: University of Michigan Press.
Montgomery, James A., and Henry S. Gehman. 1960. *A Critical and Exegetical Commentary on the Books of Kings*. Edinburgh: Bloomsbury T&T Clark.
Myers, Jacob M. 1965. *II Chronicles*. AB 13. Garden City: Doubleday.
Newsom, Carol. 2014. *Daniel: A Commentary*. OTL. Louisville: Westminster John Knox Press.
Nihan, Christophe. 2013. "1 Samuel 8 and 12 and the Deuteronomistic Edition of Samuel." In *Is Samuel Among the Deuteronomists? Current Views on the Place of Samuel in a Deuteronomistic History*, edited by Cynthia Edenburg and Juha Pakkala, 225–273. Ancient Israel and its Literature 16. Atlanta: SBL Press.
Noth, Martin. 1943. *Überlieferungsgeschichtliche Studien: Die sammelnden und bearbeitenden Geschichtswerke im Alten Testament*. Tübingen: Max Niemeyer.
Olyan, Saul M. 2008. *Disability in the Hebrew Bible: Interpreting Mental and Physical Differences*. Cambridge: Cambridge University Press.
Otto, Susanne. 2011. *Jehu, Elia und Elisa: Die Erzählung von der Jehu-Revolution und die Komposition der Elia-Elisa-Erzählungen*. BWANT 152. Stuttgart: Kohlhammer.

Owen, David. 2008. *In Sickness and in Power: Illness in Heads of Government in the Last 100 Years*. Westport: Praeger.

Post, Jerrold M., and Robert S. Robins. 1993. *When Illness Strikes the Leader: The Dilemma of the Captive King*. New Haven: Yale University Press.

Raphael, Rebecca. 2008. *Biblical Corpora: Representations of Disability in Hebrew Biblical Literature*. New York: Bloomsbury T&T Clark.

Rosenberg, Charles E., and Janet Golden, eds. 1992. *Framing Disease: Studies in Cultural History*. New Brunswick: Rutgers University Press.

Schipper, Jeremy. 2006. *Disability Studies and the Hebrew Bible: Figuring Mephibosheth in the David Story*. LHBOTS 441. London: Bloomsbury T&T Clark.

Schipper, Jeremy. 2007. "Disabling Israelite Leadership: 2 Samuel 6:23 and Other Images of Disability in the Deuteronomistic History." In *This Abled Body: Rethinking Disabilities in Biblical Studies*, edited by Hector Avalos, Sara J. Melcher, and Jeremy Schipper, 103–114. SemeiaSt 55. Atlanta: SBL Press.

Scurlock, JoAnn, and Burton R. Andersen. 2005. *Diagnoses in Assyrian and Babylonian Medicine: Ancient Sources, Translations, and Modern Medical Analyses/ translated and with commentary*. Urbana: University of Illinois Press.

Seybold, Klaus. 1973. "Elia am Gottesberg." *EvTh* 33:3–18.

Sweeney, Marvin A. 2007. *I & II Kings: A Commentary*. OTL. Louisville: Westminster John Knox Press.

Tsumura, David T. 2007. *The First Book of Samuel*. NICOT. Grand Rapids: Eerdmans.

Wendell, Susan. 2001. "Unhealthy Disables: Treating Chronic Illnesses as Disability." *Hypatia* 16(4):17–33.

Williamson, Hugh G. M. 1982. *1 and 2 Chronicles*. The New Century Bible Commentary. Grand Rapids: Eerdmans.

Würthwein, Ernst. 1984. *Die Bücher der Könige. Teil 2: 1. Kön. 17–2. Kön. 25*. ATD 11/2. Göttingen: Vandenhoeck & Ruprecht.

IV: **Comprehensive Aspects of Leadership in Prophetic and Chronistic Literature**

Sarah Schulz
Zerubbabel, Joshua and the Restoration of the Temple – A Comparative Approach to the Concepts of Leadership in Haggai/Zech 1–8 and Ezra 1–6

Large parts of the present volume are dedicated to the investigation and analysis of concepts of leadership in Haggai/Zechariah and Ezra/Nehemiah, respectively. Here, a major intersection between Haggai and Zech 1–8 on the one hand and Ezra 1–6 on the other immediately stands out: Haggai/Zech 1–8 and Ezra 1–6 present two accounts of the rebuilding of the Jerusalem temple. For the purpose of the present volume, a comparison of the two accounts promises valuable insights, as they reflect distinct concepts of leadership. Although they describe the same event, they differ from each other in almost every other respect. The differences even extend to the most basic facts concerning the temple's restoration. For example, Haggai/Zech 1–8 and Ezra 1–6 provide different information about when the building measures began: during the reign of Cyrus (Ezra 1–6) or during the reign of Darius (Haggai/Zech 1–8). Interestingly, although the personnel involved also varies between the two accounts,[1] they both attest to the involvement of Zerubbabel and Joshua as leading figures during the restoration period. The mention of both Zerubbabel and Joshua is the closest point of contact between the two texts, which thus also forms the crucial issue in the comparison. However, apart from their agreement that Zerubbabel and Joshua played a major role in the events surrounding the temple restoration, there are also some notable differences between Haggai/Zech 1–8 and Ezra 1–6 regarding the role of these two figures, which further complicates the undertaking. The differences might hint to a complex interplay of the leadership agendas associated with the references to Zerubbabel and Joshua in Haggai/Zech 1–8 and Ezra 1–6, respectively. Thus, this article seeks to investigate the concepts of leadership found in Haggai/Zech 1–8 and Ezra 1–6 and to trace their development and relationship to each other, in order to allow for a comparative perspective on the concepts of leadership in general and the function of Zerubbabel and Joshua in particular. However, for a general orientation, the main differences between the two texts will

---

[1] Ezra 1–6 mention a certain Sheshbazzar and the elders of the community, with whom the account in Haggai/Zech 1–8 does not seem to be familiar. According to Haggai/Zech 1–8, a mysterious "shoot" plays a role in the context of the temple building instead.

first be outlined before the references to Zerubbabel and Joshua are considered in more detail in light of the concepts of leadership in Haggai/Zech 1–8 and Ezra 1–6 respectively. The literary analyses are moslty based on my *Habilitation* thesis (Schulz forthcoming).

1 Zerubbabel and Joshua in Haggai/Zech 1–8 and Ezra 1–6

A particularly obvious difference between Haggai/Zech 1–8 and Ezra 1–6 concerns the diversity and complexity of leadership concepts associated with Zerubbabel and Joshua. Throughout the books of Haggai and Zechariah, the building of the temple is time and again linked to the books' protagonists. They can be mentioned each on their own (e.g., Zerubbabel in Hag 2:20–23; Zech 4:6–10* and Joshua in Zech 3; Zech 6:9–15) or together (especially in the narrative passages which frame the prophetic sayings of Haggai in Hag 1:1–3*, 14, 15a; 2:2). Thus, over the course of these two books, many different leadership roles are ascribed to them. Compared to this variety in Haggai/Zech 1–8, Zerubbabel's and Joshua's leadership roles seem to be less complex in Ezra 1–6 (though not necessarily less cryptic). The two of them are always mentioned together as leading figures during the time of the restoration of the temple.

Moreover, two differences that are likely relevant to the underlying concepts of leadership in the two textual corpora are easily detectable at first glance. The first concerns the absence of the titles "governor" and "high priest" in Ezra 1–6. In contrast, Haggai/Zech 1–8 provide a variety of combinations regarding the information given about Zerubbabel and Joshua. While Joshua always bears the title "high priest," the title "governor" for Zerubbabel is sometimes absent (Hag 1:12; 2:4; Zech 4:6–10*). The filiation is missing for Joshua in Zech 3 and for Zerubbabel in Hag 2:4, 20; Zech 4:6–10*. When the two of them are mentioned together, normally filiation and title are provided for both (Hag 1:1, 14; 2:2).[2] However, the combination found in Ezra 1–6 (no titles but filiation for both) does not occur in Haggai/Zech 1–8. Given that in Haggai/Zech 1–8 far-reaching reflections on leadership and authority are related with the respective offices, the absence of the titles in Ezra 1–6 should be regarded as significant.

---

2 The only exception is Hag 1:12, where the title for Zerubbabel is missing. This variation can possibly be explained redaction-critically.

A second difference regarding the two protagonists affects the chronology of the reported events. While Ezra 5–6 relate to Haggai/Zech 1–8 at least as far as the protagonists' appearance during the reign of king Darius is concerned, Ezra 3 describes a previous appearance of Zerubbabel and Joshua during the early phase of the temple's rebuilding that began, according to Ezra 1–6, during the reign of the Persian king Cyrus. This difference, too, has to be considered when evaluating and comparing the concepts of leadership in Haggai/Zech 1–8 and Ezra 1–6.

Before being compared, however, the (themselves complex) concepts of leadership in Haggai/Zech 1–8 and Ezra 1–6 must first be critically examined independently from each other.

2 Concepts of Leadership Related to Zerubbabel and Joshua in Haggai/Zech 1–8

Within the limits of this article, it is impossible to trace the entire redaction history of Haggai/Zech 1–8, even if the selection of relevant texts is reduced to the instances where Zerubbabel and Joshua are mentioned. However, already a first glimpse reveals that throughout the two books, Zerubbabel and Joshua are connected to the events surrounding the restoration of the temple in such a variety of ways that there is reason to assume that the respective texts contain distinct redactional layers: While the framing passages in Haggai (Hag 1:1–3*, 14, 15a; 2:2) express the shared responsibility of governor and high priest for the building measures, according to Zech 4:6–10* Zerubbabel alone (mentioned without filiation and title) is in charge. Zechariah 6:9–15 instead promote the view that Joshua (or, alternatively, the Davidic "shoot")[3] builds the temple. This variety of viewpoints shows that the building of the temple plays a pivotal role in the leadership debate in Haggai/Zech 1–8 and, at the same time, makes a dialectical development of the concepts of leadership very likely.

As the idea of Zerubbabel's and Joshua's shared responsibility for the project reflects an important stage of this process (and the most important stage in view of the comparison with Ezra 1–6), it seems appropriate to begin the overview of the concepts of leadership in Haggai/Zech 1–8 with the framing passages in Haggai.

---

3 On the redaction history of Zech 6:9–15 see below.

2.1 The Framing Passages in Haggai (1:1–3*, 14, 15a; 2:2)

Haggai 1:1, 14; 2:2 mention Zerubbabel and Joshua with filiation and title in an equal position: The prophet addresses them together as officials responsible for the temple's restoration. In that respect, these passages framing the prophetic sayings are sometimes evaluated in terms of a diarchic constitution, which could either exist in reality or be regarded as an ideal.

Indeed, it cannot be denied that the respective verses, at least to a certain degree, express the parity of the governor and the high priest. In general, the juxtaposition of these two offices might even reflect actual political conditions in the province of Yehud during the late Persian or early Hellenistic period as can be concluded from the correspondence between the Judeans from Elephantine and Bagohi, the governor of Yehud, from the end of the fifth century BCE and from the Yehud coinage which suggests that the governor of Yehud and the high priest simultaneously minted small denominations in the second half of the fourth century BCE. Not surprisingly, the external evidence is thus often used as an argument for the historicity of the concept of diarchic leadership that is suspected behind the framing passages in Haggai. However, a diarchy (in terms of equal authority) of governor and high priest cannot easily be deduced from the Elephantine correspondence or from the Yehud coinage.

TAD A4.7 // TAD A4.8, a request for a letter of recommendation in the matter of the rebuilding of the temple of *Yhw* from the Judeans of Elephantine to Bagohi, the governor of Yehud, refers in passing to a previous letter to Bagohi[4] and the elites of Jerusalem, who are headed by Johanan, the high priest, to which the Judeans of Elephantine did not receive any response. Thus, albeit indirectly, this reference probably attests to a certain shared responsibility of the governor and the nobility in Jerusalem in affairs concerning the cult in Elephantine. However, the actual and only preserved letter to Bagohi clearly documents that the Judeans of Elephantine regard the governor of Yehud as the crucial authority even in this cultic matter. Whatever significance the mention of the former writing is given, it should not be evaluated in terms of a general dyarchy of governor and high priest in the province of Yehud (*pace* Lemaire 2002, 218; Granerød 2016, 42).

---

[4] TAD A4.7, 18–19 // TAD A4.8, 17–18. The view that "our lord" is Bagohi (Porten 1996, 142 n. 58; Granerød, 2016, 41) is sometimes contested. Another possibility is to identify the "lord" with the Egyptian satrap Arsham (Kottsieper 2002, 163–164; Joisten-Pruschke 2008, 68; Rohrmoser 2014, 400). However, the appellation of Bagohi as "lord" in other passages of the letter, together with the fact that Arsham is referred to by name at the end of the letter (A4.7, 30) clearly speaks in favor of the first option.

The same probably applies to the numismatic evidence of Yehud during the fourth century BCE. Even if a simultaneous release of coinage by the governor and the high priest is indeed very likely,[5] this does not necessarily point to an increasing political authority of the high priest and/or a diarchic form of leadership of governor and high priest towards the end of the Persian period or in early Hellenistic times.[6] It seems safe to conclude that the temple and the local authorities in Jerusalem did not play an important economic role within the Persian Empire. The temple did not function as a tax collection center for the province,[7] nor is there evidence that it was the main (or only) foundry in Yehud (*pace* Schaper 1995; 2000).[8] Thus, the release of coinage by the high priest cannot be interpreted in terms of a close relationship to the central Persian administration. On the other hand, it certainly does not signify any degree of independence from the Persian authorities either. There was no crisis of the Persian Empire in the fourth century which left room for autonomy of the local authorities *in opposition* to the Persian authorities. As Wiesehöfer states

> There was no downhill slide and no existential crisis of authority, but there were tensions in the imperial structure that in certain circumstances could grow into regional instability or temporary weakness of royal power. None of these crises threatened the existence of the Achaemenid Empire. Even the loss of Egypt for approximately 60 years did not really change anything with regard to the excellent position of the Great King in the power structure of the Eastern Mediterranean and the Near East (Wiesehöfer 2007, 23).[9]

However, the "explosion" of the Yehud coinage in the second half of the fourth century fits the political situation of the province within the Persian empire very

---

5 Next to coins bearing the inscription "Hezekiah, the governor," one coin bears the inscription "Jochanan, the priest" (both c. 330; cf. Gitler/Lorber 2008). Even if the evidence is limited, it seems safe to ascribe this coin to the high priest (Barag, 1985, 1986; *pace* Mildenberg 1988, 726; 2000, 381). The same probably applies to a coin which belongs to a certain "Jaddua" (before 350; cf. Spaer 1986). For a plausible reconstruction of the chronology see Kratz 2004b, 107–109, with VanderKam 1991.
6 *Pace*, among many, Spaer 1986; Schaper 2000, 157; Achenbach 2010.
7 *Pace* Lemaire 2007, 60, who concludes: "The role of the temple as the center of the collection of taxes is apparently connected to the origin of the economic and political power of the Jerusalem high priest during the Hellenistic period." The assumption that the Jerusalem temple functioned as a tax collection center is based on the comparison with Babylonian temples which is problematic as, unlike the Jerusalem temple, these temples had huge land holdings and were indeed economic centers. Moreover, archaeological evidence clearly speaks in favor of Ramat-Rahel as economic and administrative center of the province of Yehud (cf. Wiesehöfer 2011, 182).
8 Schaper's assumption is based on Zech 11:13. However, the biblical evidence is weak because the verse probably stems from much later times (cf. Schott 2019).
9 Cf. also Altmann 2016, 68.

well. It seems plausible to assume a general economic boom during the reigns of Artaxerxes II and Artaxerxes III which, in combination with the growing importance of the region due to Egypt's independence and the increased presence of Persian troops, led to an economic strengthening of the region (Lipschits/Vanderhooft 2007, 87; Mildenberg 1996, 132). When evaluating the possible political implications of the release of coinage by the high priest, it is crucial to consider the rather liberal monetary policy of the Persian Empire. The local minting authorities probably did not act in their own right, but a formal authorization by the central Persian administration did not seem to have been necessary either (Mildenberg 1979, 75; cf. also Howgego 1995, 46). "In the Persian empire one could mint coins whenever and wherever they were required as long as the material and technical means were available" (Mildenberg 2000, 377).[10] Thus, the significance of the minting of coins as an indicator for political autonomy of the minting authorities in the province of Yehud should not be overestimated. Consequently, it cannot necessarily be deduced from the simultaneous emissions of coins of the governor and the high priest in the fourth century that the latter's authority has increased in this time. Nor can we draw any conclusions about the relationship between the governor and the high priest from this. However, the possibility cannot be ruled out that the governor "may have permitted local authorities to produce mints of small denomination" (Cataldo 2009, 85).

To sum up, the assumption that the framing verses in Haggai reflect an actual diarchic constitution of Yehud in the late Persian period cannot be substantiated by external evidence. At a closer look, even the view that the framing verses in Haggai were composed in order to promote a diarchy of governor and high priest as an ideal concept does not seem to be without reasonable alternative. At least we have to consider the option that the literary juxtaposition of high priest and governor reflects a different leadership agenda which sought to assimilate one of the offices to the other one in order to give it more prestige. While Joshua always bears the title "high priest" in Haggai/Zech 1–8 (the filiation is missing in Zech 3), Zerubbabel sometimes appears as the person in charge of the temple rebuilding without the title of "governor" and without filiation.[11] The sparse information given for the two figures could suggest a rela-

---

10 "Im Perserreich konnte man Münzen prägen, wann und wo sie benötigt wurden und wenn die materiellen und technischen Mittel dafür vorhanden waren."
11 This is the case in Hag 2:4 and the epexegesis in Zech 4:6–10* which obviously has been inserted into the night vision of the menorah (cf. already Wellhausen 1963, 182–183). The missing title in Hag 2:23 is a different matter, since the distribution of title and filiation within Hag 2:20–23 seems to be intentional. Cf. Hallaschka 2011, 108–109.

tively early date of composition of the respective passages. This assumption might also be substantiated by further evidence.[12] If these passages indeed reflect literary stages that are older than the framing passages of Haggai (which will serve as a working hypothesis here), the innovation of the latter would be that the two leading figures (now each with a filiation) become associates and that Zerubbabel is given the title "governor." In theory, both directions of influence are conceivable. The framing verses could theoretically document the intention to elevate the high priest's office to the *de facto* powerful office of the governor and thus attest to, or at least support, the growing autonomy and authority of the high priest in political terms. However, the *ad hoc* addition of the title "governor" probably hints at a different agenda behind the text. It is likely that this title was introduced in order to highlight the bearer of this office himself (instead of his sidekick). By juxtaposing the governor and the high priest and amalgamating their functions, the Persian governor, a bearer of a "foreign" office on par with that of the high priest, becomes the addressee of the prophet Haggai[13] and his office is thus transformed into a Yehudite one.[14] Therefore, even if the framing passages in Haggai might reflect actual political circumstances in the late Persian period by juxtaposing the governor and the high priest,[15] the specific form of presentation attests to a certain agenda on the part of the redactor.

However, even if the verses indeed seek to highlight the office of "governor" as an indigenous Yehudite office of political leadership, this would not necessarily preclude the possibility that the high priest at least indirectly benefited from being associated with this politically powerful office. There is at least reason to assume that the "implicit diarchy" constituted in Hag 1:1, 14; 2:2 formed

---

12 Zechariah 3 formally introduces Joshua as high priest and defines the office (see below), which makes good sense if he enters stage for the first time in Zech 3. Furthermore, the role of Joshua in Zech 3 is still limited to the cultic realm, whereas it extends to the politic sphere in Hag 1:1, 14; 2:2 (and Zech 6:9–15, of course; see below). Haggai 2:4 (without the mention of Joshua, who has clearly been added to the verse; cf. Wöhrle 2006, 291–292; Wolff 1991, 53; Reventlow 1993, 20; *pace* Hallaschka 2011, 62–63) could be part of one of Haggai's original prophetic sayings. Zechariah 4:6–10 differ from all other instances where Zerubbabel is mentioned because he is not (yet) characterized as a leader.
13 This differs from Hag 2:20–23, which portray Zerubbabel as a messianic figure, and from Zech 4:6–10*, where he does not bear the title "governor."
14 The office of the "governor" is similarly characterized in terms of a Yehudite office of leadership in Neh 5; 13.
15 The office ceased to exist during the early Hellenistic period. Since the attempt to promote the "governor" as a Yehudite political leader is bound to the factual existence of the office, the end of the Persian period (or the very beginning of the Hellenistic period) can be considered the *terminus ad quem* of the framing verses (and of Neh 5; 13).

the basis for the subsequent redactional shaping not only of Zerubbabel but also (and especially) of Joshua not only as politically powerful but literally royal leaders in the course of the redaction history of the book.

While the office of the governor becomes irrelevant in the course of these rewritings for obvious reasons, a veritable discourse develops around the question of whether the high priest or the royal leader from the Davidic lineage (represented either by Zerubbabel as a messianic figure [Hag 2:20–23] or the "shoot" which can be identified as a Davidic king via the comparison with Jer 23:5; 33:15 [Zech 3:8; 6:12]).

2.2 Zech 6:9–15

This discourse becomes particularly evident from the presumed redaction history of Zech 6:9–15. Obviously, the central topic of "temple building" from Haggai/Zech 1–8 is now applied in order to debate questions of leadership. Specifically, in v. 13 the building of the temple is associated with "bearing honor" (ישא הוד), "being enthroned" (ישב על כסא), and "reigning" (משל). What remains unclear from the text in its present form is the question to whom this honor is due. The crown shall be placed on Joshua's head (v. 11), but immediately after that the high priest receives the order to address the "shoot" with the promise of royal leadership (v. 12). The complex distribution of roles, which is rather confusing with regard to concepts of leadership, makes a diachronic approach inevitable. It is sometimes assumed that the text originally did not report the crowning of Joshua alone but instead the crowning of both Zerubbabel and Joshua (Wöhrle 2006, 343) or of Zerubbabel alone (Wellhausen 1963, 185). The advantage of the first solution is that the plural noun עטרות in v. 11 could actually be understood as a plural form. Of course, the grammatical plural could imply the crowning of two individuals; however, since this solution involves other modifications to the text, the alternative to consider the plural form עטרות as an abstract plural seems more plausible. The second solution also entails arbitrary changes to the text. Moreover, its only advantage is that the crowning of Zerubbabel is in line with the messianic portrayal of Zerubbabel in Hag 2:20–23. However, it is not even certain that the author of Zech 6:9–15 already had Hag 2:20–23 in view.[16] If one therefore refrains from arbitrary modifications to the text, v. 11 never reported anything but the crowning of the high priest. Indeed, from this point, the redactional development of the text can easily be explained. Verse 12 is awkward both as a continuation of v. 11 and as preparation for v. 13. After v. 11 it comes as

---

16 On the possibly late date of origin of Hag 2:20–23 see below.

a surprise that the promise of royal leadership is not directed towards the newly crowned high priest but towards the "shoot." As regards the connection between vv. 12 and 13, v. 12bβ und v. 13a are doublets. It is stressed twice that "he," that is, the "shoot," will build the temple. The easiest explanation for this peculiarity would be to consider v. 12 a later insertion. Originally, v. 13a thus followed directly upon v. 11 and referred to the high priest, who, accordingly, is introduced as a royal leader. Verse 12 has been inserted in order to transfer the royal predications to the "shoot."[17] Verses 13b–14 probably also belong to this redaction. They locate an undefined priest next to the royal leader's throne[18] (i.e., on this level, the "shoot") and place the crown, which has formerly been put on the high priest's head, as a symbol for remembrance in the temple.

If this diachronic reconstruction is correct, Zech 6:9–15 originally portrayed the ideal of a royal high priest. He is formally crowned and receives the promise that he will rule as a royal leader, defined by the following privileges: building the temple, bearing royal honor, sitting on the throne, and reigning. While the topic of "temple building" is already predetermined from the existing text of Haggai/Zech 1–8, the most explicit royal predications are innovative and need to be taken seriously with regard to their implied concept of leadership and the text's supposed date of origin. It is plausible to assume that the redaction history of Haggai/Zech 1–8 began (not too late) in the Persian period. Of course, the possibility that the political influence of the high priest began to increase slightly during the late Persian and early Hellenistic periods cannot be ruled out completely (even if the Elephantine correspondence and the Yehud coinage should not be evaluated too favorably in this respect). However, the concept of the royal high priesthood is specific and rare and goes far beyond this. Even if Zech 6:9–15 are not interpreted as reflecting a political reality but rather understood as creating an ideal, it is highly unlikely that the text stems from the late Persian or early Hellenistic period. The next time the idea of a crowned high priest appears is in late texts such as Sir 45:12 and 1 Macc 10:2, which are the closest parallels to Zech 6:9–15. This could speak in favor of the late development of this concept (whether realistic or idealized).

---

17 Also in this case, the conspicuous repetition could have been avoided. The reason the redactor added v. 12bβ could have been to give v. 13a an adversative meaning ("Indeed, *he* will build the temple" – and not the crowned high priest as one might tend to suggest following v. 11).
18 על כסאו: The priest either sits on his own throne, which is located next to the "shoot's" throne, or is placed next to his (i.e. the "shoot's") throne. Both options are possible. In the first case, one might expect the verb "to sit" instead of "to be" (cf. v. 13a). In the second case, the repeated preposition על would have different meanings ("on his throne" or "next to his throne," respectively) in the two instances of its occurrence in v. 13aβ and v. 13bα. Either way, it is evident that v. 13b seeks to restrict the priest's authority.

In any case, the "shoot" has been inserted into Zech 6:9–15 as a competing leadership concept aimed at neutralizing the idea of a royal high priesthood and transferring the promises to a future Davidic ruler instead (a figure that is firmly rooted in the biblical tradition). However, the messiah joins the high priest in order to limit his influence on cultic matters, not to replace him. As an ideal concept, the development of this counter-offensive against the royal priesthood is conceivable at any time. Keeping in mind that the concept of a royal priesthood itself perhaps did not originate before Oniad times, it should be noted that the messianic counter-offensive strikingly resembles texts which reactivate the Davidic messiah as a traditional ruler (and thus a legitimate heir to the throne) against the Hasmoneans – the most prominent example is probably Ps Sol 17. An anti-Hasmonean intention of the "shoot" passages thus cannot be ruled out.

To sum up, as the product of a multi-staged literary discourse, Zech 6:9–15 contain two opposing concepts of leadership (royal high priest and messiah) which can be assumed to reflect late stages of the book's redaction history.

2.3 Zech 3

The same juxtaposition of the high priest and the "shoot" can be found in Zech 3. As the leadership predications are less explicit in Zech 3, a brief overview of the text's meaning and its literary development is essential in order to evaluate its implied concepts of leadership.

The actual vision comprises vv. 1–7. The core of the matter is an etiology of the high priest's office. In this context, Joshua is given great authority in cultic matters. However, as will be argued below, the competencies ascribed to him do not go beyond the cultic realm (*pace*, e.g., Hanhart 1998, 193; Delkurt 2000, 173–176; Pola 2003, 199).

The vision reports the purification and expiation of the high priest Joshua, who has been impurified by the exile.[19] While vv. 1–6 describe the preconditions for exercising the office of high priest, v. 7 defines its contours. Verse 7 includes five stipulations: two conditions and three privileges.[20] From the two condi-

---

[19] It can be considered with Kratz 2004a, 81, that Zech 3 already refers to the priestly *torah* in Hag 2:10–14 according to which a person must be undefiled in order to bring pure offerings.
[20] The peculiar construction וגם [...] וגם אתה speaks in favor of the beginning of the apodosis in v. 7aβ (Pola 2003, 174, 198; Tiemeyer 2006, 251–252; Schott 2019, 41). Alternatively, a beginning of the apodosis in v. 7b is also possible (Hallaschka 2011, 207–208; Wöhrle 2006, 334 n. 40).

tions, the first ("if you will walk in my ways") emphasizes Joshua's "expected personal piety and his sole devotion to YHWH" (Tiemeyer 2006, 252) and thus concerns his personal life. The second one ("if you will keep my requirements") is often associated with cultic personnel (priests or Levites) in Ezekiel, Chronicles, and P (cf. Hallaschka 2011, 207–208 n. 331) and, hence, is likely to address Joshua's professional life (Tiemeyer 2006, 252). If the verse's protasis is to be limited to these two conditions, Torah observance and the correct exercise of the office are the preconditions for the following three privileges. The first two affect the concrete duties of the high priest. "You shall rule my house" is likely to be understood as a metaphor[21] and to refer to the jurisdiction located at the temple district (cf. Hallaschka 2011, 208). "You shall have charge of my courts" also expresses the high priest's sole responsibility in cultic affairs (cf. Hallaschka 2011, 209; Tiemeyer 2006, 254). With these two privileges, Zech 3:7 indeed transfers formerly royal tasks to the office of the high priest (cf., e.g., Wöhrle 2006, 334; Hallaschka 2011, 208–209; Schott 2019, 41). However, it is unclear whether this serves a programmatic purpose or rather a pragmatic one. Although the monarch surely had sovereignty also in cultic affairs, already in preexilic times most of the cultic duties were probably exercised by priests (as royal officials).[22] The innovation in Zech 3 is thus not the duties ascribed to the high priest as such, but their transferral to his sole responsibility: "In Zech 3:7 the temple administration completely devolves to the high priest" (Pola 2003, 200).[23] Accordingly, Zech 3:7 probably does not transfer formerly royal privileges to the high priest in order to elevate his office, but might rather reflect the actual conditions at the temple and is thus to be evaluated as a pragmatic adoption of formerly royal duties by the high priest.

The third and last privilege transcends the cultic realm but still does not shape the high priest as a royal leader ("I will give you the right of access among those who are standing here"). It ties the execution of the high priest's office to the heavenly council.[24] In this concept of high priesthood, the boundary between the priestly office and *prophetic* authority begins to blur. In any case, this last privilege clearly intends to enhance the status of the high priest. If the priest has direct access to the heavenly assembly, the cult he exercises is an expression of the divine will.

---

21 Cf. the statement in 1 Sam 2:10 according to which YHWH judges the ends of the earth.
22 Also in Hag 2 the priest confers *torah*. Legal practice at the temple by priests is attested in Deut 17:11; 31:10–13. For an overview, see Begrich 1964. On the connection between priest and *torah*, see also Niehr 1987.
23 "Die Verwaltung des Tempels geht in Sach 3,7 nun vollgültig auf den Hohenpriester über."
24 "Those who are standing here" represent the heavenly assembly. Cf. Pola 2003, 201; Hallaschka 2011, 209.

The vision ends with v. 7. As vv. 8–10 introduce a completely new topic, it seems likely that they have been appended. The divine speech that began in v. 7 continues in v. 8, albeit with a shift in content. It is no longer concerned with the high priest's authority and duties but focuses on another person, the "shoot." The priestly class is subtly degraded by the insertion of v. 8: Joshua's priestly brothers who surround him become a symbol for the future royal reign of the "shoot."

In Zech 6:9–15 there was evidence that the "shoot" has been inserted in order to reject the ideal of a royal high priesthood. Unlike Zech 6:9–15, Zech 3:1–7 (at least as far as the basic layer is concerned) do not ascribe royal attributes to the high priest. However, this might be different in v. 9, which is admittedly cryptic as regards its content but ultimately seems to support the idea of a royal priesthood.

The perspective changes between v. 8 and v. 9, which probably marks another literary seam. While v. 8 addresses Joshua directly, v. 9 speaks about him in the third person. It is likely, then, that v. 9 was appended to v. 7 before v. 8.[25] It adds to the description of the high priest's privileges in v. 7 by placing before Joshua the very stone that Zerubbabel employs in building the temple (Zech 4:10).[26] Thus, v. 9 probably expresses the transferral of the control over the stone from Zech 4:10 to Joshua. As this stone has a crucial function in the context of the temple building, v. 9 symbolically assigns the supremacy in temple building affairs to the high priest and, thus (like Zech 6:9–15), ascribes a genuinely royal privilege to him. Therefore, the insertion of v. 9 does not function as a "sign for Zerubbabel" (Kratz 2004a, 81)[27] but rather focuses on "Joshua as the builder of the temple" (Reventlow 1993, 56).[28]

A similar royal "reshaping" of the high priest perhaps occurs in one other instance in Zech 3. Within the original vision, the provision of a clean turban (צָנִיף) for Joshua in v. 5abα[1] is conspicuous for two reasons. First, it is striking that the visionary himself in the heavenly council (!) issues the command to

---

[25] Like vv. 8 and 9, the auspicious eschatological perspective of v. 10 probably also goes back to a redactional hand. It is generally either related to the redaction of v. 8 (Schott 2019, 42) or regarded as even later than that (Schöttler 1987, 101; Hallaschka 2011, 196–197, 220).

[26] That Zech 4:10 is by no means a literary unity is a widely accepted view. The first part of the verse belongs to a reworking that inserts the involvement of Zerubbabel into the original vision of the menorah. The second half of the verse (beginning with שִׁבְעָה־אֵלֶּה) continues the vision and originally answered the question raised by the prophet in v. 4. The cryptic reading of Zech 3:7 would then result from an uncritical synchronic reception of Zech 4:10. Cf. Schott 2019, 42–43. Hence, a literary-critical differentiation within v. 9 itself is unnecessary.

[27] "Vorzeichen für Serubbabel."

[28] "Josua als Tempelbauer."

outfit the high priest with a turban.²⁹ Second, the order in which the garments are donned (headgear before the clothes) is somehow odd as it leaves the high priest at least temporarily scarcely clad with anything but a turban. Thus, there is reason to suspect that v. 5abα¹ reflects a reworking of the original vision and has been added between v. 4 and v. 5bα²β (cf. Hallaschka 2011, 206; Schott 2019, 41 n. 110).

The turban probably represents a royal garment. Whereas in Isa 3:23 צָנִיף designates quite generally a garment indicating the dignity of its wearer, Job 29:14 combines it with two royal predications: "I put on righteousness, and it clothed me; my justice was like a robe and a turban." Finally, Isa 62:3 explicitly qualifies צָנִיף as a royal garment (צְנִיף מְלוּכָה [qere]). This meaning is also predominant in Sirach, where the term is used relatively often (Sir 11:5; 40:4; 47:6). Against this background, Pola's view that it is "exaggerated to see another piece of evidence for the transferral of royal predications to the priestly realm" (Pola 2003, 217)³⁰ in Zech 3:5 because it occurs in connection with the king only in Isa 62:3 is not convincing. Rather, like Zech 3:9, which can thus be ascribed to the very same redactor, the insertion in v. 5 might reflect the intention to depict the high priest as a royal leader.³¹

It seems plausible, therefore, to assume that Zech 3 reflects on two distinct literary levels the same process that has been observed in Zech 6:9–15. First, royal predications are transferred to the high priest (vv. 5abα, 9); then, the Davidic "shoot" is established as an alternative and competing form of leadership (v. 8).

To complete the picture, it is important to note that Hag 2:20–23 are closely related to the passages concerning the "shoot." Haggai 2:20–23 present Zerubbabel no longer as governor like the framing passages of Haggai but as messiah and thus reflect the same messianic agenda as the passages concerning the "shoot."³² Due to this congruence, Hag 2:20–23 are often dated around the same time as the "shoot" passages (cf. Hallaschka 2011, 308; Schott 2019, 48).

2.4 Summary: Zerubbabel and Joshua in Haggai/Zech 1–8

To sum up, throughout the redaction history of Haggai/Zech 1–8, which has been dealt with only through a handful of examples, multifaceted and diverse

---

29 The LXX has the *lectio facilior* here; cf. Hallaschka 2011, 210–211. Thus, the first-person sg. of MT should be retained.
30 "[Es] erscheint [...] übertrieben, hier ein weiteres Indiz für die Übertragung von Königlichem auf das Priesterliche gefunden zu haben."
31 For a royal interpretation of צָנִיף see also Wöhrle 2006, 335; Reventlow 1993, 53.
32 On Hag 2:20–23 see also the contribution by Rückl to the present volume.

concepts of leadership are linked to Zerubbabel and Joshua. As it turned out, these must be evaluated separately regarding both their historical and conceptual significance. Since the present study focuses on a comparison between Haggai/Zech 1–8 and Ezra 1–6, some brief remarks must suffice.

The rebuilding of the temple is the core issue of Haggai/Zech 1–8 that determines all stages of the books' literary formation. Thus, it is possible that the older parts of Haggai/Zech 1–8 preserved some historical data about the restoration of the temple. For example, the mention of a certain Zerubbabel (who does not yet bear the title "governor") as an authorized person in the context of the rebuilding of the temple (cf. Hag 2:4; Zech 4:6–10*) does not bear any signs of an ideological or idealized concept of leadership. Thus, while it seems possible that a certain Zerubbabel was a crucial figure in the process of rebuilding the temple (yet not as governor), Joshua, who is introduced as high priest from the outset in Zech 3, initially (and unsurprisingly) has nothing to do with the building of the temple. Rather, Zech 3 as an "etiology" of the high priest's office defines the contours of the office regarding the high priest's authority and duties in the cultic realm.

At a later stage of composition, the framing passages of Haggai associate Zerubbabel (now as governor) and Joshua for the first time by ascribing them the shared responsibility for the temple building project. As outlined above, this is probably best understood in terms of a programmatic delineation of the office of the governor. Thus, the framing passages in Haggai do not aim primarily to promote a diarchic form of leadership.

Conceptually, the framing passages form the basis for the following redactional processes. The discourse in Zech 3 and Zech 6 (together with Hag 2:20–23), whether the royal high priest or the Davidic messiah is the legitimate leader, marks a high point in the discourse on leadership in Haggai/Zech 1–8. Though it is not easy to ascertain the point of origin of the two stages of this discourse, they should in any case not be dated too early. It is difficult to determine, of course, whether a text reflects actual sociopolitical circumstances or intends to shape a certain ideal. Nevertheless, it is at least conceivable that the two positions in this discourse reflect the circumstances of the Oniad and Hasmonean periods, respectively. At least, as was discussed above, the programmatic high priest texts (both in Zech 3 and in Zech 6) have their closest parallels in Sirach and could thus attest to the increased authority of the high priest in Oniad times. The messianic countermovement, however, has a parallel in texts such as Ps Sol 17, which are admittedly of later origin than the "shoot" passages but which stress in a similar way (with an anti-Hasmonean intent) the Davidic descent of the messiah.

3 Leadership Concepts Related to Zerubbabel and Joshua in Ezra 1–6

As outlined above, in Ezra 1–6 the concepts of leadership related to Zerubbabel and Joshua are less diverse than in Haggai/Zech 1–8. Zerubbabel and Joshua are always mentioned together and in connection with the temple building. However, compared to the manifold but rather clear-cut concepts in Haggai/Zech 1–8, in Ezra 1–6 it is far less obvious which concept(s) of leadership the two figures embody.

Among other things, the matter is complicated by the fact that Ezra 1–3 and Ezra 5–6 provide two chronicles on the rebuilding of the temple that are not completely compatible with each other. Regarding the references to Zerubbabel and Joshua, it is especially the chronology that is awkward: According to Ezra 3, they are involved in laying the temple's foundations during the time of Cyrus, whereas in Ezra 5, like in Haggai/Zech 1–8, they are active during the reign of Darius.

In what follows, Ezra 1–3 and Ezra 5–6 will be examined in turn, with an eye to their underlying concepts of leadership and the role allocated to Zerubbabel and Joshua. The survey begins with Ezra 5–6, which is generally considered to be the older version.

3.1 Ezra 5–6

The view that Ezra 5–6 incorporate a (relatively) old temple building account is widely accepted (cf., e.g., Gunneweg 1985, 31; Kratz 2000, 57; Pakkala 2004, 3; Grätz 2006, 417–419). This older Aramaic chronicle, which comprised at least Ezra 5:6–6:14, can be regarded as a literarily independent, albeit not necessarily coherent, narrative.[33]

Moreover, there is a general consensus that redactional processes can be traced at the margins of the chronicle. The precise literary seams, though, are a controversial issue. However, their identification is highly relevant for identifying developments in concepts of leadership.

At the beginning of the report, conflicting information is given about Tattenai's addressees. According to Ezra 5:10, the elders seem to be responsible for the project, whereas in 5:1–5 Tattenai addresses Zerubbabel and Joshua. The

---

[33] Cf. the suggestion of Kratz (2000, 60), according to which the Cyrus passage in 5:11–6:6 and the Darius correspondence in 6:6–13 stem from different authors.

easiest explanation for this variation would be to consider 5:1–2 as a redactional preamble to the older account, even if this implies that the original introduction to the narrative was lost in the course of the reworking.[34]

Thus, apart from the redaction in vv. 1–2 that harmonizes the chronicle with Haggai/Zech 1–8, the original account presents a depiction of the temple restoration that is totally distinct from the events reported in Haggai/Zech 1–8. The two main differences concern the beginning date of the construction and the persons or parties in charge of it.

According to the Aramaic chronicle, the laying of the foundation stone was carried out during the reign of the Persian king Cyrus by the Persian governor Sheshbazzar.[35] Compared to Haggai/Zech 1–8, the beginning of the temple construction has been back-dated from the time of Darius to the time of Cyrus. While there is no reason to doubt the historical reliability of the depiction of Haggai/Zech 1–8, according to which the temple still laid in ruins during the early reign of Darius, the beginning under Cyrus according to Ezra 5–6 probably aims to show that the salvific time began under Cyrus as the first king of the benevolent Persian dynasty.[36]

Apart from the retrospective on the beginning of the temple restoration under Cyrus and Sheshbazzar in Ezra 5:11–16, the report on the present events is situated in the time of Darius and thus accords with Haggai/Zech 1–8. However, contrary to Haggai/Zech 1–8, where at all redactional stages individuals are responsible for the temple restoration and/or depicted as political leaders (Zerubbabel, Zerubbabel and Joshua as governor and high priest, Joshua as royal high priest, the Davidic "shoot"), in Ezra 5–6 the collective of the elders is the local authority representing the community and corresponding with the Persians. Crucial for the understanding of the conceptual implications of this shift is the alleged emergence of the Council of the Elders in Hellenistic times according to

---

34 Cf., e.g., Rothenbusch 2006, 86. Verse 3 does not suffice as an absolute beginning of a narrative because the pronominal phrase עליהון in v. 3 lacks an antecedent. The original introduction need not have contained more than a short notion about the elders building the temple and, perhaps, a date and a reference to the Persian king Darius. Cf. Heckl 2016, 159.
35 Thus, in this first period of the temple's reconstruction, a Persian official is the person in charge. This correlates with the involvement of Zerubbabel in Haggai/Zech 1–8. Even if Zerubbabel probably did not bear the title "governor" during the early redactional stages of Haggai/Zech 1–8, it is plausible to assume that he was a Persian official. In both instances, the official does not have an autonomous leadership function. The leading role of the governor in Ezra 5–6 either has been adopted as a literary motif from Haggai/Zech 1–8 (which perhaps is not too likely in light of the general originality of Ezra 5–6) or the double record of a Persian official's authority in connection with the temple restoration preserved historically reliable information.
36 The same strategy is applied in Isa 44:19. See also Bortz, 157–159 in the present volume.

Grätz (2006, 420). If this assumption is correct, a composition of the Aramaic chronicle before the Hellenistic period is unlikely.[37] Perhaps the (anachronistic) ascription of authority to the elders in the course of the temple building is simply a way to reflect the impact of this council in the author's own present. However, in Hellenistic times, it does at least also seem possible to evaluate this shift from an individual to a collective form of leadership in terms of a critical agenda against the established individual leadership (most likely that of the high priest).[38]

Regarding the reference to Zerubbabel and Joshua in vv. 1–2, it is not easy to detect the conceptual interests behind the insertion. It introduces the protagonists of Haggai/Zech 1–8 into Ezra 5–6 and obviously draws on the prophetic tradition as a literary model: Like in Haggai/Zech 1–8, Haggai bears the title "prophet," while Zechariah's filiation is given instead. The setting has also been adopted from Haggai/Zech 1–8: the prophets prophesy, which motivates Zerubbabel and Joshua to become active. However, especially in view of the parallels, the differences deserve closer attention. In Ezra 5:1–2, the two prophets operate as a duo. In the prophetic books the references to Zerubbabel and Joshua also extend to both books, but only in the framing passages of Haggai are they addressed together by the prophet. Zechariah mentions Joshua (Zech 3) and Zerubbabel (Zech 4) in the redactional passages of the night visions. However, in these instances neither of them is addressed by the prophet. In Zech 6 the prophet is sent to Joshua with a message, but Zerubbabel is not mentioned. Thus, Ezra 5:1–2 seem to present a summary of the diverse settings of Haggai/Zech 1–8.

However, upon first glance it is difficult to say what the intention behind the assimilation is, what leadership agenda the insertion possibly advances, and why Zerubbabel and Joshua are not given titles. Considering that Ezra 5:1–2 have their closest parallel in the framing passages in Haggai, which provide the titles "governor" and "high priest," this discrepancy might be relevant to the underlying concepts of leadership in Ezra 5:1–2.

Possibly, the key to interpreting the insertion of Zerubbabel and Joshua lies in another blank space regarding the two leaders. It is striking that they are not mentioned again towards the end of the account, especially as Ezra 6:14 again refers to the significant role of the prophets Haggai and Zechariah in the temple restoration. This reduction of the personnel needs to be explained at any rate. One possibility is a diachronic differentiation between Ezra 5:1–2 and Ezra 6:14.

---

[37] Heckl (2016, 167–171) also assumes a composition of the Aramaic chronicle in the Hellenistic period.
[38] Cf. Grätz 2006, 420. On the leadership concepts of the original Aramaic chronicle, see also Bortz in this volume.

Wolfgang Oswald, for example, assumes a linear development. He assumes that Ezra 6:14 had no knowledge of Zerubbabel and Joshua and was thus composed (together with 5:1) earlier than 5:2 (Oswald 2009, 249). In contrast, Grätz considers 5:1–2 to be a unified redaction. Compared to the established combination of Zerubbabel and Joshua with the prophets Haggai and Zechariah, according to Grätz, the mention of the two individuals in conjunction with the elders in 6:14 was odd and unnatural. From this he concludes that 6:14 was written after 5:1–2 (Grätz 2006, 406–408).

However, a closer look reveals that Ezra 6:14 is conspicuous in itself. The verse reports the completion of the construction work by the elders – who are responsible for the temple restoration in the present time according to the Aramaic chronicle – and thus forms a coherent conclusion. However, the verse includes a striking doublet: The proceeding of the construction works is a consequence of the prophesying of Haggai and Zechariah, whereas the completion is connected with the God of Israel and the Persian kings Cyrus, Darius, and Artaxerxes.[39] As it is plausible to name the guarantors at the end of the verse,[40] the easiest way to explain the curious doubling is to consider the reference to the prophets in v. 14aβ to be a later addition. The insertion of the prophets probably can be ascribed to the same redactor who penned 5:1–2 (cf. Rothenbusch 2012, 87–88). Thus, the reduction of the personnel in 6:14 compared to 5:1–2 should not be explained diachronically but instead on the basis of content. The redactor's guiding interest obviously was to mention the prophets – whose activity he had already mentioned through an addition at the beginning of the account – a second time at the end of the account. Thus, in general, an evaluation of this redaction in terms of a prophetic leadership agenda seems plausible. The insertion connects the success of the project (which is predetermined by the older text) to the support of the prophets. The reference in Ezra 5:2 to the "prophets of God" who assist Zerubbabel and Joshua likewise points to a prophetic agenda ("and the prophets of God were with them helping them").

However, in the context of a supposedly prophetic agenda, the function of the reference to Zerubbabel and Joshua in Ezra 5:2 still remains obscure. As the redactor abstains from referring to their titles and mentioning them again at the end of the account, he apparently did not intend to identify them as leaders.

---

39 Cf. also Heckl 2016, 154. The modal relation is expressed in different ways: The elders prosper in building the temple through the prophesying of the prophets (בנבואת חגי נביאה וזכריה בר־עדוא v. 14aβ), but they finish building according to the God of Israel and the Persian kings ([...] מן־טעם אלה ישראל ומטעם v. 14baβ).
40 There is reason to assume that the last link of the enumeration was not a part of the original text. Cf., e.g., Oswald 2009, 249.

Thus, even if the prophetically-motivated initiative of Zerubbabel and Joshua in Ezra 5:1–2 contradicts the older account according to which the elders are responsible for the project, the redactor surely does not intend to supplant the elders with Zerubbabel and Joshua and, hence, to revise or (implicitly) criticize the leadership agenda of the Aramaic chronicle.

If Ezra 5–6 (including the redactional expansions) are seen as a stand-alone text, a second difficulty emerges alongside the conflicting ascription of leadership to the elders on the one hand and to Zerubbabel and Joshua on the other. Without an antecedent, Ezra 5:1 must be understood as an absolute beginning of the construction project. This, however, contradicts the Aramaic chronicle (beginning in Ezra 5:3), according to which the foundations of the temple were laid already during the reign of Cyrus. Thus, since Ezra 5–6 in their received form are problematic both chronologically and conceptually, it is worth considering the possibility that the redaction is related to the preceding chapters that also mention Zerubbabel and Joshua (again with filiations but without titles) at several points. This option would also eliminate the syntactic peculiarities of v. 1 which, as an absolute beginning of a narrative, lacks some crucial information (date, name of the reigning Persian king) and, with *waw* + perfect, appears to be quite clumsy (cf. also Kratz 2000, 56).

In any case, if Ezra 1–4 (or at least parts of these chapters) are regarded as a prequel to Ezra 5–6 added at the time of the redactional expansion of Ezra 5–6, most of the aforementioned problems are solved. Regarding the (complex) redaction history of Ezra 1–4, for the purpose of the present study a very brief outline must suffice. In what follows, Ezra 1–3 are first dealt with independently of Ezra 4, as the view that Ezra 4 is a stand-alone chapter within Ezra 1–6 is widely accepted (cf., e.g., Grätz 2006, 405–406).

3.2 Ezra 1–4

Ezra 1–3 constitute a longer narrative counterpart to the retrospective in Ezra 5:11–16 and present an alternative account of the first phase of the temple restoration (under Cyrus). The chapters include a variety of perspectives on leadership which could, again, hint at a relatively complex literary development. Next to the "Heads of the Ancestral Houses," the priests, and the Levites, who seem to represent the leading groups among the community of returnees according to some parts of the text, other passages also mention Zerubbabel and Joshua.[41]

---

[41] *Nota bene*: The role of the Persians in Ezra 1–3 differs from that in Ezra 5–6 (and Haggai/Zech 1–8). Cyrus only initiates the restoration, but is not involved in the rest of the project. Accordingly, Sheshbazzar does not bear the official Persian title "governor" but is called

Though this is not the place to go into the details of the redaction history of Ezra 1–3, the observation that Zerubbabel and Joshua are – like in Ezra 5–6 – only loosely anchored in the text provides a starting point for the discussion.

Zerubbabel and Joshua appear for the first time within Ezra 1–3 in Ezra 2:2a. The verse lists the names of eleven persons who apparently represent the leaders of the community. This list of leaders, which begins with Zerubbabel and Joshua, is at least dispensable in its context. After Ezra 2:1, which presents a sufficient introduction for the extensive list of returnees that begins in v. 2b, v. 2a starts over with a relative clause referring to those with whom the people returned from the *golah*, which is unexpected and unnecessary information after v. 1aα (ואלה בני המדינה העלים משבי הגולה). It is thus plausible to assume that v. 2a has been inserted between v. 1 and v. 2b (cf., e.g., Kratz 2000, 64; Bortz 2018, 114–115).

For a second time, Zerubbabel and Joshua are mentioned in connection with the construction of the altar for the burnt offerings in Ezra 3:2. Again, there is evidence that the building of the altar has been inserted into the surrounding context. First, the passage is suspicious insofar as it "anticipates the temple foundation in 3:8 ff. in many respects" (Kratz 2000, 64)[42] though by stressing the offerings sets a distinct focus. Second, beyond Ezra 3:1–7 the building of the altar plays no role and, thus, the passage appears to be somehow isolated. Therefore, the entire passage Ezra 3:1–7 is sometimes considered a later addition compared to Ezra 3:8–13 (cf. Kratz 2000, 64–65).[43] However, it seems plausible to assume with Bortz an alternative diachronic solution according to which Ezra 3:6–7 formed the original introduction to the following temple building account and only 3:1–5 were prefixed to it (Bortz 2018, 156). Verse 6 explicitly points to the fact that the foundations of the temple have not been laid yet. The instruction to the construction workers connects seamlessly to this. The focus is on the relevance of the cult that is revived immediately after the arrival in Jerusalem and even before the beginning of the temple's restoration (as is explicitly mentioned). Thus, the original text implies that the former altar for the burnt offerings was simply reused after the exile. Perhaps this idea bothered the redactor,

---

"prince of Judah" (הנשיא ליהודה, Ezra 1:8). According to Ezek 40–48, this title is compatible with the hierocracy and, thus, might have a sacral meaning (Grätz 2006, 417). It fits the concept that, in the view of Ezra 1–3, the funding of the restoration is not provided by the Persians but by the community itself (Ezra 2:68–69).

42 "[...] nimmt in vielem die Tempelgründung von 3,8 ff vorweg."

43 Possibly it is worth considering further redactional reworkings within Ezra 3:1–7. Cf., e.g., the discussion in Bortz 2018, 155–156 about the redactional nature of vv. 4–5. However, this cannot be pursued further here.

who considered the altar to be desecrated and thus inserted the account of the building of the (new) altar before the beginning of the offerings.

For the third and last time within Ezra 1–3, Zerubbabel and Joshua are mentioned in connection with the beginning of the temple restoration in Ezra 3:8. Again, the literary integrity of the verse is dubious. The long sequence of subjects who are said to install the Levites supervising the reconstruction works raises suspicion although it is generally considered to be a literary unity. However, at least a slight tension regarding the following account can be noticed: The reference to Zerubbabel and Joshua in a prominent position at the beginning of the sequence does not fit the collective action reported later on: According to v. 10, the foundations were laid by anonymous "builders." Furthermore, regarding chronology, it is striking that Zerubbabel and Joshua are active during the time of Cyrus, while according to Haggai/Zech 1–8 and Ezra 5–6 their appearance is limited to the time of Darius.[44]

Thus, if none of the passages mentioning Zerubbabel and Joshua belong to the original text, then two basic stages of composition can be identified in Ezra 1–3. In the original account, the ideal of the leadership of the people as a whole is dominant. In contrast to Ezra 5–6, the elders play no role in Ezra 1–3. The impact of the Persians has also been minimized. Instead, the restoration of the temple is presented as a collective project of the returnees. Hence, Ezra 1–3 develop the ideal of an autonomous temple community. The exiles return as a "people of God" led by priests, Levites, and the "Heads of the Ancestral Houses" and begin with the restoration of the temple.

Zerubbabel and Joshua were added later into the account of Ezra 1–3. Unsurprisingly, they are named among the heads of the community: They are already among the leaders of the returnees, they are responsible for building the altar for burnt offerings and, finally, are involved in the earliest events of the temple restoration.

However, at this stage of textual development, the redactionally expanded Aramaic chronicle in Ezra 5–6 does not connect organically to Ezra 1–3. According to Ezra 1–3, Zerubbabel and Joshua are active during the first phase of the restoration (under Cyrus), while according to Ezra 5–6 they appear on the scene during the reign of Darius, that is, the second phase of the restoration. Of course, the sequence of Ezra 1–3 and Ezra 5–6 can be interpreted as two separate appearances. Hence, it does not necessarily result in a chronological tension. However, to move directly from Ezra 1–3 to Ezra 5–6 does not fill the chronologi-

---

44 The date in Ezra 3:1 certainly refers to the last-mentioned date (which is the first year of Cyrus according to Ezra 1:1). For an alternative interpretation, see Bortz 2018, 150, 174. For a critical evaluation of this view, see below.

cal gap between Cyrus and Darius *narratively*. The date in Ezra 3:1 mentions only the month in which the following events took place but not the exact year. Though the date is admittedly vague, the only reasonable option is probably to relate it to the explicit date in Ezra 1:1, the first year of the Persian king Cyrus. Bortz (2018, 150) instead suggests an interpretation in terms of an "internal relative chronology,"[45] which (without marking the shift) refers to the time of Darius instead of Cyrus. Even if one would consider such an implicit shift possible, the dating of the events reported in Ezra 1–3 to the time of Darius certainly becomes problematic in light of Ezra 4. Ezra 4 closes the narrative gap between Cyrus and Darius through a disruption of the construction work. Hence, the author of Ezra 4 clearly regarded the events reported in Ezra 1–3 as taking place in the time of Cyrus.

For the interpretation of the composition of Ezra 1–6, it is crucial to observe that only this disruption of the construction works conceptualized in Ezra 4 produces a reasonable narrative between Ezra 1–3 and Ezra 5–6 in their present shape. According to Ezra 3, Zerubbabel and Joshua are involved in laying the foundations of the temple during the reign of Cyrus; Ezra 5–6 report (in accordance with Haggai/Zech 1–8) their activity during the reign of Darius. The disruption in Ezra 4 allows Ezra 5:1–2 to be interpreted as a *resumption* of the construction work. In this context, Ezra 4:24 (Aramaic) forms a transition to the Aramaic chronicle by explicitly stating that the disruption lasted until the time of Darius.[46]

Moreover, if Ezra 4:24 is interpreted as belonging with Ezra 5:1–2 from the outset, this solves the aforementioned syntactic problems. Ezra 4:24 provides a date and the name of the Persian king and thus functions as a sufficient introduction to a narrative. Hence, it seems likely that the most basic material in Ezra 4 and the redaction in Ezra 5–6 go back to the same author. Furthermore, it is plausible to ascribe the redactional parts which introduce Zerubbabel and Joshua into the account of Ezra 1–3 to the same hand.[47]

---

[45] "[...] interne relative Chronologie."

[46] Ezra 4:5 and 4:24 are doublets. Moreover, between 4:4 and 4:5 there is a tension as the verses provide different explanations for the disruption of the construction work. Perhaps v. 5 is the beginning of an insertion and originally v. 24 followed directly upon v. 4 (this would leave vv. 1–4, 24 as the basic layer of Ezra 4). The bilingualism of the supposed basic layer is conspicuous but would then be due to the fact that the author composed Ezra 4:24; 5:1–2 as a new introduction to the Aramaic chronicle.

[47] Beyond the limits of this paper is the question of the literary-historical relationship between Ezra 1–3 and Ezra 5–6 before the respective redaction. However, nothing precludes the possibility that Ezra 1–3 were composed as a literary preamble to Ezra 5–6 presenting (as outlined above) an alternative view of the early phase of the temple's restoration.

The comprehensive redaction in Ezra 1–6 foregrounds the fact that the restoration proceeded in two phases. The restoration as a two-step process was already predetermined by the original Aramaic chronicle, where the present events take place during the reign of Darius but the account includes a retrospect of the beginnings of the restoration under Cyrus in Ezra 5:11–16. While the Aramaic chronicle portrays two successive phases of construction that are unrelated to each other in terms of their concepts of leadership, the redaction redetermines the relation between them. It adjusts the leadership personnel (as far as possible) presumably in order to contrast the two phases. While the first phase in the time of Cyrus unsuccessfully ends in Ezra 4:4, the second phase, which ultimately results in the successful completion of the reconstruction under Darius, begins with Ezra 4:24.

Against the background of the enemies' successful offensive in Ezra 4, which temporarily disrupts the construction works, the investigation of Tattenai in Ezra 5 must appear as a critical moment. However, Ezra 5:2 marks the beginning of a new phase and slightly alters the conditions, which turns out to be decisive in the end: This time, the project is led by the prophets Haggai and Zechariah and, furthermore, Zerubbabel and Joshua have the support of the "prophets of God." As becomes clear by the insertion of the prophets in Ezra 6:14, *this* is the actual reason for the success.

Therefore, on the one hand, the redaction transfers the successful concept from Haggai/Zech 1–8 to Ezra 1–6, on the other hand, however, it sets a clearly distinct focus. In this context, the prominent leaders Zerubbabel and Joshua, whose authority is debated on various redactional layers within the prophetic books, are applied as a mere means to an end. Their insertion in Ezra 1–3 and Ezra 5–6 has the function to allow for a direct comparison of the two phases of the temple's reconstruction: The leaders known from Haggai/Zech 1–8 alone cannot induce a successful completion of the construction works. Rather, for this it needs prophetic guidance and support. Hence, what at first sight seems like an adjustment to the leadership concept of Haggai/Zech 1–8 turns out to be a gentle correction of it (or at least an alternative to it). The focus is not on the two individual leaders like in Haggai/Zech 1–8 (the omission of titles throughout Ezra 1–6 fit this agenda very well) but on the involvement of the prophets.

3.3 Summary: Leadership Concepts in Ezra 1–6

Ezra 1–6 include diverse concepts of leadership. Like in Haggai/Zech 1–8 they are sparked off by the question of who was responsible for the restoration of the temple or who represented the community during this time. Surprisingly, apart from this formal commonality, the concepts of leadership in Ezra 1–6 do not have anything in common with Haggai/Zech 1–8.

According to the Aramaic chronicle in Ezra 5–6, the restoration of the temple was initiated by the Persian king and his governor. Although the back-dating of the events to the time of Cyrus is surely idealized, the initiation of the project by the Persians can perhaps be considered historically plausible. During the narrative present (i.e., the reign of Darius), however, the elders function as representatives of the community and are responsible for the temple building. Although it might reflect the oldest part of Ezra 1–6, the Aramaic chronicle probably stems from the Hellenistic period.

Ezra 1–3 seem to react to this restoration agenda of Ezra 5–6 by presenting an alternative (probably in some way critical) report on the events. Compared to Ezra 5–6, the role of the Persians is minimized and the elders play no role at all. The restoration is presented as a project initiated and taken responsibility for by the collective of the community of returnees (with priests and Levites as *primus inter pares* but without individual leaders). This might at least indirectly reflect some kind of a priestly agenda. However, the passage is difficult to date. It fits nearly every phase in the Hellenistic period.

By introducing Zerubbabel and Joshua into Ezra 1–3 and Zerubbabel, Joshua, Haggai, and Zechariah into Ezra 5–6 (and at the same time inserting a basic version of Ezra 4 between the two accounts), a redactor linked Ezra 1–6 to the restoration account in Haggai/Zech 1–8. At this stage, Ezra 5–6 correspond to the events in Haggai/Zech 1–8. However, since Ezra 1–3 preface this with a first, unsuccessful attempt to rebuild the temple under the guidance of Zerubbabel and Joshua, Ezra 1–6 obtain a leadership agenda *sui generis*: A fresh attempt during the reign of Darius finally leads to the completion of the reconstruction due to prophetic support (which does not generally contradict Haggai/Zech 1–8 but sets a significantly distinct focus). Again, since the reworking does not show knowledge of the advanced redactional stages of Haggai/Zech 1–8, it is difficult to specify its date of origin.

4 Conclusion: Leadership Concepts in Haggai/Zech 1–8 and Ezra 1–6: A Comparative Approach

Everything in Haggai/Zech 1–8 and Ezra 1–6 revolves around the restoration of the temple, which can be regarded as "the cornerstone of postexilic Judah" (Oswald 2009, 249).[48] Hence, it does not come as a surprise that in both texts also the leadership concepts are developed against the background of this historic event. This is the common ground from which Haggai/Zech 1–8 and Ezra 1–6, largely independently of each other, begin on a narrative level. In Haggai/Zech 1–8, the formation of the manifold concepts of leadership is based on the information that a certain Zerubbabel played a crucial role in the restoration of the temple (Hag 2:4; Zech 4:6–10*) and that Joshua was high priest at that time (Zech 3*). By all means, this information could be reliable.[49] However, with regard to an evaluation of the leadership concepts, this is a rather irrelevant aspect. Zerubbabel is neither governor nor a messianic figure; Joshua has nothing to do with the restoration of the temple at all.

The actual leadership debate begins with the framing passages in Hag 1:1, 14; 2:2, which state that Zerubbabel (who has now been made governor of Yehud) and the high priest Joshua share responsibility for the rebuilding of the temple. As was argued above, this can best be understood in terms of an agenda promulgating the governor as a Yehudite political leader. Thus, it reflects an advanced stage of redaction within Haggai/Zech 1–8 and cannot be considered "historical." However, even if a diarchy of Zerubbabel and Joshua cannot be deduced from Haggai/Zech 1–8, this by no means excludes the possibility that the juxtaposition of governor and high priest generally reflects historical conditions at the time of this redaction, which is probably the late Persian period (cf. the Elephantine correspondence and the Yehud coinage).

While further ideas of leadership were attached to the two individual leaders in the course of the redaction history of Haggai/Zech 1–8 (the high priest as a royal leader; the Davidic messiah as a literary counteroffensive to fend off the priestly claim to leadership), the notions of leadership in Ezra 1–6 at first develop (and are debated) independently of the two prominent leaders from Haggai/Zech 1–8. According to the older (but presumably already Hellenistic) Aramaic chronicle in Ezra 5–6, the elders are the local leaders during the present time (which is the second phase of the temple restoration during the reign of Darius), while originally the Persians initiated the project (under Cyrus). Ezra 1–3 react to this account and present an alternative view on the first phase of the restora-

---

48 "[...] den einen Eckpfeiler des nachexilischen Juda."
49 As this is the only mention of the two figures (apart from Ezra 1–6, which are literarily dependent on Haggai/Zech 1–8) this assumption cannot be validated. However, there is no reason to doubt the historicity of the two individuals and the functions ascribed to them in the older parts of Haggai/Zech 1–8, which do not yet show any signs of an idealization. Depending on when the office of high priest emerged (during the restoration of the temple or, perhaps more likely, directly after it), Joshua's function could have slightly been back-dated.

tion (under Cyrus) which is only retrospectively looked at in Ezra 5. Ezra 1–3 focus on the returnees as a collective entity, who are led by the "Heads of the Ancestral Houses," priests, and Levites, and initiated the restoration of the temple on their own.

Zerubbabel and Joshua are introduced into Ezra 1–6 only at an advanced stage of composition. The redaction which inserts them clearly depends upon Haggai/Zech 1–8. Thus, their appearance in Ezra 1–6 cannot be cited as evidence for their involvement in the restoration of the temple, either. Perhaps the redactor was aware of the fact that the passages in Haggai that he referred to did not convey reliable information about the conditions during the restoration of the temple. In any case, he does not seem to adapt the account in Ezra 1–6 to historical events (or what he thought to be historical). Rather, he draws on the older prophetic tradition in order to establish a totally distinct concept of leadership. Unlike in Haggai/Zech 1–8, in Ezra 1–6 the focus is not (and not even implicitly) on characterizing Zerubbabel and Joshua as leaders. Instead, their role as leading figures in the temple restoration is employed as a means of advancing a prophetic agenda. Hence, even where the setting of Haggai/Zech 1–8 is transferred to Ezra 1–6, the latter forged its own path with regard to leadership and established an alternative view of the circumstances that led to the completion of the temple building, which, up to this point, is not covered by Haggai/Zech 1–8 or Ezra 1–6 at all: The success was not due to the involvement of Zerubbabel and Joshua but to the guidance and support of the prophets.

In the end, hardly anything can be deduced from Haggai/Zech 1–8 and Ezra 1–6 regarding the historical situation during the time of the temple's restoration. Instead, both texts utilize the temple restoration as a crucial event to debate issues of leadership and authority during the postexilic period. By tying contemporary ideals to this historic event, for centuries (the respective texts probably cover a time span from the late Persian period to the Oniad or even Hasmonean periods) the question "Who was responsible for the temple's restoration?" becomes a cipher for the question "Who is the legitimate leader of the community?" It is no surprise that Zerubbabel and Joshua – who are deeply rooted in the prophetic tradition as historical figures – play a crucial role in this context. Time and again, they became objects of an ideologically shaped presentation of the historic events in light of the present situation, either as representatives of different leadership agendas (the governor as an indigenous political leader, royal high priest, messiah) or as a means to an end for promoting a prophetic agenda.

Bibliography

Achenbach, Reinhard. 2010. "Satrapie, Medinah und lokale Hierokratie: Zum Einfluss der Statthalter der Achämenidenzeit auf Tempelwirtschaft und Tempelordnungen." *ZAR* 16:105–144.
Altmann, Peter. 2016. *Economics in Persian-Period Biblical Texts*. FAT 109. Tübingen: Mohr Siebeck.
Barag, Dan. 1985. "Some Notes on a Silver Coin of Johanan the High Priest." *BA* 48:166–168.
Barag, Dan. 1986. "A Silver Coin of Yohanan the High Priest and the Coinage of Judea in the Fourth Century B.C." *INJ* 9:4–21.
Begrich, Joachim. 1964. "Die priesterliche Tora." In *Gesammelte Studien zum Alten Testament*, 232–260. TB 21. Munich: Kaiser.
Bortz, Anna M. 2018. *Identität und Kontinuität: Form und Funktion der Rückkehrerliste Esr 2*. BZAW 512. Berlin and Boston: de Gruyter.
Cataldo, Jeremiah W. 2009. *A Theocratic Yehud? Issues of Government in a Persian Province*. LHBOTS 498. London and New York: T&T Clark.
Delkurt, Holger. 2000. *Sacharjas Nachtgesichte: Zur Aufnahme und Abwandlung prophetischer Traditionen*. BZAW 302. Berlin: de Gruyter.
Gitler, Haim, and Catharine Lorber. 2008. "A New Chronology for the Yehizkijah coins of Yehud." *Schweizerische numismatische Rundschau* 87:61–82.
Granerød, Gard. 2016. *Dimensions of Yahwism in the Persian Period: Studies in the Religion and Society of the Judean Community at Elephantine*. BZAW 488. Berlin and Boston: de Gruyter.
Grätz, Sebastian. 2006. "Die Aramäische Chronik des Esrabuches und die Rolle der Ältesten in Esr 5–6*." *ZAW* 118:405–422.
Gunneweg, Antonius H. J. 1985. *Esra: Mit einer Zeittafel von A. Jepsen*. KAT XIX/1. Gütersloh: Gütersloher Verlagshaus Gerd Mohn.
Hallaschka, Martin. 2011. *Haggai und Sacharja 1–8: Eine redaktionsgeschichtliche Untersuchung*. BZAW 411. Berlin and New York: de Gruyter.
Hanhart, Robert. 1998. *Sacharja 1:1–8:23*. Dodekapropheton 7/1. BK.AT XIV/7.1. Neukirchen-Vluyn: Neukirchener Verlag.
Heckl, Raik. 2016. *Neuanfang und Kontinuität in Jerusalem*. FAT 104. Tübingen: Mohr Siebeck.
Howgego, Christopher. 1995. *Ancient History from Coins*. London and New York: Routledge.
Joisten-Pruschke, Anke. 2008. *Das religiöse Leben der Juden von Elephantine in der Achämenidenzeit*. Göttinger Orientforschungen III. Reihe: Iranica, Neue Folge 2. Wiesbaden: Harrassowitz Verlag.
Kottsieper, Ingo. 2002. "Die Religionspolitik der Achämeniden und die Juden von Elephantine." In *Religion und Religionskontakte im Zeitalter der Achämeniden*, edited by Reinhard G. Kratz, 150–178. Gütersloh: Gütersloher Verlagshaus.
Kratz, Reinhard G. 2000. *Die Komposition der erzählenden Bücher des Alten Testaments: Grundwissen der Bibelkritik*. UTB 2157. Göttingen: Vandenhoeck & Ruprecht.
Kratz, Reinhard G. 2004a. "Serubbabel und Joschua." In *Das Judentum im Zeitalter des Zweiten Tempels*, edited by Reinhard G. Kratz, 79–92. FAT 42. Tübingen: Mohr Siebeck.
Kratz, Reinhard G. 2004b. "Statthalter, Hohepriester und Schreiber im perserzeitlichen Jehud." In *Das Judentum im Zeitalter des Zweiten Tempels*, edited by Reinhard G. Kratz, 93–119. FAT 42. Tübingen: Mohr Siebeck.

Lemaire, André. 2002. "Das Achämenidische Juda und seine Nachbarn im Lichte der Epigraphie." In *Religion und Religionskontakte im Zeitalter der Achämeniden*, edited by Reinhard G. Kratz, 210–230. Gütersloh: Gütersloher Verlagshaus.

Lemaire, André. 2007. "Administration in Fourth-Century Judah in Light of Epigraphy and Numismatics." In *Judah and the Judeans in the Fourth Century B.C.E.*, edited by Oded Lipschits, Gary Knoppers, and Rainer Albertz, 53–74. Winona Lake: Eisenbrauns.

Lipschits, Oded, and Vanderhooft, David S. 2011. *Yehud Stamp Impressions: A Corpus of Inscribed Impressions from the Persian and Hellenistic Periods in Judah*. Winona Lake: Eisenbrauns.

Mildenberg, Leo. 1979. "Yehud: A Preliminary Study of the Local Provincial Coinage of Judea." In *Greek Numismatics and Archaeology*, edited by Otto Mørkholm and Nancy Waggoner, 183–196. Wetteren: NR.

Mildenberg, Leo. 1988. "Yəhūd-Münzen." In *Palästina in vorhellenistischer Zeit*, edited by Helga Weippert, 719–728. Handbuch der Archäologie. Vorderasien II/I. Munich: C. H. Beck.

Mildenberg, Leo. 1996. "yĕhūd und šmryn: Über das Geld der persischen Provinzen Juda und Samaria im 4. Jahrhundert." In *Geschichte – Tradition – Reflexion: 1. Judentum*, edited by Peter Schäfer, 119–146. Tübingen: Mohr Siebeck.

Mildenberg, Leo. 2000. "Über die Münzbildnisse in Palästina und Nordwestarabien zur Perserzeit." In *Images as Media: Sources for the Cultural History of the Near East and the Eastern Mediterranean: 1st Millenium BCE*, edited by Christoph Uehlinger, 375–391. OBO 175. Göttingen and Fribourg: Vandenhoeck & Ruprecht and University Press.

Niehr, Herbert. 1987. *Rechtsprechung in Israel: Untersuchungen zur Geschichte der Gerichtsorganisation im Alten Testament*. SBS 130. Stuttgart: Katholisches Bibelwerk.

Oswald, Wolfgang. 2009. *Staatstheorie im Alten Israel: Der politische Diskurs im Pentateuch und in den Geschichtsbüchern des Alten Testaments*. Stuttgart: Kohlhammer.

Pakkala, Juha. 2004. *Ezra the Scribe: The Development of Ezra 7–10 and Nehemiah 8*. BZAW 347. Berlin and New York: de Gruyter.

Porten, Bezalel. 1996. *The Elephantine Papyri in English: Three Millenia of Cross-Cultural Continuity and Change*. DMOA 22. Leiden, New York, and Cologne: Brill.

Rohrmoser, Angela. 2014. *Götter, Tempel und Kult der Judäo-Aramäer von Elephantine: Archäologische und schriftliche Zeugnisse aus dem perserzeitlichen Ägypten*. AOAT 396. Münster: Ugarit-Verlag.

Rothenbusch, Ralf. 2012. *"Abgesondert zur Tora Gottes hin": Ethnisch-religiöse Identitäten im Esra/Nehemiabuch*. HBS 70. Freiburg i. Br.: Herder.

Pola, Thomas. 2003. *Das Priestertum bei Sacharja*. FAT 35. Tübingen: Mohr Siebeck.

Reventlow, Henning Graf. 1993. *Die Propheten Haggai, Sacharja und Maleachi*. ATD 25,2. 9th edition. Göttingen: Vandenhoeck & Ruprecht.

Schaper, Joachim. 1995. "The Jerusalem Temple as an Instrument of the Achaemenid Fiscal Administration." *VT* 45:528–539.

Schaper, Joachim. 2000. *Priester und Leviten im achämenidischen Juda: Studien zur Kult- und Sozialgeschichte Israels in persischer Zeit*. FAT 31. Tübingen: Mohr Siebeck.

Schott, Martin. 2019. *Sacharja 9–14: Eine kompositionsgeschichtliche Analyse*. BZAW 521. Berlin and Boston: de Gruyter.

Schöttler, Heinz-Günther. 1987. *Gott inmitten seines Volkes: Die Neuordnung des Gottesvolkes nach Sacharja 1–6*. TThSt 43. Trier: Paulinus Verlag.

Schulz, Sarah. Forthcoming. *Joschua und Melchisedek. Studien zur Entwicklung des Jerusalemer Hohepriesteramtes vom 6. Jahrhundert v. Chr. bis zum 2. Jahrhundert v. Chr.* Habilitation thesis. Friedrich-Alexander-Universität Erlangen-Nuremberg.

Spaer, Arnold. 1986. "Jaddua the High Priest?" *INJ* 9:1–3.
Tiemeyer, Lena-Sofia. 2006. *Priestly Rites and Prophetic Rage: Post-Exilic Prophetic Critique of the Priesthood*. FAT II/19. Tübingen: Mohr Siebeck.
VanderKam, James C. 1991. "Jewish High Priests of the Persian Period: Is the List Complete?" In *Priesthood and Cult in Ancient Israel*, edited by Gary Anderson and Saul Olyan, 67–91. JSOT.S 125. Sheffield: Sheffield University Press.
Wellhausen, Julius. 1963. *Die Kleinen Propheten: Übersetzt und erklärt*. 4th edition. Berlin: de Gruyter.
Wiesehöfer, Josef. 2007. "The Achaemenid Empire in the Fourth Century B.C.E.: A Period of Decline?" In *Judah and the Judeans in the Fourth Century B.C.E.*, edited by Oded Lipschits, Gary Knoppers, and Rainer Albertz, 11–30. Winona Lake: Eisenbrauns.
Wiesehöfer, Josef. 2011. "Achaemenid Rule and its Impact on Yehud." In *Texts, Contexts and Readings in Postexilic Literature: Explorations into Historiography and Identity Negotiation in Hebrew Bible and Related Texts*, edited by Louis C. Jonker, 172–185. FAT II 53. Tübingen: Mohr Siebeck.
Wöhrle, Jakob. 2006. *Die frühen Sammlungen des Zwölfprophetenbuches: Entstehung und Komposition*. BZAW 360. Berlin and New York: de Gruyter.
Wolff, Hans Walter. 1991. *Haggai*. Vol. 6, *Dodekapropheton*. 2nd edition. BK XIV 6. Neukirchen-Vluyn: Neukirchener Verlag.

Katharina Pyschny
Concepts of Prophetic Leadership in Chronicles and Their Relation to Prophetic Literature

1 Introduction

This volume's section on chronistic literature already provided important insights into the variety and complexity of concepts of leadership in the book of Chronicles. While those essays focus predominantly on royal and priestly figures as well as other leaders like judges, officers, and elders, the following remarks will concentrate instead on concepts of prophetic leadership in Chronicles and their relation to prophetic literature. In doing so, this essay seeks to provide some synthetic observations instead on concepts of leadership in chronistic and prophetic literature.

In his article "The Chronicler and the Prophets: Who Were His Authoritative Sources?", Louis Jonker makes a crucial observation:

> It is an ambiguous picture of prophecy that we get from Chronicles: instead on the one hand, it seems that the phenomenon of prophecy was held in high esteem by the Chronicler, who draws on prophetic voices every now and then in his reconstructions of the past. But on the other hand, our expectations of numerous allusions to and quotations from the known prophetic writings are not met by Chronicles (Jonker 2011, 145–146).

Among other aspects, it is this "ambiguous picture of prophecy" that prompted several important studies[1] on prophets in Chronicles in the last two decades.[2] While prior scholarship on postexilic prophecy has often linked the Babylonian

---

[1] See esp. Amit 2006; Beentjes 2008; 2015; Ben Zvi 2013; Gerstenberger 2004; Jonker 2011; Kegler 1993; Knoppers 2010; Person 2013; Schniedewind 1995; 1997; Warhurst 2011. On prophetic guardianship in Chronicles, see Ben Zvi 2016 and his contribution in the present volume.

[2] Ben Zvi 2013, 168 offers a list of the most important issues dealt with in this substantial corpus of recent studies: "(1) the role and status of historical prophets at the time of the author(s) of Chronicles, including the question of whether ('classical') prophecy had ceased at that time, or even what a statement such as this may mean; (2) Chronicles' representations of prophets as 'preachers' and/or 'historians'; (3) the sources that the author(s) of Chronicles may have used or purposefully ignored when writing about prophets and prophecy; (4) the question of who is a prophet in Chronicles, and the related issues of 'ad hoc' or 'temporary' prophets, Levitical singers as prophets, and whether divinely inspired messengers were conceptually understood as 'prophets'; (5) prophecy and cult; and (6) the status of prophetic utterances vis à vis Mosaic Torah and the general question of what was authoritative for Chronicles."

exile and the Persian period with some sort of decline, demise, or even the end of prophecy,³ current research highlights the continuity in prophecy throughout history,⁴ particularly regarding the postexilic period, as evidenced by contemporary prophetic compositions such as Joel, Jonah, Haggai, Zechariah, and Malachi. Thus, instead of assuming an "end" of prophecy, it is more accurate to recognize new developments – or, more precisely, transformations – of "traditional" or "classical" prophecy during the postexilic period.⁵ Being on the one hand *"an interpretation of classical prophecy* and, on the other hand, *a reflection of post-exilic prophecy itself"* (Schniedewind 1997, 210, emphasis original),⁶ Chronicles can be considered one, but not the only, important source for retracing these processes of transformation and their relationship to (earlier and contemporary) prophetic literature.

Before turning to the issue at hand, some short remarks are in order concerning the composition of Chronicles. First, although it seems plausible that Chronicles has been rewritten and expanded in the course of its transmission, there is no reason to assume substantial successive redactions.⁷ Thus, the following study refrains from literary or redaction criticism, assuming that the scope of the original composition of Chronicles was more or less the same as that of its received form. Second, even though there are also good arguments for a later date, I situate the origins of Chronicles in the late Persian or early Hellenistic period, that is, the 4th or 3rd century BCE (cf. Knoppers 2004, 101–117). Third, I consider Chronicles a sophisticated retelling or rewriting of Samuel–Kings.⁸ It is a historiographic work describing the monarchic period of ancient

---

3 For a discussion of the different views and arguments concerning postexilic prophecy, see Schniedewind 1997, 205–210.
4 To put it frankly with Blenkinsopp 1996, 195: "A great deal of misunderstanding has arisen from the once commonly accepted assumption that for all practical purposes prophecy came to an end with the Babylonian exile."
5 Just to name one example, see Blenkinsopp 2004, 199: "The 'end of prophecy' thesis cannot therefore be explained as an account of what actually happened to prophecy, but it is itself a historical datum calling for an explanation in the context of wide-ranging political and social changes in the late biblical period." See also Knoppers 2004, 404–405.
6 Even though there are subtle differences between the aforementioned studies on prophets and prophecy in Chronicles, they all conclude that the Chronicler's literary portrayal of prophets is based on the notion of traditional or classical prophecy in Samuel–Kings and reflects a postexilic understanding of prophecy. This consensus was recently challenged by Person 2013, 187, who considers "the Deuteronomic History and the book of Chronicles […] as contemporary historiographies that were produced by different scribal guilds that nevertheless have a common institutional ancestor in the Deuteronomic school of the Babylonian exile."
7 For a general discussion of this issue, see Steins 2016b, 322–324.
8 As was convincingly shown by Nihan 2013, the Chronicler's version of Samuel–Kings was not identical to the Masoretic text of these books.

Israel but written at a time when the monarchy no longer existed. This new context influenced Chronicles' narrative compositions, particularly its portrayal of prophecy and prophets. In addition, its literary scope is characterized by a productive use of biblical traditions which include not only Samuel–Kings, but also a variety of Pentateuchal and prophetic traditions. This twofold distinct character of Chronicles, being a recontextualization and an interpretation of history on the one hand and oscillating between tradition and innovation on the other, will prove to be a decisive driving force for transformations of authority and leadership.

2 Concepts of Prophetic Leadership in Chronicles

In light of the aforementioned recent studies, this essay will not rehearse the current state of scholarship on prophets and prophecy in Chronicles. Instead, the following remarks will stress some important aspects of prophetic leadership in particular by focusing on two guiding questions: How does Chronicles construe prophetic leadership? What are the specific roles and tasks of prophetic leaders and how do they relate to other figures of mediation? These questions will be approached with a rather broad understanding of prophecy that is not restricted to prophetic phenomena marked by the use of specific titles[9] or verbs. Instead, prophecy is understood as a "form of religious mediation, or divination, the purpose of which is to transmit allegedly divine knowledge to human society" (Nissinen 2013, 11).[10] As such, prophecy is not only a cross-cultural phenomenon, but a socially and historically contingent one when it comes to its phenotypes and descriptions (see Nissinen 2013; Wetter 2015). The latter holds particularly true for the portrayal of prophets:

> As socioreligious and political agents, people called prophets execute distinctive and culture-specific roles within the social and ideological structure, identity, and narrative of any given society depending on the societal interpretation and appreciation of different types of religious mediation (Nissinen 2013, 11–12).

---

9 See Blenkinsopp 2001, 180: "The designation *nābî'* ("prophet") is difficult to pin down since it underwent a semantic development in the post-destruction period, covering a wide range of activities and roles including preaching, the composition and rendition of liturgical music historiography, and the interpretation of earlier prophecy."
10 See also the approach of Knoppers 2014, 398 who understands prophecy "as speaking on behalf of the divine realm or communicating the will of God in a given setting."

2.1 Portrayal of Prophetic Leaders

The chronistic presentation of the monarchic period knows a remarkable variety of prophets and prophetic or inspired figures. While some of them are well known from other biblical texts,[11] others are distinctive to Chronicles.[12] In addition, the portrayal of the ones known from other biblical writings differs significantly from their earlier literary contexts in some cases.[13]

In its depiction of prophetic figures, Chronicles shows little interest in the biography or the private lives of prophets. The lack of prophetic commissioning narratives and the references to many anonymous prophets reinforces this observation. In addition, Chronicles usually does not refer to prophetic schools or professional prophetic training. Also, the prophet's belonging to a certain tribe of Israel or a prophetic bloodline within a tribal division is normally not mentioned. Information about a prophet's tribe is only provided when that prophetic figure is a Levite, such as Jahaziel (2 Chr 20:14–20). Furthermore, with the exception of Hanani and Jehu (2 Chr 16:7–10; 19:1–3; 20:34), Chronicles does not refer to prophecy in successive generations. All of these observations suggest that prophets are first and foremost perceived in their role as mediators of God's word and are "his messengers" (מלאכיו, 2 Chr 36:15). To put it pointedly: "The medium is not the message; the message is the message" (Knoppers 2014, 400). Perhaps this almost radical focus on communicating God's message to the king or the people is exactly the reason why prophets in Chronicles – in contrast to Elijah and Elisha in the book of Kings – do not initiate miracles and do not perform signs, wonders, or other forms of symbolic actions.

Chronicles refers to prophets using a wide spectrum of prophetic titles, including נביא ("prophet"),[14] ראה ("seer"),[15] and חזה ("visionary").[16] Most of the

---

11 In general, almost every prophet appearing in Samuel–Kings is mentioned in Chronicles in one way or another. Just to name a few: Nathan (2 Sam 7:1–16 // 1 Chr 17:1–15), Gad (2 Sam 24:11–13, 18–19 // 1 Chr 21:9–13, 18–19), Ahijah the Shilonite (1 Kgs 15:29 // 2 Chr 10:15), Shemaiah (1 Kgs 12:21–24 // 2 Chr 11:2–4), Micaiah (1 Kgs 22:8–28 // 2 Chr 18:4–27), and Hulda (2 Kgs 22:14–20 // 2 Chr 34:22–28).
12 See, for instance, Azariah (2 Chr 15:17), Hanani (2 Chr 16:7–10), Jehu (2 Chr 19:2–3), various anonymous prophets and men of God (2 Chr 34:19; 25:7–9, 15–16; 33:10; 36:15–16), and Oded, a northern prophet (2 Chr 28:9–11).
13 See, for example, Samuel (1 Chr 6:12; 9:22; 11:3; 26:28; 29:29; 2 Chr 35:18), Nathan (1 Chr 29:29; 2 Chr 9:29; 29:25); Gad (1 Chr 29:29; 2 Chr 29:25), Ahijah the Shilonite (2 Chr 9:29), Shemaiah (2 Chr 12:5), and Elijah (2 Chr 21:12).
14 This title is used for Nathan (1 Chr 17:1; 29:29; 2 Chr 9:29; 29:25), Shemaiah (2 Chr 12:5, 15), Iddo (2 Chr 13:22), Oded (2 Chr 15:8; 28:9), Elijah (2 Chr 21:12), Isaiah (2 Chr 26:22; 32:20, 32), Huldah (2 Chr 34:22), Samuel (2 Chr 35:18), and Jeremiah (2 Chr 36:12).
15 This title is used for Samuel (1 Chr 9:22; 26:28; 29:29) and Hanani (2 Chr 16:7).
16 This title is used for Gad (1 Chr 21:9; 29:29; 2 Chr 29:25), Heman (1 Chr 25:5), Iddo (2 Chr 9:29; 12:15), Hanani (2 Chr 19:2), Asaph (2 Chr 29:30), and Jeduthun (2 Chr 35:15).

prophetic figures appear to be professional prophets, but, as will be shown below, there are several cases of temporary prophets who prophesy in reaction to a specific problem or challenge. The authority of the prophets seems to be a given, either via the notion of prophecy as a divinely authorized independent institution or via *ad hoc* inspirations by the (divine) spirit. Thus, while leaders such as kings, priests, or Levites are criticized at some point in the chronistic presentation of the monarchic period, there are virtually no critical voices against prophets or prophetic figures.[17] This phenomenon goes hand in hand with the observation that Chronicles' prophets never give bad or ill-timed advice and that there is an overall lack of attention to false or illicit prophecy in chronistic historiography. As is clearly illustrated by the recontextualization of the Micaiah narrative in 2 Chr 18, where the focus shifts from issues of false prophecy (cf. 1 Kgs 22) to issues of foreign alliances, the Chronicler has little to no concern about illicit forms of prophecy (see Knoppers 2014).

Since prophets are considered *God's* messengers, they are usually not summoned by the king, other leaders, or the people. Furthermore, they are not constantly present within the chronistic presentation of the monarchic period, but "pop up" on a more or less regular basis and take the stage as the occasion warrants. Especially compared to prophetic speeches and oracles from prophetic literature, Chronicles' prophets voice their oracles – most of which are in prose rather than poetry – in a relatively concise, perfectly comprehensible, and direct way, generally refraining from mysterious or ambiguous language.

Alongside several professional prophets, Chronicles mentions four individuals who receive inspiration and function in a temporary prophetic capacity.[18] Even though Chronicles clearly and consciously distinguishes the latter from professional prophets by the use of the possession formula (see Schniedewind 1997, 215–218), and independent from the exact categorization of both prophetic "groups," there can be no doubt that the messages of these inspired persons function as genuine prophecies. In 1 Chr 12:1–23 (a list of several military groups who joined David before he became king) it is the spirit that enables Amasai, the chief of the thirty representing Benjamin and Judah, to convince David of the loyalty of his company. The formulation "and the spirit clothed PN [here:

---

[17] This does not mean, of course, that kings do not get enraged at prophets in the narrative world of Chronicles. Especially prophets who deliver words of warning or bad news to the monarch are in danger of being imprisoned (see, for instance, Asa's treatment of Hanani in 2 Chr 16) or even worse. However, these episodes aim to highlight the righteousness of the prophet on the one hand and the king's foolishness and spite on the other.
[18] This category might also include two foreign kings: Necho (2 Chr 35:20–22) and Cyrus (2 Chr 36:22–23). Due to limitations of space, these cases will not be discussed further here.

Amasai]" (את־עמשׂי לבשׁה ורוח, v. 18) is only attested twice elsewhere in the Hebrew Bible. While in Judg 6:34 the "clothing" of the spirit drives Gideon to action, in the second occurrence, also found in Chronicles, it inspires speech. When Joash listens to the bad advice provided by the officials of Judah and goes astray (2 Chr 24:17–18), Zechariah, a priest and the son of Joash's true but deceased advisor, is seized by the spirit to speak the word of God (אמר כה האלהים): "Why do you transgress the commandments of YHWH, so that you cannot prosper? Because you have forsaken YHWH, he has also forsaken you (v. 20)." This rhetorical question followed by an explanation refers to the theology of retribution and the measure-for-measure-technique characteristic of Chronicles (cf. McKenzie 2004, 318). Joash and his advisors refuse to listen to Zechariah's prophetic warning. On the contrary, they conspire against him and kill him. The crime is especially egregious: It is the murder of a prophet who is the son of Jehoiada, and it is carried out in the temple court. The manner of execution, stoning, and its being carried out "at the command of the king" suggests that the accusation against Zechariah was treason. The place of execution is ironic given Jehoiada's refusal to shed Athaliah's blood in the temple (2 Chr 23:14), and it is also a violation of the laws specifying that stoning must take place outside of the camp or town. Joash breaks the commandments of YHWH (v. 20) and gives the command to execute Zechariah, thus substituting his own order for YHWH's. The statement in v. 22 that Joash did not remember (זכר) Jehoiada's kindness towards him puns on Zechariah's name. Thus, Zechariah's last words are a cry for justice. In the case of Azariah, the son of Oded (2 Chr 15:1–7), the spirit which comes upon him is specified as the spirit of God (רוח אלהים, v. 1). His prophecy given to king Asa "is one of the best of several examples in Chronicles of an 'anthological style' – a mosaic of longer or shorter citations from existing prophetic texts, slightly altered and sophistically interwoven, to serve the new context and form a coherent statement of the Chronicler's views" (Japhet 1993, 716).[19] Azariah calls on Asa and the people to recognize the military success as a chance for spiritual renewal. The king acts immediately (cf. v. 8, "as soon as Asa heard") and complies wholeheartedly: In accordance with Azariah's demand (imperative of חזק, v. 7), he takes courage (חזק hitpael, v. 8) and initiates a comprehensive reform. This reform includes three aspects: the removal of the "abominable idols" (השׁקוצים) from his territories, the restoration of the altar of YHWH that was before the vestibule (אולם), and the celebration of the covenant in Jerusalem by a great assembly. Trust in YHWH not only grants Asa military success, but his obedience to a prophetic speech or command also assures him and his people "rest round about" (וינח יהוה להם מסביב, v. 15).

---

[19] For a detailed analysis of 2 Chr 15:1–7, see below.

In 2 Chr 20:14–20, it is the Levitical singer Jahaziel who is inspired spontaneously in the midst of the assembly in Jerusalem (בְּתוֹךְ הַקָּהָל, v. 14). Jahaziel addresses the people (כָּל־יְהוּדָה וְיֹשְׁבֵי יְרוּשָׁלַם, v. 15) and the king, Jehoshaphat, promising God's salvation in the upcoming battle. The king reacts with a powerful gesture of trust and piety. Already before the actual battle, he believes in God's promise and the prophetic assurance, prostrating himself (together with all Judah) before YHWH and worshiping him (accompanied by the Levites, v. 19). Following this, Jehoshaphat acts out the prophecy, though his actions go far beyond literal obedience. His words of encouragement to the army are not only a firm declaration of trust in YHWH but also express a strong belief in YHWH's prophets.

In light of this survey, it is clear that Chronicles not only attests to traditional or classical prophetic leaders but also includes a different type of prophetic leader with a special emphasis on the spirit. While these phenomena are distinguished by the use of the possession formula (the latter being rather atypical of traditional prophecy), in both cases the prophetic speeches are proven true in the course of subsequent events. Chronicles' point is not that all laypersons, Levites, or priests are prophets, but rather that professional prophets do not have a monopoly on divine revelation (see Knoppers 2014). Individuals who are not professional prophets may be employed by YHWH to function as a prophet.

Even though the designation as "messengers" (1 Chr 19:2, 16; 2 Chr 35:21) might allude to the Achaemenid communication system via messengers, as was argued by Gerstenberger 2004 (see also Jonker 2011), this connection to contemporary forms of political communication does not render necessary Gerstenberger's definition of Chronicles' prophetic figures as "fest angestellte Kommunikatoren des Gotteswortes, das per Dekret Jahwes an das Volk befördert werden muß," instead of "spontan auftretende, vielleicht gar ekstatische Ekzentriker" (Gerstenberger 2004, 357–358). The label "messengers" is rather to be understood as a way of (almost radically) restricting the prophet's role to delivering God's messages.[20] As far as the portrayal of prophets is concerned, Chronicles' narrative repeatedly oscillates between the notion that history is permanently accompanied and guided by prophetic figures and the fact that these figures form a rather heterogeneous group of people who appear on stage as the situation demands. In the end, becoming or being a prophet is not linked to specific conditions or requirements – it is not a profession in a narrow sense – but remains under the authority of God and his divine will (of election).

---

[20] For a certain intersection in construing prophetic and priestly leadership via the label "messenger" in late prophetic texts, see Ben Zvi 2004, 27–28.

2.2 The Role(s) and Tasks of Prophetic Leaders

As Gary Knoppers has convincingly shown, the deuteronomic law was formative in shaping the Chronicler's view of the prophet's proper role. At the same time, the Chronicler goes far beyond Deuteronomy's ideas in some respects (see Knoppers 2014). As a consequence, Chronicles paints a multifaceted picture of prophetic leadership with specific emphases.

In Chronicles, prophets are predominantly *receivers and mediators of the divine word*. In contrast to Samuel–Kings, where prophetic leaders such as Samuel, Elijah, and Elisha also act in an intercessory capacity for the people, in Chronicles this role or task rests on the king as representative of the body politic.[21] Thus, Chronicles construes the mediatory relationship of prophets in a rather unidirectional way. Their main task is to receive God's words and to deliver them to the intended audience(s), namely, the king and/or the people. Since God communicates his will via prophetic figures, heeding and believing prophets is only second to trusting in God. As is evident from Jehoshaphat's exhortation, believing in God and his prophets go together and "are in fact two facets of the same faith" (Japhet 1993, 721): "Hear me, O Judah and you inhabitants of Jerusalem: Believe in YHWH your God, and you shall be established; believe his prophets, and you shall prosper" (2 Chr 20:20*). By taking up Isa 7:9* ("If you will not believe, surely you shall not be established") and changing it into a positive request (Zenger and Steins 2016, 883), "the Chronicler transforms the belief in prophets into an essential of religious faith" (Japhet 1989, 180).

As receivers and mediators of the divine word, prophets play a significant role in *shaping Israel's history*. Several historical events are accompanied and influenced by or result from prophetic words and intervention. Saul, for instance, is anointed king by the elders of Israel explicitly in accordance with the divine will communicated by the prophet Samuel (כדבר יהוה ביד־שמואל, 1 Chr 11:3). In Chronicles' close retelling of 2 Sam 7, the foundation of the Jerusalem temple is initiated by God's words mediated by Nathan (vv. 3, 15).[22] In the context of Shishak's military campaign, the sacking of Jerusalem is only avoided thanks to the prophet Shemaiah, who incites the king and the people to do penance (2 Chr 12:5–12). The reforms of Asa and his covenant ceremony likewise result from prophetic intervention by Azariah (2 Chr 15). Through their speeches, prophets not only engage in historical events but, more importantly, seek to explain how and why God has acted, is acting, or will act in history. Thus, it is

---

21 In 2 Chr 32:20, though, king and prophet act together in an intercessory capacity.
22 "Dieses prophetisch vermittelte Gotteswort ist für die Chronik die eigentliche göttliche Stiftungsurkunde des Jerusalemer Tempels" (Steins 2016a, 850).

not surprising that prophets are frequently mentioned in the source citations of Chronicles (e.g., 1 Chr 29:29; 2 Chr 9:29; 12:15; 13:22). These references follow a twofold logic of legitimation: They establish or corroborate the prophet's role as preserver and interpreter of history on the one hand and confirm the narrative's character as authentic historiography on the other. Since biblical historiography does not aim at an objective reporting of historical events but rather at their theological interpretation, historiography and prophecy are closely interconnected.[23] In Chronicles, prophetic leaders direct the actions of the king and/or the people based on their theological interpretation of history. At the same time, this interpretation of historical events provides the rationale of the leader's social interaction(s).[24] The main goal of the prophetic speeches is not simply to announce punishment to the king and/or the people, but rather to warn them and to induce them to repent. To put it in the words of 2 Chr 24:19*: "Yet he (i.e., YHWH) sent prophets to them, to bring them back to YHWH." Since Chronicles' depiction of the monarchic period conforms to "the principal of 'no punishment without warning'" (Japhet 1989, 188), prophetic leaders are crucial in their function of warning. Only if the addressees ignore the warning and do not repent will they be punished. "Not only is it the prophet's duty to warn – it is God's duty to send a prophet" (Japhet 1989, 188). In fact, by persistently sending his prophets to Israel, YHWH expresses his enduring compassion for his people.[25] Even though transmitting warnings is not exclusively reserved for prophets and can also be done by other figures such as the king himself (2 Chr 13:12) or priests (2 Chr 26:18), the calls for repentance are particularly prominent in prophetic speeches.

In addition to the duty of warning, in Chronicles prophetic leadership also includes *the function of counseling*. This aspect is especially apparent in the Amaziah narrative in 2 Chr 25.[26] The Chronicler's account follows the parallel from the books of Kings (cf. 2 Kgs 14) with only minor changes but also embel-

---

[23] "Geschichtsschreibung ist Prophetie, weil es nicht um objektive Berichterstattung, sondern um eine theologische Interpretation geht" (Steins 2016a, 850).
[24] See also Jong 2015, 139 (without referring to Chronicles, though): "Prophecy as divination had a direct relevance to the current situation, and often took the form of divine guidance *vis-à-vis* a proposed course of action. The oracles provided the guidance the recipients needed in order to confidently take the course of action that seemed the best way to victory or survival" (emphasis original).
[25] This idea is particularly prominent in 2 Chr 36:15: "And YHWH, the God of their fathers, sent to them by his messengers [...], because he had compassion on his people and on his dwelling place."
[26] For an analysis of 2 Chr 25 in light of the broader phenomenon of counseling in the Hebrew Bible, see Pyschny 2020.

lishes it with additional episodes that highlight Amaziah's development from a king loyal to YHWH to an apostate king.[27] Interestingly enough, Amaziah's apostasy arises not only from the common deuteronomistic motif of worshipping foreign gods (v. 14) but also from not observing prophetic advice. Amaziah's apostasy is framed by encounters with different prophetic figures, whose advice he accepts the first time but rejects the second time.

Starting with a (limited) positive evaluation of Amaziah ("And he did what was right in the sight of YHWH, but not with a loyal heart," v. 2), the narrative highlights the king's righteousness and his compliance to the Torah (v. 4). In preparation for a military campaign, Amaziah musters the men of Judah who are fit for military service (v. 5). When he seeks to enlarge his army with mercenaries from the northern kingdom (v. 6), an unnamed man of God comes to him and advises him against enlisting Israelite mercenaries in the Judean army: "O king, do not let the army of Israel go with you; for YHWH is not with Israel, not with any of the children of Ephraim. But if you go, be gone! Be strong in battle! God shall make you fall before the enemy; for God has power to help and to overthrow" (v. 7–8*). While the narrative clearly aims at the theological question of trust in God, an interesting subtext can be discerned as far as issues of leadership are concerned. Even though Amaziah is well aware of the economic loss, he trusts YHWH, obeys the prophetic word and sends the already paid mercenaries back to the northern kingdom. With his victory over the Edomites, his reward for trusting in God and complying with prophetic counsel follows immediately. But when Amaziah, after returning from the victory over the Edomites, sets up the gods (statues) he brought with him, worships them and sacrifices to them, the tables turn. YHWH's anger arises and he sends another unnamed prophet to Amaziah saying, "Why have you sought the gods of the people, which could not rescue their own people from your hand?" (v. 15*). Before the prophet can finish speaking, Amaziah harshly interrupts him, "Have we made you the king's counselor (הליועץ)? Cease! Why should you be killed?" (v. 16*). Thus, Amaziah not only doubts the prophet's advisory function but also threatens him with death if he continues with his prophetic speech. The prophet ceases and says, "I know that God has determined/planned (יעץ) to destroy you, because you have done this and have not heeded my advice (לעצתי)." The triple use of the root יעץ in v. 16 is striking and underscores all the more the foolish behavior of the king, who rejects the advice of the prophet sent by YHWH but then immediately deliberates by himself (cf. the beginning of v. 17: ויועץ אמציהו), which ultimately leads to a crushing defeat at the hands of the

---

27 For a synopsis, see Bae 2005.

northern king Joash. The subsequent conquest of Jerusalem by the Israelite king is thus not only a punishment for apostasy from God, but also for the failure to heed prophetic advice. Heeding prophetic advice is tantamount to complying to the divine will.

In accordance with Samuel–Kings, Chronicles sees the prophet in juxtaposition to the king. While the prophet's role in relation to the monarch is strongly defined by the function of warning in Samuel–Kings, the Chronicler supplements and transforms the prophetic profile with aspects of preaching, exhortation, and counseling. Furthermore, the relationship between prophet and king appears to be far less strained and asymmetrical in Chronicles. In fact, in terms of social hierarchy, the king holds a special position as the ruler of the body politic, but he does not stand above the prophet. Prophet and monarch are rather on a level playing field, as is evident from the joint prayer of Hezekiah and Isaiah in 2 Chr 32:20. Moreover, Chronicles portrays the prophet not only as a spokesman to the king but also considers the people or its representatives (see, for instance, the leaders of Judah in 2 Chr 12:5) as the addressees of prophetic speech. Typically, traditional prophets address the king alone,[28] while the prophetic speeches of the inspired messengers reach out to the people as a whole (and the king as part of this audience).[29] Thus, Chronicles chips away at the traditional notion of an organic relationship between prophecy and kingship, transforming the prophet's role into one of giving instructions and exhortations to the people. Especially in these contexts, prophetic speeches show an extensive appeal to and citation of the Torah in particular, but also to prophetic literature. By addressing the community as prophets who cite and midrashically transform Scripture, prophetic leadership is characterized by proclaiming God's will (in correspondence to the Torah) and interpreting it (in light of its "actualization" in the Prophets). As such, the prophetic speeches of Chronicles aim at instructing the community in civil and religious matters and clearly follow a pedagogical purpose: to guide, teach, and warn the people by interpreting Scripture.

Considering that prophetic figures are conceptually linked to the Torah and that prophetic speeches in particular closely engage with the Mosaic Torah, it is all the more surprising that prophets are not mentioned in Jehoshaphat's

---

[28] Oded, the northern prophet, is an exception as he does not address the king. This might be due to the fact that, for Chronicles, there is no (legitimate) northern monarch to reach out to (see Schniedewind 1997, 218–219).

[29] If one considers Pharaoh Neco an inspired messenger (see Ben Zvi 2009, 221–222), then he is an exception to this pattern as well. The pharaoh speaks, indeed, to king Josiah as his direct peer (see Schniedewind 1997).

mission of instruction (2 Chr 17:7–9). Instead, this set of instructors linked to the "book of the Torah of YHWH" (ספר תורת יהוה) includes three categories: five royal officials, eight Levites, and two priests. This composition of "'wandering professors'" (Japhet 1993, 750) teaching the Torah among the people is unusual, since transmitting and teaching the Torah is often ascribed to the priests (Jer 18:18; Hag 2:11; Ezek 7:26; Lev 10:11).[30] Irrespective of the question of whether this composition provides a descending (Gerstenberger 2004) or ascending (Japhet 1993) order of authority, the lack of prophets is striking. This might, in fact, hint at a special role of prophets in relation to the Torah. For Chronicles, prophets not only proclaim, interpret, and teach God's Torah but are – inspired by the (divine) spirit – capable of receiving additional revelations of the divine will which are, of course, in a Torah-like style. Thus, prophetic utterances are not only an instrument for teaching and actualizing the Torah, but hold an autonomous, albeit necessarily Torah-oriented, role for the postexilic community. The Mosaic Torah and prophetic utterances are considered qualitatively the same, insofar as both reveal the authoritative and normative words of YHWH (Gerstenberger 2004; Jonker 2011). However, the legitimacy of prophetic speech in Chronicles is demonstrated by reference not only to the Pentateuch but also to prophetic traditions.

3 Conceptualizing and Legitimating Prophetic Leadership by Engaging with Prophetic Traditions

Even though, as Jonker has argued, the reader's expectations with respect to Chronicles' quotations from and allusions to the known prophetic literature are not met (Jonker 2011, 145–146), there are several indications that the Chronicler thought of his historiography as participating in the larger prophetic tradition. The Chronicler's literary strategies of engaging with prophetic literature are various, often subtle, and cannot be reduced to explicit intertextual links. Using two case studies, 2 Chr 36 and 2 Chr 15:1–7, the following remarks will demonstrate how Chronicles engages with prophetic traditions in order to conceptualize and legitimate prophetic leadership.

---

30 Obviously, the priestly function of teaching (the Torah) is a complex issue within recent biblical scholarship (see Pyschny 2021).

3.1 Jeremiah as a Prophetic Figure in Chronicles

While Isaiah is significantly "downscaled" in Chronicles (see Jonker 2008), Jeremianic prophecies play a crucial role in Chronicles' depiction of Judah's demise. Accordingly, explicit references to Jeremiah as a prophetic figure are restricted to the final chapter of Chronicles.[31] In the portrayal of the end of Judah, Chronicles makes the contemporary king Zedekiah and his generation responsible for the exile and provides a detailed list of sins and transgressions of the king (2 Chr 36:12–13), the leaders/officers of the priests (שׂרי הכהנים, v. 14) and the people (והעם, v. 14). Zedekiah not only did what was evil in the eyes of YHWH but also "did not humble himself before Jeremiah the prophet, who spoke from the mouth of YHWH" (v. 12). Such a reference is absent in the evaluation of the king in both the deuteronomistic account (2 Kgs 24:18–20) and in the parallel text in the book of Jeremiah (Jer 52:1–3). Yet, when introducing Zedekiah as new king, Jer 37:2 mentions in a rather general way that "neither he nor his servants nor the people of the land gave heed to the words of YHWH which he spoke by the prophet Jeremiah." In fact, refusing to listen to the prophets sent by YHWH is the most accentuated transgression in the list of 2 Chr 36. It is repeated and even intensified in vv. 15–16 by highlighting the active and aggressive stance of the people against the messengers and prophets of YHWH. After YHWH persistently sent messengers with a last chance for repentance (cf. Jer 7:25; 25:3–4; 29:19), the people "mocked the messengers of God, despised his words, and scoffed at his prophets" (v. 16). The term used here, מלאך, does not denote superhuman messengers but human ones (Japhet 1993) and can also be found in contemporary prophetic literature (e.g., Isa 42:19; Hag 1:13). Second Chronicles 36:16 uses the term parallel to נביא without any kind of qualitative distinction or social status. Even more interestingly, messengers and prophets alike are directly, immediately, and unequivocally linked to God's word (דבריו).

When compared to its *Vorlagen* in 2 Kgs 24:20b–25:21; Jer 39:1–10; 52:3–30, it becomes abundantly clear that 2 Chr 36:15–21 includes three distinctive and new elements: the fulfilment of the word of YHWH by the mouth of Jeremiah, the land keeping the Sabbath, and the fulfilment of 70 years (see Jonker 2009). Interestingly enough, all of these elements show or result from a creative usage of Pentateuchal and prophetic tradition. In 2 Chr 36:15–21, this concentration or

---

31 In total, Jeremiah is mentioned four times in Chronicles. The first reference can be found in the death notice of king Josiah (2 Chr 35:25), where Jeremiah does not feature as a prophetic figure but is referred to as the author of a lament. This reference is absent in the deuteronomistic *Vorlage* (2 Kgs 23:28–30). The other three occurrences are found in 2 Chr 36.

distillation of traditions (*Traditionsverdichtung*)[32] is crucial for conceptualizing and legitimizing prophetic leadership using the figure of Jeremiah.

Even though the texts in question are not quoted as such, for Chronicles the exile and Judah's demise is the fulfillment of Jeremianic prophecies (cf. Jer 25:11; 27:7; 29:10). This is evident from the reference to Jeremiah in 2 Chr 36:20–21[33]:

> [20] And those who escaped from the sword he carried away to Babylon, where they became servants to him [i.e., the king of the Chaldeans] and his sons until the rule of the kingdom of Persia, [21] to fulfill the word of YHWH by the mouth of Jeremiah, until the land had enjoyed her sabbaths. As long as she lay desolate she kept Sabbath, to fulfill seventy years.

With Jer 25:11–12; 27:7–8; 29:10 and possibly Zech 1:12; 7:5 in mind, this passage interprets the Babylonian reign over Judah and its duration of seventy years as a fulfillment of Jeremiah's words and thus highlights Jeremiah's legitimacy as a prophet of YHWH. In doing so, the Chronicler creates and accepts a chronological discrepancy, since the time span from the destruction of Jerusalem (587/6 BCE) until the beginning of Persian rule (539 BCE) covers around fifty and not seventy years (see Berner 2006, 78–84). Linking the exile to Jeremiah and his words seems to be far more important than "historical accuracy." Interestingly enough, 2 Chr 36:20–21 not only refers to prophetic traditions but also includes some phraseology from Lev 26.[34] While Gerhard von Rad considered this combination of Pentateuchal and prophetic traditions a "Beschlagnahme der alten Propheten für das Gesetz" (von Rad 1930, 115), Sara Japhet convincingly showed that it is rather a sophisticated combination of two different notions of exile: "The 'seventy years' of Jeremiah are the necessary time for the land 'to keep its deserved sabbaths.' For the Chronicler, then, 'seventy years' is not a chronological datum which may be explained by various calculations, but a historical and theological concept: a time limit for the duration of the land's desolation, established by a divine word through his prophet" (Japhet 1993, 1076). Written at a time in which the return from exile had become a reality, in Chronicles the exile does not carry the same finality as in the books of Kings

---

[32] For a definition of the phenomenon *Traditionsverdichtung* (albeit with reference to the book of Numbers), see Frevel 2020. With regard to 2 Chr 36:15–21, see Jonker 2009, 225: "Quotations and allusions to other sources were used to invoke whole traditions. What is presented in the last chapter of Chronicles is not a whole new narrative, but rather a concise attempt to bring together different earlier religio-historical traditions with the purpose of interpreting those traditions for a new context."

[33] For a detailed analysis of 2 Chr 36:20–23, see Kartveit 1999.

[34] For a synopsis, see Jonker 2009, 229 and Maskow 2019, 142.

(see esp. 2 Kgs 25). Instead, the exile only presents a hiatus, a phase of sabbath rest (v. 21), which is necessary for redemption, purification, renewal, re-orientation, and restitution.

The concept of "desolation" (שׁמם) links v. 21 not only to Lev 26 but also to Jeremiah, again merging Pentateuchal and prophetic traditions together. In v. 21, the Chronicler does not put words from the Torah into Jeremiah's mouth (cf. Maskow 2019) but rather links his legitimacy (represented in the text by the motif of fulfillment) to both the Torah and the Prophets. Thus, for Chronicles, prophecy has to conform not only to the Torah but, in a way, also to prophetic traditions. The historical and theological impact of prophetic leadership is further accentuated in the last reference to Jeremiah in v. 22. By indicating that the stirring up of Cyrus's spirit by YHWH and the resultant promulgation of the edict that allowed the exiles to return to their land is also in fulfillment of the word of YHWH spoken through Jeremiah, Israel's entire captivity is framed by Jeremianic prophecies. Jeremiah's prophetic agency transforms a time of judgment and separation from God into a time of reconciliation for God's people. The end of Chronicles is thus marked by a twofold fulfillment of Jeremiac prophecies, as Christoph Berner (2006, 79–80) points out: "Einerseits ermöglicht die Exilierung eine Erstattung der versäumten Sabbate (36,21), und andererseits verwirklicht sich mit der Machtübernahme der Perser sowie mit der im Kyrosedikt eingeleiteten Restitution das Ende der Zeit Babels (36,22 f.)."

3.2 Quotations from and Allusions to Prophetic Literature in Prophetic Speeches: 2 Chr 15:1–7 as a Case Study

Even though Chronicles as a whole does not meet the expectation of numerous allusions to and quotations from earlier and contemporary prophetic literature, there is one significant exception to this pattern. The prophetic speeches of the inspired figures in particular are not only characterized by the Chronicler's own language and theology but also imbued in models, ideas, and idioms taken from the known prophetic writings. Thus, in Chronicles, prophecies are in continuity with both the Pentateuchal and prophetic traditions. It is precisely this "scribal prophetic leadership" (*schriftgelehrte prophetische Führung*) that characterizes prophetic agency and at the same time constitutes the prophet's legitimacy. Using 2 Chr 15:1–7 as a case study, the following remarks will elaborate on this phenomenon.

Azariah's oracle in 2 Chr 15:1–7 seems to be motivated by Asa's faithfulness and prompts Asa, in turn, to enact even greater reforms (vv. 8–15). Sara Japhet (1993) convincingly demonstrated the anthological character of this prophetic speech borrowing from, alluding to, and recalling a broad range of prophetic traditions. After addressing the king and the people with the typical introduction for speeches in Chronicles ("Hear me"), the prophet states an axiom that is the underlying principle of all history: "YHWH is with you while you are with him" (v. 2*). It follows a parallel sequence of two conditional clauses with their pending results. While the subject of the (positive and negative) protasis is the people, the subject of the apodosis is God: "If you seek him, he will be found by you; but if you forsake him, he will forsake you." The two complementary verbs used in the first condition, דרשׁ ("seek") and מצא ("find"), are a common word pair in biblical texts. However, a special connection to Jer 29:13–14* is apparent: "And you will seek me and find me, when you search for me with all your heart. I will be found by you, says YHWH." A certain affinity to Isa 65:1 ("I was sought by those who did not ask for me; I was found by those who did not seek me") and Isa 55:6 ("Seek YHWH while he may be found, call upon him while he is near") might be also at play here. The second condition uses twice the same verb, עזב ("forsake"), thus highlighting the principle of measure for measure. The point of the whole sentence makes it abundantly clear that everyone's fate in history depends on the quality of the relationship between God and his chosen people.

After this declaration of a theological principle, the prophet continues with a sort of historical review in order to illustrate the validity of the axiom in the past. The time period chosen as an example is not mentioned explicitly, but the features given in vv. 3–6 correspond most probably to the premonarchic period, the so-called time of the Judges.

Interestingly, especially the theological principles of vv. 3–4 build on models and ideas from the book of Hosea:

2 Chr 15:3–4	Hos 3:4–5
³ For a long time Israel had been without the true God, without a teaching priest, and without law;	⁴ For the children of Israel shall abide many days without king or prince, without sacrifice or sacred pillar, without ephod or teraphim.
⁴ but when in their trouble they turned to YHWH, God of Israel, and sought him, he was found by them.	⁵ Afterward the children of Israel shall return and seek YHWH their God and David their king. They shall fear YHWH and his goodness in the latter days.

As is evident from the direct comparison of 2 Chr 15:3–4 and Hos 3:4–5, the similarities are not primarily lexical but instead concern aspects of syntactic structure and the overall argumentative logic of the passages. Both texts begin with a lengthy state of chaos; for Chronicles this time is in the past, while Hosea formulates in the future. This state of anarchy is characterized in both passages by the absence (see the threefold use of ללא in 2 Chr 15 and the fivefold use of

אין in Hos 3:4) of three fundamental institutions. Hosea 3:4 contains three couplets referring to the political (שׂר, מלך), cultic (מצבה, זבח), and particularly priestly (תרפים, אפוד) realms. Second Chronicles 15:3 mentions three single elements (two of which are phrased in two words) which are religious/spiritual rather than political or cultic in nature. Special emphasis is given to teaching (כהן מורה) and the law (תורה). Even the only element shared by both passages, the priestly function, is understood in different ways. In its reference to the ephod and the teraphim, Hos 3:4 has priestly oracles in view, while 2 Chr 15:3 focuses on the priestly function of teaching (the law). Second Chronicles 15:4 continues the historical review by stating that Israel turned to YHWH, when its distress became unbearable. This verse recalls 2 Chr 15:2 on the one hand and Hos 3:5a on the other (again with the aforementioned change of tense). Both passages emphasize that even at the worst of times, repentance is possible if one seeks God.

Even though the wording "in my/your/their distress" can be found throughout the Hebrew Bible in several contexts, 2 Chr 15:4 shows a distinct resemblance to Hos 5:15–6:1, whose elements are taken up in a different order (cf. Japhet 1993, 720):

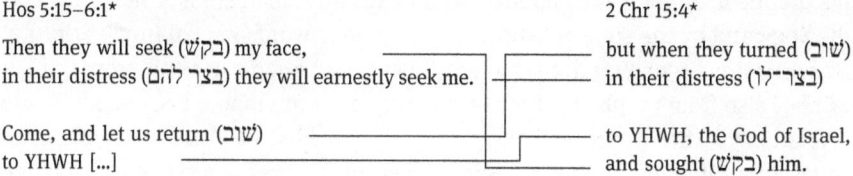

Hos 5:15–6:1*
Then they will seek (בקשׁ) my face,
in their distress (בצר להם) they will earnestly seek me.

Come, and let us return (שׁוב)
to YHWH [...]

2 Chr 15:4*
but when they turned (שׁוב)
in their distress (בצר־לו)

to YHWH, the God of Israel,
and sought (בקשׁ) him.

Second Chronicles 15:5–6 does not turn to the present but keeps its focus on "those times," laying the foundation for the conclusion in v. 7 (see the antithetic structure "In those times [...]" in v. 5 and "But you [...]" in v. 7). The prophet elaborates on the chaotic and anarchic situation of these times, which is characterized by the lack of security, great turmoil, and strife between nations and cities. These well-structured verses (each sentence describing the situation consists of two clauses, one indicative and one causative) show a familiarity with various prophetic traditions. The phrase "and there was no peace for the one who went out, nor for the one who came in" (אין שׁלום ליוצא ולבא) takes up Zech 8:10, chiastically: "For the one who went out and for the one who came in there was no peace" (ליוצא ולבא אין־שׁלום). "Great turmoil" (מהומת רבות) might be borrowed from Amos 3:9 (see also רבת המהומה in Ezek 22:5 and מהומת־יהוה רבה in Zech 14:13). The "inhabitants of the lands" (יושׁבי הארצות) and the particular statement of the verse calls to mind several prophetic texts, such as

Jer 6:12; 10:18; 25:30; Ezek 7:7; Joel 2:1; and Zeph 1:18. Furthermore, the beginning of v. 6, "They were crushed/broken in pieces (כתת), nation against nation," is reminiscent of Zech 11:6: "For I will no longer pity the inhabitants of the land [...] I will give everyone into his neighbor's hand [...] and they shall crush (כתת) the earth." The prophecy culminates in the conclusion of v. 7, which finally returns to the present with a second person imperative: "But you, be strong/take courage!" In this specific context, this encouragement calls to mind Zech 8:9, 13, while the call not to let one's hands become weak is even a literal quotation of Zeph 3:16 with a shift into the plural ("let not your hands be weak"). Finally, the prophecy concludes with "for your work shall be rewarded," a citation of Jer 31:16, where this sentence is found in the singular: "For your work shall be rewarded, says YHWH."

In sum: Based on the example of the prophetic speech in 2 Chr 15:1–7, it is clear that Chronicles' prophetic utterances engage extensively with earlier or contemporary prophetic literature. The parallels and similarities are numerous and vary significantly in their nature (quotation, allusion, etc.). In many cases, a clear classification of the intertextual links is not possible. However, an identification of the borrowed prophetic tradition(s) does not seem to be intended by or even relevant for the Chronicler. Instead, the Chronicler aims at presenting his prophetic utterances as imbued both by his own characteristic language and theology and by the style of "authentic" prophetic words known from Scripture. By borrowing argumentative structures, ideas, and idioms not only from the Torah but also from prophetic writings, the prophetic utterances become authentic revelations of the divine will. Even though this kind of *Traditionsverdichtung* works in a different way than we have seen in the previous section, it has the same function: namely, to legitimate prophetic leadership by embedding it within Pentateuchal and prophetic traditions.

4 Conclusions

As this essay has shown, Chronicles not only holds the phenomenon of prophecy in high regard but also engages theologically and literarily with a broad range of prophetic traditions. Against this background, the notion of the demise or decline of prophecy in the postexilic period is shown, once again, to be a rather problematic oversimplification (of the phenomenon itself and of the narrative of Chronicles).

By focusing on the conceptualization of prophetic leadership, it becomes clear that Chronicles knows a remarkable variety of prophets and prophetic or inspired figures. These figures are first and foremost perceived in their role as mediators of God's words. Their designation as "messengers" stresses this almost radical focus on delivering divine messages. Interestingly, within the narrative world of Chronicles, the authority of prophetic leaders seems to be a given, either via the notion of prophecy as a divinely authorized institution (in the case of prophets known from Samuel–Kings) or via *ad hoc* inspiration by the divine spirit (in the case of inspired figures). Because of their closeness to God, prophetic leaders cannot give bad or ill-timed advice (especially since the problem of false or illicit prophecy almost does not exist in Chronicles). The remarkable presence of prophetic figures not only serves to legitimize the Chronicler's presentation and interpretation of history; it also reflects a transformed concept of prophetic leadership characterized by a twofold democratization. First, Chronicles attests to "traditional" or "classical" prophets as well as prophetic leaders with a special emphasis on the spirit. Becoming a prophet is not linked to specific conditions or requirements, but is reserved for God and his divine will of election. Second, prophetic leadership is not conceptualized with an organic relationship between prophecy and kingship in mind. Instead, the people or its representatives increasingly become the main audience of prophetic leaders.

Chronicles also attests to several transformations and distinctive emphases regarding prophetic functions. This is especially true of their role as preserver and interpreter of history, which is very pronounced in Chronicles. In addition, the prophetic function of warning is transformed into acts of counseling, preaching, and teaching.[35] Especially in these contexts, prophetic speeches show an extensive appeal to and citation of the Torah in particular but also to prophetic literature. By portraying prophets as figures who cite and midrashically transform Scripture, prophetic leadership is characterized by proclaiming God's will (in accordance with the Torah) and interpreting it (in light of its "actualization" by the Prophets). Furthermore, prophetic utterances are not only an instrument for teaching the Torah but are qualitatively on a par with the Torah insofar as they likewise reveal the authoritative and normative words of God.

Significantly, this authenticity and legitimacy of prophetic utterances is constituted by the Chronicler's engagement with Pentateuchal and prophetic traditions. The ways of engaging with these traditions are subtle and varied and cannot always be classified with certainty (citation, allusion, etc.). The chosen case studies presented two different literary strategies in the "condensation or distillation of tradition" (*Traditionsverdichtung*), one using the prophetic figure of Jeremiah in order to transform a time of judgment into a time of reconciliation and restitution, and the other drawing on models, ideas, and

---

[35] These aspects are certainly not an innovation of the Persian period. However, they are definitly more nuanced in postexilic times.

idioms from earlier and contemporary prophetic literature in order to deliver prophetic utterances in a specific style. For Chronicles, prophetic agency is, thus, closely linked to the interpretation of Scripture ("scribal prophetic leadership"). Especially in the case of the inspired figures, it is exactly this phenomenon that not only characterizes prophetic agency but at the same time constitutes the prophet's legitimacy.

Bibliography

Amit, Yairah. 2006. "The Role of Prophecy and Prophets in the Chronicler's World." In *Prophets, Prophecy, and Prophetic Texts in Second Temple Judaism*, edited by Michael H. Floyd and Robert D. Haak, 80–101. OTS 427. London: T&T Clark.

Bae, Hee-Sook. 2005. *Vereinte Suche nach JHWH: Die Hiskianische und Joschijanische Reform in der Chronik*. BZAW 355. Berlin and New York: de Gruyter.

Beentjes, Pancratius C. 2008. *Tradition and Transformation in the Book of Chronicles*. Studia Semitica Neerlandica 52. Leiden and Boston: Brill.

Beentjes, Pancratius C. 2015. "King Asa and Hanani the Seer: 2 Chronicles 16 as an Example of the Chronicler's View of Prophets and Prophecy." In *Prophecy and Prophets in Stories: Papers Read at the Fifth Meeting of the Edinburgh Prophecy Network, Utrecht, October 2013*, edited by Bob Becking and Hans M. Barstad, 141–151. OTS 65. Leiden and Boston: Brill.

Ben Zvi, Ehud. 2004. "Observations on Prophetic Characters, Prophetic Texts, Priests of Old, Persian Period Priests and Literati." In *The Priests in the Prophets: The Portrayal of Priests, Prophets and Other Religious Specialists in the Latter Prophets*, edited by Lester L. Grabbe and Alice Ogden Bellis, 19–30. JSOT.S 408. London: T & T Clark.

Ben Zvi, Ehud. 2009. "When the Foreign Monarch Speaks." In *The Chronicler as Author: Studies in Text and Texture*, edited by M. Patrick Graham and Steven L. McKenzie, 209–228. JSOT.S 263. Sheffield: Sheffield Academic Press.

Ben Zvi, Ehud. 2013. "Chronicles and Its Reshaping of Memories of Monarchic Period Prophets: Some Observations." In *Prophets, Prophecy, and Ancient Israelite Historiography*, edited by Mark J. Boda and Lissa M. Wray Beal, 167–188. Winona Lake: Eisenbrauns.

Ben Zvi, Ehud. 2016. "Memory and Political Thought in the Late Persian/Early Hellenistic Yehud/Judah: Some Observations." In *Leadership, Social Memory and Judean Discourse in the 5th–2nd Centuries BCE*, edited by Diana V. Edelman and Ehud Ben Zvi, 9–26. Worlds of the Ancient Near East and the Mediterranean. Bristol: Equinox.

Berner, Christoph. 2006. *Jahre, Jahrwochen und Jubiläen: Heptadische Geschichtskonzeptionen im Antiken Judentum*. BZAW 363. Berlin and New York: de Gruyter.

Blenkinsopp, Joseph. 1996. *A History of Prophecy in Israel*. Louisville: Westminster John Knox Press.

Blenkinsopp, Joseph. 2004. "'We Pay No Heed to Heavenly Voices': The 'End of Prophecy' and the Formation of the Canon." In *Treasures Old and New: Essays in the Theology of the Pentateuch*, 192–207. Grand Rapids: Eerdmans.

Blenkinsopp, Joseph. 2017. "Social Roles of Prophets in Early Achaemenid Judah." In *Essays in Judaism in the Pre-Hellenistic Period*, 178–191. BZAW 495. Berlin and Boston: de Gruyter.
Gerstenberger, Erhard S. 2004. "Prophetie in den Chronikbüchern: Jahwes Wort in zweierlei Gestalt?" In *Schriftprophetie: FS für Jörg Jeremias zum 65. Geburtstag*, edited by Friedhelm Hartenstein, 351–367. Neukirchen-Vluyn: Neukirchener Verlag.
Frevel, Christian. 2020. "Traditionsverdichtung – eine Tora im Werden: Einblicke in die gegenwärtige Numeriforschung." *ThLZ* 145:267–279.
Japhet, Sara. 1989. *The Ideology of the Book of Chronicles and Its Place in Biblical Thought*. BEATAJ 9. Frankfurt a. M. et al.: Peter Lang.
Japhet, Sara. 1993. *I & II Chronicles*: A Commentary. OTL. Louisville: Westminster John Knox Press.
Jong, Matthijs J. de. 2015. "Rewriting the Past in Light of the Present: The Stories of the Prophet Jeremiah." In *Prophecy and Prophets in Stories: Papers Read at the Fifth Meeting of the Edinburgh Prophecy Network, Utrecht, October 2013*, edited by Bob Becking and Hans M. Barstad, 124–140. OTS 65. Leiden and Boston: Brill.
Jonker, Louis. 2008. "Who Constitutes Society? Yehud's Self-Understanding in the Late Persian Era as Reflected in the Books of Chronicles." *JBL* 127:703–724.
Jonker, Louis. 2009. "The Exile as Sabbath Rest: The Chronicler's Interpretation of the Exile." In *Exile and Suffering: A Selection of Papers Read at the 50th Anniversary Meeting of the Old Testament Society of South Africa OTWSA/OTSSA, Pretoria August 2007*, edited by Bob Becking and Dirk Human, 213–229. OTS 50. Leiden and Boston: Brill.
Jonker, Louis. 2011. "The Chronicler and the Prophets: Who Were His Authoritative Sources?" In *What Was Authoritative for Chronicles?*, edited by Ehud Ben Zvi and Diana V. Edelman, 145–164. Winona Lake: Eisenbrauns.
Kartveit, Magnar. 2009. "2 Chronicles 36.20–23 as Literary and Theological 'Interface'." In *The Chronicler as Author: Studies in Text and Texture*, edited by M. Patrick Graham and Steven L. McKenzie, 395–403. JSOT.S 263. Sheffield: Sheffield Academic Press.
Kegler, Jürgen. 1993. "Prophetengestalten im Deuteronomistischen Geschichtswerk und in den Chronikbüchern: Ein Beitrag zur Kompositions- und Redaktionsgeschichte der Chronikbücher." *ZAW* 105:481–497.
Knoppers, Gary N. 2004. *I Chronicles 1–9: A New Translation with Introduction and Commentary*. AncB 12. New York: Doubleday.
Knoppers, Gary N. 2014. "Democratizing Revelation? Prophets, Seers and Visionaries in Chronicles." In *Prophecy and the Prophets in Ancient Israel*, edited by John Day, 391–409. LHBOTS 531. New York: T&T Clark.
McKenzie, Steven L. 2004. *I & II Chronicles*. Abingdon Old Testament Commentaries. Nashville: Abingdon Press.
Maskow, Lars. 2019. *Tora in der Chronik: Studien zur Rezeption des Pentateuchs in den Chronikbüchern*. FRLANT 274. Göttingen: Vandenhoeck & Ruprecht.
Nihan, Christophe. 2013. "Textual Fluidity and Rewriting in Parallel Traditions: The Case of Samuel and Chronicles." *JAJ* 4:186–209.
Nissinen, Martti. 2013. "Prophecy as Construct, Ancient and Modern." In *"Thus Speaks Ishtar of Arbela": Prophecy in Israel, Assyria, and Egypt in the Neo-Assyrian Period*, edited by Robert P. Gordon and Hans M. Barstad, 11–35. Winona Lake: Eisenbrauns.
Person Jr., Raymond F. 2013. "Prophets in the Deuteronomic History and the Book of Chronicles: A Reassessment." In *Israelite Prophecy and the Deuteronomistic History:*

Portrait, Reality, and the Formation of a History, edited by Mignon R. Jacobs and Raymond F. Person Jr., 187–199. SBL AIL 14. Atlanta: Society of Biblical Literature.

Pyschny, Katharina. 2020. "Versammlung, Beratung und Entscheidung im Volk Gottes. Alttestamentliche Perspektiven." In *Synodalität in der katholischen Kirche: Die Studie der Internationalen Theologischen Kommission im Diskurs*, edited by Markus Graulich and Johanna Rahner, 13–41. QD 311. Freiburg: Herder.

Pyschny, Katharina. 2021. "Die Macht der Auslegung. Zum priesterlichen Anspruch auf Toraauslegung und -lehre im Pentateuch." *Cardo* 19:12–17.

Rad, Gerhard von. 1930. *Das Geschichtsbild des chronistischen Geschichtswerk*. BWANT 54. Stuttgart: Kohlhammer.

Schniedewind, William M. 1995. *The Word of God in Transition: From Prophet to Exegete in the Second Temple Period*. JSOTS 197. Sheffield: Sheffield Academic Press.

Schniedewind, William M. 1997. "Prophets and Prophecy in the Books of Chronicles." In *The Chronicler as Historian*, edited by M. Patrick Graham, Kenneth G. Hoglund, and Steven L. McKenzie, 204–224. JSOTS 238. Sheffield: Sheffield Academic Press.

Steins, Georg. 2016a. "Das 1. Buch der Chronik." In *Stuttgarter Altes Testament*, edited by Christoph Dohmen, 797–850. Stuttgart: Katholisches Bibelwerk.

Steins, Georg. 2016b. "Die Bücher der Chronik." In *Einleitung in das Alte Testament*, edited by Christian Frevel, 312–320. KStT 1,1. 9th edition. Stuttgart: Kohlhammer.

Warhurst, Amber K. 2011. "The Chronicler's Use of the Prophets." In *What Was Authoritative for Chronicles?*, edited by Ehud Ben Zvi and Diana V. Edelman, 165–181. Winona Lake: Eisenbrauns.

Wetter, Anne-Mareike. 2015. "The Prophet and the King: Is there Such a Thing as Free Prophetic Speech?" In *Prophecy and Prophets in Stories: Papers Read at the Fifth Meeting of the Edinburgh Prophecy Network, Utrecht, October 2013*, edited by Bob Becking and Hans M. Barstad, 29–44. OTS 65. Leiden and Boston: Brill.

Willi, Thomas. 1972. *Die Chronik als Auslegung: Untersuchungen zur literarischen Gestaltung der historischen Überlieferung Israels*. FRLANT 106. Göttingen: Vandenhoeck & Ruprecht.

Zenger, Erich, and Georg Steins. 2016. "Das 2. Buch der Chronik." In *Stuttgarter Altes Testament*, edited by Christoph Dohmen, 851–915. Stuttgart: Katholisches Bibelwerk.

List of Contributors

Bob Becking is Professor Emeritus for Old Testament Studies at the Utrecht University (The Netherlands).

Ehud Ben Zvi is Professor Emeritus at the Department of History and Classics at the University of Alberta (Canada).

Anna Maria Bortz is Senior Lecturer in Old Testament and Biblical Archaeology at Johannes Gutenberg-Universität Mainz (Germany).

L. Juliana M. Claassens is Professor of Old Testament and Head of Gender Unit, Faculty of Theology, Stellenbosch University (South Africa).

Isabel Cranz is Assistant Professor of Hebrew Bible at the University of Pennsylvania (United States of America).

Johanna Erzberger is holder of the Laurentius Klein Chair at the Jerusalem School of Theology (Israel).

Hervé Gonzalez is Research Associate in Hebrew Bible and its Contexts at the Collège de France, Paris (France).

Louis C. Jonker is Distinguished Professor of Old Testament at the University of Stellenbosch (South Africa).

Yigal Levin is Associate Professor in the Department of Jewish History at Bar-Ilan University (Israel).

Christl M. Maier is Professor of Old Testament at Philipps-Universität Marburg (Germany) and Extraordinary Professor in the disciplinary group Old and New Testament at the University of Stellenbosch (South Africa).

Katharina Pyschny is Junior Professor for Biblical Theology at the Humboldt-University of Berlin (Germany).

Jan Rückl is Research Fellow in Old Testament at Charles University Prague (Czech Republic).

Martin Schott is Senior Lecturer in Old Testament at Friedrich-Alexander-Universität Erlangen-Nuremberg (Germany).

Sarah Schulz is Senior Lecturer in Old Testament at Friedrich-Alexander-Universität Erlangen-Nuremberg (Germany).

Index of Biblical References

Hebrew Bible

Gen 6:3   194
Gen 20:11   191
Gen 22:17   52

Exod 5   230
Exod 14:19   119
Exod 18:21–26   228

Lev 17–26   225
Lev 18:24–30   178
Lev 19:15   225
Lev 26   306 f.

Num 2   165
Num 2:3–30   162
Num 6:7   230
Num 7   162, 165
Num 11:16   230
Num 22:26   180
Num 25:5   225
Num 31   228
Num 34:18–28   162
Num 35:24   225

Deut 1:15   230 f.
Deut 1:15–16   228
Deut 1:16–17   224
Deut 3:18   191
Deut 7   177
Deut 7:1–3   178
Deut 11:8   178
Deut 16:18–20   224, 229
Deut 17:16   89
Deut 17:18–20   29
Deut 20:5–8   230
Deut 21:19   224
Deut 22:15–19   224
Deut 23:6   178
Deut 26:17–19   50
Deut 29:9   230
Deut 31:28   230

Deut 34:7   194, 247
Deut 34:10   178

Josh 1:10   230
Josh 3:2   230
Josh 6:15   225
Josh 8:33   225
Josh 20:6   225
Josh 23:2   225, 230
Josh 24:1   225, 230
Josh 24:25   225

Judg 2:16–19   226
Judg 3:10   226
Judg 3:12   26
Judg 4:4   224
Judg 6:34   298
Judg 11:27   226
Judg 17:1–21:25   197
Judg 18:7   226

1 Sam 2:13   226
1 Sam 7:6   226
1 Sam 7:11   227
1 Sam 7:15   226
1 Sam 7:17   226
1 Sam 8   226
1 Sam 8:1–2   226
1 Sam 8:3   226
1 Sam 8:5–6   226
1 Sam 8:5–8   197
1 Sam 8:9   226
1 Sam 8:11   226
1 Sam 9:2   245
1 Sam 12:7   226
1 Sam 14:52   191
1 Sam 16:12   246
1 Sam 16:14   246
1 Sam 16:18   246
1 Sam 18:10   246
1 Sam 18:17   191

Index of Biblical References

1 Sam 19:9   246
1 Sam 24:12 226
1 Sam 24:15 226
1 Sam 30:25 226
1 Sam 31   214

2 Sam 5   232
2 Sam 6   233
2 Sam 7   72, 227
2 Sam 7:3   300
2 Sam 7:9   48, 56
2 Sam 7:15   300
2 Sam 8:15   226
2 Sam 15:2–6 226
2 Sam 18:19 226
2 Sam 18:31 226
2 Sam 23:3   191
2 Sam 24   233
2 Sam 24:17 234

1 Kgs 1:1   247
1 Kgs 1:3–4 247
1 Kgs 2:4   56
1 Kgs 3:9   226
1 Kgs 3:17–28 226
1 Kgs 7:7   226
1 Kgs 8:32   226
1 Kgs 10:9   226
1 Kgs 12   234
1 Kgs 14:1–18 250
1 Kgs 15:1–8 210
1 Kgs 15:9–24 212
1 Kgs 18   127
1 Kgs 19:15–18 249
1 Kgs 20:40 226
1 Kgs 22   297

2 Kgs 1:3–4 248
2 Kgs 8   213
2 Kgs 8:7–15 248 f.
2 Kgs 11:17 194
2 Kgs 14:21 190
2 Kgs 15:1   190
2 Kgs 15:5   226
2 Kgs 15:6–8 190
2 Kgs 15:13 190
2 Kgs 15:17 190
2 Kgs 15:23 190
2 Kgs 15:27 190
2 Kgs 15:30 190
2 Kgs 15:32 190
2 Kgs 15:34 190
2 Kgs 16   211
2 Kgs 20   250
2 Kgs 20:6   251
2 Kgs 22   177, 231
2 Kgs 22:30 22
2 Kgs 23:22 227
2 Kgs 23:30–34 21
2 Kgs 24:1   234
2 Kgs 24:6   23
2 Kgs 24:18–20 305
2 Kgs 24:20–25:21 305
2 Kgs 25   307
2 Kgs 25:22–24 167
2 Kgs 25:27–30 22

Isa 1:1   190
Isa 3:23   275
Isa 6:1   190
Isa 7:1   190
Isa 7:9   300
Isa 16:5   180
Isa 44:28   158, 162
Isa 55:6   308
Isa 62:3   275
Isa 65:1   308

Jer 1:8   37
Jer 1:19   37
Jer 14:13   75
Jer 21:11–12 26
Jer 21:12   29
Jer 22:1–5   28
Jer 22:10–12 21
Jer 22:13–19 22
Jer 22:15   25
Jer 22:15–16 28
Jer 22:15–17 24
Jer 22:19   23
Jer 22:24   68
Jer 22:24–30 22
Jer 23:1–4   27
Jer 23:5   56, 270
Jer 23:5–6   25, 47
Jer 29:13–14 308

Jer 31:16   310
Jer 31:31–34   54
Jer 31:31–37   48
Jer 31:35–37   53 f.
Jer 33:1–13   54
Jer 33:14–26   47, 121
Jer 33:15   270
Jer 35   42
Jer 36   35
Jer 36:30   23
Jer 37:2   305
Jer 38   38
Jer 39:1–10   305
Jer 40:5   167
Jer 40:7   167
Jer 40:11   167
Jer 41:2   167
Jer 45:5   37
Jer 52:1–3   305
Jer 52:3–30   305

Ezek 1:1–4   156
Ezek 10:14   236
Ezek 34:23   92
Ezek 40–48   123
Ezek 44:3   162
Ezek 45:7–8   162

Hos 1:1   190
Hos 3:4   309
Hos 3:4–5   308 f.
Hos 5:15–6:1   309

Amos 1:1   190
Amos 3:9   309

Zeph 2:14–16   102
Zeph 3:12   103
Zeph 3:14–17   102
Zeph 3:16   310

Hag 1:1   59, 77, 79, 159, 266, 269, 287
Hag 1:1–3   77
Hag 1:2–11   78
Hag 1:12   59, 79, 159, 164
Hag 1:12–14   78
Hag 1:14   59, 79, 159, 164, 266, 269, 287
Hag 2:2   59, 77, 79, 159, 266, 269, 287

Hag 2:3   164
Hag 2:3–9   61, 75
Hag 2:4   59, 73, 77, 79, 159, 268 f., 276, 287
Hag 2:6   61
Hag 2:8   164
Hag 2:11   65
Hag 2:12   77
Hag 2:14   77
Hag 2:20–23   59, 65, 90, 94, 141, 268, 270, 275 f.
Hag 2:21   159
Hag 2:23   64, 159

Zech 1–8   141
Zech 2:14   89
Zech 2:14–16   100
Zech 3   159, 269, 272, 276, 287
Zech 3:6   10, 90, 94
Zech 3:7   273
Zech 3:8   270
Zech 4:1–14   80
Zech 4:6–10   90, 265, 268 f., 276, 287
Zech 4:7–10   159
Zech 4:9   73
Zech 4:9–10   164
Zech 4:10   274
Zech 6   276
Zech 6:9–15   80, 142, 159, 265, 270, 274
Zech 6:12   90, 94, 270
Zech 7:9   236
Zech 8:4   236
Zech 8:9   310
Zech 8:10   309
Zech 8:13   310
Zech 8:16   236
Zech 9–10   130
Zech 9–14   132
Zech 9:8   111
Zech 9:9–10   85, 97, 100
Zech 9:11–17   108, 110, 138
Zech 9:13   93
Zech 9:13–15   108
Zech 10   110
Zech 10:1–3   97
Zech 10:4   109
Zech 10:11   94
Zech 11   97, 130

Index of Biblical References

Zech 11:4–14   92
Zech 11:4–16   136
Zech 11:6   310
Zech 11:15–17   92, 94
Zech 12   141
Zech 12:1–13:1   10, 97, 112, 129
Zech 13:2–6   127
Zech 13:3   127
Zech 13:7–9   97
Zech 14   97
Zech 14:1–2   92
Zech 14:4   102
Zech 14:5   190
Zech 14:9   86, 91, 94 f.

Mal 1:8   236
Mal 2:17   236

Ps 2:7   119
Ps 18:36   102
Ps 20:8   106
Ps 33   106
Ps 44:4–8   106
Ps 45:2   180
Ps 45:5   102
Ps 45:7   119
Ps 72:8   87, 110
Ps 132   72

Job 29:14   275

Lam 5:12   232

Dan 7:13   85

Ezra 1–3   161, 281, 286, 288
Ezra 1–4   281
Ezra 1–6   77, 155
Ezra 2:2   163–165, 282
Ezra 2:63   164 f.
Ezra 2:70   163
Ezra 3   277
Ezra 3–6   173
Ezra 3:1–7   282
Ezra 3:2   163 f., 282
Ezra 3:6   164
Ezra 3:8   163 f., 283
Ezra 3:9   164

Ezra 3:12   163 f.
Ezra 4   284, 286
Ezra 4:8   155
Ezra 4:23   175
Ezra 4:24   284
Ezra 5   64
Ezra 5–6   277, 283, 286 f.
Ezra 5:1–2   156, 159, 165, 279, 284
Ezra 5:1–6:18   156
Ezra 5:2   160, 164
Ezra 5:3   157, 281
Ezra 5:3–17   158
Ezra 5:3–6:13   158
Ezra 5:5   160
Ezra 5:6–6:14   277
Ezra 5:14   157
Ezra 5:16   158 f.
Ezra 6:3–5   158
Ezra 6:13   158
Ezra 6:14   157, 160, 279, 285
Ezra 6:16–19   157, 163, 166
Ezra 7–10   171, 176
Ezra 7:1–5   167, 177
Ezra 7:6   180
Ezra 7:11–28   173
Ezra 8   167
Ezra 8:1   178
Ezra 8:15–30   176
Ezra 9:1–5   176
Ezra 9:6–15   176
Ezra 9:10–11   178
Ezra 9:10–13   177
Ezra 9:14   177
Ezra 9:15   177

Neh 1:3   175
Neh 2:3   175
Neh 3–4   172
Neh 5:9   191
Neh 5:15   191
Neh 8   171, 175
Neh 8–12   172
Neh 8:1–12   179
Neh 8:2   176
Neh 12:10–11   64

1 Chr 2:3–4:23   214
1 Chr 3:12   190

1 Chr 3:17–18   22
1 Chr 3:17–24   63
1 Chr 4:38–43   195
1 Chr 5:7–10   195
1 Chr 5:18   191
1 Chr 5:18–22   195
1 Chr 5:27–41   64, 177
1 Chr 6:1–15   177
1 Chr 8:1–40   214
1 Chr 8:33–40   198
1 Chr 9:1–34   214
1 Chr 9:35–44   214
1 Chr 9:39–44   198
1 Chr 10:1–14   214
1 Chr 11:3   23 f., 300
1 Chr 11:22   191
1 Chr 12:1–23   297
1 Chr 12:18   298
1 Chr 13   233
1 Chr 13:1   233
1 Chr 15–16   233
1 Chr 15:25   233, 235
1 Chr 17   227, 229
1 Chr 21   215, 233
1 Chr 21:16   233, 235
1 Chr 22:6–10   207
1 Chr 23   229
1 Chr 23:2–5   227
1 Chr 23:4   230
1 Chr 23:13   216
1 Chr 26   229
1 Chr 26:29   228, 231
1 Chr 27:1   231
1 Chr 28:2   208

2 Chr 1:2   228 f.
2 Chr 5   234
2 Chr 5:2   233
2 Chr 5:4   233
2 Chr 5:5   216
2 Chr 5:7   216
2 Chr 5:11   216
2 Chr 12:5   303
2 Chr 12:5–12   300
2 Chr 13:1–14:1   13, 210
2 Chr 13:8   196
2 Chr 13:12   301
2 Chr 13:22   194

2 Chr 13:23–16:14:   212
2 Chr 15:1   298
2 Chr 15:1–7   298, 304, 307, 310
2 Chr 15:1–19   212
2 Chr 15:2   309
2 Chr 15:3   309
2 Chr 15:3–4   308
2 Chr 15:3–6   308
2 Chr 15:4   309
2 Chr 15:5   309
2 Chr 15:5–6   309
2 Chr 15:6   310
2 Chr 15:7   298, 309 f.
2 Chr 15:8   298
2 Chr 15:8–15   307
2 Chr 15:15   298
2 Chr 16:7–10   296
2 Chr 16:7–11   254
2 Chr 16:12   254
2 Chr 17:7–9   304
2 Chr 18   297
2 Chr 19   228 f.
2 Chr 19:1–3   296
2 Chr 19:11   231
2 Chr 20:14   299
2 Chr 20:14–20   296, 299
2 Chr 20:15   299
2 Chr 20:19   299
2 Chr 20:20   300
2 Chr 20:34   296
2 Chr 21:2–22:1   212
2 Chr 21:14–15   253
2 Chr 21:19–20   253
2 Chr 23:1   193
2 Chr 23:6   216
2 Chr 23:14   298
2 Chr 23:16   193 f.
2 Chr 24:2   193
2 Chr 24:3   193
2 Chr 24:11–14   193
2 Chr 24:14   193
2 Chr 24:15   194
2 Chr 24:15–16   193
2 Chr 24:15–22   193
2 Chr 24:17–18   298
2 Chr 24:17–19   193
2 Chr 24:17–22   191
2 Chr 24:19   192 f., 301

2 Chr 24:20   192, 298
2 Chr 24:20–22   191, 193
2 Chr 24:22   192, 298
2 Chr 24:27   193 f.
2 Chr 25:2   302
2 Chr 25:4   302
2 Chr 25:5   302
2 Chr 25:6   302
2 Chr 25:7–8   302
2 Chr 25:14   302
2 Chr 25:15   302
2 Chr 25:16   302
2 Chr 25:17   302
2 Chr 26:3   190
2 Chr 26:5   191–193
2 Chr 26:7   190
2 Chr 26:8–9   190
2 Chr 26:11   190
2 Chr 26:14   190
2 Chr 26:15   190
2 Chr 26:16–21   190
2 Chr 26:17   190
2 Chr 26:18   301
2 Chr 26:18–19   190
2 Chr 26:20–21   306
2 Chr 26:21   224

2 Chr 26:21–23   190
2 Chr 26:22   192
2 Chr 27:2   190
2 Chr 28:5–15   211
2 Chr 28:8–15   197
2 Chr 28:9–15   195
2 Chr 29–32   215
2 Chr 32:20   303
2 Chr 32:24   255
2 Chr 32:25   256
2 Chr 32:26   256
2 Chr 34–35   216
2 Chr 34:13   231
2 Chr 34:29   234
2 Chr 35:20–22   196
2 Chr 36   304
2 Chr 36:12   305
2 Chr 36:12–13   305
2 Chr 36:14   196, 305
2 Chr 36:15   296
2 Chr 36:15–16   305
2 Chr 36:15–21   305
2 Chr 36:16   253, 305
2 Chr 36:20–21   306
2 Chr 36:21   307
2 Chr 36:22–23   156

New Testament

Matt 1:12–13   77

Luke 3:27   77
Luke 9:33   178

Apokrypha

1 Esd 4:13   77
1 Esd 5–6   77

1 Macc 10:2   271

Sir 11:5   275
Sir 40:4   275
Sir 45:12   271
Sir 47:6   275
Sir 49:11   77

www.ingramcontent.com/pod-product-compliance
Lightning Source LLC
Chambersburg PA
CBHW031420150426
43191CB00006B/340